A Daily Dose of
PROVERBS

Dr. John W. Stanko

11/3/03

Natalie,

Grow in wisdom!

Joel Stee

Prov 2:2-5

Ev ergreen
PRESS

A Daily Dose of Proverbs
by Dr. John W. Stanko
Copyright ©1997, 2003 Dr. John W. Stanko.

ISBN 1-58169-130-0
Printed in the U.S. for worldwide distribution.

Evergreen Press
P.O. Box 191540, Mobile, AL 36619
1-800-367-8203

Dedication

To Kathryn, my wife of 28 years. Thank you for your love, support, and friendship during those exciting and sometimes trying years.

Other books by Dr. John W. Stanko
published by Evergreen Press:

Life Is a Gold Mine—Can You Dig It?

I Wrote This Book on Purpose

So Many Leaders...So Little Leadership

Strictly Business

Introduction

Not long after I met the Lord, a wise person advised me to read a chapter from the book of Proverbs every day. That was in 1973, and a day has rarely gone by that I haven't followed that advice. You've probably done the same. In fact , throughout the ages, countless people have begun the day by seeking the timeless counsel in this book of the Bible.

With that devotional practice intact in my life, I've written this daily devotional taking the chapter for the day, choosing one verse from it and relating it to the rest of the Bible and, hopefully, to life itself. The result is 366 days and verses that incorporate many verses from other books of the Bible that are practical exhortations for contemporary living. Use this book along with your daily reading from Proverbs and it will help make your reading more focused and applicable.

Some months focus on one topic for the entire month, while others jump from topic to topic, much as the book of Proverbs does. Since Proverbs is not a book of right doctrine but of right behavior, each day is written so that you can apply what you read that very day.

Solomon and others wrote the verses in Proverbs,

For attaining wisdom and discipline; for understanding words of insight; for acquiring a disciplined and prudent life, doing what is right and just and fair; for giving prudence to the simple, knowledge and discretion to the young—let the wise listen and add to their learning, and let the discerning get guidance—for understanding proverbs and parables, the sayings and riddles of the wise (Proverbs 1:2-6).

Who doesn't need more wisdom to live in this modern era? Who couldn't use more discipline and insight? Who wouldn't want to add to their storehouse of wisdom? This devotional book is offered to help the reader grow in wisdom and grace.

Thanks goes to Diana Scimone, my sister-in-law and editor, for her constant encouragement and editorial insight. Special thanks is reserved for my wife, Kathy, who checked all the Scripture references and offered great suggestions and changes to my text. She saw things I never would have seen, which is why we've been a great team for more than two decades.

If Proverbs is part of your regular reading, then I hope you will enjoy reading this book as much as I enjoyed writing it. If you don't currently take a "daily dose of Proverbs," this is a great time to start. So dig in and let's grow in wisdom as we study this book together.

JANUARY 1

"For acquiring a disciplined and prudent life,
doing what is right and just and fair." — 1:3.

I was sitting with my pastor for what seemed like the hundredth time. I had gone with him as he ministered to a church, and now we were in the home of that church's pastor. My pastor was answering questions and I was listening to answers I had heard many times before. I was a little angry that I had no role in that exchange. I knew I could answer, but the Lord had me sit there, doing and saying nothing.

Yet I really wasn't "doing nothing." The Spirit of God was teaching me how to think and respond. The Lord was working in me love for the church and answers for the problems that people and leaders face. I was also learning how to keep my mouth closed, how to listen, and then how to respond. As much as those times frustrated me, they taught me much and prepared me for what I'm doing today.

As you begin another year, could you use more prudence and wisdom? Would you like to know what's right, just and fair? You don't get that kind of wisdom and knowledge only by reading books. You get them by allowing the Spirit to work them into you. James wrote, "The wisdom that comes from heaven is first of all pure; then peace loving, considerate, submissive, full of mercy and good fruit, impartial and sincere" (James 3:17-18).

That description of godly wisdom closely resembles the list in Galatians outlining the fruit of the Spirit: "The fruit of the Spirit is love, joy, peace, patience, kindness, goodness, faithfulness, gentleness and self-control" (Galatians 5:22). As I sat there with my pastor and listened, the fruit of the Spirit was being worked in my life. I gained godly wisdom from that fruit and I apply it regularly today as I minister and teach.

To get the wisdom and fruit you need requires self-discipline. Proverbs was written, as today's verse tells you, so that you can lead a more disciplined life. Most people set New Year's resolutions to be more disciplined in their study, prayer life, or spiritual habits. Whatever your resolutions, know that the goals you desire will only come through the Spirit working in your life. Paul wrote in Romans, "If by the Spirit you put to death the misdeeds of the body, you will live" (Romans 8:13).

I urge you to make it your goal to submit to the work of the Holy Spirit in your life in a new way for the coming year. Whatever resolutions you make must be carried out in the power of the Spirit or they will fail miserably. A more disciplined life, knowledge of what to do, wisdom, and fruit all come from and through the Holy Spirit. Set your will not to try to do more this year in your own strength, but vow to allow the Holy Spirit more room to do what He wants in your life.

JANUARY 2

"For the Lord gives wisdom, and from his mouth
come knowledge and understanding." —2:6.

My friend was weeping on the other end of the phone, telling me of his wife who wanted a separation. It was a complicated situation and I hurt for both of them, not sure of what to tell him. Life can be complex, and the problems created by sin and human nature are often nasty. Seldom do pat, easy answers minister to the problems of life or the dilemmas in which people find themselves.

Take Solomon, for example. He asked the Lord for wisdom to rule the people. Immediately he was put in a trying situation:

> Two prostitutes came to the king and stood before him. One of them said, "My lord, this woman and I live in the same house. I had a baby while she was there with me. The third day after my child was born, this woman also had a baby. During the night this woman's son died because she lay on him. So she got up in the middle of the night and took my son from my side while I your servant was asleep. She put him by her breast and put her dead son by my breast" (1 Kings 3:16-20).

The other woman involved denied the story, and both women appealed to Solomon for a "just" ruling. What was he to do and say? He couldn't just say they had to love one another and learn to get along. He couldn't give them joint custody of the living baby. He needed the wisdom of God. In other words, he needed what he had asked the Lord to give him, and he needed it right away.

"The king said, 'Bring me a sword.' So they brought a sword for the king. He then gave an order: 'Cut the living child in two and give half to one and half to the other'" (1 Kings 3:24-25). The second woman agreed with this ruling, but the first woman rejected it, asking instead that the child be given alive to the other woman. Solomon then ruled, "Give the living baby to the first woman. Do not kill him; she is the mother" (1 Kings 3:26). Solomon knew the real mother would give up her child before she would see it killed. "When Israel heard the verdict the king had given, they held the king in awe, because they saw that he had wisdom from God to administer justice" (1 Kings 3:28).

I want that kind of wisdom. I want the world to come to the church and be in awe of the wisdom to be found there. I'm tired of trite, religious phrases that don't meet the needs of people where they are. Hearing the voice of God like Solomon did, I want to see the Church bring justice and help to hurting people. How about you? Are you willing to devote yourself to a life that carries the wisdom of God to a needy world? Solomon asked God for the answers to a problem that he had never faced before and received the answers. You too must learn to listen for the wisdom that God promises to give, and then deliver it so that the world and the Church can be in awe, not of you, but of the God who has and gives that wisdom.

JANUARY 3

*"By wisdom the Lord laid the earth's foundations,
by understanding he set the heavens in place."* — *3:19.*

George Washington Carver has been my hero ever since I read his biography. Carver was an African-American scientist who lived after the American Civil War. In a time when many of his fellow blacks were struggling for existence, this man helped to put Tuskegee University in Alabama on the map by almost single-handedly revolutionizing Southern agriculture. He encouraged farmers to plant peanuts. When there was no market for those nuts, he prayed and discovered more than 300 uses for the peanut, including paint, paper, and peanut butter! Along the way he also found more than 100 ways to use the sweet potato.

Today's verse says that the Lord used wisdom to create the earth. If you and I can tap into that wisdom, then we too can unlock the secrets of creation. We, like our brother George Washington Carver, can creatively solve problems and do tasks that seem impossible.

King Solomon did this with the wisdom God gave him.

God gave Solomon wisdom and very great insight, and a breadth of understanding as measureless as the sand on the seashore. Solomon's wisdom was greater than the wisdom of all the men of the East, and greater than all the wisdom of Egypt. He was wiser than any other man, including Ethan the Ezrahite—wiser than Heman, Calcol and Darda, the sons of Mahol. And his fame spread to all the surrounding nations. He spoke three thousand proverbs and his songs numbered a thousand and five. He described plant life, from the cedar of Lebanon to the hyssop that grows out of walls. He also taught about animals and birds, reptiles and fish. Men of all nations came to listen to Solomon's wisdom, sent by all the kings of the world, who had heard of his wisdom (1 Kings 4:29-34).

Solomon's wisdom wasn't confined to spiritual things, nor did he have wisdom just to conduct the affairs of the Temple or the Levites. He had wisdom about all of God's creation, and that same wisdom is needed today. There are still inventions and cures to be discovered through the wisdom of God. There are songs to be written and sung. There are management techniques and new business opportunities that remain to be discovered.

Don't limit God's wisdom to church matters. You need and can get God's wisdom for every area in which you're involved. Begin to believe God for creative wisdom. You can find the better way to do something if you'll seek the Lord and believe that He will give you that wisdom. Let the world once again come to the Church for answers not just in spiritual things, but in practical things. After all, creation is God's creation and He cares for it. He wants to give answers and reveal secrets to those who ask. Be the one to hear what He has to say.

3

JANUARY 4

*"When I was a boy in my father's house, still tender,
and an only child of my mother, he taught me." — 4:3-4.*

Solomon is an example of the grace of God. His father was David and his mother was Bathsheba. David got Bathsheba pregnant, killed her husband, and then took her as his wife. The Lord judged David and the baby Bathsheba bore died. The next child born to David and Bathsheba was Solomon. What an example of the grace and mercy of God!

Notice that David didn't neglect his fatherly duties to his son, Solomon. David could have been distraught over his failure and been slack or negligent, saying, "What's the use?" But today's verse tells us that David taught Solomon when he was young. He raised him in the nurture and admonition of the Lord. Solomon's wisdom wasn't given only by God, but also imparted by his father. Those two sources of input made Solomon the wisest man on earth.

When Solomon began construction on the Temple, he quoted what his father had obviously told him:

> You know that because of the wars waged against my father David from all sides, he could not build a temple for the Name of the Lord his God until the Lord put his enemies under his feet. But now the Lord my God has given me peace on every side, and there is no adversary or disaster. I intend, therefore, to build a temple for the Name of the Lord my God, as the Lord told my father David, when he said, "Your son whom I will put on the throne in your place will build the temple for my Name" (1 Kings 5:3-5).

You need to teach your children the wisdom of God. They need to know what you've learned and how to seek the Lord for their own wisdom. Proverbs again and again appeals to "my son" and "my child." The earliest chapters seem to be a summation of the wisdom that a father imparted to his son. Will there be a body of wisdom that you leave to your son or daughter?

This implies first of all that you have wisdom to give and second that you know how to give it away. David had the wisdom and took the time to pass it on. You don't know what you may say to your children that they will quote for the rest of their lives, so be diligent and faithful. Tell them your testimony and share with them the lessons you've learned. Give them a body of wisdom that will guide them, and then encourage them to add their own wisdom to the collection. When they have children, they will then pass on the godly heritage that you began.

"He will die for lack of discipline,
led astray by his own great folly."— 5:23.

The Bible never hides the failures of God's people. It doesn't contain stories of good people pursuing God, but of a good God pursuing people. Most of the Bible's "heroes" had serious flaws and made mistakes that cost them dearly. Solomon, unfortunately, is no exception to this.

King Solomon, however, loved many foreign women besides Pharaoh's daughter—Moabites, Ammonites, Edomites, Sidonians, and Hittites. They were from nations about which the Lord had told the Israelites, "You must not intermarry with them, because they will surely turn your hearts after their gods." Nevertheless, Solomon held fast to them in love. He had 700 wives of royal birth and three hundred concubines, and his wives led him astray. As Solomon grew old, his wives turned his heart after other gods, and his heart was not fully devoted to the Lord his God, as the heart of David his father had been. He followed Ashtoreth the goddess of the Sidonians, and Molech the detestable god of the Ammonites. So Solomon did evil in the eyes of the Lord; he did not follow the Lord completely, as David his father had done (1 Kings 11:1-6).

Solomon had great wisdom, but it led him to believe he could "cut corners" in his obedience to the Lord. He was above the law, or so he thought, and consequently acted unwisely even though he had all that wisdom. The story of his demise is written for your instruction so you can learn from his mistakes since, "Everything that was written in the past was written to teach us, so that through endurance and the encouragement of the Scriptures we might have hope" (Romans 15:4). If Solomon, along with Moses and David, encountered difficulties with evil in their personal lives, then you should watch for the same tendency in yours and learn from their lives.

Paul taught the Galatians, "If someone is caught in a sin, you who are spiritual should restore him gently. But watch yourself, or you also may be tempted" (Galatians 6:1). The writer of Hebrews encouraged you to "throw off everything that hinders and the sin that so easily entangles" (Hebrews 12:1). You need to be watchful that the folly in your own heart not lead you astray in the midst of the wisdom that God has given you.

A good prayer is found in Psalm 139:23-24, where David wrote, "Search me, O God, and know my heart; test me and know my anxious thoughts. See if there is any offensive way in me, and lead me in the everlasting way." That's a wise prayer. It must be prayed or else you risk believing that the wisdom God gives you is a sign of your holiness or spiritual stature. God's wisdom is given like His grace to all who ask for it. You must pursue the necessary discipline that will allow His wisdom to reside in a holy and righteous vessel. Study Solomon and determine not to repeat his mistakes as you pursue godly wisdom and holiness.

JANUARY 6

"My son, keep your father's commands
and do not forsake your mother's teaching." — 6:20.

Solomon didn't follow his own proverbs. He did just what today's verse warned not to do by abandoning his parent's teaching and turning from the Lord. All his wisdom couldn't stand against the wiles and wishes of his many wives, and his life ended in tragedy:

> The Lord became angry with Solomon because his heart had turned away from the Lord, the God of Israel, who had appeared to him twice. Although he had forbidden Solomon to follow other gods, Solomon did not keep the Lord's command. So the Lord said to Solomon, "Since this is your attitude and you have not kept my covenant and my decrees, which I have commanded you, I will most certainly tear the kingdom away from you and give it to one of your subordinates" (1 Kings 11:9-11).

Yet the Lord was mindful of His promises to David, Solomon's father. The passage continues:

> Nevertheless, for the sake of David your father, I will not do it during your lifetime. I will tear it out of the hand of your son. Yet I will not tear the whole kingdom from him, but will give him one tribe for the sake of David my servant and for the sake of Jerusalem, which I have chosen (1 Kings 11:12-13).

The Lord is ever mindful of His word to do what He has promised. God made a promise to David and would keep it even when David's son disobeyed. As a parent, you can't guarantee what your children will do with the training you give them. You can never be sure that they'll remain true to the Lord. But you can follow the Lord with all your heart, and trust that His promises to you will sustain them when they need it most.

The New Testament instructs parents to "bring them [children] up in the training and instruction of the Lord" (Ephesians 6:4). The Old Testament has stronger direction for parents when it says, "These commandments that I give you today are to be upon your hearts. Impress them on your children. Talk about them when you sit at home and lie down and when you get up. Tie them as symbols on your hands and bind them on your foreheads. Write them on the door frames of your houses and on your gates" (Deuteronomy 6:6-9).

If you are a parent, make sure your children have your instruction, even if they choose to walk away from it. Don't neglect your duty but be diligent to present to them what's dear to you. Don't rely on the Church or Christian school to do it for you. Do all you can, and then trust that the promises the Lord made to you will carry over to the next generation.

*"My son, keep my words
and store up my commands within you."* — 7:1.

While Solomon strayed from the words of his father, Daniel did not. Daniel was a young man when disaster fell on Jerusalem. Judah's disobedience over hundreds of years finally caused the Lord to act in judgment:

> In the third year of the reign of Jehoiakim king of Judah, Nebuchadnezzar king of Babylon came to Jerusalem and besieged it. And the Lord delivered Jehoiakim king of Judah into his hand, along with some of the articles from the temple of God. These he carried off to the temple of his god in Babylonia and put in the treasure house of his god (Daniel 1:1-2).

Daniel saw his hometown devastated and the temple he loved ransacked. If that wasn't enough, his whole future was changed through no fault of his own, for he was a righteous young man:

> Then the king ordered Ashpenaz, chief of his court officials, to bring in some of the Israelites from the royal family and the nobility—young men without any physical defect, handsome, showing aptitude for every kind of learning, well informed, quick to understand, and qualified to serve in the king's palace. He was to teach them the language and literature of the Babylonians. The king assigned them a daily amount of food and wine from the king's table They were to be trained for three years, and after that they were to enter the king's service. Among these were some from Judah: Daniel, Hananiah, Mishael and Azariah (Daniel 1:3-6).

Daniel was carried off to Babylon and forced to serve a heathen king and country, learning an entirely new culture in the process. But notice Daniel's response. He wasn't bitter, nor did he forsake the teaching of his parents: "Daniel resolved not to defile himself with the royal food and wine, and he asked the chief official for permission not to defile himself this way" (Daniel 1:8). Daniel was concerned with keeping the dietary laws. He remembered what he had been taught, and didn't use the difficulty of his circumstances as an excuse to abandon what he knew to be right.

You need to have the resolve of Daniel. Tight finances don't excuse you from giving—or tithing. Pressures on the job or at home don't exempt you from praying and worshiping the Lord. A threat of loss doesn't give you the right to compromise your integrity on your taxes or in other business or personal decisions. You need to store up God's commands within you and then do them regardless of the circumstances in which you find yourself. God deserves your best no matter what's taking place in your life. Determine that you'll give it to Him, for He is God and deserving of your total obedience.

JANUARY 8

"Blessed is the man who listens to me,
watching daily at my doors, waiting at my doorway."—8:34.

As soon as Daniel was promoted to serve the king, a crisis arose in the royal court. King Nebuchadnezzar had a dream that disturbed him. He wanted the interpretation, but refused to tell the dream to his wise men and counselors. He wanted them to tell him both the dream and the interpretation so he would know the interpretation was correct. His advisers told him that this was impossible, so the king ordered all the wise men to be executed unless they could do what he asked.

He [Daniel] asked the king's officer, "Why did the king issue such a harsh decree?" Arioch then explained the matter to Daniel. At this, Daniel went in to the king and asked for time, so that he might interpret the dream for him. Then Daniel returned to his house and explained the matter to his friends Hananiah, Mishael and Azariah. He urged them to plead for mercy from the God of heaven concerning this mystery, so that he and his friends might not be executed with the rest of the wise men of Babylon (Daniel 2:15-18).

Daniel understood the principle behind today's verse. He realized that God could reveal both the dream and the interpretation. Daniel knew that real wisdom rested with the God of heaven and, in His mercy, He would reveal it to men. First, Daniel knew that he had to ask God for wisdom. Second, he had to listen in faith, trusting that God would give him what he asked.

Today you are faced with many complex problems of modern life. They are complex to you but not to the Lord. It may seem like a situation is impossible to you, but the truth is that "nothing is too hard for you[the Lord]" (Jeremiah 32:17). If you have faith and know how to listen, there's no telling what the Lord can reveal to you. There are inventions, new business ideas, solutions to family problems, and answers for church dilemmas that rest in God and His wisdom. All He is waiting for is someone who will watch and listen on a daily basis.

Daniel's faith was rewarded, as yours will be: "During the night the mystery was revealed to Daniel in a vision. Then Daniel praised the God of heaven" (Daniel 2:19). Daniel did what no wise man thought possible—He discovered both the dream and the interpretation. That's the nature of the God you serve. He's able to do the impossible, and wants to do it for those who believe He can.

Seek the Lord today and listen. Take seriously that God can unlock for you the mysteries of the universe. He can show you the secrets of men's hearts. He can reveal the nature of a problem and give the solution. Let the spirit of Daniel rest on you and give you the faith to believe the Lord for what everyone else says is impossible.

JANUARY 9

"The fear of the Lord is the beginning of wisdom,
and knowledge of the Holy One is understanding." — 9:10.

Daniel had wisdom because He knew how to get more wisdom. He didn't try to figure out Nebuchadnezzar or become an expert in psychology, nor did he read books on dreams or seek out experts on dream interpretation. He also didn't study Babylonian folklore or culture. Daniel had wisdom because He knew the Lord. The phrase "knew the Lord" didn't pertain to the fact that Daniel was saved and going to heaven. Daniel understood who the Lord was and how He worked. Daniel was a success not because he was an expert in government, but because he was an "expert" in knowing how to pray to and hear from God. That's true wisdom.

When Daniel received revelation concerning the dream and its interpretation, he worshiped the source of that revelation:

Praise be to the name of God for ever and ever; wisdom and power are his. He changes times and seasons; he sets up kings and deposes them. He gives wisdom to the wise and knowledge to the discerning. He reveals deep and hidden things; he knows what lies in darkness, and light dwells with him. I thank and praise you, O God of my fathers; you have given me wisdom and power, you have made known to me what we asked of you, you have made known to us the dream of the king (Daniel 2:20-23).

Daniel praised God for His wisdom and power. He worshiped God because He had answered his prayer. For Daniel then and for you now, wisdom isn't an abstract thing. It's not a body of knowledge to be studied and mastered. For you, wisdom is a relationship. It's knowing the God of all wisdom, who then according to His mercy imparts that wisdom to those who ask. Paul wrote, "Christ Jesus has become for us wisdom from God" (1 Corinthians 1:30) and "in whom [Christ] are hidden all the treasures of wisdom and knowledge" (Colossians 2:3).

Do you need wisdom and understanding for your job, home, school, or neighborhood? Then seek the Lord. Continue to cultivate your relationship with Him. Learn about Him and you will be building a bridge with the One who holds the key to your success. In Jesus are hidden treasures of wisdom and knowledge. Get to know Him and you'll discover those treasures as a miner discovers gold nuggets in the ground he mines. There's no worship like that which follows God's revelation. Daniel praised God for answered prayer and the wisdom he received. Let your praise be enhanced by the wisdom you find for your life as you seek to know the Holy One of Israel.

JANUARY 10

"Blessings crown the head of the righteous,
but violence overwhelms the mouth of the wicked." — 10:6.

I sat down at my desk, looking for $25,000! I had been assigned by the public relations association I belonged to the task of finding out what had happened in their accounting. The bank statements were off, the director had resigned, and a lot of questions were being asked. I didn't know where to begin or what to do, so I prayed. I prayed and God led me to the exact spot I needed to begin. From there I unraveled a complicated (but not illegal) series of events that led to the shortage.

When I reported back to the State Board of Directors, they were amazed at how quickly I had found the problem. They asked me how I had done it, and I told them I had prayed. They were dumfounded, and then laughed nervously as people tend to do when you bring up spiritual things in a secular setting.

When Daniel received the answer he was seeking, he too went before his own "State Board." When he went in, the king asked him if he could indeed tell the king not only the meaning but the dream itself. Daniel's response showed his humility:

> No wise man, enchanter, magician or diviner can explain to the king the mystery he has asked about, but there is a God in heaven who reveals mysteries. He has shown King Nebuchadnezzar what will happen in days to come. Your dream and the visions that passed through your mind as you lay on your bed are these (Daniel 2:27-28).

Daniel gave glory to God for the answer he had received. You need to do the same. God is the source of all things. James wrote, "Every good and perfect gift is from above, coming down from the Father of the heavenly lights, who does not change like shifting shadows" (James 1:17). Whatever you have is from the Lord. He's generous and bestows gifts and blessings on all. There can be no room for pride when you see something that God showed you.

Yet God rewards His people for their obedience and faithfulness, and He will reward you with blessings. Look what happened to Daniel:

> Then King Nebuchadnezzar fell prostrate before Daniel and paid him honor and ordered that an offering and incense be presented to him. The king said to Daniel, "Surely your God is the God of gods and the Lord of kings and a revealer of mysteries, for you were able to reveal this mystery." Then the king placed Daniel in a high position and lavished many gifts on him (Daniel 2:46-48).

Your God will reward you for being available to him as a righteous vessel. Even though Daniel acknowledged that the interpretation was a gift from God, he was rewarded handsomely. God desires to bless you as you become a source of His wisdom to a world that's lost and without hope. Seek His wisdom, credit the source, and watch God bless you in ways that will surprise you.

JANUARY 11

"When pride comes, then comes disgrace,
but with humility comes wisdom." — 11:2.

Daniel interpreted the king's dream and in that dream, there was a statue with a head of gold. Daniel explained:

> You, O king, are the king of kings. The God of heaven has given you dominion and power and might and glory; in your hands he has placed mankind and the beasts of the field and the birds of the air. Wherever they live, he has made you ruler over them all. You are the head of gold (Daniel 2:37-38).

From there, Daniel went on to explain the other parts of the statue.

Nebuchadnezzar probably never heard the rest of the interpretation. He got stuck on the head of gold, because that was who he was. Nebuchadnezzar also never heard that God had made him the head of gold by giving him power and dominion. Instead, this king began to think how great he was and pride quickly set in.

After that meeting, the king went to work. "King Nebuchadnezzar made an image of gold, ninety feet high and nine feet wide, and set it up on the plain of Dura in the province of Babylon" (Daniel 3:1). If a head of gold was good, then Nebuchadnezzar felt a ninety-foot statue of gold would be even better! So he went to work to produce a monument worthy of his glory.

The king ordered everyone to bow down and worship the statue. His pride led him to idolatry. When Daniel's friends refused, Nebuchadnezzar ordered them burned alive. His pride led him to murder. He had the furnace heated so hot that the soldiers who threw Daniel's friends in were burned up. His pride led him to disregard the value of those around him who were serving his vision.

The only way to get wisdom is through humility. Pride only brings disgrace. Pride clings to human nature and is often man's toughest problem to overcome. Even though Nebuchadnezzar was told that God had made him great, he believed that he was somehow responsible for his own greatness. Jesus warned, "Everyone who exalts himself will be humbled, and he who humbles himself will be exalted" (Luke 18:14).

Daniel humbled himself, received wisdom, and was exalted. Nebuchadnezzar exalted himself and was disgraced. How about you? Has pride crept into your walk? Are you proud of your accomplishments and talents? Are your feelings hurt when someone is promoted over you and that person seems less talented and deserving?

If you want God's wisdom, you must humble yourself. You must empty yourself of self-importance and focus on God and His will. If you humble yourself, then God won't have to. If you don't, then God will do it for you. Choose the humble road and be like Daniel. Otherwise you will choose the road Nebuchadnezzar chose, and that leads only to disgrace.

JANUARY 12

"A man is praised according to his wisdom,
but men with warped minds are despised." — 12:8.

When Nebuchadnezzar built his ninety-foot statue, his thinking was "warped." He did the wrong thing with the message from his dream. You can assume that he wasn't the most popular king, for he treated people with contempt and brutality. You might also say that he was and still is despised and looked upon as a foolish man.

Yet the three men he threw into the fiery furnace ended up being praised and promoted. They remembered that the beginning of wisdom is the fear of the Lord and they refused to bow down to the statue of gold. When the angel of the Lord appeared in the fire with those three, everyone was amazed, including the king. The king called them out of the fire, observed that they were safe, and proceeded to praise them according to their wisdom:

> Praise be to the God of Shadrach, Meshach and Abednego, who has sent his angel and rescued his servants! They trusted in him and defied the king's command and were willing to give up their lives rather than serve or worship any god except their own God. Therefore I decree that the people of any nation or language who say anything against the God of Shadrach, Meshach and Abednego be cut into pieces and their houses be turned into piles of rubble, for no other god can save in this way (Daniel 3:28-29).

The king certainly went overboard in his praise, but he was impressed nevertheless with their stand and consequent deliverance. The wisdom of Daniel and his three friends wasn't given for them to write books or teach seminars. Their wisdom was to be applied in the arena of life. When it was shown to be true and godly before all men, they were praised, promoted, and exalted above their fellow men. Wisdom is such a precious commodity that it promotes its owner to the highest places.

Someone once said there are three kinds of people in life: those that make things happen, those that watch things happen, and those that ask, "what happened?" Into what category do you fit? If you seek and get wisdom, then you'll make things happen. You'll make a difference on your job, in your neighborhood and home, and in your church. I've made a concerted effort to seek the Lord for wisdom. That wisdom has delivered me from some tough situations and I've been praised for it. You need to do the same.

O Lord, I ask you for godly wisdom as I serve where you have placed me. I don't want to think with a "warped" mind. I want to speak and act with godly wisdom. I ask you to teach me, like you did Shadrach, Meshach and Abednego. I want to be like them in a crisis, not panicking but showing forth Your wisdom. I promise to turn any praise I receive toward You, the source of all wisdom and understanding. Amen.

JANUARY 13

"He who scorns instruction will pay for it,
but he who respects a command is rewarded."— 1:13.

If I had a dream that was interpreted by a stranger and then saw three men survive a fiery furnace, I think I would have known that someone was trying to get my attention. Nebuchadnezzar continued in his pride and arrogance, however, and "was at home in my palace, contented and prosperous" (Daniel 4:4). The Lord, however, continued to pursue him and reveal Himself to the king.

After the dream and furnace incidents, the king had yet another dream. This time he saw a tree, "large and strong and its top touched the sky. Its leaves were beautiful, its fruit abundant, and on it was food for all" (Daniel 4:11-12). But then a messenger appeared in the dream with instructions to "cut down the tree and trim off its branches, strip off its leaves and scatter its fruit" (Daniel 4:14). The stump of the tree stayed intact. That stump was then drenched with dew and lived among the animals.

The king sought Daniel for an interpretation, and Daniel "was greatly perplexed for a time, and his thoughts alarmed him" (Daniel 4:19). He continued,

> You, O king, are that tree!...You will be driven away from people and will live with the wild animals; you will eat grass like cattle and be drenched with the dew of heaven....Therefore, O king, be pleased to accept my advice: Renounce your sins by doing what is right, and your wickedness by being kind to the oppressed. It may be that then your prosperity will continue (Daniel 4:22, 25, 27).

Today's verse warns that he who scorns and ignores advice will pay for it, and that's just what happened to the king. He ignored Daniel's advice and made no changes in his life. One day he was surveying his kingdom and in his pride said: "Is not this the great Babylon I have built as the royal residence, by my might power and for the glory of my majesty?" (Daniel 4:30). Instantly he was reduced to a madman, crawling around on all fours, living outdoors, and eating grass. After seven years, his sanity was restored and he made this declaration about God:

> His dominion is an eternal dominion; his kingdom endures from generation to generation. All the peoples of the earth are regarded as nothing. He does as he pleases with the powers of heaven and the peoples of the earth. No one can hold back his hand or say to him: "What have you done?" (Daniel 4:34-35).

Don't learn the hard way that it's not good to ignore advice. Listen to the counsel of others who are capable of giving godly counsel. The promise is that those who respect a command are rewarded. Don't be like the king and harden your heart, but rather be open to the God who, in His mercy, wants to see all prosper and come to the knowledge of Him and His will.

JANUARY 14

"The house of the wicked will be destroyed,
but the tent of the upright will flourish."— 14:11.

While Nebuchadnezzar eventually came to confess the Lord as sovereign over all, his son Belshazzar did not. This son sponsored a drinking party for his friends when he became king and "gave orders to bring in the gold and silver goblets that Nebuchadnezzar his father had taken from the temple in Jerusalem....As they drank the wine, they praised the gods of gold and silver, of bronze, iron, wood and stone" (Daniel 5:2,4).

Not only did the king show disrespect for the holy utensils, but he mocked the God of heaven with his idolatry. The king had a surprise visitor to his party, however:

> Suddenly the fingers of a human hand appeared and wrote on the plaster of the wall, near the lamp stand in the royal palace. The king watched the hand as it wrote. His face turned pale and he was so frightened that his knees knocked together and his legs gave way (Daniel 5:5-6).

At first, perhaps everyone thought they were just drunk and seeing things, but this was no hallucination. No one could interpret what the writing on the wall meant, and panic set in. It's interesting that the queen was the one who suggested that the king find Daniel. That says Daniel wasn't serving in the king's court at the time. He had been demoted or fired after Nebuchadnezzar had died. After all his faithful and superior service, this young king had ignored him.

Today's verse, however, promises that the tent of the upright will flourish. Daniel may have been temporarily put aside, but his tent was about to prosper once again. What's more, the house of the wicked was about to be destroyed.

The king summoned Daniel to interpret the writing, promising him gifts and a promotion for doing so. Daniel told him to keep his gifts, but he did interpret it:

> But you his [Nebuchadnezzar's] son, O Belshazzar, have not humbled yourself, though you knew all this. Instead, you have set yourself up against the Lord of heaven. You had the goblets from his temple brought to you, and you and your nobles, your wives and your concubines drank wine from them. You praised the gods of silver and gold, of bronze, iron, wood and stone, which cannot see or hear or understand. But you did not honor the God who holds in his hand your life and all your ways. Therefore he sent the hand that wrote this inscription (Daniel 5:22-24).

That night, the king was assassinated and his kingdom given to another man. Don't fret if you've been demoted for a season and it appears that the wicked are prospering. Today's verse contains a powerful promise that God personally fulfills. The tent of the upright will flourish in the long run, so don't despair. Continue to be faithful, and God will bring you from the lowest depths to a place of honor.

JANUARY 15

"A gentle answer turns away wrath,
but a harsh word stirs up anger." — 15:1.

The man walked past the pulpit where I was standing, went to the table behind me, threw down his notes in disgust, and stormed out of the chapel. I had just finished preaching the opening message at a weekend retreat for inmates, and this man was furious. I watched him go and then continued to talk with the others.

A few minutes later I turned around and the man who had gotten so angry was standing right behind me. I didn't realize it was him at first, and naively asked, "How did you enjoy the message?" That gave him the opportunity to let me have it. He began yelling and was none too kind to my message, delivery, and theology. All the while he was fuming, I was thinking of today's verse.

I made up my mind to listen to the man. I refused to cross my arms or do anything with my body language that would say I was on the defensive. I quietly asked him questions to help clarify what he was saying. Part of me wanted to smack him, and another part just wanted to walk away. But I spoke gently and looked him right in the eye. Gradually his tone calmed down and eventually we parted with a handshake. And he was back for the next day's sessions.

Gideon understood this principle long before today's verse was penned. At the direction of the Lord, Gideon had just routed the Midianite army with only 300 men! They were pursuing their enemies when a group of Ephraimites approached Gideon and said, "'Why have you treated us like this? Why didn't you call us when you went to fight Midian?' And they criticized him sharply" (Judges 8:1).

Now Gideon could have said a lot of things in response. He could have told them that the Lord didn't want to use them and that he was just following the Lord's command. He could have complained that he took the risk in battle and now they were fussing at him. Instead, he responded gently:

"What have I accomplished compared to you? Aren't the gleanings of Ephraim's grapes better than the full grape harvest of Abiezer? God gave Oreb and Zeeb, the Midianite leaders, into your hand. What was I able to do compared to you?" At this, their resentment against him subsided (Judges 8:2-3).

One of the most difficult things to do is not react to someone who is angry with you. If they begin to raise their voice, the tendency is for you to raise yours as well. What started out as a disagreement can quickly turn into a full-scale battle. I have found this to be especially true at home, where everyone tends to be "real."

Anyone can get into a argument, but it takes godly skill to avoid one. Determine today not to react when someone comes on strong. See if a gentle answer doesn't soften their approach. Take today's practical approach and make it part of your daily relations with people. Defusing a hostile situation can be tough, but it's pleasing to God when you're able to do so.

JANUARY 16

"Better to be lowly in spirit and among the oppressed
than to share plunder with the proud."— 16:19.

Yesterday Gideon entered the picture as we looked at his response to his angry brothers. It would be good to study this man's life for the next several days, and learn from his experiences. Remember, "everything that was written in the past was written to teach us, so that through endurance and the encouragement of the Scriptures we might have hope" (Romans 15:4). As we study Gideon, I pray you'll be encouraged to endure and find hope.

In Gideon's day, Israel was in a tough place. They had sinned and God had turned them over to the wrath of their neighbors. "Whenever the Israelites planted their crops, the Midianites, Amalekites, and other eastern peoples invaded the country. They camped on the land and ruined the crops all the way to Gaza and did not spare a living thing" (Judges 6:4).

Israel cried out to the Lord, and He sent a prophet to rebuke them for their disobedience. But He also sent an angel to Gideon, and Israel's deliverance was about to begin.

"When the angel appeared to Gideon, he said, 'The Lord is with you, mighty warrior'" (Judges 6:12). At the time, Gideon was threshing wheat in a winepress, trying to hide from the Midianite food thieves. Gideon's response was blunt: "'But sir,' Gideon replied, 'if the Lord is with us, why has all this happened to us? Where are all his wonders that our fathers told us about?'" (Judges 6:13). If God is with us, he was saying, why are things so bad? Why isn't He helping us more if He is with us?

Gideon had lost perspective. Things were so bad that he was in a "famine mentality." He was just trying to get by, and wasn't concerned with the Lord or his spiritual heritage. The angel called him a mighty warrior, but he saw himself as just a poor farmer trying to eke out an existence. His proud enemies were prospering, and he would just as soon have been with them than suffering with God's people.

Today's verse tells you that it's better to have a right heart and be in a tough place, than to share plunder with the proud. Gideon was mighty because God was with him. The same is true for you. You may be in a "famine mentality," wondering where the Lord and all His miracles are. You may be thinking that it would be better to be somewhere else, sharing some of the plunder with the proud. The fact that He's with you, however, makes you a mighty warrior. "God raised us up with Christ and seated us with him in the heavenly realms in Christ Jesus" (Ephesians 2:6).

"If God is for us, who can be against us?" (Romans 8:31). That's the lesson Gideon was about to learn. It's the lesson you need to learn as well. Times may be tight and things pressing in, but a right heart attitude and God's presence bring you above the times. Begin to see that your might comes from who is with you, and not the circumstances you are in. If you can see that, then you will indeed be a mighty warrior as Gideon.

JANUARY 17

"He whose tongue is deceitful falls into trouble." — 17:20.

We were battling it out in what one pastor referred to as "the arena of truth." Things had been building up between my wife and me, and a time of airing things out was at hand. I spoke first and in no uncertain terms let her know how I felt about some things. She took her turn and did the same. This went on for several hours. An amazing thing happened, however, when we had both emptied ourselves of what was on our hearts.

I suddenly saw what my wife was saying. I saw how wrong I'd been and began to ask forgiveness. At the same time, she began to see and do the same. That intense session ended in peace, and I learned a valuable lesson about communication between two people. If you're both committed to speak and listen to the whole truth (as each sees it), then the real truth has a chance to break through. If one or the other holds back, then the chances of coming to grips with reality are limited.

Today's verse warns against a deceitful tongue. A deceitful tongue says one thing, but means another. You can use a deceitful tongue with men and even with God. Take Gideon, for example. The angel appeared to him and announced a greeting. But Gideon spoke his heart. There was no deceitful tongue in him. In essence he said, "If God is with us, why are things so bad?" His perspective was wrong, but his tongue was honest. He concluded, "But now the Lord has abandoned us and put us into the hand of Midian" (Judges 6:13).

"The Lord turned to him and said, 'Go in the strength you have and save Israel out of Midian's hand. Am I not sending you?'" (Judges 6:14). Gideon was still not impressed and spoke honestly though inaccurately: "'But Lord,' Gideon asked, 'how can I save Israel? My clan is the weakest in Manasseh, and I am the least in my family'" (Judges 6:15). Notice that the Lord didn't rebuke Gideon or withdraw from him. He accepted him right where he was and continued to reveal to him the truth of Gideon's situation: "The Lord answered, 'I will be with you, and you will strike down the Midianites, as if they were but one man'" (Judges 6:16).

Don't ever be afraid of speaking with honesty to the Lord. Just be ready for the Lord to speak honestly to you. If you're willing to have a dialogue and not just a monologue with God, then God welcomes your honesty. In fact, your honesty prepares the way for His truth. Remember also that your perspective isn't the final or correct one. It's yours, however, and you should present it and not try to present one that you think the Lord would want you to have (especially if it isn't what's really in your heart). Be like Gideon, and be honest. But then hold on for the honesty and truth that will come back your way.

JANUARY 18

"He who answers before listening—
that is his folly and his shame." — 18:13.

Finally I realized that the Lord was trying to get my attention. Since my ministry position had been phased out, I was sitting at home, praying about what to do. For months, my friend had been inviting me to come pastor his church in Orlando. I turned down his invitation three times, but now I saw that the Lord was directing me there. Wanting to be sure, I asked for, and received, clear confirmation.

In some sense, Gideon was in the same place that I was. While beating out wheat in the winepress, perhaps Gideon was thinking of how he could deliver his people from their oppressors. Suddenly a stranger appeared and promised to go with Gideon to empower him to be that deliverer. So

> Gideon replied, "If now I have found favor in your eyes, give me a sign that it is really you talking to me. Please do not go away until I come back and bring my offering and set it before you." And the Lord said, "I will wait until you return" (Judges 6:17).

Gideon suspected that he was speaking with the Lord Himself, but he also wanted to be sure. So he brought an offering of food and laid it at the stranger's feet.

> The angel of the Lord said to him, "Take the meat and the unleavened bread, place them on this rock, and pour out the broth." And Gideon did so. With the tip of the staff that was in his hand, the angel of the Lord touched the meat and the unleavened bread. Fire flared from the rock, consuming the meat and the bread. And the angel of the Lord disappeared. When Gideon realized that it was the angel of the Lord, he exclaimed, "Ah, Sovereign Lord! I have seen the angel of the Lord face to face!" But the Lord said to him, "Peace! Do not be afraid. You are not going to die" (Judges 6:20-23).

Gideon followed the advice in today's verse: He didn't answer before he had listened and was sure. Israel's deliverance was important, and he wanted to make sure that he had heard from the Lord before he acted. Notice that the Lord wasn't offended by his request for confirmation. The Lord waited for him to return, accepted his offering, and then provided the necessary proof that it was indeed the Sovereign Lord who was commissioning him.

In fact, the Lord helped him in his quest by telling him to wet down the food. The Lord knew that when the soggy food was consumed by fire, Gideon would know he was dealing with the Lord. You also need to be sure that it's the Lord speaking to you. If you suspect that God is directing you, then ask Him to confirm it in the clearest terms. Don't be afraid to ask for something significant before you act on a major decision. The Lord doesn't mind confirming His word, and you will need and rely on that confirmation later during times of doubt or trouble.

JANUARY 19

"A foolish son is his father's ruin." — 19:13.

After the Lord called Gideon, He directed his attention to the condition of his father's household.

> That same night the Lord said to him, "Take the second bull from your father's herd, the one seven years old. Tear down your father's altar to Baal and cut down the Asherah pole beside it. Then build a proper kind of altar to the Lord your God on the top of this bluff. Using the wood of the Asherah pole that you cut down, offer the second bull as a burnt offering" (Judges 6:25-26).

It seems that Gideon's family had engaged in the idolatry prevalent in Israel. Gideon's father had his own altar to Baal and Asherah. If you have any family who don't know the Lord, you understand how tough it is to confront the error of their ways. They know you so well and tend to dismiss what you say or do.

The Lord wanted Gideon to confront and tear down his family's idols, and he, like most sons, was hesitant to do so: "So Gideon took ten of his servants and did as the Lord told him. But because he was afraid of his family and the men of the town, he did it at night rather than in the daytime" (Judges 6:27). Gideon hoped to do the will of God anonymously—he wanted to be God's undercover agent.

But he was discovered:

> In the morning when the men of the town got up, there was Baal's altar, demolished, with the Asherah pole beside it cut down and the second bull sacrificed on the newly built altar. They asked each other, "Who did this?" When they carefully investigated, they were told "Gideon son of Joash did it" (Judges 6:28-29).

The people were angry and demanded that Joash, Gideon's father, do something about what his son had done. Gideon's bravery and obedience to the Lord, however, turned his father's heart:

> But Joash replied to the hostile crowd around him, "Are you going to plead Baal's cause? Are you trying to save him? Whoever fights for him shall be put to death by morning! If Baal really is a god, he can defend himself when someone breaks down his altar" (Judges 6:31).

Today's verse says a foolish son is his father's ruin. In Gideon's case the opposite was true—the wise son was his father's salvation. Gideon's father defended his son from the attacks of the crowd. Because of Gideon, Joash started to come back to his senses. You may have family members who are far from the Lord. Continue to pray for them. Don't be intimidated, but realize that you have a unique position from which to affect them for the Lord. The obstacles may seem to be large, but have courage. Your boldness may be the very thing that will win them all to Jesus.

JANUARY 20

*"It is a trap for a man to dedicate something rashly
and only later to consider his vows." — 20:25.*

The mechanic saw us coming and had to be thinking, "Not them again!" I had gone with one of the single ladies to help her purchase a used car. When we found one, everything seemed to indicate that this car was "from the Lord." But it had been nothing but problems. In looking back, I realized that I had rushed her while we were looking (to get the whole thing over with), and she also wanted a new car as quickly as possible. We had declared that car as "holy" and later had to reconsider our "vows" as we pulled into the mechanic's shop for the umpteenth time.

Gideon didn't fall into the same trap and was in no hurry to declare that he was on a mission from God. He had asked the Lord for a sign when the angel appeared to him at the winepress. Now Gideon was asking for even more evidence that the Lord was with him. He wanted to know before he went to war that he wasn't walking in deception:

Gideon said to God: "If you will save Israel by my hand as you have promised—look, I will place a wool fleece on the threshing floor. If there is dew only on the fleece and all the ground is dry, then I will know that you will save Israel by my hand, as you said." And that is what happened. Gideon rose early the next day; he squeezed the fleece and wrung out the dew—a bowlful of water (Judges 6:36-38).

Gideon wasn't going to fall into the trap discussed in today's verse. He wasn't going to be rash, only to later regret his commitment. As he proceeded, he asked the Lord for proof of His call and purpose. After the water was on the fleece and not on the ground, Gideon asked for one more sign:

Then Gideon said to God, "Do not be angry with me. Let me make just one more request. Allow me one more test with the fleece. This time make the fleece dry and the ground covered with dew." That night God did so. Only the fleece was dry; all the ground was covered with dew (Judges 6:39-40).

It's amazing how patient the Lord was with Gideon during this time. God wanted to confirm for Gideon what His will was so that Gideon would be strengthened for the battles that were ahead. And Gideon didn't want just ordinary confirmation before he gave his vow to proceed. He asked God for the impossible.

Your God is an awesome God who can do anything. When you're at a crossroads and aren't sure which way to turn, ask the Lord for confirmation. Choose something that will prove to you that the Lord is directing you. Once you have your proof, then move in confidence and without fear, using the proof as incentive to carry out the will of God with speed and certainty.

JANUARY 21

*"The horse is made ready for the day of battle,
but victory rests with the Lord." — 21:31.*

Now Gideon was ready, or so he thought. He had three miraculous confirmations of the Lord's call. Having torn down his father's altar, he erected a new one for the Lord. He assembled 32,000 fighting men and pitched camp, waiting for further orders. Those orders, however, proved to be totally unexpected:

> The Lord said to Gideon, "You have too many men for me to deliver Midian into their hands. In order that Israel may not boast against me that her own strength has saved her, announce now to the people, 'Anyone who trembles with fear may turn back and leave Mount Gilead.'" So twenty-two thousand men left, while ten thousand remained (Judges 7:2-3).

Gideon's army was reduced by almost 70 percent! But he still had a large fighting force, and maybe thought himself better off without those who were fearful. The Lord, however, wasn't finished.

> But the Lord said to Gideon, "There are still too many men. Take them down to the water, and I will sift them for you there. If I say, 'This one shall go with you,' he shall go; but if I say, 'This one shall not go with you,' he shall not go.'" So Gideon took the men down to the water. There the Lord told him, "Separate those who lap the water with their tongues like a dog from those who kneel down to drink." Three hundred men lapped with their hands to their mouths. All the rest got down on their knees to drink (Judges 7:4-6).

So now Gideon's army was reduced from 32,000 to 300! "The Lord said to Gideon, 'With the three hundred men that lapped I will save you and give Midian into your hands'" (Judges 7:7). Gideon had his horses and riders prepared for battle, but the victory belonged to the Lord. God was prepared to save Israel and wasn't ready to share the glory of His victory with Gideon or his men. The same is true in your life as today's verse reminds you.

When you think you have figured out how God is going to act, He usually does the unexpected. When you think you know where the money is going to come from, God brings it from a totally unexpected source. When you think you know how God is going to deliver you, He makes you wait a little longer and uses means you thought impossible. By doing this, God keeps your focus on Him so that you can't say you had anything to do with the outcome. Stop trying to figure God out, and stand in His promise that you'll be victorious. Then stand back and see God move in ways you never thought possible.

JANUARY 22

"Teaching you true and reliable words, so that you can give sound answers to him who sent you." — 22:21.

Gideon and his 300 soldiers went to sleep that night with mixed emotions. At the start of the day, they had been part of a 32,000-man army. Now there were only 300 commandos, hand-picked by the Lord to defeat the Midianites. Perhaps they were honored to have been chosen, but the odds had definitely changed, and it seemed like the Midianites were in a much stronger position. Everyone else had gone home, and now they were left alone with their thoughts and fears.

The Lord knew they needed further confirmation, so He decided to encourage them:

> Now the camp of Midian lay below him in the valley. During that night the Lord said to Gideon, "Get up, go down against the camp, because I am going to give it into your hands. If you are afraid to attack, go down to the camp with your servant Purah and listen to what they are saying. Afterward, you will be encouraged to attack the camp."...Gideon arrived just as a man was telling a friend his dream. "I had a dream," he was saying. "A round loaf of barley bread came tumbling into the Midianite camp. It struck the tent with such force that the tent overturned and collapsed." His friend responded, "This can be nothing other than the sword of Gideon son of Joash, the Israelite. God has given the Midianites and the whole camp into his hands" (Judges 7:8-11, 13-14).

Today's verse states that the Lord will give you true and reliable words so you can have confidence. "When Gideon heard the dream and its interpretation, he worshiped God" (Judges 7:15). Returning to the camp with confidence, he awakened his band of 300 and encouraged them. He was able to give them "sound answers" because of what the Lord had showed him in the Midianite camp.

The Lord understands you and all your needs. David wrote, "As a father has compassion on his children, so the Lord has compassion on those who fear him; for he knows how we are formed, he remembers that we are dust" (Psalm 103:13-14). The Lord knew when Gideon needed instruction and encouragement, and He knows when you need it, too.

Don't fret over guidance. If you're facing a major decision, you aren't alone. The Lord knows your fears and confusion. He's able to direct, confirm, and adjust your course. Put your complete trust in Him and then move according to what He shows you. Gideon returned to the camp confident, knowing what God wanted him to do. The Lord wants you to have that same confidence as you do His will, and will do whatever it takes for you to know that He's with you as you go.

JANUARY 23

"For their Defender is strong;
he will take up their case against you." — 23:11.

When the Lord goes to battle, there's no need for smart bombs, lasers, or stealth bombers. He's capable of winning without any help from technology. Calling Gideon to deliver His people, the Lord sent more than 31,000 troops home. He used 300 men to prove the truth of today's verse—the Lord defends His people by His strength.

Gideon and the hundred men reached the edge of the camp at the beginning of the middle watch, just after they had changed the guard. They blew their trumpets and broke the jars that were in their hands. The three companies blew the trumpets and smashed the jars. Grasping the torches in their left hands and holding in their right hands the trumpets they were to blow, they shouted, "A sword for the Lord and for Gideon!" While each man held his position around the camp, all the Midianites ran, crying out as they fled. When the three hundred trumpets sounded, the Lord caused the men throughout the camp to turn on each other with their swords. The army fled to Beth Shittah toward Zererah (Judges 7:19-22).

Gideon's army didn't even have to fight! The confusion caused by the trumpets and jars smashing threw the Midianites into a panic, and they started killing one another. As they fled, Gideon called the people to pursue and overtake them.

Paul wrote, "The Lord will rescue me from every evil attack and will bring me safely to his heavenly kingdom" (2 Timothy 4:18). Jude wrote about "him who is able to keep you from falling and to present you before his glorious presence without fault and with great joy" (Jude 24). The psalmist wrote,

"Because he loves me," says the Lord, "I will rescue him; I will protect him, for he acknowledges my name. He will call upon me, and I will answer him; I will be with him in trouble, I will deliver him and honor him. With long life will I satisfy him and show him my salvation" (Psalm 91:14-16).

What glorious news! Your God is able to protect and defend you and has the power to preserve you.

If God is for us, who can be against us?...Who shall separate us from the love of Christ? Shall trouble or hardship or persecution or famine or nakedness or danger or sword?...No, in all these things we are more than conquerors through him who loved us (Romans 8:31,35,37).

Gideon was a conqueror and you are too, through the power of your mighty God. He will take up your case against any who come against you. Armed with that good news, you can face your enemies knowing that God is on your side!

JANUARY 24

"Know that wisdom is sweet to your soul; if you find it, there is a future hope for you, and your hope will not be cut off." — 24:14.

The Arabs were talking tough and Russia was siding with them. The Middle East was about to explode, or so I thought shortly after I met the Lord. I had read a few books about biblical prophecy, and they both fascinated me and made me pessimistic. I stopped praying for our government since I thought it was evil and of the antichrist. Furthermore, I looked at any established institution as evil and part of the world system that was going to be destroyed.

Then the Lord began to change my perspective. I stopped looking for proof of the end of the world in everything I read and stopped criticizing anyone who saved money or planned for the future. I began to realize that every generation has felt it was the one that would see the return of the Lord. While we are closer today to His return than any other generation, there's no way of knowing for sure. I came to understand that the best way to be prepared for His coming wasn't by looking at the newspaper but rather by doing His will.

A passage that helped me during this time is found in Jeremiah's letter to the exiles in Babylon. This group had been carried off by Nebuchadnezzar after his first siege of Jerusalem. Far from home in a land that they undoubtedly hated, they received the following instructions from Jeremiah:

> Build houses and settle down; plant gardens and eat what they produce. Marry and have sons and daughters; find wives for your sons and give your daughters in marriage, so that they too may have sons and daughters. Increase in number there; do not decrease. Also seek the peace and prosperity of the city to which I have carried you into exile. Pray to the Lord for it, because if it prospers, you too will prosper...."For I know the plans I have for you," declares the Lord, "plans to prosper you and not to harm you, plans to give you hope and a future" (Jeremiah 29:4-7,11).

For those in exile, it must have seemed like the end of the world. But the Lord directed them to be optimistic and have hope. The Lord is saying the same to you today. Today's verse says that if you find wisdom, it will help secure your future and you'll not be cut off. If those exiles could have hope, how much more can you? Not only did he command them to have hope, but also instructed them to pray for their captors. Don't take an adversarial posture toward the world or society, and don't be a "doom and gloom" believer. Walk in hope and pursue wisdom. Wisdom will help secure your future and cause you to see things from the Lord's perspective. When you see that, it will bring a bright, fresh outlook to your life and walk.

JANUARY 25

"These are the proverbs of Solomon,
copied by the men of Hezekiah king of Judah." — 25:1.

As a teenager, I tried on numerous occasions to read the Bible and remember a time when I had a booklet that only contained Paul's first letter to Corinth, complete with commentary and pictures. I thought this booklet was just what I needed to help me read. It turned out to be no different than any other time I tried to read the Bible, however, as I fell asleep reading it. When I surrendered my life to the Lord a few years later, He gave me a hunger for His Word that hasn't been satisfied for more than 20 years!

There was a time in the life of Israel that they too fell asleep on the word of God and didn't read it. The nation and the temple were unclean and the people were lax in their service to God. But a revival took place under King Hezekiah, and the nation began to serve the Lord according to His word:

Hezekiah was twenty-five years old when he became king, and he reigned in Jerusalem twenty-nine years....He did what was right in the eyes of the Lord....When they had assembled their brothers and consecrated themselves, they went in to purify the temple of the Lord, as the king had ordered, following the word of the Lord (2 Chronicles 29:1-2, 15).

After they cleansed the temple, they offered sin and burnt offerings, the Levites played instruments and sang the words of David, the people worshiped, and the nation celebrated the Passover for the first time in many years. They had a revival and it was according to the word of the Lord. The king and priests must have studied the Law and been diligent to carry out what it said.

Someone during this revival undoubtedly discovered the proverbs of Solomon and undertook to copy and preserve them. Hezekiah ruled 200 years after Solomon, so these proverbs were probably unavailable and neglected during those years. Yet the revival touched the nation so deeply that it began to recapture its heritage, and Solomon's proverbs were a part of that. This revival was a work of God's Spirit and the word of God.

How deep is your commitment to the word of God? How much time do you spend reading the Word compared to watching television? How many books written about the Bible do you read during a given year? Are you growing in the knowledge of the word of God? Are you praying for revival?

Revival will come from the word of God. It takes place as people desire to know God's will as it's revealed in His Word and then set out to do it. Let's focus on the word of God over these next few days. Accept the challenge that the Lord is issuing to become even more committed and absorbed in His Word and its commands. Be like Hezekiah's men and work to make the word of God the guiding light in your life and the lives of those after you.

25

JANUARY 26

"A malicious man disguises himself with his lips,
but in his heart he harbors deceit." — 26:24.

The disciples were gathered around the table with Jesus for what was to be their last meal together. Jesus shocked them by making a startling prediction: "'You will all fall away,' Jesus told them, 'for it is written: 'I will strike the shepherd and the sheep will be scattered.' But after I have risen, I will go ahead of you into Galilee" (Mark 14:27-28).

The disciples were unaware of what was ahead and what was truly in their hearts. "Peter declared, 'Even if all fall away, I will not'" (Mark 14:29). Peter, as was his habit, spoke boldly and was the first to declare his loyalty. "'I tell you the truth,' Jesus answered, today—yes, tonight—before the rooster crows twice you yourself will disown me three times'" (Mark 14:30). Peter still wouldn't trust the word of Jesus. Instead he trusted his own deceitful heart: "But Peter insisted emphatically, 'Even if I have to die with you, I will never disown you.' And all the others said the same" (Mark 14:31).

Peter wasn't the only one who disguised himself with his lips. Perhaps none of the disciples believed that it would come down to a "deny him or die" situation, so they made brave statements. Or perhaps they really believed what they were saying. In any case, within a matter of hours they had all fled and Peter had denied the Lord three times. God knows the heart of men.

He knows your heart as well. Knowing it better than you do, He has provided something to help you know the truth of what's there—the word of God. Consider this from the writer of Hebrews: "For the word of God is living and active. Sharper than any double-edged sword, it penetrates even to dividing soul and spirit, joints and marrow; it judges the thoughts and attitudes of the heart" (Hebrews 4:12).

The word of God is living and "active." The Greek word for active is *"energes,"* from which we get our word "energy." The Word is a divine energy that enters your heart. Like a computer virus that gobbles up information when it's introduced, the Word consumes those things in the heart that are contrary to its will. The Word doesn't just feed the mind but also judges your thoughts and attitudes. That makes it a powerful book. You can read a passage and it can judge you as selfish, greedy, or a liar. It can do that because it's alive and active—it's more than just words on a page.

Peter and the others didn't know how to rely on the word of God. They rejected its truth where they were concerned to their own pain. Don't be like that. Don't disguise what's in your heart by using religious phrases and cliches. Let the living Word search your heart and life. Give it access to every area—your speech, thought life, giving habits, and attitudes. When you do, it has the power not just to reveal the truth, but to change you into what that truth represents.

JANUARY 27

"He who is full loathes honey,
but to the hungry even what is bitter tastes sweet." — 27:7.

What a world we live in! Technology has changed life dramatically. There are more books, magazines, and newspapers (not to mention compact discs, videos, and audio tapes) at our disposal than at any time in history. Cable television and satellite dishes give us hundreds of channels to choose from. Computers and the internet put worlds of information at our fingertips. Has all this information, however, really improved man and his spiritual life? In some ways it has deadened him, for the constant bombardment of messages has dulled him to those that are really important.

Today's verse refers to this dilemma. It tells you that those who are "full" hate even the sweet taste of honey. You can be so full of information and messages that you have no room for the word of God. I noticed a few years ago that I had too many things going into my mind and heart. Making an effort to cut back, I tried to give the Word the position it rightly deserved. I haven't always been successful, but I have made the effort.

Ezekiel had this experience when the Lord called him to the ministry:

Then I looked, and I saw a hand stretched out to me. In it was a scroll, which he unrolled before me. On both sides of it were written words of lament and mourning and woe. And he said to me, "Son of man, eat what is before you, eat this scroll; then go and speak to the house of Israel." So I opened my mouth, and he gave me the scroll to eat. Then he said to me, "Son of man, eat this scroll I am giving you and fill your stomach with it." So I ate it, and it tasted as sweet as honey in my mouth (Ezekiel 3:1-3).

The word of the Lord tasted sweet to Ezekiel. Even though it was a hard word, it was the word of God nonetheless. He wasn't too busy, nor were his taste buds ruined by the taste of other scrolls. Jeremiah did the same thing, for he said: "When your words came, I ate them; they were my joy and my heart's delight, for I bear your name, O Lord God Almighty" (Jeremiah 15:16). He too ate the word of God, and it was a delight for him.

Where do you stand with the word of God? Is it as sweet as it once was, or have you developed a taste for other "foods"? Do you enjoy the Bible or do you eat it? Do you read to feed your mind, or do you digest it so that it becomes a part of your life and being? Take steps to reduce your intake of sports, fiction, music, or movies, and then replace them in your diet with the sweet taste of the word of God.

JANUARY 28

"If anyone turns a deaf ear to the law,
even his prayers are detestable." — 28:9.

It was the hardest thing my friend ever had to endure. Being active in prison ministry, he had ministered to a believer on death row. They became good friends and the inmate opened many doors for ministry with the others on death row. They all prayed and worked to get his execution overturned. The day of reckoning came, however, and all their efforts were for naught as this man was executed.

At one time in his life, this death-row inmate had turned a deaf ear to the law of God and man. He had taken someone's life. He was sentenced to death and, even though there were unusual circumstances surrounding his case, he had to pay the penalty. His prayers were ineffectual in having his sentence overturned.

Today's verse speaks to that dilemma. If you turn a deaf ear to God's laws, your prayers are hindered. God's law is contained in the Bible, so there's a strong relationship between the Bible and prayer. For instance, Peter wrote to husbands: "In the same way be considerate as you live with your wives, and treat them with respect as the weaker partner and as heirs with you of the gracious gift of life, so that nothing will hinder your prayers" (1 Peter 3:7). He gave added incentive for husbands to obey God's will in the home—if they don't, God won't listen to them when they pray!

As you would expect, Jesus spoke to this connection between the word of God and prayer: "If you remain in me and my words remain in you, ask whatever you wish, and it will be given you. This is my Father's glory, that you bear much fruit, showing yourselves to be my disciples" (John 15:7-8). If the words of Jesus are in you, then you can ask what you wish (according to the will of God) and it shall be done for you. That's a powerful promise. But if that's true, then so is the converse—if His words don't abide in you, then what you ask won't be done.

The psalmist wrote,

Come and listen, all you who fear God; let me tell you what he has done for me. I cried out to him with my mouth; his praise was on my tongue. If I had cherished sin in my heart, the Lord would not have listened; but God has surely listened and heard my voice in prayer. Praise be to God, who has not rejected my prayer or withheld his love from me! (Psalm 66:16-20).

The writer knew that sin would hinder prayer. The good news is that the word of God confronts and has the power to eradicate sin. When that happens, your prayer line to the Lord remains open.

Open your ear to the law of God. The study of God's Word is just as important as your prayer life. In fact, the Word prepares you for a more powerful prayer life as you are filled with the knowledge of God's will. Don't let your life be either study of the Word or prayer. Let your life be balanced between the two. Your prayers will be answered in many exciting ways and you will grow in the knowledge of God!

*"The poor man and the oppressor have this in common:
the Lord gives sight to the eyes of both." — 29:13.*

The headlines in the *Jerusalem Times* would have read something like this: "Religious Leader and Prophet Dead Three Days. Followers Try to Figure Out What Went Wrong." Of course, there was no newspaper in Jesus' day, but that could have been the headline had there been one. As the two disciples walked on the Emmaus road, "they were talking with each other about everything that had happened. As they talked and discussed these things with each other, Jesus himself came up and walked along with them; but they were kept from recognizing him" (Luke 24:14-15).

Today's verse says that the Lord gives sight to everyone. That's true of both natural and spiritual sight. On the Emmaus Road, the two men were kept from recognizing him. The Lord chose to "blind" them for a time. Unaware of who was with them, they walked on as Jesus questioned them about His death. Finally,

> He said to them, "How foolish you are, and how slow of heart to believe all that the prophets have spoken! Did not the Christ have to suffer these things and then enter his glory?" And beginning with Moses and all the Prophets, he explained to them what was said in all the Scriptures concerning himself (Luke 24:25-27).

Arriving at their house, Jesus went in to eat with them. When He took bread and broke it, "their eyes were opened and they recognized him, and he disappeared from their sight. They asked each other, 'Were not our hearts burning within us while he talked with us on the road and opened the Scriptures to us?'" (Luke 24:31-32). First their eyes had been blinded, but now their eyes were opened to see the truth in the Word. They saw Jesus who had been there all along because the Lord gave sight to their eyes.

If you are to comprehend the word of God, you must have your eyes opened as well. Who better to open them than the One who created them. The psalmist understood this and wrote, "Open my eyes that I may see wonderful things in your law" (Psalm 119:18). You should be praying that very prayer, as well as the one that Paul penned: "I pray also that the eyes of your heart may be enlightened in order that you may know the hope to which he has called you, the riches of his glorious inheritance in the saints" (Ephesians 1:18).

The Bible contains what you need for life and godliness. But you can't just understand it by picking it up and reading it. The same Spirit who wrote it must open your heart and eyes to comprehend it. Let your prayer be that the Lord will open your eyes to behold the great things contained in His Word. Approach the Word with humility and God will exalt you with revelation and understanding as He did for the disciples on the Emmaus road.

"This is the way of an adulteress: She eats and wipes her mouth and says, 'I've done nothing wrong.'" — 30:20.

Those statistics couldn't be correct, I thought, but there they were, in black and white. A study reported that fifty percent of all recently married couples had lived together for some period prior to marriage. Fifty percent! When my wife and I discussed this, we began to list all the couples she knew from work or who had visited our church, all of whom were indeed living together. We concluded that maybe the study was right.

It's no surprise that there are no standards of behavior in our modern society. Today's verse speaks to that very problem—a woman does wrong and then brazenly denies any wrongdoing. That's typical of the world we live in—wrong is right and right is wrong. There are no standards because the word of God has been eliminated as a source for those standards. The Ten Commandments have become the "Ten Options," and many are opting not to obey their directives.

Paul warned that

The time will come when men will not put up with sound doctrine. Instead, to suit their own desires, they will gather around them a great number of teachers to say what their itching ears want to hear. They will turn their ears away from the truth and turn aside to myths. But you, keep your head in all situations (2 Timothy 4:3-5).

The way to keep your head in all situations is to align your life with the word of God. Any other standard is a myth and leads down the wrong road.

The psalmist asked, "How can a young man keep his way pure?" He answered his own question, "By living according to your word" (Psalm 119:9). The writer went on to pray and make some vows that you would do well to speak out as well:

I seek you with all my heart, do not let me stray from your commands. I have hidden your word in my heart that I might not sin against you. Praise be to you, O Lord; teach me your decrees. With my lips I recount all the laws that come from your mouth. I rejoice in following your statutes as one rejoices in great riches. I meditate on your precepts and consider your ways. I delight in your decrees; I will not neglect your word (Psalm 119:10-16).

Don't accept standards that are the creation of modern myths. Let the word of God be, as the Psalmist wrote, "a lamp to my feet and a light for my path" (Psalm 119:105). Walk on solid ground and stay away from the quicksand of modern morality.

"Lest they drink and forget what the law decrees,
and deprive all the oppressed of their rights." — 31:5

There are generally two categories of churches. The first are Word churches—they are strong in the Word and defend the Bible as the inspired and inerrant word of God. Some call them "Bible thumpers" because they preach with power and conviction. The second are Spirit churches—they are strong in the gifts of the Holy Spirit. They are "holy rollers" who tend to be more exuberant in worship, believing in prophecy and other public manifestations of the Spirit's power.

Word churches usually need more "spirit," and the spirit churches usually need more "word." Today's verse speaks to the tendency to drink something that can distort the supremacy of the law in one's life. I have seen some so taken with the gifts and the power of the Spirit that they allow the word of God to take a secondary role as they are led by prophesy. "The Lord spoke to me" is their favorite phrase.

Now I believe that the Lord speaks to people, but He never speaks anything contrary to His Word. You can't "drink" anything that perverts your ability to discern God's Word; it must be given the highest place in your life to guide and instruct you.

Peter wrote in his second epistle of being on the Mount of Transfiguration with Jesus. While there, Peter spoke prematurely and tried to erect tents for Jesus, Elijah, and Moses. In 2 Peter 1:16-19, he wrote about that experience (emphasis added):

We were eyewitnesses of his majesty. For he received honor and glory from God the Father when the voice came to him from the Majestic Glory, saying "This is my Son, whom I love; with him I am well pleased." We ourselves heard this voice that came from heaven when we were with him on the sacred mountain. *And we have the word of the prophets made more certain, and you will do well to pay attention to it, as to a light shining in a dark place, until the day dawns and the morning star rises in your hearts.*

Peter said he heard the voice of God affirm Jesus on that mountain. Then he said that we have the word of the prophets made more certain. He's saying that the written Word is supreme. You can be led astray by "voices" but the Word is more certain, and you do well to heed its every command. As we close this month, make a new commitment to the word of God. Let it be your guiding light. There's still time this year to read the entire Bible. Purchase some study guides, do more in-depth study, and memorize some verses. Make this year the year of the Word in your life and house, and combine your spiritual gifts with a strong foundation from the word of God.

FEBRUARY 1

"Do not give in to them. If they say, 'Come along with us; let's lie in wait for someone's blood, let's waylay some harmless soul.'" —1:10-11.

"But Dad, everybody's going!" That's what my daughter says when she wants to do something with her friends. Peer pressure is a strong force, not only in the lives of children, but also adults. "Keeping up with the Jones" is an old saying that describes the peer pressure to buy something because a friend or neighbor has it.

But peer pressure can be more serious than just a purchase; it can affect your mind and moral judgment. When he was spreading the Gospel to the Gentile world, Paul had to contend with some powerful peer pressure. For instance, in Lystra, "some Jews came from Antioch and Iconium and won the crowd over [and] stoned Paul" (Acts 14:19); in Philippi, "the crowd joined in the attack" (Acts 16:22); in Thessalonica, "they rounded up some bad characters from the market-place, formed a mob and started a riot" (Acts 17:5); and in Berea, "they went there too, agitating the crowds and stirring them up" (Acts 17:13).

Most of the people in those crowds probably didn't know Paul or care about what he was doing. They gave in to a few agitators, however, and persecuted Paul and his companions from a "mob mentality." They did exactly what today's verse warns *not* to do: They gave in to what the majority was doing. "Everybody was going," so they went along.

David was destined to be king of Israel, and the Lord took time to teach him how to lead and not just follow the crowd. One day, David's enemy Saul was trying to kill him. David had a rag-tag bunch of followers who were camping in a cave. Without knowing it, Saul came into that very cave to use it as a "rest stop." There was David's pursuer, unaware and vulnerable in the darkness of that cave.

David's advisers said to him:

This is the day that Lord spoke of when he said to you, "I will give your enemy into your hands for you to deal with as you wish." Then David crept up unnoticed and cut off a corner of Saul's robe. Afterward, David was conscience-stricken for having cut off a corner of his robe. He said to his men, "The Lord forbid that I should do such a thing to my master, the Lord's anointed, or lift my hand against him; for he is the anointed of the Lord." With these words David rebuked his men and did not allow them to attack Saul (1 Samuel 24:4-7).

David didn't go along with the desires of the mob. Rather he followed the principles the Lord had taught him and stood alone. Not being swayed by the crowd, David did what was right for him to do. How about you? Can you stand alone and do what God wants, or are you easily swayed by what everyone is doing? Are you affected by peer pressure, even though you know the godly thing to do? Let the crowd go its way and you go yours and, like David, follow the voice of your Shepherd and not that of the mob.

FEBRUARY 2

"My son, if you accept my words
and store up my commands within you...." —2:1.

I can remember driving along with the window open, the warm summer air hitting my face and hair. Driving late at night, my dad and I were returning home well past my bedtime from an appointment. My father worked many late nights, so this was a rare occasion to be with him.

As we drove, he told me about his teen and early adult years. He shared his fun times and disappointments, and told me how he met my mother by "chance" at a church social gathering. Opening his heart to me that night, he also gave me two or three pearls of wisdom that I've never forgotten. I can't remember where we went that night, but I'll never forget that ride as a time when I stored up my father's words.

I've tried to duplicate that talk with my own children. Remembering how those times with my dad impacted me, I've tried to give them the same special moments. I have to believe that whoever wrote the book of Proverbs also had some father-and-child talks. The phrase "my son" appears 23 times in the book. The writer must have learned from his father, and then wrote and taught his own children in the same manner.

Let us assume that Solomon compiled and wrote many of the verses of Proverbs. Is it safe to assume then that he learned many of these truths from his father David? With that in mind, we will use this month to study the life of David. As we study a verse, we'll see how David learned various principles.

The first mention of David in the Bible is in 1 Samuel 16. The Lord had rejected Saul as king and directed Samuel the prophet to go anoint Saul's replacement: "Fill your horn with oil and be on your way; I am sending you to Jesse of Bethlehem. I have chosen one of his sons to be king" (1 Samuel 16:1). Samuel went off to the house of Jesse, but after reviewing seven of his sons, he didn't find the Lord's chosen among them: "So he asked Jesse, 'Are these all the sons you have?'" (1 Samuel 16:11).

Jesse replied that he had another son—the youngest—named David, "but he is tending the sheep" (1 Samuel 16:11). Samuel had them bring David to him, and when he saw him, he "took the horn of oil and anointed him in the presence of his brothers" (1 Samuel 16:13). David learned that the Lord was watching him while he served his father's interests. He was the only one not home when the prophet arrived, but that didn't thwart the Lord's choice. David was still "discovered."

You too can serve your Father's interests with confidence. Store up His words and commands, knowing that He will accomplish what concerns you. There's no need for politics or anxiety in your Father's house. He will find you even if you're on some obscure hillside tending a few sheep. Knowing this, you can teach your own children to have that same confidence in their parents' God. Pass your testimony on to the next generation and watch it work in them as it did in you.

FEBRUARY 3

*"He mocks proud mockers but gives grace
to the humble." — 3:34.*

As we made our way through several tunnels and long hallways, the security guard stopped us at the entrance to another corridor. Finally the team emerged from their locker room. The Pittsburgh Steelers, led by "Mean Joe" Greene, made their way onto the playing field. I was at Three Rivers Stadium in Pittsburgh as a volunteer handing out programs, and we were being taken to our box seats. I'll never forget those huge men filing past me on their way to the playing field. I'm over six feet tall, but felt like a dwarf compared to those giants in uniform.

That's probably nothing compared to what David experienced shortly after being anointed by Samuel. Having been recruited as a personal aide to Saul, he was still being sent "back and forth from Saul to tend his father's sheep at Bethlehem" (1 Samuel 17:15). One day his father sent him to take some food to his brothers who were in Saul's army, and to bring him back a report about them.

When David arrived, he ran to greet his brothers.

As he [David] was talking with them, Goliath, the Philistine champion from Gath, stepped out from his lines and shouted his usual defiance, and David heard it. When the Israelites saw the man, they all ran from him in great fear (1 Samuel 17:23-24).

David was perplexed that no one in the army would fight this Goliath and decided to challenge him all by himself. When Goliath looked David over, he mocked him saying, "'Am I a dog, that you come at me with sticks?' And the Philistine cursed David by his gods. 'Come here,' he said, 'and I'll give your flesh to the birds of the air and the beasts of the field!'" (1 Samuel 17:43-44).

David, on the other hand, took a more humble approach by calling on the name of His God. He said, "This day the Lord will hand you over to me, and I'll strike you down and cut off your head" (1 Samuel 17:46). And, as you know, that's exactly what happened. Your enemy the devil operates through intimidation, mockery, and pride. To defeat him, Peter instructs you to

Humble yourselves, therefore, under God's mighty hand, that he may lift you up in due time. Cast all your anxiety on him because he cares for you. Be self-controlled and alert. Your enemy the devil prowls around like a roaring lion looking for someone to devour. Resist him, standing firm in the faith (1 Peter 5:6-9).

God will give you grace to overcome the devil if you humble yourself. You can't beat him by playing according to his rules, but you'll be victorious, as David was, if you humble yourself under God's mighty hand. Stand firm in your faith that today's verse is true; God will give grace to the humble and give them the victory in every situation, no matter how impossible.

FEBRUARY 4

"Do not set foot on the path of the wicked
or walk in the way of evil men." — 4:14.

I had rehearsed my speech and was now ready to go in. It had been several years since I had received a raise, and I was going to ask for one. Halfway through my pitch, my boss interrupted me and agreed to give me the raise. When the raise didn't turn up in the next pay, I thought it was an oversight. When it failed to show up in the next two, I knew that I had been tricked. My boss got me off his back by agreeing to something he had no intention of doing. I never got that raise.

That was a difficult time for me as I tried to decide how to react to my boss from then on. I found myself studying David since he encountered a similar situation with his boss, King Saul. After David defeated Goliath, he was again recruited for personal service to the king as a musician. David would play the harp whenever an evil spirit came on Saul. We're told that

> The next day an evil spirit from God came forcefully upon Saul. He was prophesying in his house, while David was playing the harp, as he usually did. Saul had a spear in his hand and he hurled it, saying to himself, "I'll pin David to the wall." But David eluded him twice (1 Samuel 18:10-11).

That passage tells us a two important things: Saul didn't want to deal with reality. Rather than deal with the source of his evil spirit, he tried to find comfort in music. And secondly, David stayed after Saul tried to run him through with his spear. He eluded Saul twice, which is one more time than you or I would have dodged Saul's spear. After one spear incident, I would have been out the door on my way home to dad's house.

Today's verse warns you not to walk in the way of evil men. I had to find the righteous way to relate to my boss when he wronged me, and David had to learn how to honor the king after his own brush with death. It's critical that you not walk in the path of evil men as you try to deal with their evil. David stayed on his job and I stayed on mine because of the principles found in 1 Peter 1:19-21:

> It is commendable if a man bears up under the pain of unjust suffering because he is conscious of God. But how is it to your credit if you receive a beating for doing wrong and endure it? But if you suffer for doing good and you endure it, this is commendable before God. To this you were called, because Christ suffered for you, leaving you an example, that you should follow in his steps.

That advice is contrary to the world's way of doing things, and will distinguish you as a follower of Christ. For that advice to be followed, God will allow evil men to come against you so that you can learn this principle. If that's happening to you, don't use the wrong tactics, but follow in Christ's footsteps and suffer with a righteous attitude.

FEBRUARY 5

"But in the end she is bitter as gall,
sharp as a double-edged sword." — 5:4.

When Saul saw that he couldn't kill David, he tried another tactic. "Saul said to David, 'Here is my older daughter Merab. I will give her to you in marriage; only serve me bravely and fight the battles of the Lord.' For Saul said to himself, 'I will not raise a hand against him. Let the Philistines do that!'" (1 Samuel 18:17).

But David wasn't killed by the Philistines. So Saul tried to ruin David's life by getting him into a troublesome and political marriage. David was spiritually sensitive enough to rebuff Saul's efforts: "But David said to Saul, 'Who am I, and what is my family or my father's clan in Israel, that I should become the king's son-in-law?'" (1 Samuel 18:18). After this response, Saul gave Merab to someone else and tried again with another daughter.

Now Saul's daughter Michal was in love with David, and when they told Saul about it, he was pleased. "I will give her to him," he thought, "so that she may be a snare to him and so that the hand of the Philistines may be against him." So Saul said to David, "Now you have a second opportunity to become my son-in-law" (1 Samuel 18:20-21).

Then Saul had his servants talk to David and convince him to give the king the foreskins of 100 Philistines, hoping that David would be killed in the process. Instead of being killed, David was highly successful.

Then Saul gave him his daughter Michal in marriage. When Saul realized that the Lord was with David and that his daughter Michal loved David, Saul became still more afraid of him, and he remained his enemy the rest of his days (1 Samuel 18:27-29).

Although Michal loved David, she proved to be trouble for him on several occasions. Michal fulfilled today's verse, for in the end she was bitter as gall and caused the pain of a two-edged sword. When Saul came to their house to kill David, "Michal took an idol and laid it on the bed" (1 Samuel 19:13). When asked by Saul why she had helped David to escape, she lied, saying that David had threatened to kill her if she didn't.

Later Michal saw David dancing and worshiping the Lord with all his might and she criticized him. The result was that "Michal daughter of Saul had no children to the day of her death" (2 Samuel 6:23). Well could David warn his son Solomon to marry wisely but, unfortunately, Solomon didn't heed his father's warnings. If you aren't married, then be certain to seek the Lord to find the mate He has chosen for you. If you're married, then study the Scriptures to structure your marriage according to God's will. Don't marry out of passion or with undue haste, for even the great can be brought down in the end by a relationship begun or not built on the will of God.

FEBRUARY 6

"If you have been trapped by what you said,
ensnared by the words of your mouth." — 6:2.

The phone rang and, for a change, it wasn't a pastoral call. My friend of 20 years was on the other end, and it was great to hear from him. Even though we live hundreds of miles apart, we keep in touch regularly. Our relationship has withstood the test of time and distance and has remained strong over the years.

David had a friend like that in Jonathan. Even though Jonathan was Saul's son, he remained faithful to both David and his father without compromising his convictions as a friend or son. Today's verse warns of the seriousness of verbal commitments that are made, urging you to get permission to change them rather than try to ignore them. Jonathan made a commitment of loyalty to David and wasn't about to change it, even though it would eventually cost him his life.

When David had to flee from Saul's presence to save his life, he and Jonathan

kissed each other and wept together—but David wept the most. Jonathan said to David, "Go in peace, for we have sworn friendship with each other in the name of the Lord, saying, 'The Lord is witness between you and me, and between your descendants and my descendants forever'" (1 Samuel 20:41-42).

Neither man ever went back on his word that he gave that day.

How about you? Have you made similar commitments of friendship in the emotion of the moment, only to have gone back on those commitments as time went on? It's a godly trait to be a friend and keep fresh the love and affection between you and your friend. Just how good of a friend are you?

Later in David's life, Jonathan came to see him when it seemed that Saul was about to overtake David. Jonathan told David,

"Don't be afraid," he said, "My father Saul will not lay a hand on you. You will be king over Israel, and I will be second to you. Even my father Saul knows this." The two of them made a covenant before the Lord. Then Jonathan went home, but David remained at Horesh (1 Samuel 23:17-18).

We aren't told whether they ever saw one another again, for Jonathan was later killed with his father as they fought the Philistines.

What an encouragement that visit from Jonathan must have been to David! Your friends may need your encouragement also. Make a note today to call, write, or visit a friend. Make an effort to renew the warmth that was once between you and them. It may take some work, but be true to what the Lord did in your life when He brought you and your friend together. Be a friend like Jonathan and don't make vows of commitment one day only to forget them the next!

FEBRUARY 7

"With persuasive words she led him astray;
she seduced him with her smooth talk." — 7:21.

While David was playing the harp for Saul, Saul tried to kill him on three separate occasions. Then Saul had his men surround David's house to capture and kill him, but David escaped. Finally, Jonathan discovered his father's hatred and murderous intent toward his friend, warning David to flee. Through all this, the Lord preserved David and kept him safe from harm.

This constant pressure began to wear on David. He was being squeezed like a toothpaste tube, and what was in him was coming out. Perhaps he was thinking: "It's just a matter of time before he gets me. I have been so good to him and his family and this is my reward. How many more times can I give him the slip? I'd better do something!"

Today's verse points out how persuasive words and smooth talk can lead a man astray. In spite of how strong the Lord had shown Himself on David's behalf, this young man succumbed to the fear in his heart, and was led astray by the persuasive words of his own thinking.

That day David fled from Saul and went to Achish king of Gath. But the servants of Achish said to him, "Isn't this David, the king of the land? Isn't he the one they sing about in their dances: 'Saul has slain his thousands, and David his tens of thousands?'" David took these words to heart and was very much afraid of Achish king of Gath. So he pretended to be insane in their presence; and while he was in their hands he acted like a madman, making marks on the doors of the gate and letting saliva run down his beard (1 Samuel 21:10-13).

David fell prey to what prison inmates refer to as "stinkin' thinkin'." A guided missile can start out just a hair off target, but be hundreds of miles off when it finally lands. David started out just a little off in his thinking, but the end result was a long way from where the Lord wanted him to be. Like Paul, we must learn to

Demolish arguments and every pretension that sets itself up against the knowledge of God, and we take captive every thought to make it obedient to Christ. And we will be ready to punish every act of disobedience, once your obedience is complete (2 Corinthians 10:5-6).

"Once your obedience is complete" means that you are responsible to establish your own obedience before looking to deal with others. One day David would command the obedience of his subjects. On this day, God wanted to secure his obedience and faith in God's protection. Have you allowed unbelief, fear, or cynicism to creep in as you respond to what is perhaps an ongoing assault of the enemy? Don't let the smooth and persuasive words of your mind lead you astray, but be strong in the Lord and in His ability to protect His people.

"You who are simple, gain prudence;
you who are foolish, gain understanding." — 8:5.

From Gath, David escaped to the cave of Adullam. A cave is a good place to go when you want to hide out. David was running from Saul, so the cave seemed as good a place as any to be. But David's cave turned into a motel:

When his brothers and his father's household heard about it, they went down to him there. All those who were in distress or in debt or discontented gathered around him, and he became their leader. About four hundred men were with him (1 Samuel 22:1-2).

David was trying to hide, and word spread that he was in the cave. Four hundred people showed up at a time when he was trying to lay low. Just when David and his men began to get comfortable in that cave, the word of the Lord came to him through the prophet: "But the prophet Gad said to David, 'Do not stay in the stronghold! Go into the land of Judah.' So David left and went to the forest of Hereth" (1 Samuel 22:5).

According to today's verse, David was being simple and foolish. I'm not criticizing David, for I would have probably been doing the same thing. I've wanted to retreat into the cave of my mind, hiding my fears, insecurities, and doubts there. I, like David, have preferred darkness to light just as John wrote:

This is the verdict: Light has come into the world, but men loved darkness instead of light because their deeds were evil. Everyone who does evil hates the light, and will not come into the light for fear that his deeds will be exposed. But whoever lives by the truth comes into the light, so that it may be seen plainly that what he has done has been done through God (John 3:19-21).

But thanks be to God, who doesn't allow us to remain in the cave. He always sends His word to lead and guide us, so we can gain prudence and understanding.

For he has rescued us from the dominion of darkness and brought us into the kingdom of the Son he loves, in whom we have redemption, the forgiveness of sins....Once you were alienated from God and were enemies in your minds because of your evil behavior. But now he has reconciled you by Christ's physical body through death to present you holy in his sight, without blemish and free from accusation—if you continue in your faith, established and firm, not moved from the hope held out in the gospel (Colossians 1:13, 21-23).

Have you been alienated "in your mind" from God? Then there's good news for you. God has found you in your cave and has sent His word to set you free. God told David to leave the cave and return to the light, and He will help you to do the same.

FEBRUARY 9

"Leave your simple ways and you will live;
walk in the way of understanding." — 9:6.

Prior to his arrival in Gath where he acted like a madman, David visited Abimelech the priest. When the priest asked why he had come, David lied and said he was on official business. David asked for food and a sword and the priest gave him some consecrated bread and Goliath's sword that David himself had captured.

While there, David was spotted by one of Saul's servants named Doeg the Edomite who went to Saul and said, "I saw the son of Jesse come to Ahimelech son of Ahitub at Nob. Ahimelech inquired of the Lord for him; he also gave him provisions and the sword of Goliath the Philistine" (1 Samuel 22:9-10). This made Saul, who was already unstable, very angry, and he accused the priest of conspiring with David against him. The priest denied any wrongdoing:

> Who of all your servants is as loyal as David, the king's son-in-law, captain of your bodyguard and highly respected in your household?...Let not the king accuse your servant or any of his father's family, for your servant knows nothing at all about this whole affair (1 Samuel 22:14-15).

But Saul didn't believe Ahimelech and ordered him and his family killed including 85 priests. Doeg carried out the king's madness.

> But Abiathar, a son of Ahimelech son of Ahitub, escaped and fled to join David. He told David that Saul had killed the priests of the Lord. Then David said to Abiathar: "That day, when Doeg the Edomite was there, I knew he would be sure to tell Saul. I am responsible for the death of your father's whole family. Stay with me; don't be afraid; the man who is seeking your life is seeking mine also. You will be safe with me" (1 Samuel 22:20-23).

Today's verse urges the reader to forsake simple ways and walk in ways of understanding. David had visited the priests, needlessly involving them in his flight from Saul. Furthermore, he had lied to them that he was on the king's business. Having defeated Goliath with only a slingshot, David now took Goliath's sword, foolishly thinking that the sword would be of help against Saul and his army. David's trust in the Lord was wavering and his unbelief caused him to go astray.

But look at David's response when confronted with the results of his actions. He took full responsibility and admitted that 85 people were dead because of his foolishness. Walking in faith again, he invited Abiathar to stay with him. David walked once again on the path of understanding, knowing full well that the Lord and not Goliath's sword would protect them all. If you're confronted today with the consequences of a wrong decision, be like David. Take responsibility, abandon your wrong thinking, and then immediately get back on the right path. Learn from David, and make course corrections as quickly as possible.

FEBRUARY 10

"Hatred stirs up dissension,
but love covers over all wrongs." — 10:12.

The man stormed out of the McDonald's, infuriated by our discussion. He had fallen on difficult economic times, so my family and church had been helping him get back on his feet. As we ate, I asked if he felt it was right for him to purchase Pittsburgh Steeler football season tickets (as was his custom for many years) since so many people had sacrificially given to his needs. At that simple suggestion, he stormed out of the restaurant and never returned. I was amazed and hurt that he had reacted so strongly after all that we and others had done for him.

David encountered that same response at least once in his career. Let's look at this particular story:

> When David was told, "Look, the Philistines are fighting against Keilah and are looting the threshing floors," he inquired of the Lord, saying, "Shall I go and attack these Philistines?" The Lord answered him, "Go, attack the Philistines and save Keilah"....So David and his men went to Keilah, fought the Philistines and carried off their livestock. He inflicted heavy losses on the Philistines and saved the people of Keilah (1 Samuel 23:1-2, 5).

When Saul heard that David was in Keilah, he saw his opportunity to trap and defeat him. Instead of being grateful that someone was defending his territory, Saul saw his chance to kill his enemy. Even if Saul was not appreciative of what David did, you would expect that the residents of Keilah would have been. That, however, wasn't the case:

> When David learned that Saul was plotting against him, he said to Abiathar the priest, "Bring the ephod." David said, "O Lord, God of Israel, your servant has heard definitely that Saul plans to come to Keilah and destroy the town on account of me. Will the citizens of Keilah surrender me to him? Will Saul come down, as your servant has heard? O Lord, God of Israel, tell your servant." And the Lord said, "He will" (1 Samuel 23:9-11).

Today's verse reminds you that love covers all wrongs. Keilah owed David its life and existence. Yet they were willing to sell him out to Saul just as that man I mentioned was willing to break with those who had helped him over some football tickets. David didn't destroy Keilah over its lack of appreciation and you can't become angry or embittered with those who wrong you. Today's verse reminds you that love covers all wrongs.

Paul wrote, "Do not repay anyone evil for evil" (Romans 12:17) and "Bear with each other and forgive whatever grievances you may have against one another. Forgive as the Lord forgave you" (Colossians 3:13). Life is full of those who forget to say thanks or repay good with evil. Let your love be such that you are free to bless those who may have spitefully used you, just as Jesus (and David) did.

FEBRUARY 11

"The Lord detests men of perverse heart
but he delights in those whose ways are blameless." — 11:20.

On the first day of this month, we saw how Saul wandered into a cave, not realizing that David and his men were there as well. His men urged David to kill Saul, trying to convince him that the Lord had sent Saul there for that very reason. In response to their advice, "David crept up unnoticed and cut off a corner of Saul's robe" (1 Samuel 24:4).

That seemingly simple and harmless action, however, caused David to be "conscience stricken....He said to his men, 'The Lord forbid that I should do such a thing to my master, the Lord's anointed'" (1 Samuel 24:5-6). What an amazing attitude from one who had endured such persecution from another. David recognized that Saul's authority was given by God and would rest there until God, not David, took it away.

Today's verse says that the Lord delights in those whose ways are blameless, and David certainly must have delighted the Lord by his actions in that cave. Proper treatment of those in authority is an important issue ignored by too many believers.

Paul wrote,

Everyone must submit himself to the governing authorities, for there is no authority except that which God has established. The authorities that exist have been established by God. Consequently, he who rebels against the authority is rebelling against what God has instituted, and those who do so will bring judgment on themselves (Romans 13:1-2).

It's important that you learn to treat authorities with honor and respect, not because they have necessarily earned it, but because God requires it. No one was more mistreated than Jesus. He stood before the corrupt government of Rome and its equally corrupt representative, Pilate, and chose not to say very much to him at all: "'Do you refuse to speak to me?' Pilate said. 'Don't you realize I have the power [authority] either to free you or to crucify you?'" (John 19:10). "Jesus answered, 'You would have no power over me if it were not given to you from above. Therefore the one who handed me over to you is guilty of a greater sin'" (John 19:11). Jesus was saying here that he was unconcerned with how Pilate used the authority God had given him. Pilate would answer to God the Father for that. Jesus, however, was more concerned with Judas who betrayed him than Pilate who was about to sentence Him to death! David had that same attitude when he let Saul escape his hand that day in the cave.

How about you? Do you "cut off the corner of the robe" worn by your authorities? Do you feel free to criticize and put down those over you, whether on the job, in the church, or family? Repent of any rebellious attitude you may have, for if Jesus could face Pilate with a proper attitude, He expects you to do the same no matter what problem you may be facing with those over you in the Lord.

FEBRUARY 12

*"A wife of noble character is her husband's crown,
but a disgraceful wife is like decay in his bones." — 12:4.*

After David spared Saul in the cave, he found himself in the Desert of Maon. There was a wealthy man in that region named Nabal. Since it was shearing time and there would be plenty of food for the shearers, David sent some of his men to Nabal to ask for some provisions. David had protected this man and his interests previously and assumed that this was a small request.

But Nabal (which means "worthless fool") answered David's men harshly and sent them away empty-handed. "David's men turned around and went back. When they arrived, they reported every word. David said to his men, 'Put on your swords!'" (1 Samuel 25:12-13). David had just been noble and kind to Saul. But now he found himself in a desert being mistreated again by someone to whom he had shown kindness. David was fed up so he took matters into his own hands.

Nabal's wife, Abigail, however, heard about what had happened. Quickly gathering a load of food,

> [she] loaded them on donkeys....As she came riding her donkey into a mountain ravine, there were David and his men descending toward her....When Abigail saw David, she quickly got off her donkey and bowed down before David with her face to the ground (1 Samuel 25:18, 20, 23).

Abigail was a wife of noble character, while her husband was true to his name and made a fool of himself. Seeing all this, Abigail didn't stand back and let him perish. Instead she interceded for him with David, talking David out of taking revenge. When she had finished, "David said to Abigail, 'Praise be to the Lord, the God of Israel, who has sent you today to meet me. May you be blessed for your good judgment and for keeping me from bloodshed'" (1 Samuel 25:32-33).

Abigail didn't have the New Testament, but she knew all about what Peter wrote centuries later: "Wives, in the same way be submissive to your husbands so that, if any of them do not believe the word, they may be won over without words by the behavior of their wives, when they see the purity and reverence of your lives" (1 Peter 3:1-2).

Nabal wasn't won over, for when Abigail told him what had almost happened, he went into shock and died! When David heard about Nabal's death, he immediately sent for Abigail and proposed marriage. Having been impressed with her behavior, he couldn't pass up the chance to make her his own. Abigail went from the house of a worthless man to that of a king because she acted right in a wrong situation. My sister, if you are married, let the spirit of Abigail affect all you do for your husband. My brother, if you have been mistreated by someone close to you, let Abigail's gracious intercession for one who was unworthy lead you to do the same. Whether you are a bride or part of the bride of Christ, let your noble character be a crown worn by your husband, whether he be a man or Christ!

"The teaching of the wise is a fountain of life,
turning a man from the snares of death." — 13:14.

"John Stanko, John Stanko, where's John Stanko?" I winced as I heard what I had heard many times before—my supervisor looking for me in his usual demeaning fashion. Having worked at this business for nearly a year, I had just about enough of his style and behavior. This man cheated, lied, stole, and wore a crooked toupee, while I was a "righteous" man. This had gone far enough.

Then my finances got really tight. Seeking the Lord one morning, I felt him tell me to get my attitude right toward that supervisor before I could expect a financial breakthrough. I remember how angry I got at hearing that. Feeling smug and self-righteous, I knew I was justified in my contempt for him. Then I found a verse of Scripture that changed my life: "Slaves, submit yourselves to your masters with all respect, not only to those who are good and considerate, but also to those who are harsh" (1 Peter 2:18).

I faced for the first time how relative my obedience was. If this man (or others, for that matter) treated me right, I would treat him right. Since he treated me wrong, I felt correct in treating him wrong. In a sense, this man controlled me, for his behavior determined mine. I had to change and I prayed that the Lord would change me into the employee that He wanted me to be.

David encountered this same dilemma. Saul, having promised not to pursue David any longer when David spared his life in 1 Samuel 24, continued to hunt David down. When Saul pitched camp in the Desert of Ziph,

> David and Abishai went to the army by night, and there was Saul, lying asleep inside the camp with his spear stuck in the ground near his head. Abner and the soldiers were lying around him. Abishai said to David, "Today God has delivered your enemy into your hands. Now let me pin him to the ground with one thrust of my spear; I won't strike him twice" (1 Samuel 26:7-8).

What was David to do? Was hatred going to run his life, or was the will of God? He was standing there with nothing but his principles to guide him and fortunately (for him and us), he made the right choice. "But David said to Abishai, 'Don't destroy him! Who can lay a hand on the Lord's anointed and be guiltless?'" (1 Samuel 26:9). The same is true for you—you can't lay a hand on the Lord's anointed without it bringing trouble on you.

Let the Lord deal with your boss, teacher, pastor, choir director, or foreman. You focus on doing the Lord's will and keeping a righteous attitude. Paul wrote, "Do not be overcome by evil, but overcome evil with good" (Romans 12:21). David didn't get promoted by getting rid of Saul; he got the throne by trusting God. In that same godly tradition, you'll see God's promises for you fulfilled as you do God's will no matter what people, and especially those in authority, do to you.

FEBRUARY 14

"He who fears the Lord has a secure fortress,
and for his children it will be a refuge." — 14:26.

What a great spiritual victory for David! Having resisted the temptation to kill Saul, he had shown great wisdom and insight. Yet sometimes great spiritual highs are followed by spiritual valleys, and David encountered a low that would lead to eventual trouble.

The Lord had preserved David from the hand of Saul, even though there had been several close calls. "But David thought to himself, 'One of these days I will be destroyed by the hand of Saul. The best thing I can do is to escape to the land of the Philistines. Then Saul will give up searching for me anywhere in Israel, and I will slip out of his hand'" (1 Samuel 27:1).

David was discouraged, assuming that Saul would successfully pursue him once again. His discouragement led to a wrong conclusion that in turn led him to take wrong action. Today's verse teaches that those who fear the Lord have a strong fortress. Abandoning this truth, David sought refuge with the Philistines. He reasoned that they would protect him and Saul wouldn't venture into the land of his enemies to find David. Swapping the security God could give for that which he could find for himself, David made a bad decision.

One sin usually leads to another and it was no exception for David. When he arrived in Philistia, Achish (the same king in whose presence David feigned madness) gave him Ziklag as a base of operation. From there David went and attacked the surrounding peoples.

Whenever David attacked an area, he did not leave a man or woman alive, but took sheep and cattle, donkeys and camels, and clothes. Then he returned to Achish. "When Achish asked, 'Where did you go raiding today?' David would say, 'Against the Negev of Judah' or 'Against the Negev of Jerahmeel' or 'Against the Negev of the Kenites.' He did not leave a man or woman alive to be brought to Gath, for he thought, they might inform on us and say, 'This is what David did'" (1 Samuel 27:8-11).

David lied to Achish about his activities. Having wrongly concluded that he must flee Saul for safety, he now resorted to unnecessary violence and falsehood.

What about you? Have you come to any wrong conclusions about God's faithfulness and His ongoing ability to preserve and protect you? Has one wrong action led to another? Have you stopped giving because things are tight? Stopped working hard because your job is going nowhere? Stopped reading the Word because you see the wicked prospering while you walk through tribulation? Whatever your situation, be encouraged today. The Lord is a strong tower for those who trust in Him, and that tower is for you and yours. Run into Him today and abandon any other tower to which you have run. In time, He'll deliver you just like He did David.

FEBRUARY 15

*"The Lord detests the way of the wicked
but he loves those who pursue righteousness." — 15:9.*

Saul and David provide an interesting contrast. While David grew in God's favor and knowledge, Saul went in the opposite direction. We see David's mistakes and God's redemptive work in spite of them. On the other hand, we see Saul's stubborn rebellion and gradual demise. While David was discouraged and wandering in the land of the Philistines, Saul was resorting to ungodly ways, trying desperately to save his throne and his life!

The Philistines assembled and came and set up camp at Shunem, while Saul gathered all the Israelites and set up camp at Gilboa. When Saul saw the Philistine army, he was afraid; terror filled his heart. He inquired of the Lord, but the Lord did not answer him by dreams or Urim or prophets (1 Samuel 28:4-6).

First, Saul was overcome with fear and then joined the ranks of Herod and Pilate—men to whom God had nothing to say. Faced with this situation, Saul felt he had only one choice: "Saul then said to his attendants, 'Find me a woman who is a medium, so I may go and inquire of her'" (1 Samuel 28:7). Even though a forbidden practice, Saul resorted to witchcraft to calm his fears.

Saul consistently chose ungodly solutions to problems in his life. When he was faced with an evil spirit from the Lord, he sought relief in David's music. He then tried to use illicit spiritual knowledge to obtain guidance and comfort when dealing with fear. It's no wonder the Lord rejected him as king.

David wasn't a perfect man, but he pursued righteousness and was a man after God's own heart. Because of this, the grace of God was always evident in his life, even when he made wrong decisions. That's why David wrote:

I will instruct you and teach you in the way you should go; I will counsel you and watch over you. Do not be like the horse or the mule, which have no understanding, but must be controlled by bit and bridle or they will not come to you. Many are the woes of the wicked, but the Lord's unfailing love surrounds the man who trusts in him (Psalm 32:8-10).

Saul was like a mule; the Lord had to lead him by circumstances (the bit and bridle). David was a son; the Lord led him by His grace. Isn't the grace of God wonderful? Where would David have been, and where would you be, without it? "The Lord is compassionate and gracious, slow to anger, abounding in love. He will not always accuse, nor will he harbor his anger forever; he does not treat us as our sins deserve or repay us according to our iniquities" (Psalm 103:8-10).

Those verses can just as easily be your testimony. Count on the grace of God today. The Lord isn't angry with those who fear Him! Pursue righteousness and enjoy God's favor. He loves you and His grace is abundantly available to you.

FEBRUARY 16

"There is a way that seems right to a man
but in the end it leads to death." — 16:25.

It seemed the right thing to do, so David went to Ziklag in the land of the Philistines. Now he had an opportunity to see the word of the Lord fulfilled. Having won the confidence of the Philistines through falsehood, David offered himself and his troops to fight against Saul and his army.

I don't know whether David was serious or whether that offer was another part of his deception. Pretending to be the friend of Achish the king had won the king's favor in the past. Maybe now David offered his help with no intention of fighting Saul's armies. Or maybe David saw this as the opportunity for which he had waited. If the Philistines could defeat Saul, then David would ascend to the throne of Israel. Whatever David's motives, it was a bad idea that probably made sense to him at the time.

When David returned to Ziklag, his home base, he found it ransacked and his family gone. Invaders had come and carried off his loved ones and those of his men. What had seemed like such a good idea was now a mess. The way that had seemed right to David had ended in "death."

I can identify with David, and you probably can as well. Some of my best ideas have turned out to be a bust. This is because I haven't heeded what Paul wrote: "So we fix our eyes not on what is seen, but on what is unseen. For what is seen is temporary, but what is unseen is eternal" (2 Corinthians 4:18). I've had to learn, sometimes the hard way, that my way isn't always the best way. Seeking the Lord for His will, and then following it, has always led to life.

Through Moses, the Lord told His people:

See, I set before you today life and prosperity, death and destruction. For I command you today to love the Lord your God, to walk in his ways, and to keep his commands, decrees and laws; then you will live and increase, and the Lord your God will bless you in the land you are entering to possess....This day I call heaven and earth as witnesses against you that I have set before you life and death, blessings and curses. Now choose life, so that you and your children may live and that you may love the Lord your God, listen to his voice, and hold fast to him (Deuteronomy 30:15-16, 19-20).

The Lord wants you to choose life. Choosing your own ways can be disastrous as David learned. Choosing God's ways always leads to good but not necessarily easy things. Examine your paths today and determine if you've made any decisions that seemed good at the time but have led to your Ziklag being overrun. If you have, seek the Lord for a new path that will lead you from Ziklag back to the promised land.

FEBRUARY 17

"A wicked man listens to evil lips;
a liar pays attention to a malicious tongue." — 17:4.

The man I was talking to had killed his parents. In a drug-induced frenzy, he had beaten his parents to death and then charged a police blockade armed only with a starter's pistol, sustaining numerous bullet wounds. To everyone's amazement, he lived and was on trial for murder. During that time, this man met the Lord and he was in my Bible study.

Mercy and grace do not flow easily from my personality, and this man taxed my ability to be civil, let alone gracious. But as time went on, I found the Lord working in me a sense of love and concern for him that surprised me. As I have faced my own shortcomings, sins, and failures over the years, I'm realizing that

It is by grace you have been saved, through faith—and this not from yourselves, it is the gift of God—not by works, so that no one can boast. For we are God's workmanship, created in Christ Jesus to do good works, which God prepared in advance for us to do (Ephesians 2:8-10).

David had to learn to give grace as I have. When he and his men pursued those who had taken their families and possessions, we are told that 200 men stayed behind because they were too exhausted to continue. David and the band that continued on were successful and returned to the others they had left behind:

Then David came to the two hundred men who had been too exhausted to follow him....But all the evil men and troublemakers among David's followers said, "Because they did not go out with us, we will not share with them the plunder we recovered. However, each man may take his wife and children and go" (1 Samuel 30:21-22).

There was no grace among some of David's men. Having done the work, they didn't want to share the results with those who stayed behind. They had evil lips and a malicious tongue as mentioned in today's verse. But David showed mercy and grace, since it was his fault that the whole rescue operation had to take place.

David replied, "No, my brothers, you must not do that with what the Lord has given us. He has protected us and handed over to us the forces that came against us....The share of the man who stayed with the supplies is to be the same as that of him who went down to the battle" (1 Samuel 30:23-24).

How about you? How is the grace level in your life? Do you freely dispense God's grace or give it according to the merit of those with whom you work, live, or worship? Make an effort today to give away some of the grace that God has given to you. Look for an "unworthy" candidate and share with him or her some of the spoils of your victories. Don't listen to the voices around you that tell you to grudgingly give grace, but rather give it away freely, just as it has been given to you.

FEBRUARY 18

*"It is not good to be partial to the wicked
or to deprive the innocent of justice."* — 18:5.

This month we're studying the life of David, trying to see when David learned the lessons that he in turn imparted to Solomon in the book of Proverbs. Today we come to the end of Saul's tragic life. He was given every opportunity to repent and rule righteously, but could not do so.

Today's verse expresses the heart of God. Being a just God, He can't be partial to the wicked or keep justice from the innocent. God wishes all men to repent and come to a knowledge of the truth. God's patience isn't without limits, however, and there's a day of reckoning for everyone. Saul had been ruling on borrowed time, yet he persisted in wickedness and rebellion. Judgment day was now at hand.

Now the Philistines fought against Israel; the Israelites fled before them, and many fell slain on Mount Gilboa. The Philistines pressed hard after Saul and his sons, and they killed his sons Jonathan, Abinadab and Malki-Shua. The fighting grew fierce around Saul, and when the archers overtook him, they wounded him critically....Saul took his own sword and fell on it....So Saul and his three sons and his armor-bearer and all his men died together that same day (1 Samuel 31:1-4, 6).

Paul wrote, "Do not be deceived: God cannot be mocked. A man reaps what he sows. The one who sows to please his sinful nature, from that nature will reap destruction" (Galatians 6:7-8). Saul had sown bad seed for years. Hatred, lying, witchcraft, and deceit had been his companions. Having sown to his sinful nature, Saul reaped a harvest from that nature. One day the Lord had had enough. When that day came, it was a bad day for Saul.

Meditate today on the words of Peter:

But do not forget this one thing, dear friends: With the Lord a day is like a thousand years, and a thousand years are like a day. The Lord is not slow in keeping his promise, as some understand slowness. He is patient with you, not wanting anyone to perish, but everyone to come to repentance. But the day of the Lord will come like a thief (2 Peter 3:8-10).

If you're waiting for the Lord to move in your situation, take heart. The Lord may be slow to you, but when He moves, the results are often swift and just. If you're persisting in some attitude or sinful practice, then repent. Don't mistake His patience for His approval. Peter wrote that His patience is to lead you to repentance, not to endorse what you're doing.

God won't be partial to the wicked for long. Desiring that they repent, He wants them to turn toward Him. God will also not let the righteous suffer beyond their time. He will act for His people with power and justice. Take encouragement from David's life and put your trust in the God who acts without partiality to all.

FEBRUARY 19

"A false witness will not go unpunished,
and he who pours out lies will perish." — *19:9.*

"No, Daddy, I wasn't playing with the pen." I had warned my three-year-old not to play with the ball-point pen she had in her hand. Retreating to her room for a while, she emerged with pen marks all over her face. When I asked her if she had been playing with that pen, she gave me that answer with a straight face! At first she couldn't understand how I knew she had been playing until I lifted her up to look in the mirror. Then she received the punishment for her lie.

David had to deal with a similar situation. When Saul killed himself, a young Amalekite man took off running to bring David the news of Saul's death. As he went, he decided to alter the story of what really happened so that his own position in David's eyes would be enhanced.

This young man started with the truth: "Saul and his son Jonathan are dead" (2 Samuel 1:4). When David asked him for details, the lies began:

> "I happened to be on Mount Gilboa," the young man said, "and there was Saul, leaning on his spear, with the chariots and riders almost upon him. When he turned around and saw me, he called out to me, and I said, 'What can I do?'...Then he said to me, 'Stand over me and kill me! I am in the throes of death, but I'm still alive.' So I stood over him and killed him, because I knew that after he had fallen he could not survive" (2 Samuel 1:6-10).

Of course, Saul had really killed himself, but this young man saw an opportunity for promotion. He thought (incorrectly) that he would make himself look good by telling David how he had put Saul out of his misery. When you think of it, most lies are told for one of two reasons: to make a person look good or to hide some bad deed. This young man wanted to look good and bragged of a good deed that was neither good nor founded in truth. This young man, like my daughter, had pen marks all over his face. David asked him,

> "Why were you not afraid to lift your hand to destroy the Lord's anointed?" Then David called one of his men and said, "Go strike him down!" So he struck him down, and he died. For David had said to him, "Your blood be on your own head. Your own mouth testified against you when you said, 'I killed the Lord's anointed'" (2 Samuel 1:14-16).

That man paid for his lie with his life. I'm glad that every lie isn't punishable by death or I wouldn't be writing this book (and you wouldn't be reading it)! Today's verse tells you that liars are punished for their lies. Commit yourself to tell the truth today. Eliminate exaggeration and false claims from your job resume or stories of the past, and answer inquiries accurately. Don't suffer the punishment for lies, but rather endure the cost of truth and you'll be the better for it.

FEBRUARY 20

"Love and faithfulness keep a king safe;
through love his throne is made secure." — 20:28.

I'm always surprised by some of the stories of those who have worked for ministries and churches. Many times they tell me tales of low pay, difficult work conditions, long hours, and pressures brought about by the character flaws of supervisors, management, and yes, even pastors. Of course, no work situation is perfect because all people are imperfect. Yet it has always seemed to me that ministry work need not be that traumatic.

A pastor or ministry worker is a leader just like David was a king. A position of leadership, however, isn't maintained solely by the anointing or calling on that person's life. Rather it's made secure through love and faithfulness as today's verse teaches. Ministry environments should be bathed in love and brotherly kindness (along with good business practices), and through those virtues provide meaningful experiences and fun for all involved.

David understood this principle and taught it to his son Solomon. After Saul's death, David took his first step toward becoming king of all Israel: "Then the men of Judah came to Hebron and there they anointed David king over the house of Judah" (2 Samuel 2:2-4).

What was David's first act as king of Judah? Did he search out and destroy his opponents? Build himself a palace? Set up a retirement account or give himself a pay raise? The answer is "no" to all those. Instead David showed love to someone:

When David was told that it was the men of Jabesh Gilead who had buried Saul, he sent messengers to the men of Jabesh Gilead to say to them, "The Lord bless you for showing this kindness to Saul your master by burying him. May the Lord now show you kindness and faithfulness and I too will show you the same favor because you have done this" (2 Samuel 2:4-6).

David wasn't kind to *just anyone*, but to those who had been gracious to Saul, David's personal enemy. He could have ignored the efforts of those men who had honored King Saul, but instead recognized and rewarded their faithfulness. David was establishing his own leadership by honoring the noble efforts of others.

If you're a leader or in training to be one, remember what Jesus said:

The kings of the Gentiles lord it over them; and those who exercise authority over them call themselves Benefactors. But you are not to be like that. Instead, the greatest among you should be like the youngest, and the one who rules like the one who serves (Luke 22:2526).

Don't be puffed up if you're a leader and don't try to hold on to your authority by exerting it. Instead look to be faithful and create an atmosphere of love, for love and service will allow you to continue in leadership for as long as the Lord wills.

FEBRUARY 21

"Haughty eyes and a proud heart,
the lamp of the wicked, are sin!" — 21:4.

There I was, dressed in my Sunday best and waiting my opportunity to preach. I was singing praises to the Lord while reflecting on several failures I had encountered during the past week. As I stood there in God's presence, the Lord spoke these words: "You're proud!" Now pride wasn't something that was on my mind or heart, but the Lord cut through my religious thinking to get to the heart of the matter—I was arrogant.

Pride has been a problem since the beginning of my walk. Fueling a critical spirit in me, my arrogance has caused me to make some bad decisions. Today's verse says that haughtiness is the lamp of the wicked. How dim my way has been when lit by my arrogance! I've stumbled over all manner of small obstacles that could have been easily hurdled in the power of God.

David understood the principle behind today's verse and surely taught it to Solomon. Having been anointed king over Judah only, David waited in Hebron for more than seven years to become the king over all Israel. Humbling himself under God's mighty hand, he patiently endured.

Not everyone in Israel was as patient and humble as David. Some couldn't wait on God, and in their pride decided to help God do what He had promised. Two such men were Baanah and Recab. We read that

> Recab and Baanah...arrived there in the heat of the day while he [King Ish-Bosheth] was taking his noonday rest. They went into the inner part of the house as if to get some wheat, and they stabbed him in the stomach. Then Recab and his brother Baanah slipped away (2 Samuel 4:5-6).

Having assassinated the king, they proceeded to cut off his head, run to David, and present the proof of their loyalty. When they arrived at David's court, they said, "Here is the head of Ish-bosheth son of Saul, your enemy, who tried to take your life. This day the Lord has avenged my lord the king against Saul and his offspring" (2 Samuel 4:8).

The Lord was capable of avenging David against Saul, but the lamp of pride had illuminated the path of these two men. They had reached a logical conclusion, but had started out with the wrong premise! In their arrogance, they concluded that God needed them. After all, how could God get David to the throne without their help? They paid for their sin with their lives, as do all who walk in arrogance.

O Lord, cleanse me from any arrogance. Where I walk in haughtiness, replace it with humility. Show me those areas that are dimly lit by the lamp of my pride and let the light of Your Word light the paths of my feet. What I have accomplished, You have done for me. I freely admit that and my ongoing dependence on You. Deliver me from the pride of life, and lead me into a new understanding of Your love and care. Amen.

FEBRUARY 22

"Humility and the fear of the Lord
bring wealth and honor and life." — 22:4.

Snow flurries were in the air and there I was, kneeling on the sidewalk outside my family's church. I was a teenager participating in Easter services at our Byzantine Catholic Church and I was more than a little embarrassed. As traffic went by on this busy street, I was in a long line of worshipers who were responding to the priest's blessing. As I knelt there, I kept wondering, "What if any of my friends see me?" I did my best to shield my face from public view.

For a long time, I held that image of kneeling on the sidewalk in public as my concept of humility. To me serving God wasn't a pleasant practice. Most of the time you ended up doing a lot of what you didn't really want to do. Then I met the Lord and He changed my wrong impression. I found out it wasn't all as negative as I thought; in fact, it was fun! I learned that after every unpleasant season or test comes a period of blessing, and the blessing is worth the trip getting to it.

After David passed the test with those two assassins, he was ready to be king. David had endured many years of hardship and discouragement on his way to the throne in Jerusalem. Having walked in humility and the fear of the Lord, he was now ready for the rewards mentioned in today's verse—wealth and honor and life.

All the tribes of Israel came to David at Hebron and said, "We are your own flesh and blood. In the past, while Saul was king over us, you were the one who led Israel on their military campaigns." And the Lord said to you, "You will shepherd my people Israel, and you will become their ruler"....And in Jerusalem he reigned over all Israel and Judah thirty-three years (2 Samuel 5:1-2, 5).

Be encouraged today that the Lord doesn't bring trials into your life forever. David wrote, "For his anger lasts only a moment, but his favor lasts a lifetime; weeping may remain for a night, but rejoicing comes in the morning" (Psalm 30:5). James wrote,

Consider it pure joy, my brothers, whenever you face trials of many kinds, because you know that the testing of your faith develops perseverance. Perseverance must finish its work so that you may be mature and complete, not lacking anything (James 1:2-4).

After trial comes blessing; after death comes life. Be encouraged today that your trials are for a purpose. They've come to prepare you for the wealth and honor and life that's yours. Don't despair, for when you have endured, you'll have a coronation just like David did. And you know that the blessing at the end is far better than the journey you took to get there. Our God is a good God, and His desire is to bless, not burden, His people. Walk in the hope of His promises today and be assured that serving God is a lot more than kneeling on a sidewalk in the snow!

FEBRUARY 23

*"Apply your heart to instruction
and your ears to words of knowledge." — 23:12.*

Can you imagine David's excitement when he finally ascended the throne? Having waiting all those years, he saw that God's promise was at hand. First, there was the revelation on the part of the leaders. As we saw yesterday, they came to David and had words of knowledge: "We are your own flesh and blood....And the Lord said to you, 'You will shepherd my people Israel, and you will be their ruler'" (2 Samuel 5:1-2).

Those statements had always been true, but now the Lord opened their eyes. You can't just decide to understand the things of God—God has to show them to you. Once God shows them to you, you must make them an integral part of your life.

But the leaders weren't the only ones getting instruction. After hosting a dinner, David announced his first plan of action and the people, with his new subjects, took action: "The king and his men marched to Jerusalem to attack the Jebusites, who lived there. The Jebusites said to David, 'You will not get in here; even the blind and the lame can ward you off.' They thought, 'David cannot get in here.' Nevertheless, David captured the fortress of Zion, the City of David" (2 Samuel 5:6-7).

David must have been meditating on the words of God spoken to Moses:

When you cross the Jordan into Canaan, drive out all the inhabitants of the land before you. Destroy all their carved images and their cast idols, and demolish all their high places. Take possession of the land and settle in it, for I have given you the land to possess...if you do not drive out the inhabitants of the land, those you allow to remain will become barbs in your eyes and thorns in your sides. They will give you trouble in the land where you will live. And then I will do to you what I plan to do to them (Numbers 33:51-53, 55-56).

Those words were 400 years old, and Israel had ignored them. According to today's verse, however, David applied his heart and ears to instruction. David read those words and acted on them. Having received the commitment of the people to his God-given position as king, he marched them to Jerusalem and took it as the Lord had commanded Moses.

For David, the word of the Lord wasn't for amusement, but for action. He didn't become conservative or careful once on his throne, but began to use his position and authority to carry out the will of God. What's your situation? Has God promoted you, and you find yourself being cautious? Or are you still aggressively applying your heart to understand what God wants so that you can do it, no matter the cost or odds against you?

Someone once said that the church isn't a rest home for saints. You're a soldier in God's army and every soldier goes on the battlefield every now and then. Determine today to apply your heart to understand what God's doing in the earth and in your life, and then play an active part in seeing His will carried out.

"The schemes of folly are sin, and men detest a mocker." — 24:9.

I was young, but I'll never forget the drama of America's football championship in Super Bowl III. That game matched the powerful Baltimore Colts against the upstart New York Jets, led by quarterback Joe Namath. Baltimore bragged that they would easily defeat the Jets, while Namath guaranteed a victory for his team, which was a serious underdog. In the end, the Colts' overconfidence was their undoing and Namath led his team to victory.

That must have been what it was like when David met the Jebusites. The Jebusites were powerful by virtue of the fact that they held the high places. So great was their confidence, they didn't post guards or protect the entrances to their stronghold. They were like the Baltimore Colts.

Then there was David, like Namath, predicting a victory for his people. David turned his men loose, they found a way up, and they defeated the Jebusites, overcoming tremendous obstacles with faith and skill.

On that day, David said, "Anyone who conquers the Jebusites will have to use the water shaft to reach those 'lame and blind' who are David's enemies." That is why they say, "The 'blind and lame' will not enter the palace." David then took up residence in the fortress and called it the City of David (2 Samuel 5:8-9).

Nothing has changed in more than 3,000 years. The enemies of God still hold some high places and discourage God's people from trying to dislodge them. But we have "divine power to demolish strongholds" (2 Corinthians 10:4). The pornography industry in your city mocks you and says, "Our lawyers and the organized crime who own us can defeat you." The abortionists laugh and hide behind the Supreme Court and other legal strongholds. Drugs and crime in the inner city mock your efforts to make a difference, claiming that the high place of poverty, racism, and despair are more powerful than your puny spiritual efforts.

But take courage today. Learning from David, you too must find their "water shaft." You must find and exploit the weakness of your enemies as they mock and boast from their high place. Refuse to be intimidated and attack them in the Spirit. You don't have to be mean or take to the streets in protest, but you can aggressively pray and work to see your mocking enemies pulled down from their place of confidence.

"Remove the wicked from the king's presence, and his throne will be established through righteousness." — 25:5.

"When you're hot, you're hot" was a popular expression of the 70s. If that saying was popular in David's day, it would have been applied to him. Having captured Jerusalem and made it his headquarters, David continued on with his conquests. His list of victories was impressive:

> In the course of time, David defeated the Philistines and subdued them....David also defeated the Moabites....Moreover, David fought Hadadezer son of Rehob, king of Zobah...[and] captured a thousand of his chariots, seven thousand charioteers and twenty thousand foot soldiers....When the Arameans of Damascus came to help Hadadezer king of Zobah, David struck down twenty-two thousand of them....And David became famous after he returned from striking down eighteen thousand Edomites in the Valley of Salt....The Lord gave David victory wherever he went (2 Samuel 8:1-5, 13-14).

As we saw a few days ago, David was committed to carry out the word of the Lord given to Moses to destroy all the people in the land. He knew the truth of today's verse—he needed to deal ruthlessly with the wicked nations around him or his throne would be brought down as he and his people mingled with and adopted the practices of the people in the land.

The same is true for you. Since you are a son or daughter of the King (making you royalty), you must work to put away all unrighteousness in your own life: "If by the Spirit you put to death the misdeeds of the body, you will live" (Romans 8:13).

Paul explained why this war must be carried out: "The mind of sinful man is death, but the mind controlled by the Spirit is life and peace; the sinful mind is hostile to God. It does not submit to God's law, nor can it do so. Those controlled by the sinful nature cannot please God" (Romans 8:6-8).

The reality of life for you is that "the sting of death is sin, and the power of sin is the law. But thanks be to God! He gives us the victory through our Lord Jesus Christ" (1 Corinthians 15:56-57).

The Lord wants to take you, like He took David, from victory to victory. Your walk isn't just to be a few victories and then a period of rest on the throne. Using your authority and power in the Spirit, you're to enjoy a life of victorious warfare as you defeat your enemies in and around you. Don't grow weary of the battle and don't look for the royal retirement home. Know that war is a part of your royal inheritance and fight the good fight. Let your testimony be that of David's, for God gave him victory wherever he went.

FEBRUARY 26

"Though his speech is charming, do not believe him,
for seven abominations fill his heart." — 26:25.

I felt so bad for this woman who was sitting across from me in a restaurant as we shared a meal together. She was a widow and I had become friends with her, occasionally counseling her. One time she had taken me to meet her financial counselor and he seemed like a fine man and brother. He was articulate, knowledgeable, and gracious, and she had invested all her money in his company.

This dinner was painful because my widow friend explained how she had lost all her money through this man's investments. This man had been a smooth talker, but he was a fraud and had covered his duplicity very well. She had hoped for a good return on her money, only to have lost it all to a con man.

David had to face a con man in his own day. When David was established on his throne, he asked, "Is there anyone still left of the house of Saul to whom I can show kindness for Jonathan's sake?" (2 Samuel 9:1). The king called for Ziba, a servant in Saul's house and put that question to him. Ziba informed David that there was one surviving son of Jonathan named Mephibosheth. This son was lame in both feet, having been crippled while fleeing during the days after Saul's demise.

David summoned this son and said, "I will surely show you kindness for the sake of your father Jonathan. I will restore to you all the land that belonged to your grandfather Saul, and you will always eat at my table" (2 Samuel 9:7). The king order Ziba "to farm the land for him and bring in the crops, so that your master's grandson may be provided for" (2 Samuel 9:10). Ziba responded, "Your servant will do whatever my lord the king commands his servant to do" (2 Samuel 9:11). Ziba gave the right answer, but seven abominations filled his heart as today's verse points out.

Later when David fled before his rebellious son Absalom, Ziba appeared before him and lied about Mephibosheth (see 2 Samuel 16:1-4). Trying to con David, Ziba told David that Mephibosheth was hoping for David's defeat to avenge his grandfather Saul's death. Upon hearing this, David gave Ziba all that he had given previously to Mephibosheth. David later discovered the truth when he returned to Jerusalem and was able to give Mephibosheth back what was his.

Have you ever been fooled by someone who was a good talker? Knowing what to say and how to say it, they convinced you of their credibility, integrity, or knowledge. Later you found, however, that they were smooth operators and you had purchased something you didn't need or want. There is only one remedy for that problem—remember that talk is cheap and seek the Lord diligently as you consider major life decisions.

God knows the hearts of all and you and I must learn not to rely on our instincts where people are concerned. Pray about what you hear, and take your time. In the end, you'll be glad you waited for God to reveal what was really in men's hearts after you heard what was coming from their mouth.

FEBRUARY 27

*"Like a bird that strays from its nest
is a man who strays from his home."* — 27:8.

"In the spring at the time when kings go off to war, David sent Joab out with the king's men and the whole Israelite army" (2 Samuel 11:1). Thus begins the most tragic segment of David's life. Having survived Saul's treachery, the dangers of battle, and his own youthful mistakes, David was about to succumb to the power of his flesh.

David should have gone out with his army but instead strayed from his "nest." Not being in the place God had for him, he was vulnerable to problems and temptations. The rest is history:

> One evening David got up from his bed and walked around on the roof of the palace. From the roof he saw a woman bathing. The woman was very beautiful, and David sent someone to find out about her....Then David sent messengers to get her. She came to him, and he slept with her....The woman conceived and sent word to David, saying, "I am pregnant" (2 Samuel 11:2-5).

Jesus said, "I am the vine; you are the branches. If a man remains in me and I in him, he will bear much fruit; apart from me you can do nothing" (John 15:5). That verse tells you where your home is—in Christ. If you wander from that home, you're in the same danger David was in. There's no time when you can say, "That's okay, Lord. I can handle this." Regardless of your past success, you must continue to abide in Christ and allow Him to be your life and strength.

Paul understood this fact and wrote:

> Do you not know that in a race all the runners run, but only one gets the prize? Run in such a way as to get the prize. Everyone who competes in the games goes into strict training. They do it to get a crown that will not last; but we do it to get a crown that will last forever. Therefore I do not run like a man running aimlessly; I do not fight like a man beating the air. No, I beat my body and make it my slave so that after I have preached to others, I myself will not be disqualified for the prize (1 Corinthians 9:24-27).

David got out of his lane assignment as he ran his race, and was disqualified for a time. Don't fall into the same trap. Make sure you're abiding in the Vine, not just when you're in trouble, but all the time. When you're in Christ, you're where you're meant to be. Don't stray from that place for any reason. Pray, read, give, meditate, serve, worship, and pray some more. Maturity doesn't replace the need for those things; it only serves to heighten the need for them in the mind of the wise person.

"He who conceals his sins does not prosper, but whoever confesses and renounces them finds mercy." — 28:13.

I rehearsed my speech for the umpteenth time as I nervously sat in my pastor's living room, waiting for him to come downstairs. Convinced that my spiritual condition was critical, I braced for the worst. When he came, I shared my recent failures and lack of spirituality. He listened, prayed for me, and then gave me some new responsibility in the church.

I was convinced that my honesty with my pastor would keep me from being used by God and him. Instead I discovered that God was more comfortable with my human frailty than I was, giving me mercy and grace in my failures. Today's verse says that mercy is available to those who freely confess, but those who don't are cut off from the grace they so desperately need. David had to learn this lesson the hard way.

Once David found out Bathsheba was with child, he manipulated circumstances so that her husband Uriah was killed in battle.

When Uriah's wife heard that her husband was dead, she mourned for him. After the time of mourning was over, David had her brought to his house, and she became his wife and bore him a son. But the thing David had done displeased the Lord (2 Samuel 11:26-27).

David tried to go on with his life without addressing the wrongs he had committed. A son was born to him so we know that he went almost a year without dealing with what he had done. Then Nathan the prophet came and confronted him, and David finally confessed that he was guilty: "Then David said to Nathan, 'I have sinned against the Lord'" (2 Samuel 12:13).

When David said he sinned, "Nathan replied, 'The Lord has taken away your sin. You are not going to die. But because by doing this you have made the enemies of the Lord show utter contempt, the son born to you will die'" (2 Samuel 12:13-14).

Yes, there were consequences from his sin, but there was also mercy when David confessed. The Lord doesn't want to rub your face in what you've done, but He does want you to "face the music" and get on with your life.

John wrote:

If we claim to be without sin, we deceive ourselves and the truth is not in us. If we confess our sins, he is faithful and just and will forgive us our sins and purify us from all unrighteousness. If we claim we have not sinned, we make him out to be a liar and his word has no place in our lives (1 John 1:8-10).

Be honest with yourself, be honest with God. That honesty puts you in a place where God can grant you mercy, grace, and yes, even prosperity.

FEBRUARY 29

"By justice a king gives a country stability,
but one who is greedy for bribes tears it down." —29:4.

The Lord told David that, because of his sin with Bathsheba, "the sword will never depart from your house" and "out of your own household I am going to bring calamity upon you" (2 Samuel 12:10-11). David's son Absalom was the "chosen" instrument to fulfill those promises and the pain and loss from Absalom's actions were indeed great.

> He [Absalom] would get up early and stand by the side of the road leading to the city gate. Whenever anyone came with a complaint to be placed before the king for a decision, Absalom would call out to him, "What town are you from?" He would answer, "Your servant is from one of the tribes of Israel." Then Absalom would say to him, "Your claims are valid and proper, but there is no representative of the king to hear you." And Absalom would add, "If only I were appointed judge in the land! Then everyone who has a complaint or case could come to me and I would see that he gets justice" (2 Samuel 15:1-4).

Absalom set out to fulfill the truth in today's verse. Being ambitious and greedy for power, position, and money, he "stole the hearts of the men of Israel" (2 Samuel 15:6) by planting the seeds of doubt and discord. He wasn't interested in justice but rather in being king. Not willing to pay the price that his father paid to come into a leadership position, Absalom tried to cut corners and take what his father had patiently waited to attain.

The result was a rebellion against David that cost many lives. Absalom did tear down the country as today's verse warns, and it was only preserved by the grace of God. Ambition is destructive, as James warned:

> Who is wise and understanding among you? Let him show it by his good life, by deeds done in the humility that comes from wisdom. But if you harbor bitter envy and selfish ambition in your hearts, do not boast about it or deny the truth. Such "wisdom" does not come down from heaven but is earthly, unspiritual, of the devil. For where you have envy and selfish ambition, there you find disorder and every evil practice (James 3:13-16).

James warned us not to deny ambition when it is present. It's easy to disguise ambition as something else like spiritual insight or justification for trying to compensate for the poor job someone else is "obviously" doing. Absalom hid ambition behind his outward concern for the needs of the people in his father's kingdom.

Is there disorder on your job, in your church or home? Then start to look for envy or selfish ambition, first in your own heart. Be ambitious to serve God, but don't be zealous for position or power. Don't let the spirit of Absalom get a foothold in your mind or heart, for its fruit is bitter. Don't take matters into your own hands but let God do the promoting in your life and ministry.

MARCH 1

"Such is the end of all who go after ill-gotten gain;
it takes away the lives of those who get it." — 1:19.

The Bible contains so much about David that one month isn't enough to cover all that needs to be said. So we will borrow a few days from March to complete our study. We left off in February as Absalom had stolen the hearts of the men of Israel. Standing at the gate, he told the people that if he were in charge, things would be better for them.

Then one day he made his move:

A messenger came and told David, "The hearts of the men of Israel are with Absalom." Then David said to all his officials who were with him in Jerusalem, "Come! We must flee, or none of us will escape from Absalom. We must leave immediately, or he will move quickly to overtake us and bring ruin upon us and put the city to the sword" (2 Samuel 15:13-14).

Absalom was so hungry for power that he would have killed his own father to get it! The spirit of Absalom still shows up in life, sometimes even in churches. There are always those who say, "If I were in charge, things would be different." Often the youth director wants to be the associate pastor, the music director wants to be the pastor, and the associate pastor wants to be bishop. There may be plenty of gossiping, backbiting, and political maneuvering to go along with the ambition, sometimes making churches less than pleasant places to work.

Today's verse tells us that power achieved through wrong means takes away the life of those who get it. Absalom paid for his ambition with his life. Contrast his death with that of Jesus, who gave His life as a ransom for many:

Your attitude should be the same as that of Christ Jesus: Who, being in very nature God, did not consider equality with God something to be grasped, but made himself nothing, taking the very nature of a servant, being made in human likeness. And being found in appearance as a man, he humbled himself and became obedient to death—even death on a cross! (Philippians 2:5-8).

Absalom lost his life, but Jesus showed us how to find it. Jesus endured the cross and

Therefore God exalted him to the highest place and gave him the name that is above every name, that at the name of Jesus every knee should bow, in heaven and on earth and under the earth, and every tongue confess that Jesus Christ is Lord, to the glory of God the Father (Philippians 2:9-11).

The choice is yours. You can follow the world's prescription and promote yourself, or follow Jesus' example of humility and long-suffering. Ask God to empty you today of conceit and selfish motives. Look to serve the Lord and others, and let God handle your career or ministry. By so doing, you may lose your life in the short run, but gain it back and enjoy many years of fruitful service.

MARCH 2

"Wisdom will save you from the ways of wicked men...who leave the straight paths to walk in dark ways." —2:12-13

I was on my knees praying my best religious prayers and reminding God of His promises to provide for my family and me. But the more I prayed, the poorer I got! Then one day the Lord spoke to me; it was my attitude that had hindered the provision and not His ability to provide! When my attitude improved, so did my finances. God gave me wisdom and it saved me from the ungodly path I was on.

After David had put Absalom's rebellion behind him, he faced a new dilemma: "During the reign of David, there was a famine for three successive years; so David sought the face of the Lord. The Lord said, 'It is on account of Saul and his blood-stained house; it is because he put the Gibeonites to death'" (2 Samuel 21:1).

Joshua had made a covenant with the Gibeonites that they would dwell with Israel in safety, although they would serve Israel as "woodcutters and water carriers for the house of my God" (Joshua 9:23). Hundreds of years later, Saul took it upon himself to break that covenant by destroying the Gibeonites.

We aren't told what Saul did to them or when he tried to do it. According to today's verse, Saul left the straight paths he inherited from his fathers and walked in dark ways. "But Saul in his zeal for Israel and Judah had tried to annihilate them" (2 Samuel 21:2).

Today's verse promises that wisdom will save you from the ways of men who have departed from the straight paths. David received the wisdom that broke the famine, but it took three years of suffering in the land for him to ask! I'm sure David tried everything before then; perhaps he prayed for rain, rationed food, and tried to import food from neighboring lands. Having done all he could, David finally asked for wisdom and discovered the source of the famine.

The predicament in which you may find yourself might seem complicated, but God's answer to solve it seldom is. It won't take the mind of a rocket scientist to apply the simplicity of God's wisdom to the most challenging of situations. The first step is to ask and the second step is to listen. Of course, by asking for God's wisdom you admit that you need help and that the answer isn't within your grasp. Take that step of humility and show God that you're willing to face reality, even if it means that you're wrong. Then count on His wisdom to deliver you from darkened paths that you or someone else may be walking.

MARCH 3

"When you lie down, you will not be afraid;
when you lie down, your sleep will be sweet." — 3:24.

I hear many people say that they have trouble sleeping. Even though they are spiritual, they go to bed worried and stay up because they're burdened or anxious. Now there are times when the pressures of life or the emotions from a traumatic experience can get to anyone. But this should be the exception and not the rule.

When David had been delivered "from the hand of all his enemies and from the hand of Saul" (2 Samuel 22:1), he composed a long song found in 2 Samuel 22. The song began with:

> The Lord is my rock, my fortress and my deliverer; my God is my rock, in whom I take refuge, my shield and the horn of my salvation. He is my stronghold, my refuge and my savior—from violent men you save me (2 Samuel 22:2-3).

David faced some life-threatening situations and learned that God was indeed his refuge. Fleeing from Absalom, David wrote:

> O Lord, how many are my foes! How many rise up against me! Many are saying of me, "God will not deliver him." But you are a shield around me, O Lord; you bestow glory on me and lift up my head. To the Lord I cry aloud, and he answers me from his holy hill. I lie down and sleep; I wake again, because the Lord sustains me (Psalm 3:1-5).

If David could sleep while going through all his troubles, how about you? Solomon learned this lesson from David, for he said: "In vain you rise early and stay up late, toiling for food to eat—for he grants sleep to those he loves" (Psalm 127:2). You can rest because "He who watches over Israel will neither slumber nor sleep" (Psalm 121:4).

The key to overcoming anxiety is found in Philippians 4:6: "Do not be anxious about anything, but in everything, by prayer and petition, with thanksgiving, present your requests to God." When worries press you, don't ignore them but pray them through. Pray until God lifts the burden from you, for the promise in the next verse states, "And the peace of God, which transcends all understanding, will guard your hearts and your minds in Christ Jesus" (Philippians 4:7). You'll know you've prayed them through when you have peace.

Today's verse promises peaceful rest and freedom from fear for those who walk in wisdom. Seek His wisdom in prayer and then go to bed. Leave your burdens beside the bed and get some rest. When you awake, you'll be fresh and the burdens that you left there will have diminished some time during the night.

MARCH 4

"She will set a garland of grace on your head
and present you with a crown of splendor." — 4:9.

He was 15 and she was 23 when they got married. It was a marriage destined to fail, or so it would seem. But today that couple, after 25 years of marriage, are pastoring a church. They have seven children, most of whom are serving the Lord. This couple has a wonderful ministry and bless many people on a daily basis.

If I were God, I would not have blessed that relationship. But God blesses people I wouldn't bless (and that's why you should be glad I'm not God). There are some people with whom I disagree or in whom I see some major flaws. Yet the grace of God is on them, and I've had to learn to give grace to those with whom God is also gracious. And this has been an important lesson for me, for as I've matured, I've come to realize that God has been just as kind to me as to those whom I've judged.

Solomon is a wonderful example of God's grace. As you know, David got Bathsheba pregnant while her husband Uriah was off to battle. David then tried to cover his sin by having her husband come home and sleep with her. When that didn't work, David conspired to have Uriah placed in the thick of a battle. Uriah was consequently killed and David immediately took Bathsheba as his wife.

Bathsheba gave birth to a son and it seemed as if David had pulled off this nasty scheme without getting caught. But Nathan the prophet confronted him, exposing his sin. The baby from that illicit union died and the promise came to David that the sword would never depart from his house. It seemed as if the Lord would have nothing but trouble for David the remaining days of his life.

Yet at that point the grace of God showed up:

> Then David comforted his wife Bathsheba, and he went to her and lay with her. She gave birth to a son, and they named him Solomon. The Lord loved him; and because the Lord loved him, he sent word through Nathan the prophet to name him Jedidiah (2 Samuel 12:24-25).

The son born after the one who died was Solomon, one of the greatest kings that the world has ever known! What an example of God's grace!

The Lord sent word through the same prophet who had confronted David that the child was "Jedidiah," which means "loved by the Lord." How could God love this child whose parents had been so wrong? He loved him because He's a God full of grace and compassion.

If He could bless that child, who can *you* bless? Are you a channel of God's grace or do you want to be like Nathan when he confronted David with his sinful behavior? All too often the church has chosen to preach judgment and not grace. God doesn't ignore sin, but He doesn't dwell on it either. Instead He pours out His grace to those who sometimes least deserve it, and He then expects you to do the same. Look for how you can give away some grace today.

MARCH 5

"Now then, my sons, listen to me;
do not turn aside from what I say." — 5:7.

It was one of those teachable moments. My young son and I were sharing a bed while on a family vacation. In the early morning hours, we both found ourselves awake and began to talk. It was a special time when my son was asking all the right questions and I had all the right answers. We both eventually fell back to sleep, but I still remember that talk in a San Francisco motel room. I would like to think that David had similar times with his own sons, especially Solomon.

Today's verse exhorts sons not to turn aside from what their father is telling them. This assumes, of course, that the father has something to say that's worth holding onto. Mothers and fathers should have a philosophy of life centered on who God is and what He does. Once they have that philosophy, they must communicate it every chance they get in accordance with the command of Moses: "Only be careful, and watch yourselves closely so that you do not forget the things your eyes have seen or let them slip from your heart as long as you live. Teach them to your children and to their children after them" (Deuteronomy 4:9).

You saw the day before last how David composed a long song to commemorate his many deliverances from his enemies. After testifying about God's power to deliver, he then made this statement:

> To the faithful you show yourself faithful, to the blameless you show yourself blameless, to the pure you show yourself pure, but to the crooked you show yourself shrewd. You save the humble, but your eyes are on the haughty to bring them low (2 Samuel 22:26-28).

While you can't manipulate God to do what you want, you can help determine how He will respond to you. If you're faithful, He'll show Himself faithful toward you. If you try to outsmart God, He'll only meet you in the same manner and, of course, outsmart you every time.

You'll do yourself and your children a favor by coming to grips with this truth. God is gracious, but He's also just. James wrote, "Come near to God and he will come near to you" (James 4:8). You may need God to come near to you, but first you must come near to Him. James went on to write, "Humble yourselves before the Lord, and he will lift you up" (James 4:10).

Are you feeling as if the Lord hasn't been responding to you as you would like? Then ask yourself how you've postured yourself toward Him. Your attitude and actions will determine to a great extent God's attitude and action toward you. Maybe today you need to stop complaining about God and repent of your own behavior. The promise holds that if you draw near to Him, He'll draw near to you. Draw near today, and prepare the way for the Lord to show Himself near to you.

MARCH 6

*"For these commands are a lamp, this teaching is a light,
and the corrections of discipline are the way of life." — 6:23.*

This would be the plot Hollywood movies are made from. Picture the movie's hero, a brave king, lying on his deathbed. He summons his son and, in the midst of tears and hugs, gives the next king final instructions. As he finishes, the old king dies and everyone lives happily ever after to the sounds of dramatic music.

That was the exact scene (without the music) described in 1 Kings 2:2-4 as David talked to Solomon for the last time:

> "I am about to go the way of all the earth," he said. "So be strong, show yourself a man, and observe what the Lord your God requires: Walk in his ways, and keep his decrees and commands, his laws and requirements, as written in the Law of Moses, so that you may prosper in all you do and wherever you go, and that the Lord may keep his promise to me: 'If your descendants watch how they live, and if they walk faithfully before me with all their heart and soul, you will never fail to have a man on the throne of Israel.'"

The last words of a dying person can contain something significant, and these were no exception. In those few sentences, David summed up what he felt to be the most important advice to the new king. Today's verse reiterates his last words, for the writer maintains that the commands and teaching of the Lord are the most critical elements for a successful kingdom, ministry, or life.

Perhaps David's most profound statement was, "I am about to go the way of all earth." The end of any ministry, reign, or life is at hand even from the beginning. Someone once said, "We are born to die." The psalmist wrote, "Do not put your trust in princes, in mortal men, who cannot save. When their spirit departs, they return to the ground; on that very day their plans come to nothing" (Psalm 146:3-4).

David gave Solomon good advice. He acknowledged his own limitations and then pointed Solomon in the right direction. Reminding him of God's promise, he urged his son to obey the Lord with all his heart. Solomon's throne would not be preserved through being the son of David, but rather as a son of God.

That's good advice to you as well. If you "watch how you live" and walk before the Lord with all your heart and soul, you'll prosper. But no matter how much you prosper, the end will come one day and you'll have to pass on to another your position and what you've done. The knowledge of your ultimate end will keep you humble as God blesses you now according to the faithfulness of your walk.

MARCH 7

"Now then, my sons, listen to me;
pay attention to what I say." — 7:24.

My heart went out to him and my hand started for my pocket. I'd met the man standing before me when I ministered in a jail. Now he stood before me and convincingly poured out his heart. It was our church's policy, however, not to give to anyone (in most cases) until they had attended church and established a relationship with some of the members. Several weeks later I got the word: He was a con man, and the few dollars we had given him had been poorly invested.

In David's last words to Solomon, he gave final instructions concerning some of the men in his own administration. About Joab, David said, "He killed them, shedding their blood in peacetime as if in battle....Deal with him according to your wisdom, but do not let his gray head go down to the grave in peace" (1 Kings 2:5-6).

Then there was Shimei, and David had this to say:

You have with you Shimei son of Gera...who called down bitter curses on me the day I went to Mahanaim....Do not consider him innocent. You are a man of wisdom; you will know what to do to him. Bring his gray head down to the grave in blood (1 Kings 2:8-9).

Now these statements may come across as harsh and vindictive, and I suppose to some extent they are. But Joab had murdered innocent men and Shimei had cursed the king when he was fleeing from Absalom. Neither man had repented, although their fear of David seemed to keep them in line. Now that David was dying, he was saying to Solomon, "Watch out for these two. They will talk a good talk, but you can't trust them. You may want to trust or ignore them, but don't."

True to David's words, Joab wasn't to be trusted, for he soon conspired against Solomon. Solomon gave Shimei orders not to leave Jerusalem, but he ignored that order and went off to capture some runaway slaves. Solomon then put both men to death according to his father's instructions. He was true to today's verse; he paid attention to what his father said and it helped to establish his throne.

As a leader, pastor, or supervisor, you must deal with the tendency to trust those who have proven themselves untrustworthy in order to maintain a peaceful relationship with them. You must still give grace and be kind, but you can't be naive. Paul warned the Ephesian elders, "I know that after I leave, savage wolves will come in among you and will not spare the flock. Even from your own number men will arise and distort the truth in order to draw away disciples after them" (Acts 20:29-30). You can't make a wolf into a pet; you must keep the wolf away.

If there are those who have proved themselves unworthy of trust, require that they earn it back. If they're unwilling to do that, but want to talk their way back into your good graces, resist them even though your heart may want to do the opposite. Believing in Jesus shouldn't make you an easy mark, but rather should make you one who has discernment and wisdom in your dealings with others.

MARCH 8

"Listen to my instruction and be wise; do not ignore it." — 8:33.

I had heard stories about this, but never thought it would happen to me. There I was, in the darkness of early morning, going to retrieve my son. He had done something stupid and I was called to go get him. Not knowing what to expect or how to handle it, I was partially relieved to hear him say to me, "You were right. I never thought it would ever come to this." He had ignored my advice and now he was paying for it. Fortunately, the consequences of his mistake weren't serious.

Yesterday we studied David's advice to Solomon concerning Joab and Shimei and how Solomon followed through on that counsel. But David also had these words to say just before he died: "Show kindness to the sons of Barzillai of Gilead and let them be among those who eat at your table. They stood by me when I fled from your brother Absalom" (1 Kings 2:7).

The Bible doesn't tell whether or not Solomon did anything for the sons of Barzillai, but we know that the Lord did. When the exiles returned from captivity five hundred years later, there was a priest named Barzillai in their number. We are told that he was "a man who had married a daughter of Barzillai the Gileadite and was called by that name" (Ezra 2:61).

The Lord rewarded the loyalty of that family by preserving their family line for centuries. When they had no sons among the faithful, a son-in-law who was a priest took the family name and returned with the remnant from Babylon. Now if the Lord did all that to reward faithfulness and loyalty, shouldn't you do the same?

If you're an employer, how have you rewarded and honored your faithful employees? "Look! The wages you failed to pay the workmen who mowed your fields are crying out against you" (James 5:4). As a parent, have you tried to be "fair" and do the same for all your children, or have you rewarded faithfulness where it was demonstrated? As a spiritual leader, have you promoted those who have worked the hardest, or have you given rewards to family members or those who "look" the best (or who make you look good)?

David's advice to Solomon is good advice for today. Make it your goal to reward loyalty and performance. If you, with the best of intentions, reward those who meant well but didn't produce, you're not helping them or being fair to those who have been faithful. In one of Jesus' parables, the master rewarded those who took what they had and produced more, while he chastised those who maintained only what they had. Look today to do good to those who have been productive and you will please the Lord by blessing what He has already blessed.

MARCH 9

"For through me your days will be many,
and years will be added to your life." — 9:11.

This may be my last day on earth. That is something I think about from time to time as I work, fellowship, spend time with my family, or get uptight. I also think of the verse in the Amplified Bible describing David's life: "He died in a good old age [his seventy-first year] full and satisfied with days, riches, and honor; Solomon his son reigned in his stead" (1 Chronicles 29:28 NAS).

After all the battles David fought and arrows he dodged, he lived to be in his 70s. In spite of all the pressure and mistakes, he survived and prospered. It says he was "full of days." That means he didn't spend his life in front of the television set or collecting stamps. He wasn't a sports junkie, nor did he retire and travel the world. David didn't retire from serving the Lord, but was productive to the end. He even made a huge contribution toward the building of the temple as he turned the plans for its construction over to Solomon.

I want to die satisfied with my days, knowing that I did the most I could with the time and opportunities I had. I want it said about me what Paul said about David: "For when David had served God's purpose in his own generation, he fell asleep" (Acts 13:36). When I fall asleep, I want to have given my all to accomplish my purpose to my own generation.

Today's verse says that wisdom will add days and years to your life. Your days are numbered already, so wisdom can't actually prolong your life. Wisdom can, however, help you make the most of the days that you do have, keeping you from wasting them or investing them where they don't count.

Wisdom will help you heed Paul's warning: "Be very careful, then, how you live—not as unwise but as wise, making the most of every opportunity, because the days are evil" (Ephesians 5:15-16). The wise take advantage of every opportunity; fools don't even notice as chances to do great things pass them by.

What's your purpose in life? Is it a condo in Florida after so many years of work? Or is it to see the kingdom of God advanced on earth with you playing a role in it happening? I encourage you to make the most of your time. Be faithful with what's before you, and God will increase your sphere of influence.

As we close the study of David's life, I challenge you to impact your generation as David did his. Build something that you can turn over to your spiritual children after you. Don't waste your life on trivial things, but rather lay up treasures in heavenly places. When you die, be "full of and satisfied with days," having no regrets for having missed the opportunities that came your way.

MARCH 10

"The fear of the Lord adds length to life,
but the years of the wicked are cut short." — 10:27.

I have a sure way to add years to your life. No, it isn't an exercise program, diet, secret potion, or vitamin supplement. Everyone has access to it and it doesn't cost a thing. Curious? You can prolong your life, as we discussed yesterday, by the efficient use of your time.

When you think of it, everyone has the same amount of time in a day. While life spans will vary according to individuals, each day you share with every other human being has 24 hours in it. If you could find 30 minutes a day to study the Bible, in one year you would have spent almost eight 24-hour days reading the Word. In 20 years, you would have spent the equivalent of six full months reading by just spending 30 minutes every day.

Yesterday we looked at Ephesians 5:16: "Be very careful, then, how you live— not as unwise but as wise, making the most of every opportunity, because the days are evil." The Amplified Version translates that verse, "Making the very most of your time—buying up each opportunity." The Living Bible says, "Make the most of every opportunity to do good." The New American Standard says, "Making the most of your time." You can lengthen your life by making the most of every moment you have.

This takes a commitment to discipline yourself on a daily basis, something that you may not want to do. You can make the most of your time only if you want to do so. I've tried to help people manage their time more effectively but have discovered I'm wasting my time unless that person is committed to change and make the most of the minutes they have.

If you're serious about making the most of your time, the first thing I recommend is a time management system. This includes a notebook with a calendar and pages for every day of the year and some blank paper to insert. Without this basic tool, you can't manage your time effectively. All day long you will be at the mercy of the phone and other interruptions. At night, you'll suddenly remember a phone call or report that you forgot. You'll also tend to forget birthdays, miss family times, and feel frustrated and tense without a system. You and I have all experienced that and it's not pleasant.

I'm convinced (and research proves) that after financial difficulties, poor time mismanagement is the greatest stress producer in your life. You cut short the quality of the days you have if they are spent being anxious about how time is slipping away. Over these next few days, make a commitment to study your time and how you use it. Determine to make changes so that you can begin to master time instead of it mastering you. Over the next few days let's study some biblical principles that will help you make the most of every opportunity by using your time wisely.

"Like a gold ring in a pig's snout
is a beautiful woman who shows no discretion." — 11:22.

What a picture today's verse paints. Imagine going to a state fair or farm show to view the animals. As you walk among the pigs wallowing in the mud, you notice they have gold rings in their snouts. How ridiculous that would be! Yet a beautiful woman without sense is just like a pig with that nose ring; her beauty is wasted because she lacks the discretion to go with it.

Proverbs 31 paints another picture, this time of a woman with sense. In the midst of all she is, it stands out that she knows how to manage her time. Consider these traits of the Proverbs 31 woman:

1. "She selects wool and flax" (verse 13). She knows how to set a goal (sewing) and carry out the necessary steps to accomplish it (getting the materials together to sew).

2. "She gets up while it is still dark" (verse 15). No staying in bed for this woman.

3. "She sets about her work vigorously" (verse 17). There's no procrastination.

4. "Her lamp does not go out at night" (verse 18). She plans well so as not to be caught off guard (here she has plenty of oil for light at night).

5. "She can laugh at the days to come" (verse 25). She has learned to anticipate the future and plan accordingly.

6. "She does not eat the bread of idleness" (verse 27). Her time is well-planned for maximum output.

If this is the standard for a godly woman, you can be sure the same standard holds for a godly man. Many have misinterpreted the words of James when he wrote,

> Now listen, you who say, "Today or tomorrow we will go to this or that city, spend a year there, carry on business and make money." Why, you do not even know what will happen tomorrow. What is your life? You are a mist that appears for a little while and then vanishes. Instead, you ought to say, "If it is the Lord's will, we will live or do this or that" (James 4:13-15).

James didn't say not to plan your time. Rather he warned not to plan like everything depends on you and appealed to include the Lord in the planning process. My sister, if you want to be a Proverbs 31 woman at home or on the job, then learn how to manage your time. My brother, if you want to be successful at what you do, then learn to do the same. Manage your time well and you'll add discretion and wisdom to the other gifts the Lord has given you.

MARCH 12

"The plans of the righteous are just,
but the advice of the wicked is deceitful." — 12:5.

Rather than take out my computer, I decided to do some work with my planning notebook as the plane took off. I started working, first setting a prioritized daily task list for the next several days. Finishing that, I reviewed the sheets I have for each staff member of items on which they were working. Then I looked at the days of the past month to check for any projects that hadn't been completed. As I finished all this, the plane landed and I never got to my other work.

Yet this time was well spent because I spent it planning my work and life. People have commented on my ability to get a lot done, and there's no secret to that trait. I've learned to plan, and the more work I have, the more time I must devote to planning. In fact, there's a saying, "If you want something done, give it to a busy person to do." The busy person usually knows how to plan and will find the time to do what's being assigned.

Today's verse declares that the plans of the righteous are just. As proof of this, consider Joseph when he came before Pharaoh. Having interpreted Pharaoh's dreams, he said:

Now let Pharaoh look for a discerning and wise man and put him in charge of the land of Egypt. Let Pharaoh appoint commissioners over the land to take a fifth of the harvest of Egypt during the seven years of abundance. They should collect all the food of these good years that are coming and store up the grain under the authority of Pharaoh, to be kept in the cities for food. This food should be held in reserve for the country, to be used during the seven years of famine that will come upon Egypt, so that the country may not be ruined by the famine (Genesis 41:33-36).

Joseph combined the direction of the Lord with his ability to plan and it got him promoted:

The plan seemed good to Pharaoh and to all his officials. So Pharaoh asked them, "Can we find anyone like this man, one in whom is the spirit of God?" Then Pharaoh said to Joseph, "Since God has made all this known to you, there is no one so discerning and wise as you. You shall be in charge of my palace, and all my people are to submit to your orders. Only in respect to the throne will I be greater than you" (Genesis 41:37-40).

If you learn to plan under the direction of the Holy Spirit, you too will be promoted. Decide today that you'll commit fifteen minutes every day to plan your day. Stop reaching the end of your day feeling frustrated at how time got away from you. Begin to plan your work, and then work your plan. If you become skilled at it, you may appear before the Pharaoh of your day because of your reputation for wisdom to plan.

MARCH 13

"He who ignores discipline comes to poverty and shame,
but whoever heeds correction is honored." — 13:18.

Why aren't you more organized or using your time to the fullest? Isn't it due, at least in part, to lack of discipline? First of all, using your time wisely requires the desire to do so. Then it requires personal change so you can make the necessary adjustments. Finally, it takes the grace to discipline yourself to do what you *need* to do instead of what you *want* to do. But if what you need and want to do are the same, then your time management becomes a joy instead of a chore.

Paul's last letter to Timothy should help you as you seek to manage your time: "For God did not give us a spirit of timidity, but a spirit of power, of love and of self-discipline" (2 Timothy 1:7). You're not alone as you attempt to discipline yourself because the Holy Spirit is there to help you. But you must want that help, or life will continue to pass you by while you feel as if things are out of control.

Today's verse warns that those who ignore discipline will reap a bad harvest of poverty and shame. The most important discipline for effective time management, once you have identified a notebook or some system to use, is to construct a daily list of things to do. The prophet Habakkuk said,

I will stand at my watch and station myself on the ramparts; I will look to see what he will say to me, and what answer I am to give to this complaint. Then the Lord replied: *"Write down* the revelation and make it plain on tablets" (Habakkuk 2:1-2 emphasis added).

You must "make it plain" and write it down so that you know where to invest your time. Don't just record the things you don't want to forget, but write down everything. My daily list includes prayer, reading, and exercise. If I choose not to do any or all of those three things, at least they're written down and "call out" for attention all day.

From there, I list my book-writing duties, family times, phone calls, business meetings, and school assignments. I do this every day, including Sunday. I seldom face a day where my proposed duties aren't written out for me to study and follow. Having done this, I can take all the interruptions that are certain to come my way because I have my list to help me get back to what I need to do.

But all that comes from self-discipline. If you don't manage your time, it will manage you and torment you when things get out of control. After you have your system notebook, begin to develop the habit of writing things down every day. Ask the Spirit to help you develop self-discipline and start taking back the days that you have lost to lack of discipline.

MARCH 14

*"But those who plan what is good
find love and faithfulness." — 14:22.*

Securing and using a notebook is the first step toward effective time management. Making a daily list every day is the second step. But the planning process isn't complete until you give some structure to that task list by assigning priorities to the things on your list.

Today's verse promises that if you plan what's good, you'll find love and faithfulness. Good things don't always just happen, but rather require planning and diligence. If you approach your day with no plan, then chances are that you will be blown in whatever direction the wind blows that day. If you plan your day by setting priorities, you're more likely to achieve those things you really desire to do.

There's no system you can learn to help you set daily priorities. Obviously, the number one thing on your list should be prayer and devotional reading. Write those things down and put a number "one" and "two" next to them. Then begin the prayerful process of numbering the other items.

I've found that setting priorities after that is often a listening process. Because of family or work commitments, not all your time can be planned, for some is planned for you. But in the time that's yours you'll have to determine what you should do next that will please the Lord most or that will follow the law of love and bless your neighbor. Is it rest? Is it writing a letter? Calling a friend? Working on one of your long-term goals? Spending time with your children, spouse, or pastor? Repairing your car or home?

Jesus said, "My food is to do the will of him who sent me and to finish his work" (John 4:34), and "I always do what pleases him [the Father]" (John 8:29). Furthermore, He stated, "By myself I can do nothing; I judge only as I hear, and my judgment is just, for I seek not to please myself but him who sent me" (John 5:30).

Jesus didn't carry a notebook to keep track of his priorities, but rather listened and did what the Father directed Him to do. Jesus' sole desire was to please the Father, so He sought to do only what the Father wanted—that became His highest priority at all times. Until you get that focused, learn to write everything down and study it to determine where you should invest yourself. Even when an interruption comes, you can refer back to your list and get back to what you were doing.

"One of those days Jesus went out to a mountainside to pray, and spent the night praying to God" (Luke 6:12). Jesus put a higher priority on praying than sleeping. How about you? Are you willing to go through the discipline of comparing activities and giving yourself to that which pleases the Father as often as possible? It may seem a little awkward at first, but in the long run you'll give yourself more and more to those things that make the best use of your time and are consistent with the will of God for your life.

MARCH 15

"A man of understanding keeps a straight course." — *15:21.*

I tried to watch, but the pressure was incredible as a U.S. figure skater was trying to win the gold medal at the Olympics. As the world looked on, she performed flawlessly and took home the gold. I had to watch the re-runs, for every jump and maneuver was so pressure-packed that I couldn't bear to watch it while it was really happening.

What struck me most about that skater, however, was how single-minded she had been in pursuing her sport. The "up close and personal" segment showed her driving to the rink for practice while it was still dark. Then after school it was more practice. Weekends were devoted to travel, competitions, and other related activities. She had no social life and it cost her parents plenty to get her lessons. But that night she stood on the platform as the best, and gained the admiration of the world for her achievements.

Today's verse says that a man of understanding will keep a "straight course" just like that skater did. She didn't let anything keep her from her goal. If a skater, concert violinist, ballerina, or baseball pitcher devotes everything to keep a "straight course," how much more should you who have a purpose ordained by God.

Jesus was single-minded, for it was written of Him, "When the days were approaching for His ascension, that He resolutely set His face to go to Jerusalem" (Luke 9:51 - NAS). Isaiah also described this trait in Jesus by writing, "Because the Sovereign Lord helps me, I will not be disgraced. Therefore *have I set my face like flint*, and I know I will not be put to shame" (Isaiah 50:7 emphasis added).

I like that phrase, I set my face like flint. It speaks of many things, including proper time management. When your face is like flint, you're not easily sidetracked by lesser things. Jesus did what He did because He kept a straight path, doing only those things that led Him to the goal. Paul was like His Lord, for he wrote, "I press on to take hold of that for which Christ Jesus took hold of me....Forgetting what is behind and straining toward what is ahead, I press on toward the goal to win the prize for which God has called me heavenward in Christ Jesus" (Philippians 3:12-14).

Do you have what it takes to succeed, or are you willing only to dream of greatness? When you have something to do, can you set your fact like flint, or are you easily discouraged? Jesus had the stuff that champions are made of, and so did Paul. They kept their priorities straight and didn't give themselves to lesser things. Learn to do the same, and one day you'll stand on the platform to receive the prize that's reserved for those who paid the price to win it all.

MARCH 16

"The laborer's appetite works for him;
his hunger drives him on." — 16:26.

I dreaded going to another meeting, but I felt the Lord prompting me to go. I had joined a secular professional association and each get-together was difficult since I was the only "church man" who attended. I needed some incentive to keep me faithfully attending, so I decided that in five years I would be president of the organization.

I became president in four years and developed a wonderful partnership with that group by the time I moved from Alabama to Florida. If I hadn't set that goal of leadership, however, I doubt if I would have had enough incentive to endure those initial meetings.

Today's verse refers to setting a goal. If you get "hungry enough," you'll go through whatever is necessary to "satisfy your hunger." My hunger was to be president and to do that, I endured the awkwardness of feeling out of place to reach my goal.

Don't shy away from godly ambition unless you're unwilling to pay the price for the position you desire. Paul wrote: "Here is a trustworthy saying: If anyone sets his heart on being an overseer, he desires a noble task" (1 Timothy 3:1). Paul didn't rebuke anyone who wanted to be a leader in the church. Having said that, however, he outlined the requirements for such leadership. If anyone was willing to pay the price, they could indeed achieve that goal.

The hunger to be used of the Lord has caused many to be faithful in difficult and trying times. According to the writer of Hebrews, we are to "fix our eyes on Jesus, the author and perfecter of our faith, who for the joy set before him endured the cross, scorning its shame, and sat down at the right hand of the throne of God" (Hebrews 12:2). Jesus had joy set before Him (sitting at the right hand of God), so He endured the cross and looked past the shame. He had a goal and was able to focus His energies on the goal, even though He went through "hell" to achieve it.

You need some lofty goals to which you can give yourself. Your goal (or according to today's verse, your hunger) will keep you on course. Keeping the goal in sight will cause you to use your time wisely because you have somewhere to go.

Do you want God to use you? What would you like to do? When you decide that, then give yourself to the preparation process. You'll practice the piano, take your classes, learn a language, or serve your leaders in order to get where you (and God) want to go. Learn to harness your "appetite" and use it to direct you in the ways God has set aside just for you.

MARCH 17

"A discerning man keeps wisdom in view,
but a fool's eyes wander to the ends of the earth." — 17:24.

My head was swimming and my eyes were about to cross! My friend the visionary was sharing his dreams and plans for evangelizing an entire continent, and I couldn't keep up with all that he was doing and planned to do. I politely listened, but my mind had checked out!

The world needs visionaries, for they create enthusiasm and urgency around seemingly impossible goals and dreams. Yet visionaries need those who are firmly entrenched in reality, for someone will have to help them carry out their dreams. Too often, however, visionaries are off to the next big project before the last one has even gotten off the ground.

Today's verse warns that fools have a hard time focusing on what's in front of them. Their eyes tend to wander to the end of the earth while ignoring the world right in front of them. Paul was no fool, but he was a visionary. After the Lord Jesus, he did more to establish the early church than any other man. Yet the Lord had to help keep him in check so his eyes wouldn't wander too far from the task before him.

Paul wrote to the Romans:

It has always been my ambition to preach the gospel where Christ was not known, so that I would not be building on someone else's foundation. Rather as it is written: "Those who were not told about him will see, and those who have not heard will understand." This is why I have often been hindered from coming to you (Romans 15:20-22).

Paul had a ministry priority to preach to those who hadn't already heard the Gospel. Since the Roman church was established, ministry there was inconsistent with this priority. For Paul, Rome was the "ends of the earth," and he felt resisted whenever he set his sights on going there.

How much of your time is given to those things that are the "ends of the earth" for you? It's critical that you know where and when to invest yourself, and then do it with all your energy. After I order my daily task list, I either set a time limit of when to stop working on an item or stay with it until I have completed the project. By doing that, I keep myself from wandering to the ends of my desk or the earth to find something that can distract me.

Focus your attention and energies on the task before you, a task that's consistent with what you're called to do. In that manner, you'll increase in productivity and efficiency and will not be prone to go off in so many different directions.

MARCH 18

"One who is slack in his work
is brother to one who destroys." — 18:9.

The devastation was terrible and not to be forgotten. A hurricane had swept through southern Florida and homes that were standing a few hours before were no longer there. Trees, office buildings, and signs were no more and the total damage ran into the billions of dollars.

As I viewed that carnage on television, I remembered the hurricane I had lived through and identified with the pain and suffering of the people. But I also thought of today's verse and meditated.

Today's verse makes a simple yet profound statement, which could also be phrased in question form: Is there any difference between someone who builds something and then tears it down, and another who just doesn't build at all? The end result, whether it's not built or built and destroyed, is that there's nothing there in the end.

Today's verse also says that one who is slack and doesn't do anything is the same as one who would tear down what's already built. In the end, there's no difference between the two. To plant a church and then wreck it, or not to plant the church bring the same result: There's no church.

If you can't set priorities and see them through to the end, you're brother to one who destroys. Not finishing your work is the same as finishing it and then destroying it. Understanding that can help you maintain a level of diligence that enables you to finish what you start.

The Apostle Paul was certainly not slack in his work. While at Troas, Paul preached all night, so long that Eutychus fell out of the window and had to be brought back to life (see Acts 20:7). By his own testimony, he said:

I have worked much harder, been in prison more frequently, been flogged more severely, and been exposed to death again and again. Five times I received from the Jews the forty lashes minus one. Three times I was beaten with rods, once I was stoned, three times I was shipwrecked, I spent a night and a day in the open sea, I have been constantly on the move....I have labored and toiled and have often gone without sleep; I have known hunger and thirst and have often gone without food; I have been cold and naked (2 Corinthians 11:23-27).

One day you'll face Paul in the receiving line of heaven. When you do, you don't want to tell him you couldn't do more because your computer was slow or your VCR didn't work. Use Paul as your model for work and ministry and then work diligently to faithfully finish what God has put before you to do.

"Laziness brings on deep sleep,
and the shiftless man goes hungry." — 19:15.

My mother and I would sit at home, waiting for that familiar sound. Some time after 10:00 p.m., our garage door would open and my dad would finally come home. Many times, he would work from 9:00 a.m. until 9:00 p.m. for weeks at a time. He received no overtime or time off, and often went weeks with only Sunday to rest.

I also remember my mother working in the home and later at a school. She was so focused on her work that she would come home at 10:00 p.m. and tell me it was the first time she had even thought of taking a bathroom break all day. When I was young, at times I wished that they would be at home more with me. Now I appreciate just how hard they worked to provide for my sister and me. On a modest income, my parents put me through private college with no loans. They left us a legacy of hard work and diligence, and it's a legacy I want to leave to my children as well.

Paul wrote the Thessalonians on the subject of work:

For you yourselves know how you ought to follow our example. We were not idle when we were with you, nor did we eat anyone's food without paying for it. On the contrary, we worked night and day, laboring and toiling so that we would not be a burden to any of you. We did this, not because we do not have the right to such help, but in order to make ourselves a model for you to follow. For even when we were with you, we gave you this rule: "If a man will not work, he shall not eat" (2 Thessalonians 3:7-10).

Paul worked night and day to provide an example to that church and to you of what the Lord expects from His people. The Greek world of Paul's day didn't believe in "work." The Greeks used servants to work, while they spent their time in the pursuit of education or other activities. Paul warned: "We hear that some among you are idle. They are not busy; they are busybodies. Such people we command and urge in the Lord Jesus Christ to settle down and earn the bread they eat" (2 Thessalonians 3:11-12).

Today's verse warns against laziness. Nowhere does the Bible promise retirement, a vacation, leisure time, or a reduced work week. There's nothing wrong with any of those, but they're not promises. Work was assigned to man in the Garden of Eden before Adam and Eve sinned, so work didn't come as a result of the Fall. Rather work is man's purpose so that he can subdue the earth and rule over it. Embrace your God-given role today and work hard, shunning laziness in favor of the work that will prosper you and leave your children a godly heritage of hard work.

MARCH 20

"The purposes of a man's heart are deep waters,
but a man of understanding draws them out." — 20:5.

It's a common theme in this book that everyone is born with a purpose, some God-given plan that only that person can fulfill. Often this purpose is hidden from view, for it's written, "It is the glory of God to conceal a matter; to search out a matter is the glory of kings" (Proverbs 25:2). Today's verse speaks to the hidden purposes in one's heart and the need for understanding to draw them out.

If you're a son or daughter of the King, then part of your royal inheritance is to diligently seek your purpose. For the next few days, let's study how Nehemiah's life proved the truth of this matter.

Nehemiah was a cup bearer in the court of the Persian king. It was his job to taste the king's wine to make sure it wasn't poisoned. A remnant of his people had returned to Jerusalem, but the building program there had been stopped by order of King Artaxerxes (see Ezra 4:7-23). Some men came from Judah to the city where Nehemiah served and Nehemiah "questioned them about the Jewish remnant that survived the exile, and also about Jerusalem" (Nehemiah 1:2).

The report wasn't good: "Those who survived the exile and are back in the province are in great trouble and disgrace. The wall of Jerusalem is broken down, and its gates have been burned with fire" (Nehemiah 1:3). Many were undoubtedly saddened by the state of affairs in Jerusalem, but Nehemiah particularly so: "When I heard these things, I sat down and wept. For some days, I mourned and fasted and prayed before the God of heaven" (Nehemiah 1:4).

There was a purpose deep in the heart of Nehemiah and he was about to discover what it was. He sought the Lord and saw that he was the man to champion the rebuilding of Jerusalem. He was born for that reason. From that point on, Nehemiah's life changed and he recorded it for us by the inspiration of the Holy Spirit.

What's your purpose and why were you born? Don't give the old catechism answer that you were born to glorify God and serve Him forever. How are you to serve Him? Don't assume that what you see and feel is what is seen and felt by everyone. Your burdens, talents, and vision are unique and part of the package that will help you to fulfill your purpose. Others were sad by Jerusalem's disarray, but Nehemiah was burdened because his purpose was tied to that city.

Ask the Lord for understanding so that you can draw out of the depths of your heart the reason you exist. Ignore it and you'll be left to a life of drudgery and aimless wandering through fads and odd jobs. Define it and your life will change as dramatically as did Nehemiah's from the point when he realized who he was and what he was to do.

MARCH 21

*"A man who strays from the path of understanding
comes to rest in the company of the dead."* — 21:16.

As America went to war in the Persian Gulf in 1993, the world watched in wonder as a new line of weaponry was unveiled. Press conferences with video footage showed "smart bombs" and cruise missiles being launched with previously unknown accuracy at targets hundreds of miles away. Guided by laser and computer technology, these weapons found their way to air shafts and through windows of targeted objects. The face of war had been changed forever.

The Lord also wants to unleash "smart bombs" on His enemies. His weapons, however, aren't guided by sophisticated technology. The Lord's tools are His people who are guided by an understanding of who they are and what God has called them to do. Nehemiah was just such a weapon.

Girded with an understanding of his purpose, Nehemiah went to Jerusalem and began to rebuild the ruins. He imparted vision to the remnant there, set out a plan, adjusted the plan as he went along, and completed the work in an amazingly short period of time. Refusing to be a politician, diplomat, priest, or governor, he would not stray from the path of understanding as today's verse warns. Instead he was a spiritual "smart bomb," focusing on his target and pursuing it with relentless energy.

You too can be a smart bomb in the hands of the Lord if you arm yourself with your God-given purpose. Having the understanding of that purpose, you must fight every temptation to be diverted to another "target" and instead strive to stay on course. Don't waste your time pursuing trivial things. Stay on course or you'll wander into areas that take away the life that comes from accomplishing the will of God.

Nehemiah faced that problem:

When word came to Sanballat, Tobiah, Geshem the Arab and the rest of our enemies that I had rebuilt the wall and not a gap was left in it—though up to that time I had not set the doors in the gates—Sanballat and Geshem sent me this message: "Come, let us meet together in one of the villages on the plain of Ono." But they were scheming to harm me; so I sent messengers to them with this reply: "I am carrying on a great project and cannot go down. Why should the work stop while I leave it and go down to you?" Four times they sent me the same message, and each time I gave them the same answer (Nehemiah 6:1-4).

Your enemies—fear, insecurity, intimidation, unbelief—will always try to distract you. Keep your purpose before you and don't come down from the wall where you're working. If you see your work for what it is and your time as precious, then you'll stay on target and be a smart bomb under the guidance of the Holy Spirit.

MARCH 22

"Train a child in the way he should go,
and when he is old he will not turn from it." — 22:6.

Baseball great Yogi Berra once said, "Baseball is 90% mental, and the other half is physical." While not always accurate, he had a way of making sense in a "folksy" kind of way. He also said, "It ain't over until it's over." That's certainly true of life, and especially children.

My children are now teens, and we're encountering challenges with them that we never thought we would have. Having raised them in a Christian home and sent them to Christian schools, we felt sure that we would never have to deal with attitudes and behavior that we're now having to address. We assumed that our training would take root and immediately keep them from some of the mistakes that my wife and I made growing up. That hasn't always been the case.

As we have struggled at times with our children and their problems, we've tried to take Yogi Berra's words to heart—it ain't over until it's over. What our children are going through today isn't necessarily their final destiny. We've had to keep training and exhorting them in hope and faith that the Lord will do the work in their hearts that needs to be done. We've tried to stand on today's verse that when they're old, they won't depart from what we've imparted to them.

I don't know what kind of childhood Nehemiah had, but when he was old, he walked in his heritage. He must have been raised by parents who feared the Lord. While far away from home and serving a foreign king, he walked in the law of God and didn't waver. Notice his prayers and the phrases he used:

> I confess the sins we Israelites, including myself and my father's house, have committed against you. We have acted very wickedly toward you. We have not obeyed the commands, decrees and laws you gave your servant Moses (Nehemiah 1:6-7).

Nehemiah prayed "we" prayers and identified with his father's household. Being away from home, he could have separated himself from Israel's problems. Instead, he identified with them and prayed on their behalf. That gives me hope for my children and the youth of this generation. If I do my job and point them in the right direction, the God of Nehemiah will preserve them and keep them going in the right direction.

Today's verse requires faith, because it causes us to do the job of training even when the results don't seem to be there. Are *you* walking in faith for the next generation? Do you believe that the God who saved and delivered you can do the same for them? Are you expecting immediate results and, if you don't see them, becoming discouraged or withholding the training you should give?

Be encouraged by today's verse and train the next generation. Even if they seem to be asleep or ignoring you, trust the Lord that His word will penetrate their hearts and eventually produce a bumper crop of righteousness.

MARCH 23

"For drunkards and gluttons become poor,
and drowsiness clothes them in rags." — 23:21.

I heard someone say that football is played by 11 men in desperate need of rest and watched by 70,000 people in desperate need of exercise. That's how it can be in church, too. The Sunday "program" is carried by a few musicians and ministers who are overworked and underpaid. Those in the pews need to get involved, but are all too often content to watch rather than minister.

Today's verse tells you that drowsiness comes on all those who eat and drink to excess. After years of pastoring, I've come to see that this is also a spiritual truth. I've observed those who are always after spiritual experiences and a "new" word from the Lord. They eat so much that they become fat and drowsy! Having consumed as much as they could, they too often want it all for their own good without working any of it off by serving or helping others.

This generation is perhaps the best-fed body of believers the Church has ever seen. With cassettes, books, Christian television, radio broadcasts, and a host of other material, we have more at our disposal than ever before. But has it just produced a group of "drunkards"—those hungering for spiritual experiences—and "gluttons"—those feeding on the word of God without the proper response? There's nothing wrong with hungering or feeding on God's goodness. Without "exercise," however, they lead to spiritual drowsiness and "fat" believers who mistake hearing for doing.

Nehemiah had no such problem. He was a man rich in spiritual experience and the Word, yet he kept alert and active. Having been given much, he looked to produce much. Nehemiah wasn't content to talk about God; he wanted to do great things for God. He wasn't satisfied that he knew about God's greatness; he wanted others to see God's greatness in action.

When Nehemiah heard about the condition of Jerusalem, he wrote, "For some days I mourned and fasted and prayed before the God of heaven" (Nehemiah 1:4). When he went before the king, the king asked,

"Why does your face look so sad when you are not ill? This can be nothing but sadness of heart." I was very much afraid, but I said to the king, "May the king live forever! Why should my face not look sad when the city where my fathers are buried lies in ruins, and its gates have been destroyed by fire?" (Nehemiah 2:2-3).

Nehemiah wasn't just eager for another good church service, sermon, spiritual high, or revival. He wanted to fulfill his purpose and do something with what he had learned. The secret to your success lies in having that same attitude. Move out of your comfort zone and tackle a project that will bring God honor and allow you to use the gifts or knowledge you have received. When you have, the Lord will give you more so that you can effectively use that, too. If you are drowsy, then shake off your sleep and begin today using what you've been given to the glory of God.

"Do not envy wicked men, do not desire their company; for their hearts plot violence, and their lips talk about making trouble." — 24:1-2.

I've noticed two different theories of life among some believers. First, there are those who see a conspiracy in everything. The antichrist is taking over and things are getting worse and worse. Then you have the naive. They believe that love means you become a doormat for others to step on. I think the truth lies some place in the middle, for we need to show love and know how to deal with those who would abuse you.

Paul wrote, "Everyone who wants to live a godly life in Christ Jesus will be persecuted" (2 Timothy 3:12). Today's verse warns not to envy or deal too closely with wicked men for they plot and talk trouble. This shouldn't surprise you, nor should you just sit back and "love" them. You must learn to accept the reality that they'll cause you trouble and then attempt to counteract their evil, just like Nehemiah did.

Nehemiah wrote, "So we rebuilt the wall till all of it reached half its height, for the people worked with all their heart" (Nehemiah 4:6). Things were going pretty well and the people had some measure of success. When you get to that place, you become a target for God's enemies. Nehemiah continued,

> But when Sanballat, Tobiah, the Arabs, the Ammonites and the men of Ashdod heard that the repairs to Jerusalem walls had gone ahead and that the gaps were being closed, they were very angry. They all plotted together to come and fight against Jerusalem and stir up trouble against it....Also our enemies said, "Before they know it or see us, we will be right there among them and will kill them and put an end to the work" (Nehemiah 4:7-8,11).

Just as today's verse warns, the wicked men were plotting and talking evil against the people of God. This shouldn't surprise you when it happens, but you can't afford to be discouraged or to ignore it. You must then do what Nehemiah did: "But we prayed to our God and posted a guard day and night to meet this threat" (Nehemiah 4:9). When the people heard more rumors and became fearful, "Therefore I stationed some of the people behind the lowest points of the wall at the exposed places, posting them by families, with their swords, spears and bows" (Nehemiah 4:13).

Nehemiah was ready to fight his enemies if they attacked. He didn't think that a believer in God had to passively stand by while his work was threatened. You need to have the same resolve. Just because you're a believer doesn't mean that you have to ignore real threats to your life, safety, or ministry. Don't be naive and think that love will conquer all. Instead understand that you live in an imperfect world that holds many enemies to God's cause. Don't be mean, but don't be a pushover either. Pray and post a guard and stand up to your enemy's intimidation in the name of the Lord, and don't feel guilty or unspiritual when you do.

*"It is not good to eat too much honey,
nor is it honorable to seek one's own honor." — 25:27.*

Every year it was the same thing, and every year we were expected to go along with the act. At a company where I worked for four years, we would have a Christmas party. The assistant director would come around and collect a certain amount of money from each employee. He would take that money and buy gifts for the director and his wife. When the gifts were given at the party, the director would act surprised and thank us for our generosity.

But we weren't generous; we were paying an assessed fee that would bring trouble to any who refused to pay. The director and his assistant were seeking their own honor, not certain that they would get anything if it were left up to the employees to decide the gifts. According to today's verse, those gifts weren't tokens of honor but of dishonor.

Nehemiah was a godly man who wasn't seeking his own honor. He wrote:

Furthermore a hundred and fifty Jews and officials sat at my table, as well as those who came to us from surrounding nations. Each day one ox, six choice sheep and some poultry were prepared for me, and every ten days an abundant supply of wine of all kinds. In spite of all this, I never demanded the fool allotted to the governor, because the demands were heavy on these people (Nehemiah 5:17-18).

Nehemiah didn't seek his own honor, nor was he impressed with himself or his position. Instead he sought to serve the people and let the honor take care of itself. The Lord, who gives honor to whom honor is due, made sure Nehemiah's story is read by every generation by including his report in the inspired word of God.

Paul wrote of another man who didn't seek his own glory:

I hope in the Lord to send Timothy to you soon, that I also may be cheered when I receive news about you. I have no one else like him, who takes a genuine interest in your welfare. For everyone looks out for his own interests, not those of Jesus Christ. But you know that Timothy has proved himself, because as a son with his father he has served with me in the work of the gospel (Philippians 2:19-22).

Into what category do you fit? Do you serve your own interests or those of Jesus Christ? Do you seek your honor or His honor? Have you humbly served or demanded your rights as a child would? Set your heart today to be like Nehemiah and Timothy and leave the honor that may be due you in God's hands for Him to distribute when and where He wills.

MARCH 26

"As a door turns on its hinges,
so a sluggard turns on his bed." — 26:14.

I've searched the Bible, and haven't found the nine-to-five work day anywhere. God isn't limited to work within our time schedule, and you may have to work long hours to see what He wants accomplished. While many have burned out working for Jesus, others are sluggards where the work of the Lord is concerned. They're guilty of this quote from *Bits and Pieces* magazine: "Many desire greatness who cannot figure out what to do on a rainy Sunday afternoon" (April 4, 1993).

Nehemiah and his workers had no such problem. He reported:

> We continued the work with half the man holding spears, from the first light of dawn till the stars came out. At that time I also said to the people, "Have every man and his helper stay inside Jerusalem at night, so they can serve us as guards by night and workmen by day." Neither I nor my brothers not my men nor the guards with me took off our clothes, each had his weapon, even when he went for water (Nehemiah 4:21-23).

The walls at Jerusalem didn't miraculously appear, nor did the Holy Spirit do the work while everyone read the Bible. "The wall was completed in fifty-two days" (Nehemiah 6:15) because the people worked more than seven weeks from dawn to dusk while also having to stand guard at night. If you want to do great things for God, then you'll probably find yourself working long hours to see it come about.

The apostle Paul left a legacy of hard work just like Nehemiah and told of his labors to the Corinthians. First, he wrote, "The man who plants and the man who waters have one purpose, and each will be rewarded according to his own labor" (1 Corinthians 3:8). The word translated "labor" in that verse is the Greek word *"kopos."* It literally means "intense labor coupled with toil and grief." Paul knew his own "kopos." He went on to teach that everyone was assigned "kopos" and that this labor would have some grief and problems.

After that he commended himself to the Corinthians "in beatings, imprisonments and riots; in hard work, sleepless nights and hunger" (2 Corinthians 6:5). He continued by writing, "I have labored and toiled and have often gone without sleep; I have known hunger and thirst and have often gone without food; I have been cold and naked" (2 Corinthians 11:23).

What's your "kopos?" What labor have you been assigned that requires all you have? How many sleepless nights have you spent in the pursuit of your purpose? Determine now, not to work yourself to death by keeping busy, but to give yourself wholeheartedly to the work that's in the heart of God just for you.

MARCH 27

"The prudent see danger and take refuge,
but the simple keep going and suffer for it." — 27:12.

God can give insight to others for your particular situation, and I've been the recipient of such a blessing many times. One particular incident stands out in my mind that taught me an important lesson. I was sitting among a group of men with whom I was ministering and some new brothers I had just met began to speak "prophetically" into my life. Without them knowing me or my situation, they began to address some issues which I'd been praying about, so I was all ears.

What they said, however, didn't give me peace. In fact, it made me mad! I took the tape from that session, had it transcribed, and studied their words prayerfully. In counsel with my pastor and family, I determined that while some of what they said was true, some of what they said didn't reflect the will of God for my life.

I've learned that I need to judge for myself whatever input I receive from others, no matter how good their intentions may be. When it comes to spiritual things, I've paid a price for being "simple"—not taking the time to let God confirm the validity of what has been given in prophesy or counsel.

There was nothing simple about Nehemiah. He was a prudent man who carried out his work with diligence and faith. Yet he was a prudent man who didn't assume that because he was doing the Lord's work, everything would go smoothly. Having started the work of rebuilding, he had to constantly be on the lookout.

One day I went to the house of Shemaiah son of Delaiah, the son of Mehetabel, who was shut in at his home. He said, "Let us meet in the house of God, inside the temple, and let us close the temple doors, because men are coming to kill you—by night they are coming to kill you" (Nehemiah 6:10).

Nehemiah didn't naively accept what this man said to him as the truth. Shemaiah made a simple request—that they go to "church" so they would be safe from harm. Plenty of people were mad at Nehemiah, so it made sense that some could have been on their way to kill him. Nehemiah rejected his proposal, however, because he was prudent:

But I said, "Should a man like me run away? Or should one like me go into the temple to save his life? I will not go!" I realized that God had not sent him, but that he had prophesied against me because Tobiah and Sanballat had hired him. He had been hired to intimidate me so that I would commit a sin by doing this, and then they would give me a bad name to discredit me (Nehemiah 6:11-13).

If Nehemiah had assumed that this man was sent by God, he would have gotten into trouble. You also need to be careful not to naively accept what you hear without judging it for yourself. Today's verse warns that the simple proceed and suffer for it. The prudent way is to pray, wait, and allow God the opportunity to confirm the truth in what you're hearing.

*"When the righteous triumph, there is great elation;
but when the wicked rise to power, men go into hiding."* — 28:12.

I've always played to win, and have cheered for my teams with all that I have. I can remember being depressed for a week in 1972 after the U.S. Olympic men's basketball team lost to the Russians. When I played softball in a church league, I disliked late games because, if we lost, I'd be up into the wee hours of the morning replaying the game in my mind.

While some of that is carnal, some of it's spiritual as well. Consider this quote from William Temple, archbishop of Canterbury in England during World War II: "At the root of all your being, your intellectual studies, the games you play, whatever it is, the impulse to do them well is and ought to be understood as being the impulse towards God, the source of all that is excellent."

You need to think about winning and succeeding because your God does! Thank God Jesus played to win. He didn't play for a tie or to make a good showing; He played to win! He went into the arena and beat the enemy. Nehemiah didn't embark on his mission to rebuild Jerusalem hoping to accomplish some of his goals. He wanted to complete what he started for the glory of God, and thank God he too was successful.

Nehemiah wrote,

> The wall was completed on the twenty-fifth of Elul, in fifty-two days. When all our enemies heard about this and all the surrounding nations saw it, our enemies lost their self-confidence, because they realized that this work had been done with the help of our God (Nehemiah 6:15-16).

When Nehemiah first arrived, the righteous were discouraged and in hiding while the wicked were confident and in control. To reverse that situation, Nehemiah realized that he would have to be victorious and succeed at rebuilding the walls. A good showing wouldn't do!

Paul was grateful for God's victory and wrote, "Thanks be to God. He gives us the victory through our Lord Jesus Christ" (1 Corinthians 15:57). You should be both thankful for the victory in which you walk and seek to duplicate that victory in every situation. Be like Paul; be a winner.

Paul went on to achieve his own great victories, seeing successful churches planted against almost impossible odds. The apostle overcame persecution, apostasy, ignorance, idolatry, and his own weakness to do the job. Because he did, thousands of lost and oppressed rejoiced because that righteous man triumphed.

Don't settle for a loss or second place where your job, family, or ministry are concerned. Rather seek victory and watch the wicked flee and the people rejoice when good triumphs over evil.

MARCH 29

"When the righteous thrive, the people rejoice;
when the wicked rule, the people groan." — 29:2.

When Nehemiah finished the wall, he found that the work had just begun! He then had to set about organizing the city and especially reestablishing the spiritual life of the people. The people had groaned in their poor conditions for so long that they had neglected the things of the Lord. When Ezra and the Levites assembled the people to read the Law, "All the people had been weeping as they listened to the words of the Law" (Nehemiah 8:9).

Nehemiah knew what the people needed to carry on,

Then Nehemiah the governor, Ezra the priest and scribe, and the Levites who were instructing the people said to them all, "This day is sacred to the Lord your God. Do not mourn or weep"...Nehemiah said, "Go and enjoy choice food and sweet drinks, and send some to those who have nothing prepared. This day is sacred to our Lord. Do not grieve, for the joy of the Lord is your strength" (Nehemiah 8:9-10).

Joy is so important in everything that you do. Without it, you lose your strength and are unable to bear the burdens of the day. Nehemiah told the people to do whatever was necessary to celebrate and to recapture their joy. He told them to eat something special, go out to dinner, and share with those who were lacking. A modern Nehemiah may have even counseled that they watch some wholesome comedy.

Too often I have seen the servants of God weighed down in God's service. The work needing to be done tends to sap their strength. In this condition, they sometimes take themselves much too seriously and tend to look like they've been baptized in lemon juice.

I make an effort every day to laugh a lot. I have favorite comedians who make me laugh and I try to watch them regularly. I attempt to be with upbeat people who can keep me positive. I try to laugh at myself and my mistakes, and make a sincere effort to serve the Lord with gladness of heart. I even try to get other people to laugh at themselves.

I do all that I can to be happy so that others will be able to share in my joy when they are around me. It's my goal to have people leave my presence refreshed and happier than when they first encountered me. Wanting to take God seriously, I try not take myself and others quite as seriously.

Do what you need to do to regain and keep your joy. Above all, don't make the will of God a time of mourning but an occasion for celebration. When you do, you and others will thrive and have all the strength you need for the task at hand. That will make your chances for success greater and allow you to enter into the victory that God has in store for you. Laugh today and help someone else laugh. It's just what the doctor ordered.

MARCH 30

"If you have played the fool and exalted yourself, or if you have
planned evil, clap your hand over your mouth!" — 30:32.

I stayed up late, putting the finishing touches on an article for a national Christian publication. Having written for it previously, I just knew they would love the new revelation I had been receiving. To my surprise, the manuscript was returned and the Lord then showed me why it hadn't been accepted.

The Lord made it clear that I had tried to promote myself by writing the article and He had resisted its use. When they had called me to write in the past, it had been because the Lord was exalting my ministry. But I had decided to take matters into my own hands, and had "played the fool" by exalting myself.

One of the reasons Nehemiah's exploits are recorded for all time is because he didn't promote himself, but rather waited on the Lord to promote him. His humility is evident throughout the book as evidenced by this account:

> Moreover, from the twentieth year of King Artaxerxes, when I was appointed to be their governor in the land of Judah, until his thirty-second year—twelve years—neither I nor my brothers ate the food allotted to the governor. But the earlier governors—those preceding me—placed a heavy burden on the people and took forty shekels of silver from them in addition to food and wine. Their assistants lorded it over the people. But out of reverence for God I did not act like that. Instead, I devoted myself to the work on this wall. All my men were assembled there for the work; we did not acquire any land (Nehemiah 5:14-16).

Nehemiah wasn't impressed with his high position, nor did he use those 12 years as a time for personal gain. He could have said, like Paul was to say centuries later,

> I have not coveted anyone's silver or gold or clothing. You yourselves know that these hands of mine have supplied my own needs and the needs of my companions. In everything I did, I showed you that by this kind of hard work we must help the weak (Acts 20:33-35).

Nehemiah's heart was right and he was able to commend himself to the Lord, writing, "Remember me with favor, O my God, for all I have done for these people" (Nehemiah 5:19). As he closed his writings, he prayed, "Remember me, O my God, and do not blot out what I have so faithfully done for the house of my God and its services" and "remember me for this also, O my God, and show mercy to me according to your great love" (Nehemiah 13:14 and 22). He closed his account with the simple plea, "Remember me with favor, O my God" (Nehemiah 13:31).

Make up your mind not to use positions of authority for personal gain. When faced with the opportunity to receive a benefit that comes with the position, decline it. Be careful not to build your own kingdom while you're building the Lord's kingdom. Follow in the footsteps of Paul and Nehemiah and let the Lord take care of promoting you. He will do a better job of it than you could ever do for yourself.

MARCH 31

"It is not for kings, O Lemuel—not for kings to drink wine, not for rulers to crave beer...." — 31:4.

It was a revelation that changed my life and ministry. After being a pastor for a number of years, I realized one day that everyone had problems. I further came to realize that it was and would always be that way. What's more, I saw that I was called to walk with them in the midst of their problems. The bottom line was that I would always be dealing with problems!

Now that may seem like something very basic and simple, and indeed it is. Yet that represented a change in my ministry philosophy, for I was hoping to one day move beyond the problems and use my ministry to do great things for God. When I realized that dealing with people's problems was to God's glory, my ministry took on new meaning.

Today's verse simply states that kings aren't promoted for their own pleasure. Nor are they to drink "wine and beer"—dull their senses to the problems around them. Leaders like Nehemiah are appointed by the Lord to see problems and find godly solutions for them.

First, Nehemiah had to face the problem of marshaling resources to rebuild the wall. Then he had to fend off critics and opponents. While so doing, he had to face an internal problem of the rich charging interest on loans to the poor who needed the credit to feed themselves.

Once the wall was complete, Nehemiah had to devise a plan to repopulate the city. Since the temple was no more, he had to find ways to recharge the dead spiritual life of the people. After going off on a business trip, he returned only to find his enemies living in the house of God, people working on the Sabbath, and the men taking foreign wives.

Nehemiah faced all these problems and probably more that aren't recorded. He was promoted not to enjoy leisure time, but to deal with problems. And God wants to send you to deal with some problems as well. Where there are people, there are problems. But the good news is that God, in His mercy, wants to help people with their problems and He may send you to be part of the solution.

As we close this month, I hope you'll offer yourself to God in a new way. Ask God to use you, like He did Nehemiah, to solve problems and to serve. Don't look for a promotion to "easy street," but see promotion as a chance to be used by God in some tough situations. Avoid getting your hands dirty and your time at the top will be short-lived and unproductive. Work hard like Nehemiah did and your ministry or professional position will bear the kind of fruit that you've always hoped and dreamed it would.

APRIL 1

*"Since they would not accept my advice
and spurned my rebuke...." —1:30.*

It was time to sell again. We had our house up for sale, and within days a buyer appeared. He seemed to be serious, so my wife and I listened to his offer, which we thought had potential. Before we agreed to anything, however, we called a friend who had years of experience in the financial world.

As we explained the offer to him, he began to point out its weaknesses and pitfalls. Everything in us wanted to accept the offer in hopes of it all working out, but we listened to his advice and made some adjustments to the buyer's proposal. In a matter of days the deal disintegrated; since we had listened to our friend's advice, we had protected ourselves from a bad deal.

We never get too old or smart to seek and listen to advice. Our perspective is often limited, so not having advice and counsel from others may mean that we have an incomplete picture of reality.

It's a new month and time to begin study on a new topic. Having finished Nehemiah last month, let's take a few days to study another hero of the faith by the name of Esther. Esther began her "career" as queen by listening to advice.

King Xerxes had begun the selection process for a new queen. Having won the favor of the king's harem superintendent, Esther was among the finalists. She won out over all the other finalists because she listened to advice. Esther had been raised by her cousin Mordecai. "Esther had kept secret her family background and nationality just as Mordecai had told her to do, for she continued to follow Mordecai's instructions as she had done when he was bringing her up" (Esther 2:20).

According to the warning in today's verse, Esther didn't reject the advice given her. She sought and listened to Mordecai's perspective, realizing that his counsel was needed if she was going to be successful. Esther could have seen her promotion to the palace as a sign that her relationship with Mordecai had changed now that she was the "queen-in-waiting." Instead, she listened to him and was chosen from among all the maidens to be queen. Mordecai's advice helped her greatly.

Do you have a Mordecai in your life? Have you made mistakes that could have been avoided if you had tsought some counsel? Do you feel you have "arrived" in some area of life, thus allowing (or pressuring) you to act independently of others?

The book of Proverbs repeatedly recommends a "multitude of counselors." Whether you are a pastor, parent, professional, or prayer warrior, you need others to speak into your life, just as Esther did. Don't let a false sense of pride or importance keep you from accepting even a stern rebuke.

Take steps today to give others access to your life and decisions. Don't let them run your life, but don't be so independent that you make or repeat foolish blunders. By doing so, perhaps you'll also be promoted to "queen" because you listened to the advice of someone more knowledgeable in palace affairs.

APRIL 2

*"Discretion will protect you
and understanding will guard you." — 2:11.*

My heart felt as if it had jumped right up my throat as I found a letter from the IRS buried in the day's mail. With sweaty palms and pounding heart, I opened the letter only to have my worst fears confirmed: An agent was coming to audit a small ministry of which I was executive director.

One of my first steps was to seek the advice of a certified public accountant who had years of experience dealing with the IRS. I asked every question I could think of and then let him tell me things I hadn't thought of or known to ask. When the agent arrived, I was confident (and nervous). The audit ended with some recommendations and a clean bill of health for the ministry.

Esther went through an audit of sorts, for she was to be examined by the king himself. Fortunately, Esther didn't just seek the advice of her cousin who had raised her: "When the turn came for Esther (the girl Mordecai had adopted, the daughter of his uncle Abihail) to go to the king, she asked for nothing other than what Hegai, the king's eunuch who was in charge of the harem, suggested. And Esther won the favor of everyone who saw her. " (Esther 2:15-16).

Esther was one smart girl. Having no experience with kings, harems, and auditions for the throne, she found the one who had the knowledge and did what he told her to do. She found the principle in today's verse to be true—discretion guarded and protected her. The result was her promotion to the royal palace.

The New Testament speaks to this same principle. The writer of Hebrews taught, "Obey your leaders and submit to their authority" (Hebrews 13:17). Peter wrote, "Young men, in the same way be submissive to those who are older. Clothe yourselves with humility toward one another, because, 'God opposes the proud and gives grace to the humble'" (1 Peter 5:5). Paul added his wisdom when he wrote, "Submit to one another out of reverence for Christ" (Ephesians 5:21).

Submission is not a blind act of following someone; rather it's an attitude that's characterized by a "teachable spirit." Submission frees you from having to be and know all, and opens you to the abundance of wisdom that resides in others.

If you can't submit or hear from others, you are proud. If you hear only from the Spirit and not from others, you are proud. Many say, "The Lord told me," and God does indeed speak to His people. But to hear only from God is risky, for you can open yourself to deception if you aren't careful. God will speak not only through the Spirit but through the person next to you who knows more than you.

Pride makes you think you have to know it all and doesn't allow you to let someone else see your own weakness or ignorance. Real wisdom and maturity mean finding the more experienced person and submitting to his/her advice and counsel. Abandon any tendency to act as if you know it all, and begin today to find and submit to those who are able to impart the words and ways of life to you. Then discretion and understanding will guard your way, just as they did Esther's.

APRIL 3

"Let love and faithfulness never leave you; bind them around your neck;
write them on the tablet of our heart." — 3:3.

I have a spiritual father. When I was young in the Lord, he took me under his wing and raised me in the Lord. He promoted, rebuked, encouraged, cared for, and advised me. I owe him a great deal, and I always want to honor him because of how God has used and is still using him in my life.

Today's verse urges the reader to make love and faithfulness a part of life, not just for a season, but for all times. I want to do that, being careful not to use people, or get so "mature" or insecure that I can't honor those whom God has used to train me. I don't want to see people for what they can do for me, but I want to give of myself the way others have given of themselves to and for me.

The book of Esther could just as easily be called the book of Mordecai, for Esther's cousin figures prominently in its story. It seems as if Mordecai always had Esther's best interests at heart. In fact, he always had someone else's welfare at the top of his list. For instance:

> During the time Mordecai was sitting at the king's gate, Bigthana and Teresh, two of the king's officers who guarded the doorway, became angry and conspired to assassinate King Xerxes. But Mordecai found out about the plot and told Queen Esther, who in turn reported it to the king, giving credit to Mordecai. And when the report was investigated and found to be true, the two officials were hanged on a gallows. All this was recorded in the book of the annals in the presence of the king (Esther 2:21-23).

Mordecai was a faithful man who heard about a plot against an innocent person. Rather than mind his own business, he got involved because he was motivated by love. Paul wrote about love and faithfulness to the Philippian church:

> If you have any encouragement from being united with Christ, if any comfort from his love, if any fellowship with the Spirit, if any tenderness and compassion, then make my joy complete by being like-minded, having the same love, being one in spirit and purpose. Do nothing of selfish ambition or vain conceit, but in humility consider others better than yourselves. Each of you should look to not only to your own interests, but also to the interests of others (Philippians 2:1-4).

Mordecai wasn't positioning himself to be king or adviser to the queen; he was just a good man looking after the interest of others. How about you? Do you invest your time, money, and care in others? Be like Mordecai and try not to operate from selfish ambition or selfish conceit. Let the love of others be all the motivation you need to do good. Do something nice to someone today and do it in secret, trusting the Lord to reward you when He's ready to do so.

APRIL 4

"For they cannot sleep till they do evil; they are robbed of slumber till they make someone fall." — 4:16.

The Bible is a book of contrasts. Light and darkness, good and evil are often placed side by side so that the fruit of each is clearly distinguished. Cain and Abel, Saul and David, are two of those contrasting pairs with totally different fruit.

In the book of Esther, the contrast is between Mordecai and Haman. Yesterday you saw how Mordecai functioned with love and faithfulness. Haman, on the other hand, was a conniving, wicked man, who saw power as something to be amassed for personal gain.

> King Xerxes honored Haman son of Hammedatha, the Agagite, elevating him and giving him a seat of honor higher than that of all the other nobles. All the royal officials at the king's gate knelt down and paid honor to Haman, for the king had commanded this concerning him (Esther 3:1-2).

Mordecai was a good Jew who would not bow down to any man. This infuriated Haman and "having learned who Mordecai's people were, he scorned the idea of killing only Mordecai. Instead Haman looked for a way to destroy all Mordecai's people, the Jews, throughout the whole kingdom of Xerxes" (verse 6).

Haman conceived an elaborate plan to carry out his wickedness and got the king's permission to carry out his vendetta. True to today's verse, he couldn't sleep until he had carried out his evil. Haman decided to maintain his honor through his own ambition and efforts. Having been given the honor, he acted as if it were a birthright or something he had exclusively earned.

Jesus told his disciples, "Freely you have received, freely give" (Matthew 10:8). Paul cautioned the Corinthians against pride by asking, "For who makes you different from anyone else? What do you have that you did not receive? And if you did receive it, why do you boast as though you did not?" (1 Corinthians 5:7). Haman didn't see his promotion as a gift of God, but as a platform to wipe out his enemies.

Paul told the Corinthians that he had authority given to him by God, but that the authority was given to build them up and not tear them down. He further taught that the Lord "gave some to be apostles, some to be prophets, some to be evangelists, and some to be pastors and teachers, to prepare God's people for works of service, so that the body of Christ may be built up" (Ephesians 4:11-12).

You also need a ministry philosophy so that you'll know how to act as the Lord promotes and uses you. You can choose between the philosophy of Haman (one of personal promotion and gain) or the one of Mordecai (one of counsel and service given on behalf of others). Don't spend your time planning your next promotion or how you'll get even with someone who doesn't recognize or acknowledge what God is doing in your life. Rather be about the work of the ministry to reconcile the world to God.

APRIL 5

"That you may maintain discretion
and your lips may preserve knowledge." — 5:2.

Haman enlisted the support of King Xerxes to carry out his plot against the Jews. By convincing the king that the Jews were undermining his kingdom, Haman persuaded Xerxes to issue an order to annihilate the Jews. Without realizing it, the King had signed his queen's death certificate, for Esther was a Jew.

When Mordecai heard of the edict, he went to work. Today's verse states that the wise will have wisdom on their lips. Mordecai "tore his clothes, put on sackcloth and ashes, and went out into the city, wailing loudly and bitterly" (Esther 4:1). Not understanding, Esther sent her servant to console Mordecai.

But there was no consoling this servant of God:

> Mordecai told him everything that had happened to him, including the exact amount of money Haman had promised to pay into the royal treasury for the destruction of the Jews. He also gave him a copy of the text of the edict for their annihilation, which had been published in Susa, to show to Esther and explain it to her, and he told him to urge her to go into the king's presence to beg for mercy and plead with him for her people (verses 7-8).

This was tough counsel to Esther, for she risked her life by going to the king unannounced. When she responded to Mordecai, informing him of the risks involved, Mordecai's lips "preserved knowledge" with a classic response:

> Do not think that because you are in the king's house you alone of all the Jews will escape. For if you remain silent at this time, relief and deliverance for the Jews will arise from another place, but you and your father's family will perish. And who knows but that you have come to royal position for such a time as this? (verses 12-14).

Mordecai was a man for the times, understanding what needed to be done. He knew that the favor of God on Esther was for some purpose in the overall plan of God. She was in the right place at the right time and Mordecai was there to encourage her to be all that she was to be.

In a sense, Paul wanted all believers to be like Mordecai, so he wrote,

> Let the word of Christ dwell in you richly as you teach and admonish one another with all wisdom, and as you sing psalms, hymns, and spiritual songs with gratitude in your hearts to God. And whatever you do, in word or deed, do it all in the name of the Lord Jesus Christ, giving thanks to God the Father through Him (Colossians 3:16-17).

Wouldn't you like to be like Mordecai, making a difference today? Do you want people to seek you out, because you know what to do and when to do it? Is it your desire to understand what the Lord is doing and how you and others fit into that picture? Then today ask the Lord for wisdom and the ability to speak it to others.

APRIL 6

"Therefore a disaster will overtake him in an instant;
he will suddenly be destroyed—without remedy." — 6:15.

Haman was a proud, conceited rascal. The word of God reports, "Calling together his friends and Zeresh, his wife, Haman boasted to them about his vast wealth, his many sons, and all the ways the king had honored him and how he had elevated him above the other nobles and officials" (Esther 5:10-11). He also boasted of his invitation to dine with the queen, not knowing that it would be his last dinner on earth.

Yet Haman wasn't satisfied with all this honor and position because Mordecai would still not bow down before him. So his wife and friends gave him some advice: "Have a gallows built, seventy-five feet high, and ask the king in the morning to have Mordecai hanged on it.....This suggestion delighted Haman, and he had the gallows built" (verse 14).

Today's verse warns that what you plan will come back on you. If you plan good, then you'll find good. If you plan evil, then it will certainly come upon you. Haman and his wife had no idea that they were building the platform where they themselves would hang, because they had no concept of the spiritual principles involved.

David wrote,

Do not fret because of evil men or be envious of those who do wrong; for like the grass they will soon wither, like green plants they will soon die away....Be still before the Lord and wait patiently for him; do not fret when men succeed in their ways, when they carry out their wicked schemes. Refrain from anger and turn from wrath; do not fret—it leads only to evil. For evil men will be cut off, but those who hope in the Lord will inherit the land. A little while, and the wicked will be no more; though you look for them, they will not be found. But the meek will inherit the land and enjoy great peace (Psalm 37:1-2, 7-11).

Haman was a wicked man plotting evil schemes, and it seemed as if he was prospering. Instead, he perished on the very instrument he had built to carry out his plans. Praise the Lord for His sovereign works. There is none who can outsmart or escape His justice! It may seem that someone is "getting away" with something, but it's only the mercy of God extended to them so that they will repent. But His patience is not endless, and one day payday will come.

Without confidence that God will set all things right, Jesus' instructions to "turn the other cheek" seem to make believers the doormat for all. But understanding that the wicked are given every chance to repent before their destruction frees the believer to do the will of God in every situation and trust Him for the outcome. The lesson in Esther is that the good *do win* in the end. The challenge for us is to act like that is true regardless of whether we can see it happening or not.

APRIL 7

"I saw among the simple, I noticed among the young men,
a youth who lacked judgment." — 7:7.

Someone once said, "It's a shame that something like youth is wasted on the young." Another proverb states that you are "too soon old, too late smart." You undoubtedly have memories of your youth that are painful, brought about by some dumb decision made because you lacked experience and knowledge.

Many people today, not only youth, seem to lack judgment. But the Holy Spirit has come to "lead and guide you into all truth" so that you, whether young or old, have the discernment to do the right thing at the right time.

There's a story in the book of Samuel about a priest named Eli who was not a youth, but who lacked sense. One day Eli watched a woman whose name was Hannah. She had no children and would go to Shiloh with her husband every year to weep before the Lord. The Bible tells us:

> In bitterness of soul Hannah wept much and prayed to the Lord. And she made a vow, saying, "O Lord Almighty, if you will only look upon your servant's misery and remember me, and not forget your servant but give her a son, then I will give him to the Lord for all the days of his life." As she kept on praying to the Lord, Eli observed her mouth. Hannah was praying in her heart, and her lips were moving but her voice was not heard. Eli thought she was drunk, and said to her, 'How long will you keep on getting drunk? Get rid of your wine'" (1 Samuel 1:10-14).

Hannah responded that she was not drunk, but was "pouring out my soul to the Lord" (1 Samuel 1:15).

Eli didn't discern what was going on around him—like the youth mentioned in today's verse—because he judged according to what his eyes saw. As the man in charge of spiritual matters for the nation, he seriously misread this woman.

Contrast this with the ministry of Jesus as described by Isaiah: "He will not judge by what he sees with his eyes or decide by what he hears with his ears" (Isaiah 11:3). Jesus did not fall into the trap of judging only by what He saw, but rather relied on the Holy Spirit to impart the reality of the situation to Him.

Paul prayed for the Philippians and asked: "This is my prayer: that your love may abound more and more in knowledge and depth of insight, so that you may be able to discern what is best and may be pure and blameless until the day of Christ, filled with the fruit of righteousness that come through Jesus Christ—to the glory and praise of God" (Philippians 1:9-11).

Do you want to discern "what is best" and be "pure and blameless"? Then determine to stop judging only by what your eyes and ears tell you. Pray that "your love may abound more and more in knowledge and depth of insight." Determine not to be like Eli, who completely misread someone who came to the house of God.

APRIL 8

"To the discerning all of them are right;
they are faultless to those who have knowledge." — 8:9.

The stage was set for a dramatic impartation by Samuel, the prophet of God. The Lord had rejected Saul as king, and had given Samuel his marching orders: "Fill your horn with oil and be on your way; I am sending you to Jesse of Bethlehem. I have chosen one of his sons to be king" (1 Samuel 16:1).

The Lord was no more specific than that, so Samuel went off to Bethlehem and assembled Jesse's household at a sacrifice. The rest is a lesson in walking in the discernment that only the Spirit can provide:

> When they arrived, Samuel saw Eliab and thought, "Surely the Lord's anointed stands here before the Lord." But the Lord said to Samuel, "Do not consider his appearance or his height, for I have rejected him. The Lord does not look at the things man looks at. Man looks at the outward appearance, but the Lord looks at the heart" (1 Samuel 16:6-7).

Today's verse states that the discerning know what's going on. While Samuel started to trust in his own wisdom and judgment, the Spirit of God had the perfect insight that Samuel needed. Samuel focused on Eliab the eldest because he looked good, being tall and handsome. But Israel had suffered through Saul who was also a good looking specimen but lacked leadership skills, and now the nation needed a king with a heart after God. That man could be seen only by a discerning man who knew how to see beyond the external.

It's never enough to take a word from the Lord and then try to work it out in your own strength or understanding. You can't begin in the power of the Spirit and end in the flesh and expect to be successful. The Lord doesn't look at things the way you do, nor does He have the same list of criteria that you have for any situation. You must learn to hear and rely on the discernment He alone can give.

The writer of Hebrews wrote, "Solid food is for the mature, who by constant use have trained themselves to distinguish good from evil" (Hebrews 5:14). Part of your discernment will come directly from the Holy Spirit but another part will come from experience, from using your senses to discover what the will of God is. How often have you done nothing because you feared doing the wrong thing?

Paul wrote, "Therefore do not be foolish, but understand what the Lord's will is" (Ephesians 5:17). You can avoid being foolish by learning to listen to and rely on the Lord's voice in every and any situation. Don't trust your eyes or your ears. If you know you have a weakness in judging a situation, whether it's financial or concerning another person's gifts or character, then by all means seek advice.

Pray that you may hear the will of God and then be diligent to walk according to what He shows you. Be like Samuel and you'll fulfill today's verse and discern the things that are right.

APRIL 9

"'Let all who are simple come in here!'
she says to those who lack judgment." —9:4.

He was a homeless person, fleeing a family problem. Having no place to sleep, he chose a spot in an open field and had to use a rock for a pillow. During the night he had a dream that changed his life and to some extent the course of history. No, this isn't a modern story of a homeless person in some a major city. This is the story of the patriarch Jacob as he left his father's land to live with his uncle Laban.

A mama's boy all his life, Jacob had cooperated with his mother Rachel to steal his twin brother's birthright. Having tricked his father into giving him the blessing, Jacob found himself in deep trouble with his brother Esau who said, "The days of mourning for my father are near; then I will kill my brother Jacob" (Genesis 27:41). Jacob felt led to leave after he heard this!

As Jacob departed, his father, Isaac, summoned him, blessed him, and gave him some instructions about the future. On his journey to his uncle's home, Jacob had an interesting experience with the Lord:

> Jacob left Beersheba and set out for Haran. When he reached a certain place, he stopped for the night because the sun had set. Taking one of the stones there, he put it under his head and lay down to sleep. He had a dream in which he saw a stairway resting on the earth, with its top reaching to heaven, and the angels of God were ascending and descending on it. There above it stood the Lord, and he said, "I am the Lord the God of your father Abraham and the God of Isaac. I will give you and your descendants the land on which you are lying....I am with you and will watch over you wherever you go, and I will bring you back to this land" (Genesis 28:10-13).

When Jacob woke up, he uttered these words: "Surely the Lord is in this place and I was not aware of it" (Genesis 28:16). How profound that statement is for you and me. It's so easy to be distressed when you don't get that promotion you hoped for, or your vacation you planned doesn't work out, or your finances take an unexpected turn for the worse. But, like Jacob, God can suddenly show you that it was His hand that was behind that difficulty and you too can say, "God was in this and I didn't recognize that it was Him!"

Jacob was busy stealing a birthright, fleeing to another land, and then trying to get a good night's sleep. After his dream, he said, "God is here and I was so preoccupied, I didn't even know it." Is that your testimony as well?

If so, then ask the Lord to reveal Himself to you and ask Him to show you what He's doing. Today verse says that you can go to the Lord and receive wisdom and insight. Suddenly that hard rock under your head can become an altar where you can worship the Lord and find new direction and vision.

Seek the Lord today and maybe you'll have new insight into what He's doing and why. His revelation can turn an ordinary event into a powerful experience.

APRIL 10

"Wisdom is found on the lips of the discerning,
but a rod is for the back of him who lacks judgment." — 10:13.

I enjoy a good movie about the old West. I especially enjoy the ones where the cavalry arrives just as the bad guys are about to overwhelm the good guys. The sound of the bugler playing "charge" was the sound that those under siege wanted to hear.

The nation of Israel found itself surrounded one day and in need of the cavalry. Sennacherib, king of Assyria, attacked Judah and surrounded Jerusalem while Hezekiah was king. From his superior position, Sennacherib sent his messengers to read an arrogant letter requesting Jerusalem's surrender.

The Assyrian messenger read, "Do not let Hezekiah mislead you when he says, 'The Lord will deliver us.' Has the god of any nation ever delivered his land from the hand of the king of Assyria?....Who of all the gods of these countries has been able to save his land from me? How then can the Lord deliver Jerusalem from my hand?" (Isaiah 36:18-20).

While the king of Assyria was arrogantly boasting of his impending victory, Hezekiah turned to the Lord. Today's verse says that wisdom is on the lips of the discerning, and Judah's king knew he needed a word not from Sennacherib but from Isaiah.

When King Hezekiah's officials came to Isaiah, Isaiah said to them, "Tell your master, 'This is what the Lord says: Do not be afraid of what you have heard—those words with which the underlings of the king of Assyria have blasphemed me. Listen! I am going to put a spirit in him so that when he hears a certain report, he will return to his own country, and there I will have him cut down with the sword'" (Isaiah 37:5-7).

While the Assyrians spoke concerning what they saw with their eyes, Isaiah spoke from what he saw in the Spirit. The temptation often is to speak according to what you see, not according to what you discern in the Lord. Paul wrote, "It is written: 'I believed; therefore I have spoken.' With that same spirit of faith, we also believe and therefore speak" (2 Corinthians 4:13).

Those who trust in the Lord should speak from faith, not doubt. Having trusted in the Lord, you should have wisdom on your lips at all times. Those that lack sense, like Sennacherib, will receive a rod to correct their pride or unbelief. Which would you prefer—to have people seek you out because there's wisdom on your tongue coming from faith, or give you a rod for your back because you lack the discernment to understand what the Lord is doing? I know I don't want a rod. Like Paul, I'll try to speak out of what I believe and not out of what I see.

Determine today that you, too, will be like Isaiah, Paul and a host of others who have gone before you and discern what to say out of what you believe and know to be true.

APRIL 11

*"A man who lacks judgment derides his neighbor,
but a man of understanding holds his tongue." — 11:12.*

I was so mad, if I would have spit on the ground, it would have burned a hole in the carpet. An employee of mine deliberately ignored a directive and it had cost the ministry money. The whole situation was made worse by the fact that this same thing had happened before.

I felt so bad that I wanted to share with everyone what had happened, how this person had messed up, and how I had warned him. I wanted to tell his friends that he had really blown it. In short, I wanted to run my mouth and expose his mistake. Today's verse, however, warns against what I wanted to do. If you lack judgment, you'll deride your neighbor, but a man of understanding will keep quiet, even if his neighbor was wrong.

As an example of this verse, consider Jesus when He appeared before the priests and elders of His day just prior to His crucifixion. There was the King of glory standing before the corrupt representatives of God's government in the temple. Matthew wrote,

When he was accused by the chief priests and the elders, he gave no answer. Then Pilate asked him, "Don't you hear how many things they are accusing you of?" But Jesus made no reply, not even to a single charge—to the great amazement of the governor (Matthew 27:12-14).

Pilate was amazed that Jesus kept silent. It's a human trait to defend when accused or shift the blame when confronted. Here was a man who had His tongue under control. Jesus could have retaliated and even exposed the religious officials in their sin and greed. Yet He showed remarkable restraint, so much so that Rome's governor took notice because He was different from other men.

James wrote, "If anyone is never at fault in what he says, he is a perfect man, able to keep his whole body in check" (James 3:2). Peter wrote,

To this you were called, because Christ suffered for you, leaving you an example, that you should follow in his steps. "He committed no sin, and no deceit was found in his mouth." When they hurled insults at him, he did not retaliate; when he suffered, he made no threats (1 Peter 3:21-23).

It's a sign of wisdom and maturity to hold your tongue when all others are wagging theirs. Furthermore, it's a sign of tremendous discipline not to join in with others who have created a "feeding frenzy" of criticism and gossip, even if what they're saying is true.

Wouldn't it be a good idea today not to talk so much, especially about other people? Can you follow in Jesus' steps today and not verbally retaliate against others? Follow Jesus' example and keep quiet, even if you have legitimate complaints against someone. Give God room to fight your battles and give your mouth a rest.

102

APRIL 12

"A prudent man keeps his knowledge to himself,
but the heart of fools blurts out folly." — 12:23.

We should all be glad that Peter was chosen by Jesus to be one of the twelve. Peter is proof that you don't have to be perfect to serve the Lord; he also shows that God is patient and merciful when we display our human weaknesses.

After Jesus announced His impending death to His disciples, Matthew reported, "Peter took him aside and rebuked him, 'Never, Lord!' he said. 'This shall never happen to you'" (Matthew 16:22). At the Last Supper, Peter declared that he was ready to die with Jesus, only to deny his Lord and Master a few hours later.

Peter was guilty of what today's verse warns against. He was always quick to blurt out what was in his heart, not always checking to see if it was accurate. Peter would even correct the Lord Himself if he felt he knew better. Today's verse states that a prudent man learns to be quiet, even if he's right.

Of all wisdom's traits, the most remarkable is that it is willing to yield. Obviously, godly wisdom is correct, yet it is willing to yield to another way because it is so gentle and pure. Just because you are right does not mean that you are right in speaking it in every situation. Sometimes godly wisdom must yield and sometimes the one with the wisdom must be quiet. As an example of this, look at Paul as he was sailing to Rome for his trial before Caesar,

> Much time had been lost, and sailing had already become dangerous because by now it was after the Fast. So Paul warned them, "Men, I can see that our voyage is going to be disastrous and bring great loss to ship and cargo, and to our own lives also." But the centurion, instead of listening to what Paul said, followed the advice of the pilot and of the owner of the ship (Acts 27:9-11).

The result was as Paul predicted. The ship was destroyed and the trip was a disaster. Yet Paul didn't complain, nor did he (as far as we know) run off and sulk. Instead he yielded and was instrumental in encouraging the crew and saving their lives. Just before dawn Paul urged them all to eat.

> "For the last fourteen days," he said, "you have been in constant suspense and have gone without food—you haven't eaten anything. Now I urge you to take some food. You need it to survive. Not one of you will lose a single hair from his head." After he said this, he took some bread and gave thanks to God in front of them all. Then he broke it and began to eat. They were all encouraged and ate some food themselves (Acts 27:33-36).

There was no "I told you so" coming from Paul. He had spoken his word, and then went about his business, keeping quiet after his advice had been rejected for fourteen days. What discipline! Be prudent and willing to yield, seeking to be a source of blessing and encouragement in situations that could have been avoided if your original advice had been followed.

APRIL 13

"Every prudent man acts out of knowledge,
but a fool exposes his folly." — 13:16.

"Good help is hard to find," or so the saying goes. At least Elisha the prophet certainly found that to be true. He had a servant named Gehazi who ministered to the prophet's needs. One day a man from Syria by the name of Naaman came to see Elisha in hopes of having his leprosy cured.

Elisha didn't even go out to meet Naaman but instead "sent a messenger to say to him, 'Go, wash yourself seven times in the Jordan, and your flesh will be restored and you will be cleansed'" (2 Kings 5:10). I suspect that the messenger was Gehazi.

At first, Naaman rejected what he had been told to do. But when he reconsidered and dipped himself, he was healed. "Then Naaman and all his attendants went back to the man of God. He stood before him and said, 'Now I know that there is no God in all the world except in Israel. Please accept now a gift from your servant'" (2 Kings 5:15). Elisha declined and Naaman returned to his own country, happy and healed.

But according to today's verse, Gehazi went on to expose the folly in his heart. He ran after Naaman, thinking, "My master was too easy on Naaman, this Aramaean, by not accepting from him what he brought. As surely as the Lord lives, I will run after him and get something from him" (2 Kings 5:20). Gehazi did and Naaman was only too delighted to give him clothes and money.

When he returned, Gehazi lied to Elisha about his whereabouts, not knowing the other truth found in today's verse, for Elisha was a prudent man who already knew where Gehazi had been and what he had done. The prophet told him,

> Was not my spirit with you when the man got down from his chariot to meet you? Is this time to take money, or to accept clothes, olive groves, vineyards, flocks, herds, or menservants and maidservants? Naaman's leprosy will cling to you and your descendants forever (2 Kings 5:26-27).

God will create any number of situations specifically designed to reveal the folly that is in your heart. Gehazi's heart was exposed, even though he had served Elisha for years, perhaps without his greed ever surfacing. Yet Elisha knew what was going on and did not need Gehazi to tell him where he'd been; Elisha knew because he was a prudent man. You too should have supernatural knowledge that goes beyond what you can see in any given situation.

Given the choice, I want to be like Elisha rather than Gehazi. I want the Lord to expose any folly so I can serve Him with distinction, excellence and knowledge. May the Lord help me and you to always act out of knowledge rather than foolishness.

APRIL 14

"A patient man has great understanding,
but a quick-tempered man displays folly." — 14:29.

I awakened to a strange and wonderful presence in my bedroom. Just the night before, I had stood publicly and confessed that Jesus Christ was Lord, surrendering my life to His service. Now I knew the Lord was making Himself known to me and it was an awesome experience.

I sensed three things from that encounter. The first was that I would leave the church I was raised in; that happened three years later. The second was that I would go into full-time ministry; that took place five years later. Finally, I knew that I would give my life to His service, indicating that I would be expected to give my all in what I was to do. The latter has been fulfilled on an ongoing basis.

But none of what the Lord spoke that day was fulfilled quickly, and in some sense, it's all still being fulfilled. I've learned that the Lord is never in a hurry. He's patient and spends a great deal of time preparing His vessels for His use. When I sense someone with a great deal of urgency in their ministry, I try to encourage them to slow down and "smell the flowers along the way," for today's verse says that a patient man has great understanding.

If that is true, Caleb and Joshua must have both had great understanding. They were both among the 12 spies sent out by Moses. Only those two gave a good report. The others complained and panicked, telling the people that the obstacles were insurmountable. The people rebelled and the Lord ordered them to wander in the wilderness for 40 years until all those who rebelled had died.

Caleb and Joshua were allowed to enter the land, however, but had to wait those 40 years before they could receive what was theirs. What a great day it must have been when Caleb stepped forward to receive his land:

> Now the men of Judah approached Joshua at Gilgal, and Caleb...said to him, "I was forty years old when Moses the servant of the Lord sent me from Kadesh Barnea to explore the land. And I brought him back a report according to my convictions, but my brothers who went up with me made the hearts of the people melt with fear....So on that day Moses swore to me, 'The land on which your feet have walked will be your inheritance...because you have followed the Lord my God wholeheartedly'....I am still as strong today as the day Moses sent me out; I'm just as vigorous to go out to battle now as I was then. Now give me this hill country" (Joshua 14:6-12).

Just like Caleb, you never lose anything when you're patient. The Lord is able to preserve what is yours while you wait on Him. Isaiah wrote, "Those who wait on the Lord will renew their strength; they shall mount up with wings like eagles, they shall run and not be weary, they shall walk and not faint" (Isaiah 40:31). Wait on the Lord today and every day, and watch Him preserve and strengthen you until the day when He gives you what He has promised.

APRIL 15

"The discerning heart seeks knowledge,
but the mouth of a fool feeds on folly." — 15:14.

There was no way I was going back to school. I was 37, busy in ministry, had a family, and couldn't afford the time or money. So of course the Lord showed me that He wanted me to go back to school. I started out with one course in systematic theology, and seven years later finished my Masters Degree in Pastoral Ministries.

Even though I never thought I would earn another degree, I've always tried to grow in the knowledge of God and His ways. It's been my goal for many years to read one book every month on some spiritual topic. In addition, I'd make it a point to attend one seminar every year on an area in which I need to improve.

Today's verse says that the discerning heart seeks after knowledge. Discernment is not just a gift of the Holy Spirit, but can also be developed through knowledge and experience. You never "arrive" when it comes to learning; it's something that you must always pursue.

I've always admired Nicodemus the Pharisee because he was a man who sought the truth and continued to learn and grow. John wrote:

Now there was a man...named Nicodemus, a member of the Jewish ruling council. He came to Jesus at night and said, "Rabbi, we know you are a teacher who has come from God. For no one could perform the miraculous signs you are doing if God were not with him." In reply Jesus declared, "I tell you the truth, unless a man is born again, he cannot see the kingdom of God." "How can a man be born when he is old?" Nicodemus asked. "Surely he cannot enter a second time into his mother's womb to be born" (John 3:1-4).

Nicodemus was a man of stature; but he didn't feel as if he had it all together. Even though he sought out Jesus under the cover of darkness, he came asking questions. The discerning always ask a lot of questions rather than merely relying on what God will "show" them.

Nicodemus did something that showed his humility and desire to learn—he asked a dumb question! Not understanding what Jesus was saying about being born again, he asked if a man can enter his mother's womb again. Nicodemus was not afraid to show that he had no idea what Jesus was talking about. Nicodemus wanted to learn too badly to hide his ignorance.

Paul prayed that the Colossians would please the Lord by "growing in the knowledge of Him" (Colossians 1:10). Are you growing in knowledge and discernment? Has the thought of additional education crossed your mind, but you dismissed it for the same reasons I did?

I'm now pursuing my doctorate because I want to grow until I die. With my degrees, I want to add the power and insight of the Holy Spirit so that I can discern the will of God and encourage others to do the same. Won't you join me in that pursuit?

APRIL 16

"The wise in heart are called discerning,
and pleasant words promote instruction." — *16:21.*

A few days ago we looked at the story involving Elisha and Naaman, focusing on Elisha's servant named Gehazi. Today let's return to that story and look at another aspect of it. In particular, let's look at what Naaman did after he was healed.

In 2 Kings 5, you can read how Naaman came from Syria to get his leprous condition healed at the direction of the prophet. When the prophet didn't come to meet him but sent word of what he should do, Naaman almost went home in anger over what he perceived to be a snub. Naaman pressed through his disappointment, however, and was healed.

Then Naaman made an unusual request:

Please let me, your servant, be given as much earth as a pair of mules will carry, for your servant will never again make burnt offerings and sacrifices to any other god but the Lord. But may the Lord forgive your servant this one thing: When my master enters the temple of Rimmon to bow down and he is leaning on my arm and I bow there also—when I bow down in the temple of Rimmon, may the Lord forgive your servant for this (2 Kings 5:17-18).

What was even more unusual was Elisha's response. He did not preach to Naaman concerning the evil of idolatry, nor did he chastise him for just receiving a healing and not following the Lord from that point with his whole heart. Instead, Elisha told Naaman to "go in peace" (verse 19).

Today's verse says that the wise in heart are discerning. In no matter of life is wisdom more necessary than in how to respond to people. Talking to someone is in some sense like driving a car. You can have a green light and see a pedestrian crossing illegally in front of your car. At that point, you can proceed (since you are "right") and hurt or even kill the pedestrian. Or you can slow down and "discern" that it's not worth running over them to prove that you're in the right.

That's how it is in responding to people. You may have the truth and the other person may be "dead" wrong. That still doesn't mean that it's the time to respond to them with what you know. Today's verse also says that pleasant words promote instruction. Hitting someone with all you know is only half the battle in communicating the truth. Besides the truth, you need pleasant words that will best carry the message that you want to deliver.

Jesus said, "I did not speak of my own accord, but the Father who sent me commanded me what to say and how to say it" (John 12:49). If the Father told Jesus not only what to say, but how to say it, it's a safe assumption that He wants to do the same for you.

Take Elisha's example to heart and today season your words with salt. Make someone thirsty for more truth than you have presented by using gracious, pleasant words.

APRIL 17

*"A man who lacks judgment strikes hands in pledge
and puts up security for his neighbor." — 17:18.*

Theirs was an unholy alliance. Wicked King Ahab had enlisted the support of good King Jehoshaphat in attempting to recapture Ramoth Gilead back from the Aramaeans. Even though Ahab was wicked and his nation of Israel had rebelled against the Lord, we see in 1 Kings 22 that Jehoshaphat agreed to consider Ahab's request for an alliance. Jehoshaphat foolishly said, "I am as you are, my people as your people, my horses as your horses" (1 Kings 22:4). But to his credit, he also advised Ahab to "first seek the counsel of the Lord" (verse 5).

Ahab summoned a company of prophets and they all predicted victory for Ahab. But Jehoshaphat was not convinced by the words of those court prophets on Ahab's payroll. He responded, "Is there not a prophet of the Lord here whom we can inquire of?" (verse 7).

Ahab was hesitant to summon the prophet Micaiah: "I hate him because he never prophesies anything good about me" (verse 8). In spite of that, Micaiah was summoned and initially prophesied success for Ahab and his expedition. Even though the prophet spoke favorably, Ahab was angered and said, "How many times must I make you swear to tell me nothing but the truth in the name of the Lord?" (verse 16). Even wicked King Ahab knew something wasn't right.

After that warning, Micaiah went on to predict Ahab's downfall. In spite of his words, "the king of Israel and Jehoshaphat king of Judah went up to Ramoth Gilead" (verse 29). What's more, Ahab disguised himself while encouraging Jehoshaphat to wear his royal robes. As the battle unfolded, the Aramaeans surrounded Jehoshaphat only to withdraw when they realized that he wasn't Ahab. The Aramaeans then found Ahab and carried out the judgment of God that had been spoken through Micaiah.

Jehoshaphat almost lost his life because he foolishly joined forces with Ahab. Today's verse warns that a foolish man hastily shakes hands and makes a deal with another. Jehoshaphat formed an alliance that was ill-advised. Paul wrote,

> Do not be yoked together with unbelievers. For what do righteousness and wickedness have in common? Or what fellowship can light have with darkness?...What does a believer have in common with an unbeliever? What agreement is there between the temple of God and idols? (2 Corinthians 6:14-16).

How many women have ignored this to marry a man who was at best a lukewarm believer? How many others have suffered in a business partnership with someone who was not a follower of Christ? Listen very carefully before you enter into a working relationship with anyone. Get to know them first, and rely on the perspective that the Holy Spirit can give. Don't be like Jehoshaphat, hastily committing your resources to a battle that may not be yours. Instead, ask God for wisdom and discernment and avoid the pain of having to undo what you did hastily.

APRIL 18

"Before his downfall a man's heart is proud,
but humility comes before honor." — 18:12.

Kathy and I sat motionless before the television set, watching the news unfold. One of the Church's most prominent evangelists was before us and the world, being exposed for his sins. This was a blow to all of us, but in some sense we should have seen it coming. Today's verse warns that pride precedes a downfall and this brother had openly attacked others and had put his own ministry forth as a model of integrity and anointing.

I don't want to criticize this brother, for I loved him then and love him today. He served the Lord faithfully for many years, and the fruit of his ministry has been plentiful. I had the opportunity to meet with him personally for several hours one time and it was a highlight for me. But pride will undo even the greatest, and it may be the most deadly enemy that we face.

While pride is a sign that a problem is coming, humility is a sure sign that good times are ahead. I vividly remember an intense time when Kathy and I were going through some difficulties. We went to our pastor to describe all that was going on and receive some counsel.

I'll never forget his perspective, for he shared that a blessing was on the way! It was his experience that when the Lord humbles His servants, it was for a coming promotion that could produce pride if humility was not firmly in place. Kathy and I left his home encouraged in what we were encountering and watching for the "honor" that was about to come our way.

Paul, James and Peter all warned, "God opposes the proud but gives grace to the humble." When you are proud, God stands against you. It's frightening to think that God will stand in your face to oppose you, but that's what He does to the proud. But the good news is that He also gives grace to the humble. Since you are told to humble yourself, then humility isn't a feeling, but rather a conscious decision. It's up to you to watch yourself so that pride doesn't creep in.

John wrote, "For everything in the world—the cravings of sinful man, the lust of his eyes and the boasting of what he has and does—comes not from the Father but from the world" (1 John 2:16). Any boasting about what you have or do is of the world and is pride. That's why a good indicator of pride is how much you talk about yourself, even if what you say is factual. Pride always causes you to focus on self, the antithesis of the believer's walk.

Maybe today would be a good day to take a spiritual inventory and see what is stored in your heart. Is it pride in what you have done or have, not only in the world but in the church? Or is there humility of heart that realizes what you've accomplished or gained is through the grace of God. The good news is that you can humble yourself, or choose to wait for God to humble you, which means that a fall is coming that always follows a prolonged period of pride. The choice is yours—choose wisely!

APRIL 19

"Rebuke a discerning man,
and he will gain knowledge." — 19:25.

Nowhere is self more evident than when someone corrects you, especially if you feel you know better than the one rebuking you. It's hard not to be defensive when corrected and focus rather on the tone of voice, probable motives, and knowledge of the one doing the correcting.

Focusing on any of those things, however, will cause you to miss any truth that may be in the rebuke. It's better to accept the rebuke, thank the one bringing it, and then commit the entire matter to prayer in an atmosphere less heated.

To King David's credit, that's what he did when confronted by the prophet Nathan. As king he could have ignored the prophet or had him banished or killed as he did Bathsheba's husband. Instead he said simply, "I have sinned against the Lord" (2 Samuel 12:13). From that incident, David gained some much needed knowledge that he wrote about in Psalm 51:

> For I know my transgressions, and my sin is always before me. Against you, you only, have I sinned and done what is evil in your sight, so that you are proved right when you speak, and justified when you judge. Surely I have been a sinner from birth, sinful from the time my mother conceived me. Surely you desire truth in the inner parts; you teach me wisdom in the inmost place (Psalm 51:3-6).

First of all, Nathan's rebuke reminded David of his transgressions. God doesn't want you carrying around a constant awareness of your sins, nor does He want you to totally ignore your imperfections. An awareness of your need for God's mercy and grace makes you a ready channel of that same mercy to others.

Since the Lord revealed David's sin to Nathan, David knew that the Lord was grieved over what he had done. David knew that he had to accept Nathan's rebuke, for the Lord had sent him. If you dismiss the rebuker because that person is less than perfect, you're really resisting the One who sent the rebuke.

David knew that the rebuke came because God required the truth in the inner parts. That truth wasn't doctrine, but rather the truth of a person's heart that God wishes all to acknowledge. It is wisdom to accept a rebuke, for there may be truth in it that God wishes to get deep down into you.

If you want to gain knowledge and discernment, then you must learn to accept correction even in the form of a rebuke. If someone corrects you today, say thanks and express appreciation that they had the courage and concern to share what they saw. Then pray about what was said, and let the Lord confirm it or adjust it. By doing it that way, you give the Lord plenty of room to speak to you about some blind spot or to shield you from criticism that wasn't justified. Accept the rebuke as the powerful learning experience that the Lord intends for it to be.

APRIL 20

"Ears that hear and eyes that see —
the Lord has made them both." — 20:12.

It's easy to think that everyone sees things as you do. As a preacher, I've studied the Bible and then taught, all the while apologizing to the people for what I thought was obvious to everyone. After the message, I would have people tell me that they had never seen what I'd just shared, and expressed gratitude for the insight. I'm still surprised when that happens.

The Lord made your eyes to see and your ears to hear—not just the normal things of life, but the special insight unique to you and your ministry. Your gifts and calling will enable you to see and hear things that may be nothing to you, but extraordinary to others.

Consider once again Elisha and his ministry. When the king of Aram confronted his staff and accused one of them of spying for Israel, his people told him, "Elisha, the prophet who is in Israel, tells the king of Israel the very words you speak in your bedroom" (2 Kings 6:12). As today's verse states, the Lord made Elisha's ears to hear and he heard things that no one else could.

When the king sent his troops to capture Elisha and stop this bedroom espionage, Elisha prayed to the Lord: "Strike these people with blindness" (verse 18) and the Lord did just that. The same Lord who allowed Elisha and his servant to see the chariots of fire protecting them, now made the eyes of their enemies blind.

Elisha led this blind band of raiders to Samaria, the capital city of their enemies. "After they had entered the city, Elisha said, 'Lord, open the eyes of these men so they can see.' Then the Lord opened their eyes and they looked, and there they were, inside Samaria" (verse 20). Now the Lord opened their eyes and all were amazed that the prophet, without a sword or army, had rendered the Aramaeans helpless and had actually led them into the camp of the enemy.

The one similar characteristic of everyone listed in Hebrews 11 is that all who had faith "saw" something. Noah saw the warning of the Lord "about things not yet seen" (11:7); furthermore, "all these people were still living by faith when they died. They did not receive the things promised; they only saw them from a distance" (11:13); Moses "by faith left Egypt not fearing the king's anger; he persevered because he saw him who is invisible" (11:27).

The Lord doesn't play games with mankind; He desires that all men may see clearly and understand Him and His purpose. Blindness and deafness are spiritual conditions caused by sin. Faith in God removes those conditions and opens the line of communication between God and man.

What's more, God will never assign you a job in which He will not give the insight and wisdom necessary to carry it out. Elisha, Noah, and Moses heard and saw fantastic things. Their ministries affected the whole world and yours can, too, if you learn to walk in faith! Ask the Lord to allow you to hear and see as He created you to do. After that, fasten your seat belt for the ride of your life!

111

APRIL 21

"In the house of the wise are stores of choice food and oil,
but a foolish man devours all he has." — 21:20.

Yesterday we read about Elisha and how he led a band of enemy raiders (who had been struck blind by the Lord) into Israel's capital city. When they were inside the city walls, Elisha prayed that they would see again and their eyes were opened! But now the question was what to do with these men.

When the king of Israel saw them, he asked Elisha, "Shall I kill them, my father? Shall I kill them?" "Do not kill them," he answered. "Would you kill men you have captured with your own sword or bow? Set food and water before them so that they may eat and drink and then go back to their master." So he prepared a great feast for them, and after they had finished eating and drinking, he sent them away, and they returned to their master. So the bands from Aram stopped raiding Israel's territory (2 Kings 6:21-23).

Today's verse says that the house of the wise has a wealth of food and oil, while the house of a fool devours all he has. If you'll learn to see with eyes of faith, you'll realize that you haven't been shortchanged by the Lord in any way. If you'll learn to see things from God's perspective, you'll realize just how blessed you are.

The king of Israel suddenly had his enemies before him and naturally saw the chance for military victory and revenge. But the prophet had him raise his eyes higher to see the purpose of God. Israel had a wonderful chance to bless their enemies by feeding them. To have killed that scouting party would have brought some temporary relief, but another party would probably have followed. But by feeding and blessing them (and by allowing God to show forth His power in Elisha's ministry), the Aramaeans decided to stop harassing Israel altogether.

If you focus on what you don't have, you'll hold onto to what you do have and consume it on your own needs or desires. But if you walk in faith and see things from heaven's view, you'll take the many opportunities you have and seize them to do good. After all, "we are God's workmanship, created in Christ Jesus to do good works, which God prepared in advance for us to do" (Ephesians 2:10).

Paul also instructed, "Let us not become weary in doing good, for at the proper time we will reap a harvest if we do not give up. Therefore, as we have opportunity, let us do good to all people, especially to those who belong to the family of believers" (Galatians 6:9-10). Jesus told His followers to do good, and lay up treasures in heaven where moth can't eat and rust can't destroy.

Don't wait until your situation improves to do good. Ask God to open your eyes to see the many opportunities at your disposal. Ecclesiastes tells you to "sow your seed in the morning, and at evening...for you do not know which will succeed, whether this or that, or whether both will do equally well" (Ecclesiastes 11:6). Take every opportunity to draw from your rich storehouse. You don't know whether what you do today may be the key to your enemies retreating for good.

APRIL 22

"The eyes of the Lord keep watch over knowledge." — 22:12.

Have you ever thought what it was like to be alive when Jesus walked the earth? I have wondered how I would have reacted to Jesus' ministry and the reports of His miracles and teachings. I would like to think I would have become a follower, yet there were those who saw and heard His ministry and still killed him.

There was one who lived 2,000 years before Jesus came and saw Him more clearly than the Pharisee who could reach out and touch Him. That man's name was Abraham. Jesus told the Jews, "Your father Abraham rejoiced at the thought of seeing my day; he saw it and was glad" (John 8:56).

The Jews had no idea what Jesus was talking about or how that was possible. But Abraham walked in faith and was given knowledge and insight. Today's verse tells you that the eyes of the Lord keep watch over knowledge. Another verse tells you that "the eyes of the Lord range throughout the earth to strengthen those whose hearts are fully committed to him" (2 Chronicles 16:9). When the Lord finds those who are totally His, He imparts knowledge and insight reserved for those who walk in faith.

Abraham "saw" Jesus and His day when he was on the mountain to sacrifice his only son, Isaac, as reported in Genesis 22. When Isaac asked where the sacrifice was (not realizing that he was "it"), Abraham responded in faith: "God himself will provide the lamb for the burnt offering, my son" (Genesis 22:8).

As Abraham was about to slay his son, a voice from heaven spoke, preventing Abraham from doing what in his heart he had already done. At that point,

Abraham looked up and there in a thicket he saw a ram caught by its horns. He went over and took the ram and sacrificed it as a burnt offering instead of his son. So Abraham called that place, "The Lord will provide." And to this day it is said, "On the mountain of the Lord it will be provided" (Genesis 22:13-14).

While everyone else would have seen a ram in the thicket, Abraham saw the day of the Lord Jesus. He saw at that moment that one would come who would give His life as a ransom for many. Two millennia before Jesus came, a man on a mountain with his son and a ram saw Jesus more clearly than those who grew up with Jesus and sat under His ministry. That's what faith opens to those who believe.

You're a child of Abraham and his inheritance is yours. The Lord, who preserves knowledge and insight and gives it to whom He wills, wants to show you great things, perhaps long before they ever come to pass. On the mountain of the Lord—that high place of fellowship with Him—He will show you great things.

You son or daughter of Abraham, walk today in your father's faith. Don't react to what is happening to you, but get above it and see it from your heavenly Father's perspective. Everyone else may see a ram, but God wants you to see if differently. Let the Lord show you the reality of what you encounter today, and then apply your faith to understand it and maybe even impart it to someone else.

APRIL 23

"When you sit down to dine with a ruler,
note well what is before you." — 23:1.

It was late at night and I could see the hardened and sad faces of the inmates peering out from their cells as I walked that long, cold corridor. My friend had been sentenced and requested that I come visit him before he was transferred to another prison. We sat together in a small conference room and discussed the events of the last few days that had led to his hearing, sentencing, and incarceration.

Of all that had happened to him, the most upsetting and shocking was the betrayal of some of his closest friends and associates. He told me (and I knew it to be true) how much talk there had been behind his back. Friends he had trusted were talking against him; the media had reported half-truths and lies based on statements he had innocently uttered; even a former spiritual adviser turned out to be an informant.

You soon learn that prisons are full of people claiming their innocence, but my friend wasn't claiming his. He was, however, commenting on how naive he had been in trusting himself too quickly to those who had said they wanted to help him. When I got home from that visit, I read today's verse and thought of him.

Today's verse tells you to be careful when sitting down with another person. You must not be anxious to "give dogs what is sacred; do not throw your pearls to pigs. If you do, they may trample them under their feet, and then turn and tear you to pieces" (Matthew 7:6). While you can't be paranoid, suspecting anyone with whom you come in contact, you can't just casually trust yourself to any and all. It requires discernment to know what to do, keeping in mind that "Jesus would not entrust himself to them, for he knew all men. He did not need man's testimony about man, for he knew what was in man" (John 2:24).

The most painful problems are problems with people whom you trust. When they betray you, it can be hard to cope. Paul wrote Timothy, "You know that everyone in the province of Asia deserted me, including Phygelus and Hermogenes" (2 Timothy 1:15) and "At my first defense, no one came to my support, but everyone deserted me. May it not be held against them" (2 Timothy 4:16).

The good news is that man may be fickle, but the Lord is faithful and true. After Paul told Timothy of his disappointments with his associates, he continued, "But the Lord stood at my side and gave me strength, so that through me the message might be fully proclaimed and all the Gentiles might hear it" (2 Timothy 4:17). Don't be surprised when people disappoint you, but use those times to reflect on God's faithful love.

When man lets you down, it makes God's loyalty and love that much more special. While all others may desert you, He has your best interests at heart and will never forsake you or be anything less than the Comforter and Wonderful Counselor He has promised to be.

APRIL 24

"I applied my heart to what I observed
and learned a lesson from what I saw." — 24:32.

Jesus was no dummy, but was an observant man who studied life and was able to draw conclusions from what He saw that could help other people. For instance,

Jesus sat down opposite the place where the offerings were put and watched the crowd putting their money into the temple treasury. Many rich people threw in large amounts. But a poor widow came and put in two very small copper coins, worth only a fraction of a penny. Calling his disciples to him, Jesus said, "I tell you the truth, this poor widow has put more into the treasury than all the others. They all gave out of their wealth; but she, out of her poverty, put in everything—all she had to live on" (Mark 12:41-43).

Jesus had to be watching very closely to see two small coins being put into the offering. Not only did He observe that, but He was also able to immediately turn an ordinary event into a supernatural teaching about how to give.

Today's verse tells you how He was able to do that on a regular basis—He applied his heart to what He observed. He didn't just pray in the wilderness to get revelation, but also observed the everyday affairs of His generation and taught the people with examples from what He saw and learned.

Another example of this is found in Luke 7 when Jesus was dining in the home of Simon the Pharisee and the sinful woman came and anointed Jesus' feet. Simon immediately judged the situation according to his Law: "When the Pharisee who had invited him saw this, he said to himself, 'If this man were a prophet, he would know what kind of woman she is—that she is a sinner'" (verse 39).

Jesus not only knew what was in the woman's heart, but also knew exactly what Simon was thinking. Jesus was observing everything—how Simon looked, what he did and didn't say, how the woman behaved, and how she wasn't welcomed in the house. The Lord didn't apply a set of rules to that scene; He rather applied His heart to get understanding and cut right to the heart of the matter, creating an opportunity to teach an important truth about grace and forgiveness.

Jesus gave you an example of how to act when He observed the widow who gave, the woman who wept, and the Pharisee who was self-righteous. True to Isaiah's prophecy, Jesus did not "judge by what he sees with his eyes, or decide by what he hears with his ears" (Isaiah 11:3). You too must learn to observe, gain understanding, and then act on what you have understood.

Make it your goal today to serve someone before they ask; encourage one who is down and doing their best to "hide" it; give a word to someone who is hungry to hear from God. Learn to observe their eyes, actions, words, or silence, and minister out of what you have observed. Don't take "I'm doing OK" as the reality of where someone is. Rather observe them carefully and allow the Lord to reveal the truth. From there, you will minister effectively and be a source of strength to many.

APRIL 25

*"What you have seen with your own eyes do not bring hastily to court,
for what will you do in the end if your neighbor puts you to shame?"* — 25:8.

My friend and brother was on the other end of the phone, crying over his impending divorce. His wife, who is also my friend, had served him the papers a few days before, and the reality of his situation was overwhelming. We prayed and I encouraged him as best I could, but it was (and is) painful for me to see.

As sometimes happens, people began to take sides. Some observed the wife and placed the blame on her, while others were quick to cite the husband's failures as reasons for this breakup. Members of both "camps" came to me sharing their perspective as if it were the entire truth, subtly trying to get me to agree with their views on the situation. I have and will continue to avoid their attempts.

For me, this situation is too complicated for an easy assessment. Mistakes were made by both the husband and wife, and I'll never know all that they've gone through in getting to the point where they are today. I refuse to judge their motives, choosing rather to stand with both of them as they do what they feel they must do.

Today's verse cautions you not to come to a quick judgment without all the facts. You can rush into a situation, claiming to have all the truth and wanting a final verdict to be rendered in the minds of all. Yet the verse today asks what you'll do when another arrives with additional information that renders your initial assessment useless.

My goal with my friends is to let the Lord sort out the motives and mistakes in this situation. By taking this posture, I want to be their friend when the Lord reveals to them their role in what happened. I'm not condoning divorce, but neither will I make this be the fault of one over the other. I want to stand as a brother with both of them, and let God speak in righteous judgment.

Paul wrote, "Now I know in part, then I shall know fully" (1 Corinthians 13:12). I don't and can't know it all about my friends, or about anything for that matter So I've stopped trying to act as if I do. By giving situations more time, I allow the Lord room to make the thoughts and intentions of the heart clear to all who are interested in the truth.

When the apostle John saw people not doing he thought they should, he asked Jesus, "Do you want us to call fire down from heaven to destroy them?" (Luke 9:54). That attitude is still prevalent among Jesus' followers. Without having all the information and certainly not having the heart of God, it's all too easy to call down fire. Jesus rebuked John and will rebuke you if you carry the same attitude.

The Lord wants us to be people of truth and grace. We must carry the truth, but carry it gently, realizing that we don't have it all. I don't understand much of what happens and why people do what they do. I do understand that I'm called to stand with my brothers while I'm trying to figure it all out and until the Lord shows me the whole picture. With that in mind today, be a dispenser of grace and let God be the judge of the truth.

APRIL 26

"The sluggard is wiser in his own eyes
than seven men who answer discreetly." — 26:16.

It had been a year since I had been there, but I was certain where this place was located. I kept driving back and forth looking for a familiar landmark, but couldn't seem to get my bearings. My friend had wanted to give me directions, but I had confidently refused. Now I was late picking him up as I stubbornly continued to drive back and forth, refusing to admit that I was wrong.

It turned out that I was one street over from where I should have been. Returning home that night, I told my wife I would have bet her, the house, and kids that I knew exactly where that place was. Good thing I didn't bet, for my children would be fatherless and my wife a widow!

Today's verse cautions against this attitude. When you know and you know that you know, it's hard not to be cocky and arrogant. But wise men don't insist that they're correct. Leaving room for error, they answer discreetly and softly. Yet the one who knows (and knows that he knows) can see the wise as weak and uncertain and himself as the one with superior spiritual insight and maturity.

Peter had that tendency. Jesus was trying to tell him that he would soon deny the Lord, but Peter knew better than the Lord, replying, "Even if I have to die with you, I will never disown you'" (Mark 14: 31). Several hours later, Peter had to face his own wretchedness, something he had tried to avoid with brave words.

My pastor once said, "It's hard to be humble when you're good." When you're right and have proved it in the past, it's difficult not to approach every situation as if you have all you need to be the best. But your past successes can be your downfall, for you can begin to believe that you're as good as you think you are. You can then assume that you're right or will automatically succeed just because you're special or possess extraordinary insight or wisdom.

I'm learning to stand strong in what I believe, but then make room for the opinions and insight of others. While wanting to be confident, I also want to walk humbly and "softly." I don't want to be wise in my own eyes, but rather leave that assessment to others, while I stay mindful of my limitations.

I've seen too many pastors and leaders fall prey to this subtle but cocky attitude. I've heard too many subtly brag of their abilities or insight. With all that in mind, I remind myself that my greatest successes aren't nearly as much to my credit as I'd like to think. By not holding myself and my abilities in such high regard, I think I can more readily glorify the Lord who enabled me to succeed in the first place. And it gives other people more room to offer input into my decisions and direction. You would do well to watch this same tendency and to guard against pride or optimism as you enjoy the blessing and favor of the Lord.

APRIL 27

"As iron sharpens iron,
so one man sharpens another." — 27:17.

The man was driving me nuts, and there was no way I could avoid dealing with him. God had undoubtedly joined me to him so I could serve and learn from him. But he was so different from me that I found it hard to work with him, and often wanted to abandon the relationship.

This man was spontaneous and I was more prone to plan far ahead. He would eat at the strangest times and sleep in late, working into the early hours of the morning. Thinking out loud, he would share his thoughts of what he might do and then never seem to do those things, appearing to some as a man who couldn't keep his word (instead, he was one who liked to "hear" his thoughts and used me and others as a sounding board for their practicality). His buying habits, routines with his family, and tastes in clothes were almost all the exact opposite of mine.

It would have been a tragic mistake, however, for me to have backed out of that relationship. The Lord had joined us together for a reason, and I learned more in the long run than I ever could have if I had worked with someone "more like me."

That relationship gave me much-needed insight into how to build an effective team, and also spoke to the truth of today's verse. Relationships with others can keep you sharp, especially those that involve people not like you. Your tendency may be to gravitate to those who are more like you. While that may be comfortable, you may lose the giftings of those who can do what you can't.

At the same time, people who aren't like you cause you to grow in tolerance, patience, and your understanding of human nature. Being exposed to people with different tastes, schedules, and preferences in general will help you to be sharpened and more useful to the Lord, since you'll be able to look past what is convenient to what is important in building a team or a relationship.

My wife is almost the exact opposite of who I am, and I thank God that she is. She brings balance to my limited perspective; she gives me insight into the world of others who don't think anything like I do. She has shown me, just like the relationship I referred to above, that there's more to the world than my perspective.

Is there someone you are working with, whether in the church, on the job, or at school, who rubs you the wrong way? Do you avoid relationships with people who are very different from you? Perhaps you need to assess whether you aren't overlooking their God-given worth because they don't align with your thinking of what they should be like.

Today's verse says that you'll overcome dullness as you're sharpened by others. That sharpening will take place as the friction comes and the sparks fly. Don't avoid this just because it's painful, but embrace it as the necessary process that it truly is.

APRIL 28

"A faithful man will be richly blessed,
but one eager to get rich will not go unpunished." — 28:20.

I was adding my pastoral salary to the one that was being promised, and singing "Happy Days Are Here Again!" in my mind. As a part-time director of an organization, I was told that in no time I would be making $30,000 per year. I just knew that God wanted to bless me financially, and thought for sure that this was the vehicle He had chosen to do so.

That scheme, like so many other of my get-rich-quick ideas, failed because my motives were wrong. No matter how I tried to label them, they were simply ideas to make me a lot of money. Like today's verse says, I was eager to get rich. My desire to make an easy dollar actually lost me money several times and caused me to lose untold hours in pursuing a dream that wasn't to be.

There's a modern proverb that states, "If it's too good to be true, it probably is!" I've seen many other people, including committed believers, pursue riches in the name of the Lord. Network-marketing plans and other business ventures have mostly ended in frustration. I'm not against network marketing, nor am I against believers prospering financially. But whatever the scheme, I've come to realize that there's only one way to prosperity and success, and that is through hard work, faithfulness, patience, and sowing seed through giving. Today's verse promises that a faithful man will be richly blessed. Jesus taught this same principle:

> Whoever can be trusted with very little can also be trusted with much, and whoever is dishonest with very little will also be dishonest with much. So if you have not been trustworthy in handling worldly wealth, who will trust you with true riches? And if you have not been trustworthy with someone else's property, who will give you your own? (Luke 16:10-12).

It takes more than business smarts or being in the right place at the right time to be successful. Knowing this, Jesus told His followers not to focus on the business plan but on the condition of the heart.

The way to prosperity, according to Jesus, is learning to handle small things well. Be on time; do small jobs well and learn to finish them; be faithful with the little money you have at the moment; learn to serve someone else's vision and treat it as if it were your own. None of these have to do with business plans or marketing, but they have everything to do with what's important to the Lord. And since He's the one who controls your success or failure, it would be wise to learn to do things His way if you're to achieve the desired results.

Beware of any shortcuts; don't automatically try to circumvent the hard times or seeming insignificance of your everyday routine. Be faithful to what's before you, and the Lord, who is watching, can promote and prosper you from nothing to something. Let your focus be on the kingdom of God and not money, and perhaps God will grant you financial success as you serve Him with faithfulness.

APRIL 29

"A fool gives full vent to his anger,
but a wise man keeps himself under control." — 29:11.

There he was, making a fool of himself for all the world to see. I was watching a baseball game and the umpire blew a call at first base. Immediately the manager was out arguing the call, and before long, the manager went on a rampage.

He kicked dirt on the umpire and then pulled first base out of the ground and tossed it into right field. Even though the umpire had thrown him out of the game, he continued to rant and rave from the dugout, where he threw bats and helmets onto the field. I guess you could say that he definitely disagreed with the umpire!

Some would call that good baseball, for the manager was doing his job opposing the umpire and perhaps preventing another bad call from being made against his team. The Bible says, however, that the manager made a fool out of himself because he gave full vent to his anger.

Today's verse doesn't state that anger itself is wrong. Anger is a human emotion that man can experience because God gave him the capacity to do so. It's not that anger is sinful, but the behavior that comes out of anger can be. Today's verse warns that the one who gives vent to his anger is the fool; the one who feels anger but controls its expression is considered wise.

Paul instructed the Ephesians on anger: "'In your anger do not sin': Do not let the sun go down while you are still angry, and do not give the devil a foothold" (Ephesians 5:26-27). Paul didn't tell them to avoid anger, since all humans experience it, but he did tell them to deal with their anger quickly.

Perhaps you have encountered the negative effects of someone who gave vent to their anger. That so hurt or scared you that you've tried to deny or ignore your own anger. That never works, for you're trying to ignore a part of you that can play an important role. Instead of ignoring your anger (or calling it by another name like frustration, anxiety, or "having a bad day"), you need to face it and deal with it.

Anger can be positive if it can spur you to take action that otherwise you wouldn't take. If you stub your toe on the junk in your garage for the hundredth time, then your anger can move you to clean it up once and for all. Kicking the clutter and yelling at it isn't the way to give vent to your anger.

If you're angry today, then first of all recognize that you're angry, and don't feel guilty or ambivalent about it. Instead of pouting or screaming, tell the Lord, "I'm angry about this, Lord. I'm so angry I could hit something. Help me to deal with my anger and show me how I can use my anger to do something useful or constructive. I want to deal with this quickly before the sun goes down."

By not denying it or giving it room to be destructive, you'll use your anger as an incentive to act and you'll recognize it as something that's a part of you by the design of God. But if you give way to your anger so that it leads to sin, you'll feel even worse as you have to deal with the aftermath of your misdirected wrath.

APRIL 30

"The leech has two daughters. 'Give, give!' they cry." —30:15.

It was written of Abraham Lincoln that he had "plain common sense, a kindly disposition, a straight forward purpose, and a shrewd perception of the ins and outs of poor, weak human nature."** That is something the Church needs more of. Just because someone has surrendered their life to Jesus doesn't mean that their basic nature has been changed at all. It only means that they're now on the path to deal with that nature if they choose to do so.

I was scandalized in my early years to see human nature rear its ugly head among believers. Assuming that knowing the Bible would take care of every problem, I couldn't understand how offenses, grudges and selfish ambitions could happen among believers.

Then I ran across a passage that changed my perspective and my life forever:

I hope in the Lord Jesus to send Timothy to you soon, that I also may be cheered when I receive news about you. I have no one else like him, who takes a genuine interest in your welfare. For everyone looks out for his own interests, not those of Jesus Christ. But you know that Timothy has proved himself, because as a son with his father he has served with me in the work of the gospel. I hope, therefore, to send him as soon as I see how things go with me (Philippians 2:19-23).

Paul traveled with some pretty impressive company, yet he wrote that he had "no one else like [Timothy]," for everyone else was looking out for their own interests. Paul had to deal with fallen human nature among his companions and had only one man who seemed to press through it all to true service and selflessness. I saw that if Paul had only one, then I would probably not encounter many more as I walked with the Lord.

When I saw that passage, I set a life's goal to be like Timothy. If the Lord had only a few who could be genuinely interested in others, then I wanted to be one of them. I set out to serve my pastor and leadership as Timothy obviously served Paul. Seeing that Paul had the freedom to send Timothy whenever he thought best, I decided to submit to my leaders and be directed by what they felt was best for me and the body of Christ at large.

Now just because I decided to do all this doesn't mean I was successful. When I set those goals, I underestimated my own weakness and the strength of my human nature. Sometimes I was offended by not getting enough credit for work I had done; I occasionally criticized others. Given my failures, however, my goal is still the same—I want to be like Timothy and be more genuinely interested in the welfare of others than my own.

Today's verse says that the leech knows only how to take. Don't be a spiritual leech, but be a Timothy and lead a more selfless life today and everyday as a faithful disciple of Jesus Christ. **Phillips, Donald T., *Lincoln on Leadership* (New York: Warner Books), page 35.

MAY 1

"Let the wise listen and add to their learning,
and let the discerning get guidance." —1:5

The professor was five minutes late and I walked out of the classroom! That was how I treated all my philosophy classes in college. While they were required courses, I dreaded them with a passion. From my earliest years, I couldn't tolerate subjects and discussions that I believed had no apparent purpose. I didn't want to discuss what knowledge was; I wanted to do something, *anything*, with what I learned.

I dislike this same practice when I see it in the church. While the world is literally going to hell, often the church wastes time discussing issues that don't really matter. Wanting to make a difference in the world, I hope to take my theology and experience and apply them to real-world problems.

Today's verse tells us that the wise will grow in learning and the result will be guidance. The end of wisdom is guidance, which is the knowledge of what to do in a particular situation.

Paul was a great theologian; he could apply his theology to guidance for real-life situations. Consider the letter to Philemon, his shortest epistle. For years I ignored this little gem, but have recently found it to be an important statement for anyone who wants to make a difference in the world.

This letter was written to Philemon, a leader in the church at Colossae. It appears that Philemon had lost a runaway slave named Onesimus, who ended up in Rome. While there, Onesimus was converted, probably under Paul's ministry. This created an interesting dilemma.

Should Paul send the slave back to Philemon to resume his position as a slave? And what should Philemon's response be to this man whom he had once owned? Paul tackled these questions head on, not by discussing the theological merits of slavery, but rather by applying the wisdom he had gathered over the years to this thorny problem.

The world needs you to help find answers to tough questions. People are less concerned with your doctrine and more concerned with what your doctrine causes you to do to help their situation. Who better to face and address the problems of today than you?

What problem is your community facing, and how can you grow in wisdom and guidance to help out? If your employer is confronting a difficult situation, what can you do to help resolve it? Is there some other problem—a disease, human condition, procedure, or strategy—that has always troubled you? If so, can you possibly be part of seeing it resolved or cured to the glory of God?

The Lord expects you to grow in wisdom and to translate your wisdom into guidance. Seek to be a fountain of life to those who are thirsting and show your God to be the source of your life-giving and life-changing waters.

MAY 2

"Then you will understand the fear of the Lord,
and find the knowledge of God." —2:5.

George Washington Carver is one of my heroes. After the Civil War, when many African-Americans were struggling for their existence, he almost single-handedly revolutionized Southern agriculture through his creativity, wisdom, and understanding.

The story goes that Carver encouraged farmers to plant peanuts as a good crop for the region; he was quickly confronted with the fact that there was no market for this crop. Discouraged and burdened, Carver took action:

> As I prayed, I was drawn to my feet... "Oh, Mr. Creator," I asked softly, "why did You make this universe?" A wind stirred the trees a bit. "Your little mind asks to much," came the answer, "Ask something more your size." Confused, I rubbed my chin. "What was man made for?" I whispered. Once more, I seemed to hear a voice on the wind. "You are still asking too much, little man, try once more." I fell to my knees, "Dear Mr. Creator, why did You make the peanut?" Once more the breeze rustled through the trees. "Now you are asking questions your own size. Together we will find the answers."*

Carver found the knowledge of God by seeking it, and discovered over 300 uses for the peanut after his simple prayer. He knew the source of his scientific knowledge and went to Him in humility and out of a deep sense of inadequacy. The response was a tremendous breakthrough in agricultural science.

Today's verse promises that you will find the knowledge of God when you seek for it with all that you have. There are still new technologies to be discovered, new products to be developed, and simple cures for complex problems to be uncovered. Who better to do those things than you who know the source of all that knowledge?

Determine to make a difference in your world, and plug into the creative resources available to you through prayer. Don't settle for the status quo, but seek the Lord for how you can do what you do more efficiently. Who knows, you may invent something or develop a procedure that will save lives or change the course of history. It's not farfetched at all if you realize your own limits and then call upon your God who knows no limits.

*Collins, David R., *George Washington Carver: Man's Slave Becomes God's Scientist* (Milford, Michigan: Mott Media), pages 105-106.

MAY 3
"My son, do not forget my teaching,
but keep my commands in your heart." — 3:1.

The day before yesterday we began to discuss Paul's letter to Philemon, which urged him to receive back a runaway slave who was now a brother in the Lord. Paul wrote:

Although in Christ I could be bold and order you to do what you ought to do, yet I appeal to you on the basis of love....I did not want to do anything without your consent, so that any favor you do will be spontaneous and not forced (Philemon 8-9, 14).

Paul could have ordered Philemon to do what was right, but Paul realized that an order would not accomplish the spiritual purpose he had in mind for Philemon. He rather appealed to Philemon to do what was right, so that when he chose to do it, the decision would be of some benefit because it was unforced and voluntary.

The Lord uses the same tactics with you. God could force you to do His will but rather chooses to persuade you to obey Him. If all else fails and you resist stubbornly, He can order circumstances so that you have few options left but to do what He desires. But that's rare, for there's more benefit when you do something from love than against your will or because of fear or force.

Today's verse urges you to keep God's commands in your heart, not your head, and there's a big difference. The Lord wants to guide you willingly and without compulsion. Jesus told His disciples,

You are my friends if you do what I command. I no longer call you servants, because a servant does not know his master's business. Instead, I have called you friends, for everything that I learned from my Father I have made known to you (John 15:14-15).

Imagine, God wants you for a friend! He desires to share His most intimate thoughts with you, and then see you follow them, from no other motive than love for Him. Paul finished his letter by stating, "Confident of your obedience, I write to you, knowing that you will do even more than I ask" (Philemon 21). After Jesus called His disciples friends, He said, "You did not choose me, but I chose you and appointed you to go and bear fruit—fruit that will last" (John 15:16).

I wonder if fruit isn't what Paul was looking for from Philemon—abundant obedience beyond the minimum standard. When you do things from the head, you tend to do them legalistically, looking for the easiest way. When you do things from love, you do them from the heart and tend to do them abundantly.

I want to be like Philemon and learn to act on God's every suggestion. With the same attitude, I don't want to settle for doing the minimum required by law, but the maximum motivated by love. I invite you to join me as together we seek to please the Lord from loving hearts that look to willingly carry out His wishes.

MAY 4

"Above all else, guard your heart,
for it is the wellsprings of life." — 4:23.

It was a collect call from Hong Kong, and I was only too glad to accept the charges. My pastor and spiritual father was on the other end, having gone to Hong Kong on a ministry trip. I was honored that he called and didn't mind footing the bill for our chat while we were 10,000 miles apart!

Over the years, my times with my spiritual father have all been special as he has challenged me in the Lord. He allowed me to get close to him to see his family, ministry, and life so that I could learn. I can remember him calling when I was discouraged, or writing when I was confused. The Lord would put me on his mind at critical times and he would faithfully contact me to exhort me in the Lord. I'm the better today for that relationship and shudder to think where I would be without it.

I think that Timothy was just as excited to hear from his spiritual father as I have been to hear from mine. The two letters Paul wrote to Timothy were among his last epistles and reveal a special love and bond between the two men that was and is unique. I wish every man and woman of God could experience the joys and challenges that come from that kind of father-child relationship.

Today's verse cautions you to guard your heart, the very thing that Paul warned his son Timothy to do:

> Don't let anyone look down on you because you are young, but set an example for the believers in speech, in life, in love, in faith and in purity. Until I come, devote yourself to the public reading of Scripture, to preaching and to teaching. Do not neglect your gift, which was given you through a prophetic message when the body of elders laid their hands on you. Be diligent in these matters; give yourself wholly to them, so that everyone may see your progress. Watch your life and doctrine closely. Persevere in them, because if you do, you will save both yourself and your hearers (1 Timothy 4:12-16).

You need someone to help you keep watch over your heart. It's all too easy to get caught up in business and lose track of where your heart is and what condition your heart is in. But Timothy had (and I have) someone who can help do just that, and it's a wonderful gift from God.

I've heard many say that they want a relationship like that, but it's seldom pursued or found for a number of reasons. I urge you today to find someone to help you keep watch over your heart, someone with whom you can be yourself. You need someone with whom you can share your failures, doubts, and inner secrets and know that you'll still be loved and accepted.

Ask the Lord today for someone like that for your life. If you already have someone, then call them today to tell them how much you appreciate them. Recommit yourself to work with them to keep watch over your heart and doctrine, so that the wellsprings of life won't get clogged, but will flow freely from you to others and to the Lord.

MAY 5

"At the end of your life you will groan,
when your flesh and body are spent." — 5:11.

The water surrounding our boat was dark and murky and some of it was finding its way into the vessel. I turned around to see the man driving the boat bailing it out with a coffee can. We were on a ministry trip into a jungle river filled with piranha fish that were capable of devouring an entire cow in minutes! At that point, I wished the driver had a bigger coffee can to bail the water.

But I calmed myself with the words of Psalm 23: "Even though I walk through the valley of the shadow of death, I will fear no evil, for you are with me; your rod and your staff, they comfort me" (verse 4). I decided that I had given my life to the Lord and if He chose to claim it in the muddy waters of Guyana, South America, that was His business and His alone.

I once heard a teacher say that God's people are like currency—He spends them out of His "savings account." Once you get saved, you are cash in His hand for Him to invest wherever and whenever He wishes.

It's a fact of life that you'll spend your life on something. You can spend it on work, a hobby, sports, or relationships. When you do that, you come to the end described in today's verse: Your life is spent on something that doesn't pay any returns; your time and energy are consumed by things that are of no lasting value.

Paul was no different in that he too was currency in the Lord's hands, and the Lord spent him freely. Paul wrote, "Even if I am being poured out like a drink offering on the sacrifice and service coming from your faith, I am glad and rejoice with all of you" (Philippians 2:17). He likewise wrote to Timothy, "I am already being poured out like a drink offering, and the time has come for my departure" (2 Timothy 4:6).

Now a drink offering could be seen as a waste since it was poured into the ground. No one got the pleasure of drinking it and it was put to no practical use; it was simply poured out to the Lord. That's how Paul viewed his life and ministry; it was poured out to God through his service to the Church. Yet Paul rejoiced that, if his life was to be consumed, it was given to something that made a difference.

What if the Lord wants to cash in His investment and spend you? How will you react if He takes all that is in your cup and pours it into the lives of others? What if there is no credit or "residue" of your being poured out? Will you react like Paul and rejoice, or will you feel as if your life was a waste, having been poured out for less than you had hoped?

I urge you to spend your life wisely; better yet, let the Lord spend it however He chooses. You gave your life to Him; now let Him spend you as He sees fit. The truth is that "the body that is sown perishable, it is raised imperishable; it is sown in dishonor, it is raised in glory; it is sown in weakness, it is raised in power; it is sown a natural body, it is raised a spiritual body" (1 Corinthians 15:42-44). Pour yourself out and you will get back a spiritual return beyond description!

*"Free yourself, like a gazelle from the hand of the hunter,
like a bird from the snare of the fowler." — 6:5.*

God can be sneaky sometimes. What appears to be a wonderful opportunity may turn out to be a test to see what's in your heart. The writer of Hebrews made this interesting comment: "People who say such things show that they are looking for a country of their own. If they had been thinking of the country they had left, they would have had opportunity to return" (Hebrews 11:14-15).

That seems to say that God will always give you ample opportunity to turn away from all that He has for you. There are people who start out looking for something new in the Lord, but when they encounter the cost, turn back to a less costly lifestyle. And the amazing thing is that the Lord seems to help them return, for God wants those who willingly offer themselves to Him without reservation.

God doesn't want you to feel trapped into doing His will; today's verse actually encourages you to free yourself if that's how you feel. Paul, while being poured out as a drink offering, had no desire to turn back. He kept pressing for all he could be and do in the Lord. He wrote to the Philippians,

> But whatever was to my profit I now consider loss for the sake of Christ. What is more, I consider everything a loss compared to the surpassing greatness of knowing Christ Jesus my Lord, for whose sake I have lost all things. I consider them rubbish, that I may gain Christ and be found in him, not having a righteousness of my own that comes from the law, but that which is through faith in Christ—the righteousness that comes from God and is by faith. I want to know Christ and the power of his resurrection and the fellowship of sharing in his sufferings, becoming like him in his death (Philippians 3:7-10).

Those aren't the words of someone giving a half-hearted effort to serve the Lord, nor do they represent the heart cry of one who was looking back with fondness or nostalgia at the past. He wrote to the Corinthians,

> To keep me from becoming conceited because of these surpassingly great revelations, there was given me a thorn in my flesh, a messenger of Satan, to torment me. Three times I pleaded with the Lord to take it away from me. But he said to me, "My grace is sufficient for you, for my power is made perfect in weakness." Therefore I will boast all the more gladly about my weaknesses, so that Christ's power may rest on me. That is why, for Christ's sake, I delight in weaknesses, in insults, in hardships, in persecutions, in difficulties. For when I am weak, then I am strong (2 Corinthians 12:7-10).

Paul delighted even in a messenger from Satan if it helped him come into what the Lord had for him. Be like Paul and don't even think of turning back if things are tough, and don't automatically see an open door to go back to some comfort zone as from the Lord. But rather set your will to pay the price to walk the path that God has chosen for you.

MAY 7

"I came out to meet you;
I looked for you and have found you!" — *7:15.*

It was 4:00 a.m., and I had to go to work the next day. There was more packing to do, however, and my friend and brother was due to move the next day. I had to make a decision of whether to continue serving or to leave him on his own so I could get some rest. I decided to continue packing his belongings and went to work with only a few hours sleep.

Service is seldom convenient and there are times when the Lord will actually hide an opportunity for service to see if you're alert and committed to serve. I heard someone say that when the opportunity to serve crosses my will, it forms a perfect "cross" for me to carry. And unless I pick up my cross and follow Him, my discipleship is faulty.

Paul wrote of one man who had to aggressively pursue service to Paul, and his name was Onesiphorus:

May the Lord show mercy to the household of Onesiphorus, because he often refreshed me and was not ashamed of my chains. On the contrary, when he was in Rome, he searched hard for me until he found me. May the Lord grant that he will find mercy from the Lord on that day! You know very well in how many ways he helped me in Ephesus (2 Timothy 1:16-18).

The opportunity to serve Paul didn't just drop into Onesiphorus' lap. He had to diligently pursue the chance to minister to Paul and he did it at some cost to his own reputation, since it appears that many of the brothers were ashamed of Paul's chains and were avoiding contact with him. But Onesiphorus pressed through all that to receive a blessing—and what a blessing it was.

Twice Paul prayed that he and his household would find mercy! If you need mercy (and we all do), then a sure way to get it is to search out hard-to-find chances to serve and fulfill them. When you do, it causes the recipients of your service to mention you to the Lord with thanksgiving in their hearts.

Notice too that this service wasn't just a once-in-a-while thing with Onesiphorus. On the contrary, he gave himself many times to the ministry of being helpful and developed a wonderful habit of being sensitive to the hard-to-see needs of others. For that reason, his memory has been preserved to this day through the inspired writings of a man on the receiving end of his service.

Do you want to receive mercy and obtain a godly heritage? If you do, then determine to be a servant. Be observant and look for the chance to serve the needs of others. Today there will be chances for you to assist someone without them asking you. Make the most of those chances and follow in the footsteps of your brother Onesiphorus, the faithful servant.

MAY 8

*"Rejoicing in his whole world
and delighting in mankind." — 8:31.*

I came out of my home to find three letters scrawled next to the front door: "KKK." Since we had a Bible study in our home and the people were of mixed racial backgrounds, some of my neighbors were upset with so many people of color coming to their neighborhood and had let me know of their displeasure.

Not long after that, Kathy and I moved to Alabama, again to work with a racially-mixed group of believers. I'll never forget the stares and comments we got almost everywhere we went because we were committed to an integrated expression of the body of Christ. Unfortunately, that hasn't always been the norm for the Church or for me.

At one time, I took great pride in my lack of prejudice. Then I began to walk more closely with people of different cultures and colors and I saw that I wasn't as "clean" as I had thought. I remember one instance in particular when an African-American brother picked up and held my two-year-old daughter in public. When he did, she began to touch his hair and I was embarrassed for no reason except that he was black and she was white. I wanted to separate them, and faced at that point that I had more work to do in accepting all people.

Today's verse is a bit of wisdom that says God rejoices in the whole world and delights in all of mankind. As I write this, I'm sitting in the Honolulu airport, having a cup of coffee. I can see people with red, white, black, brown, and yellow skin all sitting in the same restaurant, speaking different languages and clad in unique dress. I think I can feel God's pleasure at the diversity that He created as it's expressed in a limited way right here.

Yet the world is full of racial prejudice and cultural pride, and violence from hatred and bigotry is increasing. Tribe fights tribe in Africa, one Asian group discriminates against another, and American society is increasingly segregated. In the midst of all this, the Church and you as a member must model and stand for the love and tolerance that God has for all His creation.

John wrote in his Revelation, "I looked and there before me was a great multitude that no one could count, from every nation, tribe, people and language, standing before the throne and in front of the Lamb" (7:9). If that's what John saw in the Spirit, shouldn't the Church see the same thing? If that's what heaven or the next age will look like, shouldn't the Church reflect that now?

What can you do to promote racial reconciliation and harmony? What steps can you take to reflect the beauty of God's diverse creation in your own life and ministry? It isn't enough to pay lip service to racial harmony; you should actively pursue it. Search your heart today and see if there's any barrier that would prevent you from rejoicing in all of God's creation. If there is, then remove it and be a source of God's love to all people, for they are indeed God's creation.

MAY 9

"Little do they know that the dead are there,
that her guests are in the depths of the grave." — 9:18.

Years ago I was in a meeting where I was one of only a few whites. An African-American pastor was asked whether he approved of interracial marriage. Without hesitation, he responded, "No!" All were quiet as they waited for an explanation to his quick reply and he finished by saying, "I don't think a believer should ever marry a non-believer." The crowd laughed and some nodded their agreement.

This pastor was in essence saying that the color of the skin shouldn't have as much to do in a marriage as the condition of the soul. While this pastor recognized the unique problems faced by any interracial couple, he wasn't ready to use those problems as an excuse for racism. Often that's the root problem behind many of the excuses given for separation in the body of Christ among ethnic groups.

As I mentioned yesterday, I led an integrated group Bible study in my early years as a believer. I was always surprised by the response to that group by outsiders who visited for the first time. I remember one couple telling me that they would like to come to the group but were afraid of who would pick up their children. I didn't understand at first, but later realized that they were afraid that a person of a different color would handle their children.

Then I moved to Florida and pastored a racially-mixed congregation, something I actively preached about and pursued. I got letters and lost members because of our open stand concerning the acceptance of all people. Some feared interracial marriages and others felt that people should only attend churches with others of the same culture or color.

There was a day when I would have condemned or judged those attitudes, but that's no longer the case. I know that the Lord has given me grace to deal with ethnic diversity, and I don't want to legalistically impose that on everyone around me. Yet I feel a sense of loss for people who don't see the gain in properly relating to the whole body of Christ.

Today's verse warns that those who lack wisdom don't realize the death their state holds for them. To walk in racial prejudice or to be cut off through bitterness or fear from another group restricts the life of God that was meant to flow between all members of the body of Christ.

Our love and acceptance for one another is to be in more ways than just lip service. It's easy to talk about welcoming and loving all people, but do you make room in your heart for their culture and legitimate differences in taste and music? Have you searched your heart, or better yet, have you asked the Lord to search your heart, for any vestige of prejudice?

Work to remove anything that could hold back your love from any group of people. By so doing you'll prepare for the next age when all the saints will worship together around the throne of God. If it's going to be like that then, work today to see the Church reflect that now.

MAY 10

"Lazy hands make a man poor,
but diligent hands bring wealth." — 10:4.

The hillside was filled with parents for the big game, but mine were missing. It was Monday night, and we were playing a crucial little league game. But my dad had to work every Monday evening, and he missed this and many other games, meetings, and concerts through no fault of his own. That bothered me when I was young, but now I understand and appreciate him all the more for his example of hard work and sacrifice.

My father never made a lot of money, but he was a great man who was rich in many other ways. He has always enjoyed good health and paid off his mortgage early. He put me through private college without resorting to student loans. Having put in his years, he was able to retire a few years early.

I didn't appreciate how hard my father worked until I started working myself. I can see that the good things that have happened to my parents weren't an accident—they were the result of hard work and diligence. Today's verse testifies to the truth that I've seen in their lives.

The life of Joseph in the Old Testament is another testimony to the reward for hard work. While Joseph had the promise and blessing of God on his life, he was still a hard worker in Potiphar's home. When Potiphar's wife lied about him, Joseph carried his diligence to his next assignment.

Joseph's master took him and put him in prison, the place where the king's prisoners were confined. But while Joseph was there in the prison, the Lord was with him; he showed him kindness and granted him favor in the eyes of the prison warden. So the warden put Joseph in charge of all those held in prison, and he was made responsible for all that was done there. The warden paid no attention to anything under Joseph's care, because the Lord was with Joseph and gave him success in whatever he did (Genesis 39:20-23).

What an unbeatable combination Joseph represented—diligence and the blessing of the Lord! The favor of God doesn't relieve you from hard work, but it causes your efforts to shine forth among men. And the favor of God doesn't guarantee you ideal working conditions. I'm sure Joseph would have preferred to apply his diligence back home with his family. The Lord had chosen his field for him, however, and he was faithful in whatever situation he found himself.

Today why not evaluate your work efforts. Do you apply the same diligence to every task, regardless of its importance? Do you let your working environment affect your diligence, or do you look beyond all that to the One you are serving? Is any financial lack you are experiencing partially due to bad work habits?

Renew your commitment to diligence today, reminding yourself that you serve the same God who rewarded Joseph for his diligence with great honor and wealth, and a special place in the history of God's people.

MAY 11

"The righteousness of the blameless makes a straight way for them, but the wicked are brought down by their own wickedness." — 11:5.

Someone once said jokingly that God has only one problem: He thinks He's God and can do whatever He wants. That certainly proved to be true in Joseph's life. First, the Lord gave Joseph a promise that he would rule over his brothers. From there, however, it was all downhill for quite a while!

First, Joseph was thrown into a pit by his jealous brothers. Through the intervention of his brother Reuben, he wasn't killed but rather sold to some Midianite traders for 20 shekels of silver, and they in turn sold him as a slave in Egypt. From there Joseph served Potiphar faithfully, only to be slandered by Potiphar's adulterous wife. That landed Joseph in prison, where he served his fellow inmates.

If Joseph had known what was ahead, I don't think he would have welcomed God's promises as he did. After many years of disappointment and hard work, Joseph was languishing in the dungeon. But instead of it being the end of the line for him, it proved to be only the beginning.

One day Pharaoh had a dream that no one could interpret. Pharoah's cup bearer, who had been in prison with Joseph, told Pharaoh of Joseph's ability to interpret dreams, and the fulfillment of today's verse was about to take place for Joseph: "So Pharaoh sent for Joseph, and he was quickly brought from the dungeon. When he had shaved and changed his clothes, he came before Pharaoh" (Genesis 41:14).

In a matter of minutes, Joseph went from the dungeon to the palace; from obscurity to fame; from menial work to world-changing labor. In the time it took to shave and change clothes, Joseph moved from being an inmate to the prime minister of the most powerful nation on earth! God can indeed do whatever He wants, using whatever means He chooses.

Today's verse promises that righteousness makes a straight path for its possessor, and that was certainly true for Joseph. He was faithful and holy, and his life, although lived in obscurity at first, took him on a path that led to the throne room:

So Pharaoh said to Joseph, "I hereby put you in charge of the whole land of Egypt." Then Pharaoh took his signet ring from his finger and put it on Joseph's finger. (Genesis 41:41-42).

If that story doesn't inspire you, then perhaps nothing will! God doesn't have to follow any set order to promote you, but can bypass the seemingly logical choices to get to you. Your righteousness can be rewarded in a moment's notice, and your dreams fulfilled in the twinkling of an eye.

Renew your faith that God's in charge of all your steps. Your situation can change quickly, if God so chooses. If it hasn't or doesn't, it's not because He can't. It's only because He hasn't chosen to do so. That knowledge should free you to continue to do the will of God with all your heart regardless of your situation.

MAY 12

"No harm befalls the righteous,
but the wicked have their fill of trouble." — 12:21.

Let's take a moment today to study the contrast between Joseph and his brothers. It's understandable why the Lord chose to promote Joseph instead of his worthless brothers. They were a jealous, vindictive, and conniving group of men. Having disposed of Joseph, they deceived Jacob into thinking that he was dead.

The truth of today's verse can be seen in the lives of Jacob's sons. On the one side is Joseph, the righteous brother. Although he was torn from his home and family, he was safe because he rested in the will of God. Slavery couldn't dampen his enthusiasm; the lies of Potiphar's wife couldn't destroy him; prison couldn't diminish his faithfulness; and being forgotten by those he helped couldn't deter him from his appointed duties. In it all, God protected him.

His worthless brothers occupied the other end of the spectrum and reaped trouble for their wickedness. First, there is the story of Judah, one of Joseph's brothers, and his shameful behavior toward his daughter-in-law, Tamar. Then we see the brothers' lack of insight concerning what to do during the famine, for their father said to them, "Why do you just keep looking at each other?" (Genesis 42:1).

Finally, we see what Joseph did to his brothers before he revealed his true identity. When I first read that account years ago, I thought Joseph to be a bit cruel and vindictive. I've since come to see that Joseph was an instrument in God's hands to repay the brothers in part for what they had done.

When they returned to their father the first time and found their money they had used to pay for their grain in their sacks, "they were frightened" (Genesis 42:35). I'm sure that Joseph had some fearful days after his betrayal at their hands, and his brothers were now getting back what they had brought on him. They were frightened again when they returned to Egypt the second time and were invited to Joseph's home, thinking, "He wants to attack us and overpower us and seize us as slaves and take our donkeys" (Genesis 43:18).

Then the brothers agonized when they thought that their youngest brother had stolen Joseph's silver cup. Joseph, having planted the cup in Benjamin's bag, ordered that Benjamin be seized and kept in Egypt. The mental anguish and fear must have been overwhelming for all of them, but they had brought it upon themselves through their corrupt and deceptive behavior.

The Lord never promised to keep you from trouble, but to preserve you in the midst of trouble. Joseph's dreams didn't exempt him from going through all that he did in Egypt. But in the end, his testimony was that God did keep him from all harm, although sometimes he came very close to being overtaken by evil.

You may find yourself in a difficult place as you read this. I can only encourage you to hang in there and see God's deliverance. Your righteousness will pay dividends if you're patient enough to see it all work out. Don't despair, but, like Joseph, watch the wicked receive their due and you, yours.

133

MAY 13

"A wicked messenger falls into trouble,
but a trustworthy envoy brings healing." — 13:17.

I felt like Moses as he re-entered the land of Egypt after his tour of the desert as a shepherd. No, I wasn't on a tour of the pyramids. While on a business trip one time, I had a chance to visit a world-renowned display of Egyptian life. This exhibit included a priceless collection of artifacts, many of which had belonged to the pharaohs of old. The most startling thing about the display was the idolatrous nature of almost all of Egyptian culture.

Every aspect of nature was a god to the Egyptians, including the crocodile, fly, beetle, sun, and the Nile River. Perhaps the most ironic was the god of wisdom who was the baboon! The Egyptians had given themselves over to all sorts of false gods, and even Pharaoh himself was a god.

How ironic that Joseph was sent to that culture and nation as an ambassador of good will. Only a loving God would overlook the sins of those people. And how foreign it all must have been to Joseph. Like Daniel would find centuries later, Joseph discovered that the Lord wasn't repulsed by these people, but rather cared enough to send His very best.

And Joseph proved to be a faithful envoy who brought healing and deliverance to his mission field. When Joseph was brought before Pharaoh to interpret his dreams, he didn't use that time as a chance to clear his name. He didn't request a meeting with Potiphar, who was one of Pharaoh's officials, to confront the evil done him by Mrs. Potiphar. When asked if he could interpret the dreams, Joseph humbly answered, "I cannot do it, but God will give Pharaoh the answer he desires" (Genesis 41:16). Joseph was a faithful messenger.

When Joseph's father died and his brothers feared for their lives, Joseph comforted them with this perspective of all that had happened: "You intended to harm me, but God intended it for good to accomplish what is now being done, the saving of many lives" (Genesis 50:20). Joseph, the faithful envoy, had saved many lives.

In this regard, Joseph was a type of Jesus, the supreme faithful envoy. Jesus entered a foreign mission field and even though the culture and habits of the people were a challenge to Him, He was faithful to His mission and message. He brought healing to a dying world that didn't deserve what He brought.

And now the baton has been passed to you. You're called to be a faithful envoy after the pattern of Jesus and Joseph. You can't allow your own opinions or bias to affect the purity of your message, and that message is the love of God. You have the capacity to bring healing if you'll be faithful to the message of the Gospel, free from your own editorial changes. Make up your mind that you'll be just that, and you'll refresh not only the ones you're sent to, but the One who sent you.

MAY 14

"The faithless will be fully repaid for their ways,
and the good man rewarded for his." — 14:14.

"When did Mary pull Jesus out of the water?" was the question, and I was stumped as to what the lady meant. I had opened the floor for questions in the ladies' jail, and that was the first one. As I questioned the woman, it turned out that she had confused Jesus with the story of Moses, which she assumed she knew by watching the movie, *The Ten Commandments.*

I wonder how many people today have formed their ideas of the Old (or New) Testament from that movie, which is shown by the television industry at Easter. The last time I watched it I noticed one scene that was probably just as it happened.

As Moses (or Charlton Heston) is leading the people out of Egypt in the movie, there's a group of old men carrying something on their shoulders. Each time they appear, a men's choir singing some sort of sad funeral dirge is also heard. While I had never paid attention before, that's Hollywood's depiction of Joseph's bones being brought back to the Promised Land.

Today's verse promises that a faithless man will be repaid for his ways. If that's true, how much more that a faithful man will be rewarded for his. Joseph was a man of faith. The writer of Hebrews even included him in the faith "hall of fame" in chapter 11: "By faith Joseph, when his end was near, spoke about the exodus of the Israelites from Egypt and gave instructions about his bones" (verse 22).

Not only was Joseph rewarded for his faith with a good life, full of honor and riches, but He was also given a place in history, making the exodus with his people, because he believed the Lord and His promises. There's no record that anyone else who died in Egypt requested to be buried in the Promised Land.

Then Joseph said to his brothers, "I am about to die. But God will surely come to your aid and take you up out of this land to the land he promised on oath to Abraham, Isaac and Jacob." And Joseph made the sons of Israel swear an oath and said, "God will surely come to your aid, and then you must carry my bones up from this place" (Genesis 50:24-25).

Perhaps Joseph's greatest act of faith was putting his future into the hands of his brothers and their children. The last time he was in their hands they tried to bury his bones in a ditch as they sold him into slavery! But he gave instructions about his bones while everyone else was getting settled and trying to earn a living.

Again the writer of Hebrews said, "All these people were still living by faith when they died. They did not receive the things promised; they only saw them and welcomed them from a distance" (Hebrews 11:13). Joseph died in faith, and the Lord honored his faith hundreds of years later by having his bones removed from Egypt and carried to the land promised to his fathers.

How about you? Are you living in faith? God is pleased only by faith, so you must walk in that faith to be worthy of His pleasure. Be like Joseph and have faith in the God of the future.

MAY 15

"The house of the righteous contains great treasure,
but the income of the wicked brings them trouble." — 15:6.

I'm a man on a mission, in search of the righteous root in my family. I'm convinced that there was someone in my family's past who served the Lord faithfully. In their service, they dedicated our future to the Lord and asked that the Lord would raise up a righteous off-shoot from what they were doing.

As a result of that, I'm now serving the Lord. I don't believe that I'm here just because the Lord likes me or simply decided to choose me. While there aren't many serving the Lord in my family, I somehow feel connected to the past and sense I am the continuation of something that began long before I came along.

I may never get to prove that theory, but I'm going to keep looking to confirm my hunch. What keeps me going in my quest is the story of Joseph and his two sons. When Jacob was dying, Joseph brought Manasseh and Ephraim to their grandfather for his blessing. What transpired was a surprise to Joseph, for Jacob knowingly and purposefully gave the blessing for the eldest to the youngest, and Ephraim walked away with the promise of abundance and fruitfulness.

Yet it occurs to me that neither Manasseh nor Ephraim had done anything to receive their blessings. They just happened to be Joseph's sons and Jacob's grandsons. The Bible doesn't tell us that they were righteous; in fact, their mother was the daughter of an Egyptian priest. They had neither done great exploits for the Lord nor gone through the trials of their father. They were simply in the right place at the right time in the will of God.

With a sense that I'm a continuation and not the beginning, I want to pass on the blessing that I've received through no merit of my own. I pray for my children regularly; I've prayed for their spouses-to-be since they were infants. Assuming that I'll have grandchildren, I've dedicated them to the Lord's service. I've asked the Lord that there will always be a Stanko serving God in the house of the Lord.

Today's verse states that there's great treasure in the household of the righteous, and part of that treasure is the ability to bless future generations. I can vividly remember dedicating my children to the Lord; I've tried to tell them that they can choose to reject that dedication, but they can never change it. Their mother and I chose to pass on the treasure that was in our house, and they're the recipients.

Seeing myself as a continuation of the Lord's work has served to temper any pride that the Lord has blessed me because of my accomplishments. And I desperately want to play a part in passing that undeserved blessing on to my offspring.

Bless your children and grandchildren today in the Lord. Pass on your blessing whether they want it or not. Give the treasure in your house to those who aren't even born yet. You have the power to continue the Lord's work that began probably before you were born. By so doing, you'll insure that your family tree will be filled with those who share a godly heritage and feed from a godly root system.

MAY 16

"Better a patient man than a warrior,
a man who controls his temper than one who takes a city." — 16:32.

I've had a rough day as I set out to travel from Australia through Hawaii to my home after a long ministry trip. My gate was poorly marked, and I huffed and puffed my way there with some heavy carry-on items. I then traveled for 4 hours next to a young man with a cold, who noisily exhaled all over me.

Then I got in the wrong line at customs and was severely delayed. I took my baggage to change flights and found out the elevator I took required that I take all my baggage off my carrier, carry it up one flight of steps, and then out to the curb.

I then boarded an all-night flight where the woman in front of me bounced on her seat during the entire trip. When I got home, my associate took my computer to make some repairs and proceeded to erase 4 days of writing, and so I'm writing this day's work for the second time.

It doesn't take a brain surgeon to figure out that the Lord is dealing with me about patience, and teaching me about it through circumstances that require it.

Today's verse states that a man who rules his temper is greater than a conqueror. Joseph never led a great military campaign; he didn't reorganize a company and make it profitable. He didn't discover the cure for a rare disease, nor did he have an invention that changed the course of history. Joseph was a man who was patient under trial, and the Lord promoted him over others who were great warriors and statesmen. James wrote,

> Consider it pure joy, my brothers, whenever you face trials of many kinds, because you know that the testing of your faith develops perseverance. Perseverance must finish its work so that you may be mature and complete, not lacking in anything....Blessed is the man who perseveres under trial, because...he will receive the crown of life that God has promised...(1:2-4,12).

I should consider it "pure joy" to encounter various trials but everything in me wanted to erupt. Then I considered Joseph, who endured the pit, Potiphar, and the dungeon before he ruled Egypt. If that's the price I have to pay for the Lord to use me, then help me, Lord, to bear up under such insignificant trials.

Perhaps you have need today of the encouragement written to the Hebrews: "You need to persevere so that when you have done the will of God, you will receive what he has promised" (10:36). Part of the doing may be to endure difficult conditions on your way to the blessing. Anyone can serve the Lord when He's giving out His promises; fewer can do it when He withholds His promises to build up endurance and perseverance.

Remember, if you learn patience, you're mightier than the fiercest warrior in the sight of God. So don't worry that you're stuck in some insignificant task or that your life seems to be filled with frustration. Let patience have its way, and God will promote you to the highest level that your endurance has prepared you for.

MAY 17

"A man of knowledge uses words with restraint,
and a man of understanding is even-tempered." — 17:27.

"I will send you out, and when you go, you will be uncomfortable." Those were the words the Lord spoke to me as I set out on my first international missions trip. Needless to say, those weren't the words I was longing to hear.

I slept for two weeks on a one-inch foam mattress resting on a piece of plywood. I slept under mosquito netting, and almost every night, I woke up with one or more mosquitoes under the net with me. At midnight, the roosters would begin crowing and hold all-night crowing vigils that rendered my earplugs useless. My roommate snored and several times we shared one bed and one mosquito net.

We bathed from a rain bucket with cold water, and had to make do with electricity that often wasn't working for up to 18 hours a day. I had to occasionally bathe in someone's backyard from a faucet, in full view of the neighbors! And the water was bad and couldn't be consumed without boiling.

Yet through all that I knew the Lord was trying to make me more even-tempered. I had to minister effectively there regardless of the circumstances and learn not to grumble or complain. As Paul wrote Timothy, "Endure hardship with us like a good soldier of Christ Jesus" (2 Timothy 2:3). The problem is that there's only one way to learn to endure hardship—you learn to endure hardship by enduring hardship. You can't get that by reading about it in a book.

Once again, the writer of Hebrews gives us some useful insight, "You need to persevere so that when you have done the will of God, you will receive what he has promised" (Hebrews 10:36). Often I want the will of God, promising the Lord I'll be able to persevere if I can only have what He has promised now.

But the Lord thinks differently than I do. He prefers that I learn to endure and then He'll give me what He has promised. To have the privilege of ministering in a far-off land, He required that I first endure some primitive conditions. And I had to endure those conditions after years of preparation that readied me to go to that land and endure new hardships! How marvelous are His ways, don't you think?

Today's verse attributes two traits to the wise: an even-temper and a closed mouth. Paul instructed the Philippians in the second chapter,

> Do everything without complaining or arguing, so that you may become blameless and pure, children of God without fault in a crooked and depraved generation, in which you shine like stars in the universe as you hold out the word of life (verses 14-16).

You must learn to endure hardship without alerting everyone to the fact that you're enduring. In that manner you'll show the world how Jesus endured. Can you learn to be even-tempered and to do all things without griping? Welcome those petty inconveniences today for what they are—God's tools to develop you into a vessel that's worthy and ready to receive the will of God.

MAY 18

"A man who isolates himself seeks his own desire;
he rages against all sound wisdom." —18:1.

"Thank you, pastor, we're just here to visit and rest." I heard that many times as I would greet visitors at my church. These folks would be seated near the rear of the church, and would let me know that they had no intentions of taking me up on my offer to get involved in the church. They had been hurt, or burned out someplace else, and were simply looking for a place to rest, but not get involved.

Evelyn Underhill, a noted British author, wrote to a friend who was asking for spiritual guidance. Her response struck me as significant, especially for those who were attending church irregularly, refusing to get involved there:

> I feel the regular, steady docile practice of corporate worship is of the utmost importance for the building up of your spiritual life: more important than reading of advanced books....No amount of solitary reading makes up for humble immersion in the life and worship of the Church. In fact the books are only addressed to those who are taking part in that life. The corporate and personal together make up the Christian ideal.

She certainly was in line with what Paul taught. In Ephesians 4:16, he wrote, "From him the whole body, joined and held together by every supporting ligament, grows and builds itself up in love, as each part does its work." Each part is to do its job in conjunction with the other parts.

It wouldn't be possible for the arm, the leg, or the eye to do its job by itself. To sever itself from the other members would be death to that part, and at least pain if not death to the body itself. So it is with the spiritual body. For a member to separate itself rages against all sound wisdom.

Hebrews 10:24-25 states, "And let us consider one another in order to stir up love and good works, not forsaking the assembling of ourselves together, as is the manner of some, but exhorting one another, and so much the more as you see the Day approaching."

Proverbs 18:1 reveals one reason for isolation, and that's self-will. Having to forgive, or walk in humility, or be patient as you wait for God to promote or deliver you, are all difficult positions in which to be. Regardless of the difficulty, however, you can't be independent and still walk in the Way that Jesus and the apostles outlined. Isolation quarrels against all sound wisdom and sets you up for your enemy.

Ask the Lord to show you if and where you've isolated yourself. Pray that He'll reveal the real motives of your heart. Pray that the Lord will lead you to the people to whom He wants to join you.When He does, become a vital part of what's going on there. Don't just warm a pew, but get involved. Yes, there will be problems, and yes, you won't always be happy with what's happening. You will, on the other hand, open yourself to the Lord's blessings that come through others and be obedient to His will for you to be involved.

MAY 19

"A man's own folly ruins his life,
yet his heart rages against the Lord." - 19:3

When you follow the Lord, it may take a while to realize that tribulation will find you, no matter where you try to hide. It's part of every believer's life as Paul warned in Acts 14:22, "We must through many tribulations enter the kingdom of God." There's a big difference, however, between God-ordained tribulation and the problems or consequences that arise from your own decisions, and it's important that you learn to distinguish the two.

For instance, you may be experiencing financial lack. You may have prayed and it just doesn't seem like God is answering your prayers. Perhaps you're a bit angered at the Lord for not helping you as you've asked and you consider what you're going through as "tribulation." But could there be another reason for your lack?

It's a fact that you'll reap what you sow. Perhaps you should also ask yourself, "Have I planted enough seed to expect a harvest at this time?" I've found that generous people always reap abundantly. Those who withhold, suffer want. 2 Corinthians 9:6 states, "He who sows sparingly will also reap sparingly, and he who sows bountifully will also reap bountifully." If you've been foolish and not sown generously, don't fuss at the Lord if you're not reaping bountifully. If you've been sowing, then continue, for "we shall reap if we do not lose heart" (Galatians 6:8).

Maybe you're discouraged today because you don't have more friends or close relationships. Ask yourself, "Have I been friendly so that I should expect to reap friends?" You may want people to make the first move toward you, and when they don't, you become hurt or angry. You may want them to understand how lonely you are, or have expectations of how they should treat you. Paul quoted Jesus and wrote, "It is more blessed to give than receive" (Acts 20:35). Your foolishness in trying to receive before you give is the real source of your problem. It's not God's fault if you don't do your part to gain whatever you need or want.

I had a seminary professor who said, "Most of the Christian walk is trying to distinguish between what only God can do and what only I can do. Too often we're waiting for God to do what only we can do, and too often we're trying to do for ourselves what only God can do for us. Maturity is learning what the difference is, and accepting responsibility for our part."

If you're in a difficult place, don't question God. Look to yourself. Ask God to show you if your own foolishness is part of the problem. Then begin to do what you need to do to reap an abundant harvest in the Lord.

MAY 20

"An inheritance quickly gained at the beginning
will not be blessed at the end." - 20:21.

State lotteries are big business in the United States and other countries. Probably everyone has thought about winning the lottery, and dreamt of how they would divide the wealth "for the Lord's work" of course. Several years ago I read of a man in Massachusetts who died right after he won his state's jackpot. His wife said that the pressure of his sudden wealth had actually killed him!

That's, of course, an extreme case, and many of us would like to face that kind of pressure. A quick fix, however, often isn't the answer to your problem, and can actually be counterproductive to what the Lord wants to do in your life. Winning the lottery would be nice, but allowing tribulation to produce in you what it came to do is even better in the sight of God.

Patience doesn't come easily for most people. If you're like me, you want a quick word, a quick escape, a quick promotion, or a quick answer to prayer. You want a word from the Holy Spirit to make all the bad go away. That may help now, but in the end it can undermine the perseverance that God is trying to work in you.

I remember hearing years ago of someone seeing a butterfly struggling to escape from its cocoon. When it was partially out, this person cut the cocoon, allowing the butterfly what he thought was a quicker and easier escape. What he found was that the butterfly wasn't able to operate its wing on the side that had been cut out of the cocoon. The struggle of the cocoon was part of the strengthening process that would allow it to do what all butterflies do—fly!

That's how it is with you. If God, or someone else, were to cut you out of the cocoon you're in, your development would be hindered. Paul wrote, "We also glory in our tribulations, knowing that tribulation produces perseverance; and perseverance, character; and character, hope" (Romans 5:3-4 emphasis added).

James wrote, "My brethren, count it all joy when you fall into various trials, knowing that the testing of your faith produces patience. But let patience have its perfect work, that you may be perfect and complete, lacking in nothing" (James 1:2-3). It seems that trials bring patience, and the whole process must be allowed to complete its "perfect" work.

Are you looking for the quick fix? Or are you content to allow your situation to work its perfect will in you? If a quick inheritance isn't blessed in the end, then an inheritance gained through patience and endurance will be blessed. The choice is yours. Choose wisely today.

MAY 21

"The king's heart is in the hand of the Lord;
he directs it like a watercourse wherever he pleases." — 21:1

It's easy for us to understand how God works through a person in authority who is also a believer, or at least a reasonable person. But do you struggle with the fact that the Lord is sovereign and works His purpose through all leaders, even the ungodly ones? This issue raises immediate questions about wicked leaders throughout history, and it seems impossible that God's purpose could be established through them.

Yet the Bible tells us that God Himself established pagan kings over the nations, and even over His own people, Israel. Nebuchadnezzar, Cyrus, and Darius are a few examples. God didn't ignore their wickedness, but He didn't hesitate to promote them even though they weren't part of the "covenant" community of Israel.

Psalm 75 tells us that promotion doesn't come from the east or west. It comes from God. That's an important principle that every believer must grasp. You didn't get the promotion, and someone else did, because God willed it. If you were meant to be the leader, heaven and hell couldn't stop your promotion. If you weren't meant to have it, no amount of praying, complaining, or political maneuvering could get you the job. God fills all positions of authority.

When I worked a secular job, my boss wasn't only difficult, but immoral. Over time, my attitude toward him got worse and worse. Gradually, my commission checks got smaller and smaller. When I asked the Lord why, He clearly showed me that it was because of my attitude toward this man. To be truthful, I got angry! I wanted God to deal with him, not with me. I was serving God; my boss wasn't. The Lord wasn't impressed, however, and kept the pressure on until I repented of my bad attitude.

If God can turn the heart of the king wherever He wishes, then you must learn to respond to leadership in a godly manner. To complain against the leader is to murmur against the God who put them there! If they're immoral or wrong, you must still be careful. You're not free to write them off or ignore them. You must at least keep a respectful attitude even if you must disobey them. They're in authority because God placed them there.

If someone over you in school, on the job, in the home, or in church isn't responding as you would like, it's time to pray. God can change their heart. If the leader doesn't respond, then accept it for now as God's choice for you. Don't resent or fight it, but claim the promise that the heart of a leader isn't out of reach of the sovereign finger of God. If you must suffer for disobeying an unrighteous command, do it with a good attitude. Give God room to work and to perhaps change your heart, and watch the Lord intervene on your behalf.

MAY 22

"Do you see a man who excels in his work?
He will serve before kings; he will not serve before obscure men." — 22:29

Proverbs contains not only instruction, but also some promises from the Lord. Today's verse contains one of the more exciting promises you can find. It's a promise that, if you excel in what you do, you'll be promoted. Excellence has its own reward, whether or not anyone notices at first. If you continue in excellence, God promises that you'll one day stand before kings and other significant leaders.

The exciting thing about this promise is that it applies to any kind of work. If you work at achieving excellence in school, banking, homemaking, auto mechanics, writing, street sweeping, or preaching, you're destined to stand before the leaders in your field, community, church, or nation!

Most employees, housewives, students, or ministers feel from time to time like they aren't adequately appreciated. There are times when you may feel as if you don't receive enough recognition or credit from those over or around you. Your work can suffer when this feeling creeps in.

This verse provides an incentive to continue striving for excellence. The Lord, who neither slumbers nor sleeps, is watching. "And whatever you do, do it heartily, as to the Lord and not to men, knowing that from the Lord you will receive the reward of the inheritance; for you serve the Lord Christ" (Colossians 3:23-24). Work unto the Lord and He, who is watching, will reward you.

"Therefore, my beloved brethren, be steadfast, immovable, always abounding in the work of the Lord, knowing that your labor is not in vain in the Lord" (1 Corinthians 15:58). Your hard work, your striving for the best, isn't in vain. If no one notices, if promotion or financial reward isn't forthcoming, or if you feel unappreciated, be comforted that the Lord is watching, and He's in control. "For exaltation comes neither from the east nor from the west nor from the south. But God is the Judge: He puts down one, and exalts another" (Psalm 75:6-7). God can and will exalt you in due time if you produce quality work in His name.

Don't settle for mediocrity. Don't do a great job only if someone is watching, or in hopes of impressing some person. Let your work reflect the excellence of the God whom you serve. Go the extra mile and do more than is expected. Then be patient. For in only a matter of time, you'll find yourself standing before great men.

MAY 23

"Buy truth and do not sell it;
get wisdom, discipline and understanding." — 23:23.

There's a price tag for almost anything you receive in the Lord, except salvation. Jesus purchased your pardon at the expense of His life. He imparts eternal life to any who repent and turn toward Him. A simple, earnest prayer of surrender purchases the greatest treasure there is. It costs you at that point very little.

As you began your walk, however, you realize that God does require you to pay some price to come into all that He has for you. You begin to see that every aspect of truth has a price tag on it. You may want that truth much like you would want a new car or stereo system. The question is whether you can and want to pay the figure listed on the price tag for that truth.

Today's verse exhorts you to obtain wisdom, discipline, and understanding. Those truths can indeed be the "costliest" to purchase. If you've ever had a serious failure—a failed marriage, business, relationship, church, or career—then you today have truth that was paid for. You learned the hard way what to do and not do in that situation.

But today you're the wiser for it. For that reason, it's best not to second-guess your past. God has ordered your steps and you're the better for the experiences you've had. You paid a high price for truth, and it's helping you do what you're doing today.

I was called to preach in 1973, but had to wait 16 years for a pulpit. During that time, I was involved in work that seemed "light years" away from the call of God. I cried real tears, and sought the Lord saying, "There must be more than this." My price tag was to walk in humility and faith during those years. I paid a high price for this truth, and I'm not going to sell it cheaply!

If you've paid a high price, don't sell what you've obtained—it's priceless. Today's verse encourages you not to sell the truth. Don't give away what you've gotten for a momentary flight into sin or rebellion. Moses sold his truth of the Promised Land by striking the rock and misrepresenting the Lord. Moses paid a high price to get to that point in his life, but he sold the truth. He regretted it until he died.

Your salvation was free, but your walk with the Lord from there is a walk through the department store of the Kingdom. Don't look for bargain-basement sales and don't shoplift. Pay the full price up front for wisdom and knowledge, and then enjoy your purchases.

MAY 24

"If you falter in times of trouble,
how small is your strength." — 24:10.

"Into every life a little rain must fall," or so the secular proverb goes. To you, it may seem like a monsoon has invaded your life and not just a "little rain." As long as you live and are tied to this sin-infested, uncertain world, you'll encounter some trouble and problems in your family, church, job, or school. It's therefore important to respond properly to these inevitable troubles.

Depression and discouragement have undoubtedly attacked you at various times in your life. If you get depressed when things get tough, however, you're doing the very thing that will allow your troubles to remain or get worse.

For example, let's assume that your house is on fire. You discover it when it's just a little fire in the garage. Having discovered the flames, you become discouraged because so many things have been going wrong lately. You go into the living room, turn on the television, and try to forget about the fire in the garage. Maybe you lie on your face before the Lord in your bedroom. You don't call for help, you don't warn your family, and you don't pour water on the fire.

What will happen? What was perhaps a small, controllable fire will now grow to something that can destroy your entire house. If you falter in time of trouble, according to today's verse, you're a weakling. The correct response toward the fire is to fight it with all you have. That's the same response required for the troubles of life that come your way.

Just the other day I was facing numerous "troubles" that threatened to overwhelm me. My finances were in poor shape, my wife was sick, and I felt like I was under spiritual attack. Everything in me wanted to give in to discouragement. I didn't want to pray or worship the Lord or prepare my Sunday message. Instead I wanted to sulk. But I forced myself to pray. I began praying out loud as I drove my car, calling on God's help and mercy. I decided not to falter in that time of trouble and continued by quoting Scripture verses audibly.

My wife is now healed, we had a great Sunday service, and my finances are recovering. All because, I believe, I didn't go limp in the day of trouble. When you're in trouble, it's the wrong time to do what comes naturally. That's the time to attack the problem with every weapon you have.

Put your fires out now and don't let them grow too big to handle. Use the strength you have, and God will give you strength you don't have. Pray, sing, call for prayer help, and press into God. Then watch the fires of life go out before your eyes.

MAY 25

"It is the glory of God to conceal a matter;
to search out a matter is the glory of kings." — 25:3

Sometimes it seems as if God is playing hide-and-seek with you and me. Our prayers aren't being answered and we lack direction. The Bible reads like any other book. We may be stuck in a situation that has no apparent escape. Having patiently sought the Lord about something, we don't see it resolve as we had hoped.

If you're in that predicament, you first need to see yourself as you really are. Something happened to you when you met the Lord—you became royalty! You're now a prince or a princess because you're related to the King of glory! You have a wonderful inheritance and will rule with Him in heavenly places. Hallelujah!!

Now that you're royalty, however, you've come into a special glory. Your glory, according to today's verse, is to "search out a matter." You realize that God will hide things from you on purpose, so that you can obtain your royal destiny through the earnest seeking of His face and will.

Hebrews 11:6 is one of my favorite verses. It states, "And without faith it is impossible to please God, because anyone who comes to Him must believe that He exists and that He rewards those who earnestly [or diligently] seek Him." God is a rewarder of those who seek Him with all their heart. He won't reward those who casually or occasionally cry out to know His will.

Even in trouble, Moses said, "If from there [trouble] you seek the Lord your God, you will find him if you look for him with all your heart and with all your soul" (Deuteronomy 4:29). Proverbs 2:3-5 further exhorts you to search a matter out with all diligence: "If you call out for insight and cry aloud for understanding, and if you look for it as for silver and search for it as for hidden treasure, then you will understand the fear of the Lord and find the knowledge of God."

If I were to guarantee you that there was a large vein of pure gold in your backyard, and you dug one hole and didn't find it, would you give up? I dare say you would not. You would dig and dig and dig until you found what I had guaranteed was there. Maybe you would enlist the help of family and friends to find those riches. Well, the word of God promises that you will find "glory" as you seek His will that may be hidden for a season. Don't give up the search. What you'll find is better than any treasure. The searching will strengthen you, and you'll find the glory of royalty, of which you've become a part.

MAY 26

"Do not answer a fool according to his folly, or you will be like him yourself.
Answer a fool according to his folly, or he will be wise in his own eyes."
— 26:4-5.

At first glance, these verses are confusing and contradictory. We're told to answer and then not to answer a fool. How can you do both at the same time?

The answer to this apparent contradiction lies in your tendency to want a system of rules that will "explain" God. Your religious heart wants to know—preferably ahead of time—how to handle each and every situation that may arise in your daily walk. In a nutshell, you want to figure God out. You want some assurances that if you do one thing, He'll always do another.

As I mentioned previously someone once said, "God has only one problem. He thinks He's God and can tell us what to do in any situation." As soon as you "figure God out," He seems to do what you don't anticipate. When you expect mercy, He rebukes. When you expect rebuke, He's merciful. He's God, and His ways aren't our ways. His ways are perfect, free from sin, and truly magnificent.

No system can contain God. The goal of a disciple's life is to be led by the Spirit. On one occasion you'll encounter a fool and the Spirit will prompt you to respond. Another time you'll encounter the same, and the Spirit will direct you to be quiet. If you assume you must answer the second just because you answered the first, you may miss the Lord and encounter trouble.

Paul wrote to the Roman church,

> Those who live according to the sinful nature have their minds set on what that nature desires; but those who live in accordance with the Spirit have their minds set on what the Spirit desires....You, however, are controlled not by the sinful nature but by the Spirit, if the Spirit of God lives in you....Those who are led by the Spirit of God are sons of God (Romans 8:5, 9, 14).

The writer of Hebrews describes the mature as those "who by constant use have trained themselves to distinguish good from evil" (5:14). Don't try to find a system into which God fits. Rather learn to sense the pleasure or displeasure of the Spirit in each life situation by constant effort. Learning to allow the Spirit to guide your decisions and actions, you must be led by the Spirit in all things, and so be a son of God.

When you're faced with a decision of what to do or how to act, by faith the Spirit will lead you into the perfect will of God. Continue to cultivate this kind of relationship with the Spirit, and you'll have something better than any set of rules could ever give you.

MAY 27

"Let another praise you, and not your own mouth;
someone else, and not your own lips" — 27:2.

I became aware several years ago of how often I used "I, me, and mine" in normal conversation. I was prone to talk about myself, my accomplishments, and my feelings, and it didn't sound right to me. From the time I saw that tendency, I determined, with God's help, to be a better listener, to start talking less about me, and to turn the conversation toward the interests and feelings of other people. This hasn't been easy.

Today's verse urges you to allow someone else to talk about you. Philippians 2:3-4 have been a tremendous help as I have sought to walk this out in my life: "Do nothing out of selfish ambition or vain conceit, but in humility consider others better than yourselves. Each of you should look not only to your own interests, but also to the interests of others."

You can't know the interests of others if you don't take time to listen to them and ask questions. If you're always talking about yourself, you can't know how to look out for your brother's needs.

As I've asked questions, I've then worked on really listening and trying to retain the information. I'm working on remembering first names. I want to be able to ask that person the next time I see them about something we discussed at our previous meeting. I also want them to feel that I'm interested in them and their world. In other words, I want to be known as a good listener.

Philippians 2:5 contains a command, which today's verse from Proverbs helps you obey: "Your attitude should be the same as that of Christ Jesus." Paul goes on to describe how Jesus emptied Himself to serve the purpose of God. He tells how Jesus gave His life to minister to the needs of others. And praise God He did!!

You're given the same task and can begin by making an effort not to talk about yourself. Don't manipulate the conversation to topics that interest you, and don't try to impress others with your wisdom, victories, or problems. If you're not receiving the credit you deserve for what you're doing, then trust the Lord. When you need recognition or encouragement, the Lord will send it. With that in mind, determine to change your way of speaking and listening.

You know how hard it is to be around people who are always talking about themselves. Today's verse gives you a good guideline by which to walk: Don't praise yourself, but wait for someone else to do it. When they do, you'll know God sent them with a basket of encouragement with your name on it. Until such time, give yourself to others. It will be difficult at first, but with practice, you'll actually be walking in Jesus' footsteps just by learning to be a good listener!

MAY 28

"He who trusts in himself is a fool,
but he who walks in wisdom is kept safe." — 28:26.

He was on the talk show, as arrogant as ever. A well-known American business tycoon was talking of his business deals and the millions of dollars he had won and lost. He was successful, but his personal life was a mess and his entire financial empire was laden with debt. It was obvious that this man had a high opinion of himself, trusting his instincts and decisions.

Today's verse seems to be saying that "walking in wisdom" and "trusting in oneself" are opposed to one another. This makes a lot of sense when you think about it. You can so easily fool yourself, tending to trust your ideas, opinions, feelings, impressions, and even anger. You tend to believe the best about yourself, and direct your suspicions toward others, especially those who don't hold you in such high esteem.

Paul wrote, "I know that nothing good lives in me, that is, in my sinful nature" (Romans 7:18). Paul didn't write this in the past tense; he wrote it in the present tense. I take that to mean that it was true for Paul when he wrote it. And I've found that to be true in my own life. I can't find anything in me in which I can put my trust. My intellect is limited, my ability to endure hardship weak, my prayer life isn't what it should be, and my love for people is too related to how they treat me.

I find myself too ready to excuse my shortcomings and too eager to please myself. Like Paul I find myself crying out, "What a wretched man I am! Who will rescue me from this body of death?" (Romans 7:24). What I want to do for God I regularly discover I can't do.

Real wisdom isn't a head full of knowledge, but a living "walk" with the Lord Jesus Christ. In 1 Corinthians 1:30 we are told, "It is because of him that you are in Christ Jesus, who has become for us wisdom from God." To walk in wisdom can only mean to walk with Jesus on a daily basis. As soon as you decide to trust yourself and go it alone, you're in for trouble. If you walk in wisdom—with Christ—you're on the road to success.

To walk with the Lord in wisdom also includes walking with our brothers and sisters. Early in our walk with the Lord, Kathy and I participated in a Monday night home group with seven other couples. We were committed to one another, and we got together to pray, counsel, confront, and encourage. Those were hard meetings! As we brought up questions and problems, each person spoke the truth to one another and sometimes the truth really hurt! When it was my turn to hear some truth, I wanted to get defensive, hide, or not bring up my problems. I grew from that experience, however, and "heard from the Lord" in that setting on numerous occasions. I still walk in some of the counsel given during those encounters.

Learn to walk with the Lord and allow Him to use others to speak into your life. There is indeed safety in numbers—and wisdom, too. But if you trust in yourself, you may sound wise, but you're on dangerous ground.

MAY 29

"Do you see a man who speaks in haste?
There is more hope for a fool than for him." — 29:20.

I have a new definition for spiritual maturity: It's the ability not to waste emotional energy over something that may never happen. Have you ever heard that something may happen, or a certain person reportedly said something offensive, or another person is supposedly planning to do something against your wishes or best interests, or a certain repair job may cost a lot of money?

Have you gotten upset, maybe even carrying the anxiety an entire weekend, only to find out on Monday that what you heard was only partially true, or not true at all? You found yourself anxious over a situation that never happened or wasn't nearly as bad you had first thought. You were hasty in forming a judgment, and that judgment may have even led you to talk to someone else, perhaps getting them upset, before you found out the whole story.

This same tendency has caused me to react and speak in haste many times. For instance, I've found myself responding to someone before they were finished speaking. Or at other times I've jumped to conclusions before I had all the facts. More often than not I was hasty in formulating an opinion and spoke out of turn. All these tendencies caused me to display my ignorance for all to see, instead of taking time to get the facts, assess the situation, and then formulate a response.

I'm gradually learning to discipline my mind and I'm using today's verse as my guide, for it tells me that there's more hope for a fool than for me if I speak in haste. And you know how little hope there is for a fool! If I don't learn to ignore rumors and half-truths and keep quiet, then I'm causing myself needless trouble.

I encourage you to address this tendency in your own life. Anxiety over what might happen is a waste of emotional energy. Don't let only a rumor of a lay-off where you work get you worried. Don't let the latest economic forecast discourage you. Until you know for sure what's wrong with the air conditioner and how much it will cost, refuse to be anxious. Make sure you understand fully what someone is saying before you respond.

Take James' admonition to heart: "Everyone should be quick to listen, slow to speak, and slow to become angry" (James 1:19). A wise man is slow to speak; a fool is all too ready to do so A wise man is slow to anger; a fool is angered by what might happen. A wise man waits to form a judgment; a fool speaks at the drop of a hat. May the Lord help you and me this day to walk as wise men, and not as a fools, by helping us keep quiet.

MAY 30

"Every word of God is flawless;
he is a shield to those who take refuge in Him." — 30:5.

When Adam and Eve were in the garden, the serpent called God's word into question. He explained why God didn't want them to eat from the tree of the knowledge of good and evil, saying that God didn't really have their best interests at heart. If they were to eat, they would be like God, and God didn't want that to happen, or so the serpent reasoned.

Adam and Eve believed the serpent, doubted God's word, ate from the tree, and the rest is history. Sin, suffering, disease, calamity, and death came into existence because two people doubted whether God's word was "flawless." They believed the word of another, and it brought disastrous results.

The same is true today. God's word to us is perfect and it will accomplish what it set out to do. God is looking for those who will believe His word to them, regardless of what the circumstances seem to say. Paul wrote,

Therefore we do not lose heart. Though outwardly we are wasting away, yet inwardly we are being renewed day by day. For our light and momentary troubles are achieving for us an eternal glory that far outweighs them all. So we fix our eyes not on what is seen, but on what is unseen. For what is seen is temporal, but what is unseen is eternal (2 Corinthians 4:16-18).

It may seem like God's word is delayed, or not coming, or can't possibly be fulfilled in your situation. That isn't the time to doubt, but rather the time to take refuge in Him who spoke the word. There are times when I've had to quote God's word in a loud voice in my car, or in the shower, or in prayer, when everything seemed to be going wrong. I've had to run into the Lord's presence when my finances were terrible; I've sung hymns, quoted Scripture, and reviewed sermon excerpts or listened to tapes of messages that ministered to me. I've had to run and hide in the Lord when the bills were due or when ministry responsibilities were overwhelming.

You don't need a shield unless something is being thrown at you. You won't know your need for the Lord, your shield, until the enemy and life throw doubt, fear, and aggravation at you. God allows the enemy to throw them so that you'll learn He is indeed a shield through which nothing can penetrate. Take cover in Him today. His word is flawless and can't fail. Don't walk by sight, but by faith, and watch and see the salvation of God as you trust in Him.

MAY 31
"The sayings of King Lemuel—
an oracle his mother taught him...." —31:1.

We aren't sure who King Lemuel was. He's mentioned in the Bible only in this chapter, and we have no idea where his throne was or how long he ruled. Some believe it's a reference to King Solomon. We do know one thing—Lemuel had good parents, or at least a good mother. She taught him practical things and they stuck with him throughout his life—so much so, that the Holy Spirit was able to make his mother's teaching a part of inspired Scripture. Now that's anointed teaching!

When you're working with children, especially your own, it often seems as if your words are "going in one ear and out the other." You preach, teach, and exhort, yet don't seem to get anywhere. But you're not called to evaluate or see the results of your training. You're called to instruct, teach, and trust the Lord for the results. You're never sure what will make a permanent impression, and you never know what quote your children will carry through life and attribute to you.

I can remember my dad talking to me as a young boy about the Lord as we drove together at night in his car. He spoke to me about all kinds of issues. One night he was telling me of a major disappointment he encountered after his graduation from high school. A college football scholarship had fallen through and he was crushed. But he ended by saying that if he had gotten that scholarship, he probably would not have met my mother. He ended by saying, "Son, God really does have a plan for your life." I'll never forget that word and it has helped me many times.

Note that Lemuel's mother didn't just prepare him for a common life, but taught him with a great destiny in mind. She taught him how to be a king before he ever became a king. Treating him like royalty, she imparted vision and a sense of purpose through her teaching. She saw him as part of the royal family and prepared him for royal duties.

Your children and those of the church are also destined for royal things. They'll lead their generation. Build them up with instruction worthy of a prince and princess. Assuming they'll be in high positions of authority, do all in your power to let them know that they're special in God's sight. Don't worry about building them up too much, for life has a way of bringing enough hard knocks that will more than balance things out. Impart vision and a sense of destiny and let God do the rest.

I've always insisted on a high standard of work from my children; I have tried to explain to them that they'll be leaders, and that leaders must produce work on a higher level. In their worst times, I've instructed them with an eye on their greatness. Their royal behavior hasn't always been good, but that doesn't take away from their royalty. Exhort the young people around you. They have enough elders and peers against them. Treat them like royalty and see if they don't begin to act like it.

JUNE 1

"For the waywardness of the simple will kill them,
and the complacency of fools destroy them." — 1:32.

Today's verse speaks of two issues—"waywardness" and "complacency." Let's consider waywardness first, which can also be translated "backsliding." You may think of backsliders as those who have walked with the Lord and now have fallen, or "slidden back," into some awful sin. The term "backslider" is much broader than that, however, and can include the spiritual state of a believer who hasn't necessarily fallen into gross sin.

Hebrews 10:38-39 says, "But my righteous one shall live by faith. And if he shrinks back, I will not be pleased with him. But we are not of those who shrink back and are destroyed, but of those who believe and are saved." I can backslide by shrinking back—not walking quite as quickly as I once did. When faced with the need to trust and have faith in God, I can instead put my faith in others, my abilities, my job, education, or whatever.

Next this verse addresses complacency, which is being self-satisfied or smug. Complacency says that everything is all right. I don't need to make any changes or exert any more effort than I already have. Complacency leads to a false sense of security.

You can be a good Christian and still be complacent. You go to church, give some money, pray, and live a moral life. What more does God want? But the believer's life is a "walk." When you go on a walk, you start out at one place to get to another place. It speaks of time and energy exerted and progress being made.

A disciple's walk with the Lord implies growing in the knowledge and grace of God. That walk contains adventures of faith that reveal your weaknesses and bring you to maturity. Jesus was always going somewhere. All His "somewheres" were leading to the big "somewhere"—the cross. There was no complacency in His walk. Nor would He allow the disciples to be complacent. He always led them into new lessons and ministry, and He does the same thing today for us.

Backsliding and complacency are enemies to your walk of faith. If you've shrunk back or become smug, shake it off and ask the Lord to stir you up. Regain your sensitivity to the Lord and His voice. Know that your spiritual life depends on it, and then commit to walk in faith again in every area of your life.

JUNE 2

*"And if you look for it [wisdom] as for silver
and search for it [wisdom] as for hidden treasure."* — 2:4.

Just last week we discussed this verse, but it's worth reconsidering. I often paint this scene for those I counsel: "If I were to guarantee for you that there was silver and gold in the backyard of your house, what would you do? If you dug one hole and did not find this promised treasure, would you quit?"

Most people tell me that they wouldn't quit until they found it, staking out the backyard and carefully digging up every square inch. They would go down six feet, and if they didn't find it, they would dig deeper. The guarantee I gave them would encourage them to do whatever was necessary to find the treasure. I'm sure that you would do the same.

The interesting thing is that we already have such a guarantee, for the Bible promises wisdom to any and all who will search for it. James instructed his readers, "If any of you lacks wisdom, he should ask God, who gives generously to all without finding fault, and it will be given to him" (James 1:5). But he also warned, "But when he asks, he must believe and not doubt...that man should not think that he will receive anything from the Lord" (James 1:6-7).

You have a role to play, however, in getting this wisdom. You must ask for it—not just once or twice, but as often as necessary and with everything in you.

Do you give up too easily in this quest? Have you allowed opposition to send you off track? Have you gotten discouraged and stopped seeking wisdom for your family, job, church, ministry, finances, and children? If so, then start digging again. You can start today by memorizing Bible verses, reading more, or listening to teaching tapes. You can begin to ask questions, fast, and pray. You need to dig and dig to fulfill this promise, and it is a promise made to you and me.

As you dig, you must dig in faith. We must believe that we will find something at the end of our searching. The writer of Hebrews said it like this: "Anyone who comes to him [God] must believe that he exists and that he rewards those who earnestly seek him" (Hebrews 11:6 emphasis added). Those who diligently seek Him will find wisdom, so start seeking and make Him your chief aim. When you do, God will reward your faith with insight and knowledge that will change your life.

JUNE 3

"Honor the Lord with your wealth, with the firstfruits of all your crops; then your barns will be filled to overflowing, and your vats will brim over with new wine." — 3:9-10.

I was surprised to discover how much of the book of Proverbs deals with money, even though it was written thousands of years ago. It makes sense, however, since so much of life, both then and now, revolves around money—or the lack of it. Since money plays such an important role, it's critical that we recognize the role that money has in helping us grow in grace.

Luke 16:11 says, "So if you have not been trustworthy in handling worldly wealth, who will trust you with true riches?" Money, and how we deal with it, are critical factors in receiving the true riches of the Kingdom. Righteousness, peace, and joy are some of the true riches, and you and I can obtain these if we handle our money properly.

When you give, you honor the Lord. He gave you all that you have. When you give, you take a portion of what He has given you and return it to its source. This is an act of faith because you acknowledge that He has given and will give again toward your needs.

When things are tight, however, there's sometimes a tendency to cut back on giving because we want to be responsible and first take care of obligations. We must resist this temptation because the firstfruits belong to the Lord in every situation. Don't honor the electric or mortgage company more than you honor God. Don't take His portion and give it to someone else in the name of "responsibility." What's more, don't stop sowing seed when times are lean, but continue to sow so that you will reap a future harvest.

Recently our church finances were lean and I hadn't been paid in several weeks. There was some money in the church account, and I was trying to decide what to do with it. After considering all my options, I decided to make sure that all our giving commitments were met. I wrote out checks to several ministries and missionaries. I didn't get paid, but we gave to the Lord what was His.

Honoring God with our giving, finances were "current" within a couple of weeks. Now I'm praying for the "true riches" since I believe we passed that financial test. I didn't "shrink back" during that dry time, but rather sowed faithfully in spite of my own needs.

Honor the Lord with your money; be faithful in good times and bad. Wait to see the Lord's blessing come from your generosity, and then watch for the true riches as you're faithful with this world's wealth.

JUNE 4

"The path of the righteous is like the first gleam of dawn,
shining ever brighter till the full light of day." — 4:18.

It has always amazed me how powerful light is. I can be in a pitch black room, light a match, and be able to see quite well. It's not surprising that Jesus likened Himself and His followers to light, because just a little of His or their presence was enough to dispel darkness. Yet it's the nature of darkness to hide from the light, for darkness is no longer what it's meant to be when it's exposed to light.

Perhaps you're encountering "darkness." No, I don't mean sin, but that you don't understand your way, or what God is doing in your life. You have two promises that will help you in your walk as you proceed on your "path" of life. The first is that the Lord promises to give you some light; God is always ready to give you encouragement or some small token of His presence.

I remember another time that our family finances were particularly tight. My wife and I were in Los Angeles with our two children and we were having to ration our remaining money to last the remainder of the trip. One morning I prayed, "Lord, I need to know that You are with me, and that this season is of You. I need to know that I haven't messed up, but that You're guiding my path."

That afternoon we took our children to an amusement park, prepared to spend what little money we had left. While we were in line, a woman turned around and asked us, "Could you use some free tickets?" and proceeded to give us four tickets. Once inside, we went to buy lunch. After I got our order, another woman came up and literally forced hot dogs, fries, and drinks on us, claiming that we had left them at the counter. In spite of my protests (and fears that she was crazy), she insisted we take them and disappeared.

It was a little sign, a little light on my way, but it was enough. I saw that God had answered my prayer. He didn't give me $10,000, but He gave me a little light to show that He was with me.

The second promise is that your light will grow if you keep walking on your current path. While the first light of dawn allows you to see, the full light of noon illuminates everything completely. From that time in Los Angeles, the Lord has revealed to me a lot more of His purpose and direction concerning finances. He has given us a house, new cars, a church building, money for orthodontics, and a whole lot more. He has allowed me to teach on the issue of finances and to bless many people.

The lesson is simple. Walk in the little light you have and God will give you more. Be faithful to the understanding you have today, and tomorrow's light will shine more brightly.

JUNE 5

"For the lips of an adulteress drip honey,
and her speech is smoother than oil." — 5:3.

The book of Proverbs is full of advice concerning sexual matters, some of which we've discussed already. Today's verse calls to mind something out of the New Testament that warrants our attention. In the New Testament, the Church is referred to as the bride of Christ and the relationship between the two is likened to a marriage covenant.

James wrote in his epistle,

> You adulterous people, don't you know that friendship with the world is hatred toward God? Anyone who chooses to be a friend of the world becomes an enemy of God. Or do you think Scripture says without reason that the spirit he caused to live in us envies intensely? (James 4:4-5).

God is a jealous bridegroom when it comes to His Church. He wants to be the only love of the Church's life. Any other relationship is considered by Him to be adulterous and is a serious matter.

The world is constantly wooing the Lord's bride to win her affections. There's a spirit in every generation, whether it be materialism, hedonism, sexual permissiveness, or secular humanism, that constantly strives to win the hearts and minds of men. There are always new "toys" and technological breakthroughs that provide the fanciest of gadgets to help with life and work. Education and philosophy produce new "ideas," such as Marxism, feminism, or evolution, which appeal to the intellect of man.

All of these things come with smooth speech and sweet talk, sounding and looking very good. They're designed, however, to cater to the carnal nature in man, and the carnal nature is always at odds with the Spirit of God.

It's possible to attend church, read the Bible, and pray, yet still be affected by some adulterous relationship with the world and her ways. James cautions you not to be fooled. You can't maintain a cozy relationship with materialism, for example, and stay friends with God, the bridegroom. Jesus issued the same warning when He said, "No servant can serve two masters" (Luke 16:13). No one is permitted to have two husbands or two wives. That's adultery. And no one can serve two spiritual masters, for that's spiritual adultery.

Take stock today. Have you made peace with a philosophy, a way of life, or a mind set that's contrary to the Spirit of Christ? Ask the Lord to show you what's in your heart. Allow the Spirit to search your innermost person and convict you of hidden sin. Your new "love" may have come with honey and oil, but the end will be bitter unless you repent.

JUNE 6

"Go to the ant, you sluggard; consider its ways and be wise!" — 6:6.

Do you remember when you were a child and you'd watch ants at work? Perhaps you kicked over their anthill with your foot and watched them frantically carry out their damage control. Or maybe you watched a group of them carry some large insect over a long distance to a mound.

Today's verse commands us to study the ant and learn from its ways. In our own society, leisure is rapidly replacing work as the goal of modern life. We can easily put more emphasis on free time than work time. This is a radical departure from the attitude of one generation ago, when work—hard work—was the standard.

I remember several years ago when I was involved in a number of diverse activities. I was pastoring a small group, administrator of our church, traveling as a fund raiser for a Christian ministry, and also involved in several community activities. I was the father of two and husband of one. I began to seek the Lord for what I could eliminate, for I thought that surely I was too busy to do it all.

As I was seeking the Lord over this matter, I woke up one morning and felt impressed to read 1 Corinthians 15:10. I didn't know what that verse said and I had not been reading the epistle. About mid-morning, I finally picked up a Bible and read these words: "But by the grace of God I am what I am, and his grace to me was not without effect. No, I worked harder than all of them—yet not I, but the grace of God that was with me."

Having read that, I knew what the Lord was saying: I wasn't going to work any less but I was going to do what was before me and more! I was underestimating my ability to work, or at least the ability of the grace of God to work in and through me. I determined that if this hard work was God's will, then I would learn how to work so I could maximize my efforts for Him.

Since then, I've studied the ant. I've tried to manage my time, set priorities, work without direct oversight, and practice self-discipline. I've made a daily "task list" list for ten years, trying to be sensitive to all the things the Lord would have me do. Today I'm as busy as ever.

Don't underestimate your ability to work. The grace of God in and through you can help you do more that you ever imagined possible. Don't limit God, and He'll empower you to do a lot of work for His glory!

JUNE 7

"Bind them on your fingers; write them on the tablet of your heart." — 7:3.

This verse requires you to do two things with the commands of God. The first is to bind them on your fingers. This means that God's commands should make a difference in your outward appearance. Have you ever noticed a woman wearing a ring on every finger? When she raises her hand, you notice her many rings. So it is with the commands of God, for they're to adorn you outwardly. In Acts 6:15, Luke describes Stephen, saying, "They saw that his face was like the face of an angel." The Holy Spirit had so filled his life that it changed his outward appearance.

When I first became a believer, I prayed that the Lord would allow people to look at me and know that I was a disciple. I wanted my outward actions to mirror the Spirit of God who had come into my life. I also wanted people to watch what I did, see how I "handled" life, and then know there was something different about me. When people have commented how peaceful I've looked during a certain trial or tribulation, it has given me a great chance to witness about the goodness of the Lord; I always thank God for answering that prayer offered in the early days of my walk.

Changes, however, can't be external only. The Pharisees tied the commands of God to their fingers. Everyone knew what they were doing and why they were doing it, for they were attracting attention to themselves with such behavior. These external acts aren't enough, for the commands of God are also to be written on your heart.

In fact, the second thing to do with God's commands, according to today's verse, is to write them on the "tablets" of your heart. Your heart was as hard as stone when you came to the Lord, somewhat like the tablets upon which the original Ten Commandments were written. You're to take the commands of God and chisel them if necessary on your heart. Real change comes only when you are changed within. When your heart is changed, your actions will naturally follow.

The Lord promises you, "I will give them an undivided heart and put a new spirit in them; I will remove from them their heart of stone and give them a heart of flesh" (Ezekiel 11:19). Part of this "stone-to-flesh" process is the chiseling of God's commands on your heart. This requires work and is a gradual process. And the command of God—His word—is what it will take to break that rock. "'Is not my word like fire,' declares the Lord, 'and like a hammer that breaks a rock in pieces?'" (Jeremiah 23:29).

Write the word on your heart today. Allow it to break up the hard places, and give it room to turn your rock to flesh. Don't just *do* the word of God, but also *be* the word of God. They're both essential to your life as a believer.

JUNE 8

"Does not wisdom call out? Does not understanding raise her voice?" — 8:1.

The book of Proverbs can be difficult to read because it jumps from subject to subject as it goes from verse to verse. When I first began to read a chapter a day, I was startled to return to the a chapter one month later and realize I didn't remember any of what I had read! It seemed like my pursuit of godly wisdom was too difficult, and that Proverbs was a disjointed, confusing book.

Today's verse contradicts that thinking, for it states that wisdom is crying out to be heard, trying to get my attention. I realized from this that the voice of godly wisdom was competing with many other voices in my life. It wasn't that wisdom was fickle or too difficult to obtain as I had thought. My inability to distinguish wisdom's voice was the real issue. The problem wasn't with God; the problem was with me.

The writer of Hebrews explained this when he wrote:

> We have much to say about this, but it is hard to explain because you are slow to learn. In fact, though by this time you ought to be teachers, you need someone to teach you the elementary truths of God's word all over again. You need milk, not solid food! Anyone who lives on milk, being still an infant, is not acquainted with the teaching about righteousness. But solid food is for the mature, who by constant use have trained themselves to distinguish good from evil (Hebrews 5:11-14).

Jesus gave His life so that you could enter into the things of God. After giving His all, will He now withhold wisdom from you? If you lack wisdom, is the problem His or yours? Unfortunately, wisdom isn't a set of rules to be memorized and followed. Godly wisdom is a listening relationship with God, in which you've learned to distinguish His voice from all the other voices vying for your loyalty.

"Whether you turn to the right or to the left, your ears will hear a voice behind you, saying, 'This is the way; walk in it'" (Isaiah 30:21). Wisdom doesn't hide herself; she simply talks in the same tone as the other voices of life. Wisdom won't yell. Searching for wisdom is simply learning to ignore or tone down the other voices so that wisdom can come through loud and clear.

To what and to whom are you listening? Commit yourself afresh to hear the voice of the Lord, and His voice only. Stifle all other voices and His voice will come through. Wisdom is crying out to you today. Listen to her voice.

JUNE 9

"If you are wise, your wisdom will reward you;
if you are a mocker, you alone will suffer." — 9:12.

You reap what you sow, and that's true the world over. If you plant corn, you'll harvest corn. If you plant wheat, you get wheat. If you don't pull weeds, they go to seed and you get more weeds. These truths can't be ignored. You can't pray for corn or wheat and you can't rebuke weeds. What you plant is what you'll enjoy. It's as simple as that.

This verse gives the basic motivation for your pursuit of wisdom. Wisdom will reward you and that's not self-serving or selfish. Wisdom blesses your life, work, and family; ignoring wisdom causes suffering. Not seeking wisdom is an attitude that keeps you from being all you can be in Christ.

Now I realize that in your flesh dwells no good thing. But in your flesh now also dwells the risen Christ through the Holy Spirit. The Holy Spirit is at work in us, and has awakened faith, gifts, and the fruit of the Spirit. Paul wrote in 2 Corinthians 5:17, "Therefore, if anyone is in Christ, he is a new creation; the old is gone, the new has come!" You're a new creation made worthy to receive the blessings of God by and through the blood of Jesus.

Paul also wrote in Ephesians 5:29, "After all, no one ever hated his own body, but he feeds and cares for it, just as Christ does the church." Self-preservation is in us for our good. It's not pride to eat or sleep since the need for those two things was put in you by God Himself. In the same way, there's nothing wrong with seeking wisdom for your own good. You're a spiritual being, a new creation, and you need wisdom. God created you to want and need it.

There's true humility and false humility. The former is a virtue while the latter is a sin. Paul wrote in Romans 12:3, "For by the grace given me I say to every one of you: Do not think of yourself more highly than you ought, but rather think of yourself with sober judgment." This verse cautions you not to go overboard in your personal estimation; it tells you not to dismiss yourself as worthless either.

Pay attention to your spiritual life by getting wisdom and feeding yourself. Stop seeing yourself as insignificant, for you're the righteousness of God! You're a new creation in Christ. Ask God to deliver you from any false sense of worthlessness. Ask His help to see yourself as He sees you. Build up your spiritual life, and fly on the wings of wisdom as high as you can!

JUNE 10

"When words are many, sin is not absent,
but he who holds his tongue is wise." — 10:19.

Some have called James' epistle the Proverbs of the New Testament. It's a letter that covers a number of subjects in short, concise terms. One of James most vivid pictures is that of the tongue. He writes in 3:2-10:

> We all stumble in many ways. If anyone is never at fault in what he says, he is a perfect man, able to keep his whole body in check. When we put bits into the mouths of horses to make them obey us, we can turn the whole animal. Or take ships for example. Although they are so large and are driven by strong winds, they are steered by a very small rudder wherever the pilot wants to go. Likewise the tongue is a small part of the body, but it makes great boasts. Consider what a great forest is set on fire by a small spark. The tongue also is a fire, a world of evil among the parts of the body. It corrupts the whole person, sets the whole course of his life on fire, and is itself set on fire by hell. All kinds of animals, birds, reptiles, and creatures of the sea are being tamed and have been tamed by man, but no man can tame the tongue. It is a restless evil, full of deadly poison. With the tongue we praise our Lord and Father, and with it we curse men, who have been made in God's likeness. Out of the same mouth come praise and cursing. My brothers, this should not be.

James said it better than I ever could, using strong language and powerful examples. We need to take what he says to heart. When we know this about our mouth, why are we so quick to use it? Earlier in his epistle, James wrote, "Everyone should be quick to listen, slow to speak and slow to become angry" (James 1:19). He's telling you and me to be quiet, learning to be a better listener and more even tempered.

Start today to control your tongue. Use it more to encourage people and don't complain. Don't respond to people or situations so quickly, and when you do respond, use only the words necessary to get the job done. Regardless of how old you are in the Lord, you'll be considered wise if you limit what you say to the bare essentials.

JUNE 11

"If the righteous receive their due on earth,
how much more the ungodly and the sinner!" — 11:31.

God is a just God and He will give to each man the fruit of his deeds. To those who work righteousness, He'll grant His favor. To those who sin, He'll grant the consequences of that sin. At times, however, it seems that the righteous are walking a hard road, and sinners are floating along with few problems.

David addressed this dilemma in Psalm 37:1-2: "Do not fret because of evil men or be envious of those who do wrong; for like the grass they will soon wither, like green plants they will soon die away." Through the Spirit, David commanded the reader not to fret over the seeming prosperity of the evildoer. Sometimes we compare the tribulation of the righteous to the external prosperity of the wicked and "fret" over it. This can lead to anger and frustration and cause us to be less than godly in our attitude and behavior.

This is especially true when someone has wronged us. We're suffering, and they proceed with life like nothing ever happened! Perhaps your neighbor wronged you, your employer messed with your pay, your car got totaled by a hit-and-run driver, or your classmate got good grades because of cheating. When those things happen, it's important to remember that God is watching, and will eventually, on the earth—in this lifetime—reward everyone according to their deeds.

Be patient and give God time to even things out. Take to heart the exhortation that Paul wrote in Romans 12:17-21:

Do not repay anyone evil for evil. Be careful to do what is right in the eyes of everybody. If it is possible, as far as it depends on you, live at peace with everyone. Do not take revenge, my friends, but leave room for God's wrath, for it is written: "It is mine to avenge; I will repay," says the Lord. "On the contrary: If your enemy is hungry, feed him; if he is thirsty, give him something to drink. In doing this, you will heap burning coals on his head." Do not be overcome by evil, but overcome evil with good.

Don't ever worry about "evening the score," because that's God's job. Keep yourself free from fretting, bitterness, and anger. Keep your focus on the Lord, and then watch and see how things turn out.

JUNE 12

"A man cannot be established through wickedness,
but the righteous cannot be uprooted." — 12:3.

Every television network was broadcasting exciting shots of "The Wall" being torn down by the people. I'll never forget the scenes of the Berlin Wall as people from both East and West Germany stood, danced, and painted graffiti on it. Desperate men build that wall to establish themselves through wickedness, but their effort lasted only 20 years.

The wicked always try to establish themselves by wickedness because that's all they know. History is full of examples of men like Hitler and Stalin who used any means possible to preserve power. They died and their plans failed. Yet men and women come along and try to replace them, destined to repeat their mistakes because they don't understand the Lord and His purposes.

The righteous, on the other hand, can't be uprooted. They're compared to a tree that puts down its roots and grows to great heights:

Blessed is the man who does not walk in the counsel of the wicked or stand in the way of sinners or sit in the seat of mockers. But his delight is in the law of the Lord, and on his law he meditates day and night. He is like a tree planted by streams of water, which yields its fruit in season and whose leaf does not wither. Whatever he does prospers (Psalm 1:1-3).

The righteous will flourish like a palm tree, they will grow like a cedar of Lebanon; planted in the house of the Lord, they will flourish in the courts of our God. They will still bear fruit in old age, they will stay fresh and green, proclaiming, "The Lord is upright; he is my Rock, and there is no wickedness in him" (Psalm 92:12-15).

Jeremiah wrote:

Blessed is the man who trusts in the Lord, whose confidence is in him. He will be like a tree planted by the water that sends out its roots by the stream. It does not fear when heat comes; its leaves are always green. It has no worries in a year of drought and never fails to bear fruit (Jeremiah 17:7-8).

Yesterday we were reminded that the wicked and righteous often are rewarded in this life. We need to hear those words again. Be like that tree to which you're so often compared by putting your trust in the Lord and not in wickedness. Don't look to money or power as your security but put your roots down deep in God. Meditate on His word night and day. Avoid shortcuts that may pay dividends now, but will cost you dearly later. Put down deep roots in the Lord and you'll prosper in any and every season of life.

JUNE 13

"A wise son heeds his father's instruction,
but a mocker does not listen to rebuke." — 13:1.

My daughter can't wait to grow up. When people would ask me how old she was, I told them, "12 going on 20." She wanted to wear makeup, run the house, cook, and be grown up in every way. Wanting to be independent, she always resisted me telling her what to do. She wanted to make decisions on her own, just like an adult.

No matter how old in the Lord you are, you're still a child of God and He's your Father. He teaches you about Himself and His will for as long as you live; you never outgrow the need for His input and discipline in your life. You'll never be on your own.

I think the writer of Hebrews put it best. In Hebrews 12:7-10, he wrote,

Endure hardship as discipline; God is treating you as sons. For what son is not disciplined by his father? If you are not disciplined (and everyone undergoes discipline), then you are illegitimate children and not true sons. Moreover, we have all had human fathers who disciplined us and we respected them for it. How much more should we submit to the Father of our spirits and live! Our fathers disciplined us for a little while as they thought best; but God disciplines us for our good, that we may share his holiness.

If you received training from your natural father, it was only the prelude to spiritual training from your heavenly Father. Today's verse touches on one form of that heavenly discipline, and that is rebuke. Jesus rebuked His followers on numerous occasions, speaking sternly concerning their lack of faith, wrong spirit, presumption, or fear, to name a few. He rebuked Peter for his lack of understanding concerning the cross. He even reattached the ear of the servant after Peter cut it off. Imagine how Peter felt, having done something in his zeal for the Lord, only to have the Lord reverse the results!

Life with the Lord will include discipline and even rebuke. What you do with these will determine your progress and growth. Accept them in humility, and you'll prosper. Avoid or mock rebuke, and you'll be found resisting the Lord in pride. The choice is between childlike faith and "adult" independence. The wise choice is to accept the discipline, and let it work God's holiness in you.

If God has been disciplining or rebuking you, rejoice! It proves you are His child, and it confirms His love for you. Don't resist it, but welcome it! Let it have its perfect way in you, and then watch for your Father's pleasure in His child who welcomes not only His blessings but also His loving rebuke.

JUNE 14

"All hard work brings a profit, but mere talk leads only to poverty." — 14:23.

Perhaps you do your best work when you feel your work is relevant and appreciated. No one likes to be doing something that's tedious, insignificant, or below their capabilities. Yet this is exactly the kind of work the Lord will give you to do for a season to prepare you for what's ahead. When you do your work, whatever it may be, for God's glory and not your own, God is free to promote you to more meaningful tasks. This concept is biblical and easily seen in the lives of several great heroes of the faith.

How did God prepare Joseph for his leadership position? Joseph had a vision of his impending exaltation above his brother and parents. After he shared that vision, his brothers sold him into slavery! First he worked as the chief household slave for Potiphar in Egypt. After that, he was falsely accused and sent to prison. In prison he was made the inmate in charge of all the other inmates. He fed them, did the chief jailer's job, and even gave out spiritual counsel. Those positions prepared him to be second only to Pharaoh in the most powerful nation on earth. For Joseph, there was profit in all his labor.

Moses was another man whom God prepared for greatness through curious means. Moses studied in Egypt and was a significant man there. At some point he discovered that he was to be the deliverer of his people. A high-ranking job in Egypt, however, didn't prepare him for this God-given task. No, but God took Moses into the wilderness; for 40 years, he served as a shepherd, caring for his father-in-law's sheep. Those desert years prepared Moses spiritually for the years in which he would lead his people out of Egypt and through the wilderness. It didn't seem like those 40 years served any purpose, but for Moses, there was profit in all his labor.

David was anointed to be king of Israel; he became a mighty warrior, skilled musician, and charismatic leader. He learned much of this while, like Moses, he served as a shepherd over a few sheep. After his anointing, he became a fugitive, caring for a rag-tag bunch of followers. He fought some battles, fled from Saul, and wandered the land as an outcast with few allies. Yet those years prepared him for the awesome task of ruling Israel. For David, there was profit in all of his labor.

The same is true for you. Work hard and don't try to figure out what you're doing and why you're where you are. Because God is preparing you for the future, you may not see the relevance. It's only important to know that God is teaching you to work hard in every situation for His sake. The hard work will train you. If you only talk about what you're going to achieve when things go as you want, however, you'll miss some great opportunities to work hard and profit from experience. Roll up your sleeves, get to work, and trust God. Your future depends on it.

JUNE 15

*"The eyes of the Lord are everywhere,
keeping watch on the wicked and the good." — 15:3.*

This verse is closely related to 2 Chronicles 16:9: "For the eyes of the Lord range throughout the earth to strengthen those whose hearts are fully committed to him." God's always watching and He'll "neither slumber nor sleep" (Psalm 121:4). He's not watching just those who are righteous or those in church. God watches all people with an eye toward judging their deeds.

This should provide us incentive to do our best in all that we do, for Jesus said in Luke 16:10: "Whoever can be trusted with very little can also be trusted with much, and whoever is dishonest with very little will also be dishonest with much."

Your tendency may be to pass over the details in favor of the "big stuff." If that's true, your perspective needs to change. You must start seeing that the little things are the proving ground for bigger things. If you can't be faithful with $10, will God give you $100? If you can't diligently prepare a Bible study for 20 people—seeing it as only 20 people—will God give you a chance to speak before 100?

According to this principle in Luke 16:10, the answer is "no" to both questions. It isn't that the Lord wants to bore you with small things and it isn't that He's a "nit-pick" and wants everything to be perfect. He wants you to learn to do all things from one motivation: The Lord is watching and has given you this task to do for His glory.

"Slaves, obey your earthly masters with respect and fear, and with sincerity of heart, just as you would obey Christ. Obey them not only to win their favor when their eye is on you, but like slaves of Christ, doing the will of God from your heart" (Ephesians 6:5,6). Your motivation should be to do a good job in the will of God. It's not to see how many corners you can cut, or whether someone is watching you.

If you need to know if someone is watching, remember that the Lord is. His eyes are everywhere and He notices how and why you did what you did. Because He's watching, He is able to reward you according to your deeds. Start "sweating" the little things and allow God to strengthen your heart. Before you know it, God will entrust you with much more.

JUNE 16

"Better a patient man than a warrior,
a man who controls his temper than one who takes a city." — 16:32.

Israel longed for a Messiah, they waited for the Anointed One to come on His horse and liberate them from foreign oppression. Some envisioned another King David who would organize and lead their troops into battle. Others pictured a more spiritual leader who would establish God's kingdom on earth. As this Messiah led them, they thought, the Lord would rout their enemies as He did in days of old.

Instead of a military genius or rabbi, God sent His Son Jesus to them. Instead of a fiery general, God sent the Lamb of God, who by His own admission was "gentle and humble in heart" (Matthew 11:29). Israel wanted someone who would recapture Jerusalem for the glory of God. Instead, they got One who wept over Jerusalem's lack of spiritual insight and repentance.

Today's verse says that patience and self-control are preferable in God's sight to your greatest exploits. Evelyn Underhill, a British author, wrote the following:

We mostly spend our lives conjugating three verbs: to Want, to Have, and to Do. Craving, clutching, and fussing, on the material, political, emotional, intellectual,—even on the religious plane, we are kept in perpetual unrest; forgetting that none of these verbs has ultimate significance, except so far as they are transcended by and included in, the fundamental verb, to Be: and that Being, not wanting, having, and doing, is the essence of a spiritual life.*

Jesus was a doer, but that alone didn't make Him great. His greatness rested in who He was. He was God-became-man who gave the Holy Spirit absolute control over His life. Jesus manifested the fruit of the Spirit—fruit that's precious in the sight of God—to show that you and I are to do the same. Jesus could have been a warrior. Instead He was a patient, humble man, and that made Him greater still.

"But the fruit of the Spirit is love, joy, peace, patience, kindness, goodness, faithfulness, gentleness and self-control. Against such things there is no law" (Galatians 5:22 23). Jesus showed forth all the fruit listed by Paul and He wants you to do the same. Take time to consider whether your emphasis is on doing or being. Yield yourself anew to the work of the Spirit, knowing that your patience and self-control are greater in the sight of God than anything you can do.

---

*Taken from *Great Devotional Classics: Selections from the Writings of Evelyn Underhill,* Published by The Upper Room, 1908 Grand Avenue, Nashville, TN, 37202.

JUNE 17

"He who covers over an offense promotes love,
but whoever repeats the matter separates close friends." — 17:9.

Someone recently sent me a newspaper article from the front page of a major metropolitan newspaper concerning a church that was experiencing trouble. The problems in this church were newsworthy, and the article was fairly objective, but it was disturbing to see how many former members were willing to talk with the reporter against the church and its pastor.

Part of the spirit of this secular age is the "right" of the people to know. Books are written baring the private lives of public figures. Investigative reporters hide with cameras behind walls and doors to capture men and women on film as they are involved in questionable or criminal business or private activities. Talk show hosts regularly feature people who are willing to "tell it all" about husbands, wives, employers, or (former) friends.

Lost in this rush to honesty is the message behind today's verse: God honors friendship and loyalty more than gossip, even if that gossip contains truth. God, who graciously "covers" our sins, wants to see us "cover" the sins of others. This raises a lot of "what if" questions about how to handle the failures of friends, acquaintances, and leaders. What's needed is an attitude of grace and mercy that's perhaps best exemplified by Joseph's treatment of Mary, the mother of Jesus.

One day Mary came to Joseph and told him she was pregnant. What a devastating blow to this young man! Here was his fiancee, the woman of his future, bearing a child that wasn't his own! Was he angry? Hurt? Confused? Would he drag her before the priests to have her stoned as to the law prescribed?

We find the answer in Matthew 1:19: "Because Joseph her husband was a righteous man and did not want to expose her to public disgrace, he had in mind to divorce her quietly." May the attitude of Joseph come on the Church. He had the right to put Mary through public humiliation, but he chose instead to cover it all as quietly as possible. Because of his godly choice, an angel appeared to him and explained all that was going on.

The zeal to expose isn't always godly; it's the spirit of this world. If God has covered your sins, then determine to help him "cover" others. Don't spread stories about others, even if they're true. Don't place doubts in people's minds about their friends. This isn't dishonesty, it's loyalty. Let God deal with the sins of others; you be a friend, or at least a brother or sister in the Lord.

JUNE 18

*"An offended brother is more unyielding than a fortified city,
and disputes are like the barred gates of a citadel." — 18:19.*

Once a month I get together with other pastors in our city for a time of fellowship and prayer. During a recent meeting, one of the pastors asked a ministry question, and several others responded. One brother quoted famous theologians, shared his viewpoint freely, and (I thought) came across much too strongly.

Everything in me wanted to respond! I wanted to share my experience, challenge his conclusions, and "get it on." Armed with Bible verses and debating skills, I wanted to "blow him out of the water." Instead, I kept quiet. I sat there, offering a few simple statements, but for the most part, I shut up.

If I had attacked, I would have offended that brother. I've learned by now that believers will never agree on doctrinal issues. I kept quiet, the conversation wound down, and we went on to a great prayer time. I've come to the conclusion that Jesus is less concerned about me being right theologically than He is about me being right in matters of the heart.

You can be driving your car and have a green light, while a pedestrian is crossing the street in front of you. The pedestrian is clearly in the wrong, but you now have a choice to make. You can keep going and run him or her over on the basis that you have a green light. Or you can slow down and stop, even though that person's wrong, because it isn't worth running them over to prove your "rightness."

That's how it can be with a fellow believer, even if you're correct. Offense between believers is a serious thing, so you need to avoid it at all costs. I've seen enough church splits to last a lifetime. I've seen family and friends divided over the silliest of issues. But the split is real and painful, and the offense becomes like bars on a castle. These are very difficult, if not impossible, to break through.

Paul exhorted the Ephesian church as he wrote from prison:

Live a life worthy of the calling you have received. Be completely humble and gentle; be patient, bearing with one another in love. Make every effort to keep the unity of the Spirit through the bond of peace. There is one body and one Spirit (Ephesians 4:1-4).

Let those words guide your relationships in the church, and make every effort to be at peace with your brethren. A spiritual feud isn't a sign of maturity, but a sign of carnality. Don't let an offense develop if at all possible, for it's both painful and almost impossible to overcome.

JUNE 19

*"Many are the plans in a man's heart,
but it is the Lord's purpose that prevails." — 19:21.*

One day I was signing in at the guard house for a weekly jail Bible study. As I was waiting for my badge, the Lord spoke to me not to preach. I panicked. What was I to do? As I went before the men I was still waiting for direction from the Holy Spirit. After the opening prayer, I felt impressed to take questions from the inmates. This worked so well that I made it part of my regular format.

The question I'm asked the most concerns guidance. Men and women want to know how they can know the will of God for their life. They recognize that, as today's verse says, their own mind has a lot of ideas and plans. They want help in sorting through all the things in their minds to find the true will of God.

My response is always the same. First, I direct them to Hebrews 11:6 and explain that they must have faith that God "rewards those who diligently seek Him." We must believe that if we seek the Lord and ask Him for His will, He will somehow make reasonably clear what that will is. Every servant has at least one right, and that right is to know the will of the master. You, as a servant of God, must know His will in order to obey His will; God must show you that will.

Proverbs 16:3 in the Amplified Version speaks to this issue. It says, "Roll your works upon the Lord—commit and trust them wholly to Him; [He will cause your thoughts to become agreeable to His will, and] so shall your plans be established and succeed." God can cause your thoughts to be His thoughts; if you're praying for His will and trusting Him, then your thoughts should come in line with His will for your life.

The second principle I share with the inmates asking about guidance is John 7:17: "If anyone chooses to do God's will, he will find out whether my teaching comes from God or whether I speak on my own." You must commit to do God's will before you find out what it is. God won't tell you His will so you can have veto power over His decision. He wants a commitment that you'll do His will—no matter what it is—before He reveals it. That requires faith, a faith that God isn't going to trick you or cause you to do something terrible or unpleasant. "Without faith it is impossible to please God" (Hebrews 11:6).

Divine guidance requires human cooperation and commitment. When those are present, God is sure to reveal His will. If you need direction, seek the Lord and tell Him you'll do His will no matter what it is. Then sit back and see the God of heaven and earth accomplish His purpose on your behalf.

"Many a man claims to have unfailing love,
but a faithful man who can find?" — 20:6.

Throughout my life it seems that people have sought me out to share their problems. As had happened so often, one day a woman I barely knew was telling me her marital difficulties. I listened as patiently as I could, and then broke off the conversation with my pat response: "I'll pray for you."

I walked away and heard the word "liar" go through my mind, and I knew exactly what the Lord was trying to say to me. Even though I had said I would pray, chances were I would not. That "saying" had become a standard phrase I used with people. Maybe they thought I was going to pray, but I was only leaving them with a religious phrase appropriate for the situation.

It's easy to make commitments to the Lord and other people. It isn't hard to find someone who makes commitments; it's much harder to find someone who carries them out. Just today a woman called to tell me she would not be able to do a job in the church that she had committed to do. Her reasons—a sick child and lack of sleep—were real enough, but so was her inability to carry through on her commitment.

Psalm 15 has always been a special psalm for me. It starts out by asking, "Lord, who may dwell in your sanctuary? Who may live on your holy hill?" It goes on to list the characteristics of those who qualify, and verse 4 includes this person: "[he] who keeps his oath even when it hurts."

Now this includes someone who says "I'll be there at four," and is there at 3:55; she who says, "I will be glad to help you," and then helps even though things go wrong that would make her cancellation convenient; he who commits $10 a month to a missionary's support, and pays it on time or early; she who promises to help with the bake sale, and then, even though she forgot, gets up at 4:00 a.m. to bake so she can keep her promise; he who promises to play on the church softball team, and then practices and comes to the games even though he isn't playing much.

Those who keep their word, even when it's painful, can live on God's holy hill. Those who take seriously their vows, oaths, and promises to family, friends, business associates, and fellow believers have a special place with God. Those who talk a good game, but don't show up as promised, are a dime a dozen.

How is your level of commitment? Do you make promises, and then find good and legitimate reasons not to keep them? Do you "proclaim your own love," but find it hard to put that love into practice? Do you say the words that you think people want to hear, even though you have no intention of following through? You may excuse yourself, but God is listening. When the Lord looks for a faithful person, let Him find you.

JUNE 21

"The plans of the diligent lead to profit
as surely as haste leads to poverty." — 21:5.

When I first came to know the Lord, I was captivated by the fact that He could return at any time. I remember hearing a preacher tell how he had spent the previous year studying one particular book in the Bible. I remember thinking what a waste of precious time that was. After all, I thought, the Lord is returning soon, and I don't want to be found studying one book when I could be reading it all.

That was 20 years ago, and the Lord hasn't returned yet. He may be back tomorrow, or He may return in another 20 years. Even if He were to return next year, I've come to the conclusion that I need to be planning for the future, and diligently carrying out those plans.

Now I find myself imitating that preacher I criticized years ago. Five years ago, I began to take classes toward an advanced degree in pastoral ministries. These classes required 10 hours per week of class time, study, reading, and other work. I couldn't really afford that time, but I couldn't afford not to improve my knowledge of the Bible, church history, and other subjects.

Today, many class hours, research papers, and book reports later, I have an earned doctorate. Those plans, which I diligently carried out, have brought great profit to my ministry. The time spent studying improved my preaching, teaching, counseling, and every aspect of my ministry. Spending those years wishing or hoping for more knowledge would have impoverished my ministry. I set a goal of an advanced degree, planned accordingly, and did the work. It has paid off.

In his classic book, *The 7 Habits of Highly Effective People*, Stephen Covey lists his second habit as "beginning with the end first." He recommends that each person write his or her eulogy or funeral sermon. His logic is this: You must begin planning for and doing today what you want people to remember you for tomorrow. If you don't know where you're going, any road will take you there. If you have a destination in mind, then only a few roads will do. There aren't many shortcuts, either.

I hope and pray that the Lord returns quickly. If He doesn't, however, I don't want to wish for what might have been. I want to plan and work to get where I need to go. A long journey begins with one step. Take your first step today, and be diligent. With the Lord's help, you can do great things. And if He returns, you'll found doing His will, which will please Him greatly.

JUNE 22

"Do not be a man who strikes hands in pledge or puts up security for debts;
if you lack the means to pay, your very bed will be snatched from under you."
— 22:26-27.

There we were. My wife and I were lying in bed at 2:30 a.m., not able to sleep. Instead we were discussing one of the women in the church. Having contradicted counsel, she was now struggling because of some actions she took. Now we were burdened for her and her children, and couldn't believe the trouble she had gotten into.

During that time, the Lord made today's two verses meaningful to me. I had always understood them in a natural sense as a warning not to co-sign a loan for anyone unless I was truly ready to pay if they couldn't. But I'd never seen those verses in a spiritual sense. Here I was, carrying or "co-signing" for this sister's problems. I had taken on this situation and it was consuming me. My bed was literally snatched out from under me since my sleep was being affected.

I began to realize that the Lord had ordered this situation in her life. Now it wasn't His will for her to have made those wrong choices, but the Lord was using those to train her. If I wasn't careful, my involvement could actually work against what the Lord was trying to bring about. Yes, I was to be concerned, pray, exhort, and admonish. But I had to learn to be sensitive to what God wanted to do in her, and support that process.

I found confirmation of this principle in Paul's writings. In Galatians 6:2, he wrote: "Carry each other's burdens, and in this way you will fulfill the law of Christ." Then in verse 5 he wrote, "For each one should carry his own load." There were burdens I could help carry, and there were burdens only my sister could carry. I had to learn to distinguish between the two.

I've found this to be true in my family as well; there are some things I can't do for my children. Sometimes I have to let them fail or at least struggle. I have to let them go through it, for their trial is ordained of the Lord to develop something in their lives. There were also times when I was ready to give money to someone in need, only to find the Spirit telling me not to. Their lack was doing a work in them, and to "co-sign" would be wrong.

Of course, you can take this as justification to never carry your brother's burden, and that would be wrong. But you must be careful not to become so involved that you hinder their development, and hurt yourself as well. Maturity is knowing what's yours and what's not. If you've co-signed for someone, determine today to release them to the Lord's care and dealings.

JUNE 23

"Do not wear yourself out to get rich;
have the wisdom to show restraint." — 23:4.

Much success in life is determined by the ability to set correct priorities and then follow them in the midst of interruptions, changes, and distractions. Today's verse cautions us not to put too high a priority on obtaining wealth. Jesus was even more explicit than this when He said, "No one can serve two masters. Either he will hate the one and love the other, or he will be devoted to the one and despise the other. You cannot serve both God and money" (Matthew 6:24).

Jesus said that we can't serve God and money. He didn't say some could and some couldn't, nor was he speaking theoretically. He was saying it's impossible! In one of his sermons, Jesus warned against worrying about provision and care. "Therefore I tell you, do not worry about your life, what you will eat or drink; or about your body, what you will wear. Is not life more important than food, and the body more important than clothes?" (6:25). After further exhortation, Jesus closed that sermon with this command: "But seek first His kingdom and His righteousness, and all these things will be given to you as well" (6:33).

Your highest priority is to seek God's government in your life. King Jesus wants to rule every area of life, including your money. If you set off in pursuit of money— worrying about the things of this life instead of eternal life—you run the danger of putting your pursuit of money more important than the Lord and His rule in your affairs.

God wants to provide your every need and be your source. Your job, inheritance, labor union membership, intelligence, college degrees, job seniority, retirement and ability to manage money aren't to be the focus of your support. The Lord wants to have the highest place in your life. He can't have it if you are hung up on pursuing money.

I pastored a man who was invited to go to Hawaii with his in-laws. He didn't have the money for the airfare, and launched out on all kinds of projects to raise the money. Since he booked most of his company's air travel, his travel agency somehow got him one free ticket. That was a great miracle, but he still needed one more ticket. I remember him saying, "God isn't just going to open my roof and drop a ticket in. I have to work for it."

He couldn't earn the money as he had hoped, and as the time for the trip came nearer, he was anxious. Then one day he called to tell me that the travel agent had made a "mistake." The airline had somehow given him two free tickets instead of one!

Don't weary yourself to make money. God can provide for you in miraculous ways. Seek His kingdom above all else, and watch as the "things" of this life are given to you by Him who cares for you dearly!

JUNE 24

"For though a righteous man falls seven times,
he rises again, but the wicked are brought down by calamity." — 24:16.

It couldn't have happened again, or so I thought. How could I have been so stupid? I just wanted to stay in bed with the covers over me for the rest of my life. I had lied and was feeling badly. It wasn't a small lie. I was fighting condemnation, guilt, and a sense of failure. I dragged myself out of bed one morning and began to study and read the Word. As I did, I began to see "wonderful things from the law." I couldn't understand this. How could I receive revelation from the Lord after I had failed so miserably?

It was at that time that the Lord spoke to me and said, "Revelation doesn't depend on your righteousness; it depends on My grace!" When I had failed, it was then that the Lord's grace showed up so wonderfully. My failure had made me more sensitive to the Lord and my need for Him. Only the Lord can take a failure, redeem it, and actually bring good out of it. I still minister out of the insight I received from His Word on that morning years ago (I still had to go and make amends with the person involved).

Someone once told me that a "blameless" man isn't a perfect man, but rather a man who has dealt with his failures as best he could. The first way of dealing with our failures is confession, a topic that John addressed so well in his epistle.

In 1 John 1:5-10 he wrote:

This is the message we have heard from him and declare to you: God is light; in him there is no darkness at all. If we claim to have fellowship with him yet walk in the darkness, we lie and do not live by the truth. But if we walk in the light, as he is in the light, we have fellowship with one another, and the blood of Jesus, His Son, purifies us from all sin. If we claim to be without sin, we deceive ourselves and the truth is not in us. If we confess our sins, he is faithful and just and will forgive us our sins and purify us from all unrighteousness. If we claim we have not sinned, we make him out to be a liar and his word has no place in our lives.

The righteous "fall" (perhaps even frequently), go to the Lord and confess, receive His forgiveness, make any restitution necessary, and "rise" again. The wicked try to hide their sin, and eventually are brought down by calamity. This presents you with a clear choice. Make confession and cleansing a way of life, or be deceived concerning sin and your own shortcomings, thus inviting God's discipline. Examine your heart today, receive God's grace, and walk in the forgiveness and restoration that are yours as a child of God.

JUNE 25

"Do not exalt yourself in the king's presence, and do not claim a place among great men; it is better for him to say to you, 'Come up here,' than for him to humiliate you before a nobleman." — 25:6-7.

Jesus referred to these verses in Luke 14:7-11. He watched people picking places of honor at a banquet; He encouraged them to take the low seat and wait to be called up to a higher place. Jesus ended in verse 11 by saying, "For everyone who exalts himself will be humbled, and he who humbles himself will be exalted."

It seems that humility and pride are decisions. We have the capacity to choose to humble ourselves in any given situation. The problem is that pride tends to cling to us like lint to a dark wool suit. From infancy, we are the center of our universe. The world teaches us to believe that we are the most important person in any transaction. Pride is blinding and causes us to act in a way that is unbecoming to a disciple of Jesus.

Bernard of Clairvaux, a devotional writer who lived 800 years ago, wrote these thoughts in his work *The Steps of Humility and Pride.**

Humility is a virtue by which a man has a low opinion of himself because he knows himself well....Just as pure truth is seen only by the pure of heart, so also a brother's miseries are truly experienced only by one who has misery in his own heart. You will never have a real mercy for the failings of another until you know and realize that you have the same failings in your soul. When a man has been bragging that he is better than others he would feel ashamed of himself if he did not live up to his boast and show how much better than others he is....He does not so much want to be better as to be seen to be better. He is not so much concerned about leading a better life as appearing to others to do so....When a man thinks he is better than others will he not put himself before others? He must have the first place in gatherings, be the first to speak in council. He comes without being called. He interferes without being asked. He must rearrange everything, redo whatever has been done. What he himself did not do or arrange is not rightly done or properly arranged.

Has pride crept into your life and habits? Do you have an adequate or inflated opinion of yourself? Are you positioning yourself for the high place, or are you willingly and joyfully seeking the low place? You have two choices—humble yourself or face humiliation before the "king." I trust you'll choose wisely.

*Christian History Magazine, (Volume VIII, Number 4).

JUNE 26

"Do you see a man wise in his own eyes?
There is more hope for a fool than for him." — 26:12.

It was raining hard and the rental truck I was driving broke down on the Florida Turnpike. I walked to the motorist call box and then got a ride to a gas station. While waiting for a tow truck, I fought frustration, anger and even a little self pity. Here I was on a mission of mercy and this happened to me. Wrestling with these thoughts, I suddenly saw a man in a luxury car pull up in front of the rest stop restaurant. He immediately pulled into a no parking zone that was well marked with signs and bright yellow lines.

I was indignant. Here was some rich guy in a nice car violating the rules so he wouldn't get wet. But then I saw it differently. He got out of the car slowly, assisted by his wife who had run around to the driver's side. The man was crippled and walked with a cane. To make matters worse, I knew him. He was a fellow minister from my home town. How quickly my perspective changed! How ashamed I was that I had jumped to a conclusion without all the facts! I walked away without greeting them, not wanting to fully face my own stupidity.

That's how it is with someone who is wise in his own eyes. However you see a situation, it's only one perspective. You can't ever have all the facts, or enter into someone's heart to know with certainty what's there. Your judgments, opinions, and conclusions need to be tempered with the fact that you don't know for sure. Nor did God equip you to be an end in yourself, but rather to function in the body of Christ, being one member functioning among many.

Paul wrote about this to the Roman church. In Romans 12:3 he wrote, "For by the grace given to me I say to every one of you: Do not think of yourself more highly than you ought, but rather think of yourself with sober judgment, in accordance with the measure of faith God has given you." There are some things you can do well. You've been graced by God to do them. There are other things that you can't do well. You need to accept your limitations, function in your strengths, and not see yourself as a know-it-all or do-it-all.

When you do this, your assessment of a situation or, more importantly, another person will be softened. You won't be as apt to judge harshly or with an air of superiority. Knowing that you may not see it all, you'll therefore leave some room for the unknown before you pronounce your verdict.

The Bible has no use for a fool. But it says a person who is wise in his own eyes is worse than a fool! Determine today to begin walking in sober assessment of your abilities and perspective, and walk humbly in the fact that you won't ever know it all.

JUNE 27

"Anger is cruel and fury overwhelming,
but who can stand before jealousy?" — 27:4.

Every Sunday it would come over me. I would leave our small congregation and drive past the church next door. They had cars parked everywhere and had a packed house every week. I was working hard, laboring to build my church and it remained small. That other congregation didn't have (in my opinion) the spirituality, music, depth, or commitment of our church, and they were filled to overflowing.

One day as I drove by gently complaining to the Lord about this apparent inequity, I felt the word "jealousy" go across my mind. I realized that I was envious of that church. I was arrogant to compare my church to theirs, and I had a bad attitude. I also realized that I was jealous when I watched television and saw large crowds sitting under what I considered to be ministers who lacked "depth" and "content" in their preaching.

Jealousy is a cancer. It tells me that I deserve as much or more than anyone else. Jealousy doesn't rejoice in the blessing of others, but covets that blessing for personal gain. Jealousy can cause you to compare your situation to another, and then feel as if you've been treated unfairly. Envy, if left unchecked, will motivate you to build your own kingdom, and then derive your identity and security from that world.

After hearing this "word," I went to the Bible and found two verses that helped me in my battle with envy. The first is in John 3:26. John the Baptist's disciples were trying to incite him to envy when they brought this report: "Rabbi, that man who was with you on the other side of the Jordan—the one you testified about—well, he is baptizing, and everyone is going to him." His disciples were concerned that Jesus' following was bigger than theirs. John replied in verse 27, "A man can receive only what is given him from heaven." If a church is bigger than mine, it's because God gave that to them. I have no right to judge God as to how He distributes His blessings and favor.

The second is in 1 Corinthians 13:4, which states "Love is patient, love is kind. It does not envy, it does not boast, it is not proud." I was jealous because I lacked love in my life. I couldn't rejoice in my brother's good fortune, because I didn't love him. I loved myself, and that was the root of my problem.

From that time, I prayed a prayer of blessing on that church every time I drove by. I thanked the Lord for all the cars parked there, and prayed that the Lord would give them even more. The amazing thing is that I meant it when I prayed! God changed my heart, and He can change yours, too, if you're struggling with the same problem.

JUNE 28

"Blessed is the man who always fears the Lord,
but he who hardens his heart falls into trouble." — 28:14.

I have heard several messages over the years on the topic, "the fear of the Lord." One speaker told me that God doesn't want me to fear Him. The word fear creates the picture of a monster in a horror movie, or an intruder in a home. This minister reacted to that concept of fear, and instead explained that God wants us to hold Him in reverent awe. I suppose this is true to an extent. I've always felt, however, that God does want me to be afraid of Him, and that includes a healthy respect for His power to discipline me.

I was afraid of my father—in a healthy way. I didn't cower in his presence. He wasn't a mean man, nor did he ever abuse me. But I was afraid of him. I would have gotten into more trouble as a teen than I did, if I hadn't feared my father. Truthfully, he would have "killed" me if I had gone through with some things I considered. I loved him, and enjoyed being with him, but I was also afraid of his "right hook."

The same is true of the Lord. He's to be feared in the true sense of the word. Take time to read the covenant blessings and curses contained in Deuteronomy 28. There are 14 verses that outline the blessings for covenant obedience, and 54 verses explaining the curses for covenant disobedience. The curses contain some fearful things! If you have no other motivation for avoiding sin than the fear of the Lord, that's enough for now. The fear of God's discipline can keep you from trouble.

It's possible to harden your heart to this fear, and to God's ability to judge and discipline. In other words, you can get used to God. You can ignore Him, and over time your heart can grow less sensitive to His voice and will. Operating from head knowledge, your heart can be far from Him. The writer of Hebrews warns against such a heart condition. He writes, "So as the Holy Spirit says: 'Today, if you hear His voice, do not harden your hearts....' See to it, brothers, that none of you has a sinful, unbelieving heart that turns away from the living God" (Hebrews 3:7-8, 12).

This command says that your heart condition is your responsibility. You can harden it; you can also soften it. You can listen and obey, or you can listen and ignore. You can cultivate a healthy, realistic fear of the Lord, or you can treat the fear of God as an exercise in modern psychology. Once again, the choice is yours. The right choice brings blessing; the wrong choice brings trouble. Choose the fear of God, which includes a healthy respect for His "right hook."

JUNE 29

"Fear of man will prove to be a snare,
but whoever trusts in the Lord is kept safe." — 29:25.

I was dropping off Christmas packages at the local United Parcel Service office. As the line inched forward, I finally arrived at the desk where a young woman was ready to wait on me. As soon as I saw her, I sensed that the Holy Spirit was working in her life. I felt impressed to open a conversation and invite her to church.

But then my mind entered the process. She didn't physically look like she was a candidate for church. She had a tattoo, five earrings going up the outside of each ear, long hair, and a "hard" look. I was concerned about how she would react if I asked her. I was worried about the other people in line, for it would prolong their wait if we got into a long conversation. I was afraid she would tell me to get lost. In other words, my fear of man was a snare to me. I didn't do what I felt the Lord wanted me to do and I left.

It seems that every time I'm more concerned about what people think, I miss the Lord. When I trust the Lord, the results usually reflect that. I'm often too concerned about my reputation or what people are thinking of me when I am self-conscious. When I am God-conscious, however, the needs of people come first, and the Lord is in control.

There's an aspect of being led by the Holy Spirit that appears to be "foolish" to men. Preaching, praying for the sick, and giving money can "freak" some people out. Giving out tracts or personal witnessing surprises and offends some people. Paul wrote about this to the Corinthian church:

For the message of the cross is foolishness to those who are perishing....God was pleased by the foolishness of what was preached to save those who believe....For the foolishness of God is wiser than man's wisdom, and the weakness of God is stronger than man's strength (1 Corinthians 1:18, 21, 25).

The message I carry will make me look foolish at times, because the world is so messed up. The good news appears to be abnormal instead of normal, and the disciple can be seen as strange. If I'm going to carry out my mission, I can't be afraid of men and what people think of me. I must trust in the Lord, and give my reputation over to His care.

I encourage you to deliver yourself from the fear of man that has you trapped in any area of your life. It can involve your family, pastor, children, or spouse. You can be so concerned what they think of you that you're hindered in doing the will of God. Don't be arrogant and rude, but don't be intimidated either. Trust the Lord in the midst of whatever you must do, and He will prosper your way.

*"Every word of God is flawless, he is a shield to those who take refuge in him.
Do not add to his words, or he will rebuke you and prove you a liar."
— 30:5-6.*

I hear it all the time, especially among the prison population where I minister regularly. It's common for someone to say "I feel" or "it's my opinion" when interpreting and discussing a certain verse of Scripture. This especially happens when we discuss the end times and the Book of Revelation. Some of the interpretations are elaborate and farfetched, and sound more like a comic-book plot than the word of God.

In 1987, I began work on a Doctorate in Pastoral Ministries; my first course was systematic theology. While I'm no theologian, I began to see how "loosely" I had treated some Scripture verses and doctrines. I began to realize that growing in the knowledge of God and His Word didn't give me more freedom to interpret, but rather restricted me to deal with His Word more carefully and discretely.

When the serpent approached Adam and Eve in the Garden of Eden, he tempted them to do what today's verse warns us not to do. He tempted them to add to the word of God. The Lord spoke to our first parents not to eat from the tree of the knowledge of good and evil. His word was pure and good, and served as a shield to them. They could have run into His word and taken refuge.

Instead, they added to His word. They felt they saw hidden meaning in what God said and didn't say. They concluded that God didn't want them to eat because then they would be like Him. That was a fatal mistake.

Peter commented on the tendency for man to interpret the Scriptures according to his own bias and intellect: "Above all, you must understand that no prophecy of Scripture came about by the prophet's own interpretation. For prophecy never had its origin in the will of man, but men spoke from God as they were carried along by the Holy Spirit" (2 Peter 1:20-21).

If the Word wasn't given from man's perspective, neither can it be interpreted from man's perspective. The Holy Spirit who inspired the Word reserves the right to interpret, for He knows the mind of God.

The word of God is a marvelous thing, for it contains words of life. But these words only have life if they are used as God intended them to be used. Don't play "fast and loose" with God's Word by adding your own interpretations and opinions. Instead, commit yourself to live—and even be restricted by—His every word. That Word is a refuge open 24 hours a day. But it becomes no help at all if you remodel it to suit your own needs. Decide today to accept the Word for what it is and don't try to make it what you want it to be.

JULY 1

"The proverbs of Solomon son of David, king of Israel: for attaining wisdom and discipline; for understanding words of insight." —1:1-2.

I once read a statement in a book about preaching that made a significant impact on my ministry. The author said that no one should enter the pulpit until he or she is able to summarize what is to be said in one clear, concise sentence. I thought that to be impossible but began to try it when I preached. It has been difficult sometimes, but it works.

I've discovered that a one-sentence summary helps me stay focused. It makes my messages like a sharp arrow, instead of like buckshot from a shotgun. Now I can usually tell if a speaker has a summary statement, or if they are just "winging it," trying to cover as much ground as possible.

The book of Proverbs was written and compiled by Solomon and covers many different subjects. But one thing is for sure: Solomon was clear as to why he was writing the book. He had a "mission statement" for what he was doing.

You should learn to do the same. If you're serving someone, what do you hope to produce from that service? If you're speaking, what's your main point? If you're leading, what's your destination? If you're teaching, what are you trying to impart to your listeners?

Paul wrote that "we proclaim him, admonishing and teaching everyone with all wisdom, so that we may present everyone perfect in Christ" (Colossians 1:28). Paul knew his purpose when he taught: It was to form mature believers. He had a defined body of teaching that would help him accomplish that task. He wasn't just teaching as the "Spirit led," but he was instructing with some goal in mind.

Solomon was also successful because he knew why he was writing and what he wanted to produce—he desired that people grow in wisdom and insight. Thousands of years after he wrote, millions of believers read one chapter of Proverbs every day.

Ask yourself today why you're doing what you're doing. What's your purpose? Where are you going? If you aim at nothing, you're sure to hit it. Get more focused in your work, household, and ministry. It would be good discipline if you could summarize what you do in one simple statement. If that isn't clear to you, it won't be clear to other people. Follow in Solomon's footsteps, and maybe what you do will affect people 3,000 years later! Refuse to be focused, and you'll be fortunate if your work remains standing the next day.

JULY 2

"For wisdom will enter your heart, and knowledge will be pleasant to your soul." —2:10.

In college, I disliked philosophy classes. We would sit around and discuss what knowledge was, how we knew that we existed, and other similar issues of questionable importance. It was boring, and a lot of words were used to say very little. To me, it wasn't important what knowledge was; it was only important that I could learn. I didn't want to understand my existence; I was just glad I existed.

While I was still in college, I met the Lord and was immediately impressed with the practicality of the Gospel message. I soon saw that it was directed at making me a better son, husband, father, worker, and brother. I later saw that godly wisdom wasn't a philosophical discussion about life, but practical knowledge applied to real-life issues.

The main difference between philosophy and Christianity is the person of Jesus Christ. Jesus doesn't *have* wisdom—He *is* wisdom. Paul wrote that Jesus "has become for us the wisdom of God" (1 Corinthians 1:30). Today's verse tells you that wisdom enters your heart. That happens because the life of Christ is formed in you by the power of the Holy Spirit. That life isn't primarily to tickle your intellect, but to give you power to live a godly life. In the Middle Ages, Christianity made a shift to intellectual pursuits. It was believed that man could come to know God through his ability to reason. But this wasn't the tradition of the early church.

Paul wrote to Colossae,

My purpose is that they may be encouraged in heart and united in love, so that they may have the full riches of complete understanding, in order that they may know the mystery of God, namely, Christ, in whom are hidden all the treasures of wisdom and knowledge (Colossians 2:2-3).

The treasures of wisdom are hidden in Christ. You must find them not to become smart, but to be encouraged and strengthened to do His will. Paul wasn't a philosopher or a theologian. He was a church planter and pastor who applied God's wisdom to marriage, work, slavery, and other issues of the day. I like Paul; I still don't care for philosophy.

When you seek wisdom, you're not seeking an abstract thing; you're seeking Jesus. You're not seeking a body of truth; you're seeking the living Christ. And you're not seeking something outside of yourself; you're seeking the wisdom hidden in the Christ who lives in you by the Spirit.

Are you growing in wisdom? Is knowledge pleasant to your soul? Doctrine is good, but doctrine that leads to good deeds is better. Don't only seek a deeper intellectual knowledge of your faith. Seek also a deeper knowledge that leads to action. Don't be a philosopher; but be conformed to the image of Christ, the doer.

JULY 3

"Her ways are pleasant ways, and all her paths are peace." — 3:17.

I do a lot of one-on-one counseling. I keep a box of tissue handy, for often those who come end up in tears. I have heard it all in the counseling room—broken marriages, problems with children, sexual sins, bankruptcies, mental disorders, and terminal illness. I've listened to so many sad stories, and have come to know that "the way of transgressors is hard." Even though this is true, however, many have left the counseling room ignoring the counsel of godly wisdom to continue on the hard road of the transgressor.

Maturity is learning that God's ways really are the best ways. They may seem at the outset to be more difficult or troublesome. But in the long run, His ways are pleasant and bring peace, something which I'm sure you can use more of.

"Come to me, all you who are weary and burdened, and I will give you rest. Take my yoke upon you and learn from me, for I am gentle and humble in heart, and you will find rest for your souls. For my yoke is easy and my burden is light" (Matthew 11:28-30).

Jesus said His yoke is easy. When I'm burdened, tired, and anxious, I must ask what or whose yoke I am carrying, for it's certainly not Jesus' "easy" yoke.

The Lord is gently commanding you to get into His yoke. That is the appeal I also try to make in the counseling room. Yes, the yoke is restrictive, and you aren't free to go in the direction that you want. And yes, the yoke will rub you when you try to go off in your own direction. Jesus asks you to trade your burdens, which are heavy, for His burden, which is light. That's a good deal, but one that isn't easily transacted.

Are you ready for a trade-in? Are you prepared to trade the yoke you now walk in for Jesus' yoke? Are you ready to trade anxiety for peace? turmoil for rest? worry for faith? a heavy load for a light one? weariness for refreshment? Are you prepared to walk paths that are pleasant as opposed to dangerous? Are you ready to learn from Jesus?

The Lord is not a harsh taskmaster. He knows that you were not made to carry the load of sin and guilt that you sometimes do. He wants to relieve you of those burdens, but you must choose to allow Him to do so. Choose the correct road today and take on Jesus' yoke. In time, you'll learn from Him, and know joy and peace like never before.

JULY 4

"For they are life to those who find them
and health to a man's whole body." — 4:22.

My wife, Kathy, called me with the report from her doctor. She had been diagnosed as having a large cyst on her ovary. The doctor was very concerned and wanted to examine her again in two weeks to see how quickly it was growing. He also wanted to do more tests.

When Kathy called me, we immediately prayed. Together we "rejected" that cyst and refused to accept it. We weren't denying it was there, nor were we blindly ignoring what the doctor said. In the strongest terms, however, we declared that cyst to be an enemy. We were going to fight it with everything we had.

Kathy eliminated all caffeine from her diet. As we fasted and prayed, we spoke to that cyst like it had a life of its own, and cursed it, commanding it to dry up. We played Christian music to "fill" Kathy's body with godly sounds. We also asked people to pray with us against it.

When Kathy returned to the doctor, he was amazed. The cyst was gone! He was so delighted, and then told us how concerned he had been about its size. We went away rejoicing, and thanking God for His care. That cyst has never returned.

The Lord is not indifferent about your body, nor does He view it as insignificant. Jesus spent much of His ministry healing the sick. He showed that salvation and healing were closely related, and that health was a high priority for Him.

When an "evil" report comes to you about your health, don't be so ready to receive it passively. Think of it as a delivery man coming to your door with a package. He would ask you to sign for it and accept it into your home. But if he first told you the package contained cancer, arthritis, or tendinitis, would you accept it? You would undoubtedly send him away.

That is how it should be with sickness. Don't make peace with every bad report. If one comes, fight it, refusing to sign for the package. You shouldn't deny reality, but don't passively accept it either. Treat sickness as the enemy and intruder that it is. Make its life miserable by praying, singing, rejoicing, and cursing it in Jesus' name. Death and the symptoms of death are your last enemy. Don't make peace with them.

Should the Lord tarry, you and I will eventually die. But in the meantime, I will fight that enemy death and its agents as long as I live. In fact, I hope to die fighting. I want to die with faith in the Lord's commandments that bring health, and eventually resurrection life, to my body. In that spirit, I want to meet the Lord. My doctor doesn't have the last say; my God does. I'm glad to be in such good hands.

JULY 5

"For a man's ways are in full view of the Lord,
and he examines all his paths." —5:21.

When I was a young child, my parents would come to check on me after I had gone to bed. If I wasn't asleep, I would squeeze my eyes tight because I thought they couldn't see me if I couldn't see them! I wondered how they always knew that I was still awake.

I've tried the same routine with the Lord. I've tried to hide from Him and His scrutiny, only to find that He is intimately acquainted with all my ways! The psalmist wrote, "Where can I go from your Spirit? Where can I flee from your presence?" (Psalm 139:7).

Adam and Eve also tried to hide. They sewed together fig leaves to hide their nakedness. You might be laughing at how foolish that was, but do you do the same thing? Do you tie together the fig leaves of excuses or shift the blame to cover your failures? Are you trying to convince the Lord what your motives were for doing what you did? That doesn't work any more than closing my eyes did when my parents came into my bedroom.

Hebrews 4:13 states, "Nothing in all creation is hidden from God's sight. Everything is uncovered and laid bare before the eyes of him to whom we must give an account." That's a scary verse. I must give an account to Him who knows all things. There will be no room for exaggeration. I won't be able to blame anyone else or conveniently forget part of the story. Nothing is hidden from God's sight and I will give account to one who knows all things.

Paul gave instructions consistent with God's ability to see it all. He wrote,

The hour has come for you to wake up from your slumber, because our salvation is nearer now than when we first believed. The night is nearly over; the day is almost here. So let us put aside the deeds of darkness and put on the armor of light. Let us behave decently, as in the daytime, not in orgies and drunkenness, not in sexual immorality and debauchery, not in dissension and jealousy. Rather, clothe yourselves with the Lord Jesus Christ (Romans 13:12-14).

I'm not surprised that Paul wrote about sexual immorality, but I am surprised that dissension and jealousy made his list of "no-no's." God will examine not only our deeds but our heart condition as well. Act today as a disciple whose paths are in full view of the Lord. Remember that you must give an accurate account to Him who is watching. Your account is not for His benefit, for He already knows what you have done and why you did it. Your account is for your benefit to provide incentive to walk the right road. Happy trails to you as you walk the path of life today. The eyes of God are upon you.

JULY 6

"There are six things the Lord hates, seven that are detestable to him: ...a man who stirs up dissension among brothers." — 6:16,19.

I was conducting a prison Bible study a few months ago, and the men were asking questions. The issue of cigarette smoking and salvation came up, and the discussion got rather heated. In fact, for a moment I thought I would have to call in the guards to calm things down! How ironic, I thought, that we would be discussing the Bible, the book about God's love, and almost come to blows with one another!

That problem isn't unique to the prison world. The spirit of "fighting fundamentalism" has permeated the entire Church. You see it on television, hear it from the pulpit, and pick it up in conversations with other believers. It seems that some believe the more Bible you know, the more argumentative you should be. This is not the spirit of Christ. While Jesus debated His religious opponents, the majority of His ministry was spent ministering to the needs of people. He wasn't looking for a fight, but He didn't run from one when confronted.

Today's verse is a pretty clear statement that the Lord hates dissension among the brothers. He isn't honored or pleased when there are needless divisions in His body, which is to be united in love and faith. You're to work for unity, not disunity. You're to spend your energies on harmony, not discord. It's not a sign of spiritual maturity to pick someone apart; it's a sign of maturity to cover faults in love.

The most impressive example of this is a story we looked at a few months ago—the account of Joseph's engagement to Mary. Imagine Joseph's excitement as he and Mary planned their future together. He was a young man and his life was before him. That life included Mary, the woman he loved, and his excitement must have been great.

Then came the shocking news that Mary was pregnant! Joseph must have been devastated as his whole world suddenly was shaken. They had talked, dreamed and planned, and this was not supposed to happen. He was faced with several options, all of which were painful to him and embarrassing to Mary.

Matthew tells us that "because Joseph her husband was a righteous man and did not want to expose her to public disgrace, he had in mind to divorce her quietly" (Matthew 1:19). May the spirit of Joseph come on the Church! May you and I learn to treat brothers and sisters like Joseph treated Mary. God intervened and prevented Joseph from doing the wrong thing because Joseph's heart was right toward Mary who he thought had offended him. He sought to address it quietly, and God honored his ill-informed but godly response.

God hates dissension. Vow to be a source of unity and not division. Seek to bring healing to the body. Don't rejoice in open division, but rather work toward public harmony. If God hates dissension, He must love unity. You must learn to love it, too.

JULY 7

"Say to wisdom, 'You are my sister,'
and call understanding your kinsman." — 7:4.

When I enter a jail to minister, I always ask how many were believers before they were arrested. Often more than half the hands go up. That has always surprised me, for I thought that most would have met the Lord after they got in. The majority, however, went to church on the "outside" and can point to a day when they surrendered their heart to Jesus.

Like those inmates, many people have responded to an altar call, closed their eyes, and repeated the sinner's prayer—and then went back to their world, unchanged and unaffected by what they had just done. They "got saved," but it didn't affect their lives. They didn't realize—and too often no one told them—that they would have to "continue to work out [their] salvation with fear and trembling" (Philippians 2:12).

Once you become a disciple of Jesus, there's much work to do. You must learn about the Lord—His Word and will. You must seek His wisdom and forsake all other ways of life. It's interesting that the book of Proverbs refers to godly wisdom with feminine pronouns. "She" is to be esteemed and honored, and treated like one of the family. "She" isn't to be abused or ignored, but is to be treated with respect. In fact, today's verse tells you to treat wisdom like your sister.

Godly wisdom, it goes on to say in today's chapter, will keep you from the adulteress. Think of the adulteress as anything or anyone that takes the place in your life meant only for God. You have two options. The first is to cultivate a close relationship with wisdom; the second is to ignore wisdom and cultivate an "adulterous" relationship with someone or something else.

Our media is filled with reports of "saved" men and women who didn't treat wisdom like a sister. They went on to enter an "adulterous" relationship with money, fame, or another person. Our jails are full of people who did the same thing.

You must spend time with wisdom, your "sister," or risk going astray. Salvation or going to church aren't enough; those are just the beginning. Treat God's wisdom like family and make it an integral part of your life. The Lord wants to have input into every area of your life. Salvation isn't an insurance policy you purchase for the day you die. It's rather the first step in a life yielded to God.

Have you given your life to the Lord, yet rejected the study of His Word? Do you boast of salvation only to fail consistently at carrying that salvation into every area of your life? Is Jesus Lord of every area of your life? Examine yourself today, and then welcome God and His commandments as family.

JULY 8

"To fear the Lord is to hate evil;
I hate pride and arrogance." — 8:13.

I was furious and heard myself speaking in loud tones. I asked the inmate to leave my Bible study and hoped that he would never return. You see, this man had big problems in his life. He was loud, argumentative, rude, and opinionated. He would constantly ask questions and then argue with my answers. I had determined to win him to the Lord and be patient, but finally my patience had run out.

During this session I said something and he exploded in anger. He disagreed so vehemently that I angrily asked him to leave. I was so angry because I felt I had given him a lot of grace, and he rewarded my kindness by ruining my Bible study. The chaplain insisted he be allowed back into the class, but I angrily told the chaplain I didn't care if he ever came back.

My anger continued for days! I was so upset I could hardly even pray about it. I finally I took it to the Lord in prayer, and I sensed the Lord asking me one question: "Son, do you think you are smarter than he?" Of course I did, and that was the root of my problem.

I had let pride creep into my Bible study—and into me. I enjoyed being in front of the men and answering their questions. I liked how they admired me for my answers. Through this man's behavior, however, I came to see how arrogant my actions were. I had reacted to him out of pride, and that put me in a vulnerable position.

Jesus taught extensively on the need to resist pride and embrace humility. In Luke 18:9-14, He gave a parable concerning the two:

> To some who were confident of their own righteousness and looked down on everybody else, Jesus told this parable: "Two men went up to the temple to pray, one a Pharisee and the other a tax collector. The Pharisee stood up and prayed about himself: 'God I thank you that I am not like other men—robbers, evildoers, adulterers—or even like this tax collector. I fast twice a week and give a tenth of all I get.' But the tax collector stood at a distance. He would not even look up to heaven, but beat his breast and said, 'God, have mercy on me, a sinner.' I tell you that this man, rather than the other, went home justified before God. For everyone who exalts himself will be humbled, and he who humbles himself will be exalted."

I was confident in my own righteousness as I conducted this Bible study. This parable reminded me that it isn't wise to be proud or to compare myself to another. James wrote, "God opposes the proud but gives grace to the humble" (James 4:6). God opposes pride wherever and in whomever He finds it. If He finds it in your work, home, ministry, athletic ability, or possessions, He will oppose it. Examine yourself today and ask the Lord to show you any pride in your life. Then humble yourself and allow God to work with you, and not against you, once again.

JULY 9

"Wisdom has built her house;
she has hewn out its seven pillars." — 9:1.

I'm the first to admit that I'm no good at mechanical things. In fact, while I pastored in Alabama, my congregation embarked on a building project. The members and pastors volunteered their time to work on the facility to save money. When I arrived to work, the foreman usually handed me a broom and told me to stay out of the way.

I may not be able to use a hammer, but God has still called me to build spiritual things. Today's verse shows that godly wisdom is always building something. It provides a place for people to live and a shelter from the storm. The shelter that wisdom builds is secure, since it's supported by "seven pillars." I don't know what those pillars are, but they hold up what wisdom builds, and that makes it a secure place in which to dwell.

Jesus spoke to this tendency for all people to build something in the following parable:

> Therefore everyone who hears these words of mine and puts them into practice is like a wise man who built his house on the rock. The rain came down, the streams rose, and the winds blew and beat against that house; yet it did not fall, because it had its foundation on the rock. But everyone who hears these words of mine and does not put them into practice is like a foolish man who built his house on sand. The rain came down, the streams rose, the winds blew and beat against that house, and it fell with a great crash (Matthew 7:24-27)

Jesus is saying that there are two certain things in life. The first is that you'll build in your lifetime either according to or ignoring His word. The second is that storms, rain, and wind will come to test how well you have built. If you built by doing what Jesus and wisdom told you, your building will stand. If you chose to build according to your own design, the house will fall with a great crash.

Today's chapter begs you to build according to wisdom. Listen to the words of wisdom and you'll have something that lasts. Build according to the latest fad or modern theory and the storms of life will tear down what you build. You can build it well, but if your house isn't on the proper foundation, it will come down.

Check your foundation today. If you're building on sand, it isn't too late to start over. If you're building on rock—the Rock Jesus—the storms will buffet, but won't destroy. Listen to godly wisdom and let her pillars support your structure. It's the only safe place to live.

JULY 10

*"When the storm has swept by, the wicked are gone,
but the righteous stand firm forever." — 10:25.*

When I first met the Lord, I thought I had found a solution to all life's problems. I don't know where I got one particular notion from, but I assumed that since I was now a believer, I would never have car problems again. In my immature understanding, I was convinced that nothing I considered "bad" would every befall me again. The Lord was going to be my insurance policy against such difficulties. It didn't take me long to find how wrong I was.

Yesterday you read the parable of the storms coming against the house. Jesus didn't say *if* the storms come; He said *when* they come. The storms—and flat tires—will indeed come, and they'll distinguish between those who endure in the Lord and those who do not.

The Apostle Paul had storms in his life. He was persecuted, beaten, criticized, and falsely accused. He survived actual storms at sea and in his personal life and ministry. One look at 2 Corinthians 6:4-10 tells you something about Paul's storms.

Rather, as servants of God we commend ourselves in every way: in great endurance; in troubles, hardships and distresses; in beatings, imprisonments and riots; in hard work, sleepless nights and hunger; in purity, understanding, patience and kindness; in the Holy Spirit and in sincere love; in truthful speech and in the power of God; with weapons of righteousness in the right hand and in the left; through glory and dishonor, bad report and good report; genuine, yet regarded as impostors; known, yet regarded as unknown; dying, and yet we live on; beaten, and yet not killed; sorrowful, yet always rejoicing; poor, yet making many rich; having nothing, and yet possessing everything.

Paul's ministry didn't exempt him from storms. In fact, his ministry seemed to attract them like metal filings to a magnet. After the storms passed through, however, Paul was still standing. A hireling or one less committed would have retired, but Paul stood strong as an oak tree in the midst of incredible pressure.

Don't be surprised at the winds that are blowing in your life. They are sent to test you and prove the strength of your calling and commitment. I've survived the car problems I thought I would never have, and a whole lot more, since I became a believer. I have lived through storms that would have blown me away years ago. The Lord was faithful, however, and I found myself standing after they had passed through.

Don't go looking for a storm, but if one has come into your life, be assured that it will pass. Long after it is gone, you will remember the Lord's faithfulness that allowed you to stand firm.

JULY 11

"One man gives freely, yet gains even more;
another withholds unduly, but comes to poverty." —11:24.

I was in an early morning prayer meeting, which my church had held daily for the previous two weeks. We had been praying for a number of things, including a financial breakthrough. The church's finances, along with my own and others, had been lean. As we were praying, a word came through one of the brothers that today we would see our situation change. The only problem was that today was July 4.

The banks weren't open and I thought that nothing financial could happen today. To my surprise, however, something did. By the end of the day, money and other unexpected blessings had arrived. We prayed a few more days, but soon ended the prayer times, for our barns were filled to overflowing!

All during our lean time, I had given unto the Lord. I had tithed on what little I had received. I had come to learn that hard times didn't exempt me from giving my ten percent to the Lord. While some have felt that the tithe belongs to the old covenant, I have always felt the opposite. The tithe is the minimum standard of giving in the new covenant and is still the means by which we practically express our faith in God to provide for us.

The words of Malachi still apply to you and me. He wrote:

"Will a man rob God? Yet you rob me. But you ask, 'How do we rob you?' In tithes and offerings. You are under a curse—the whole nation of you—because you are robbing me. Bring the whole tithe into the storehouse, that there may be food in my house." "Test me in this," says the Lord Almighty, "and see if I will not throw open the floodgates of heaven and pour out so much blessing that you will not have room enough for it. I will prevent pests from devouring your crops, and the vines in your fields will not cast their fruit," says the Lord Almighty (Malachi 3:8-11).

The New Testament says little about the tithe because it was such an accepted practice. There was no need to teach on something that everyone agreed on. Even Jesus, when he was rebuking the Pharisees for tithing on the herbs of their garden while neglecting the weightier matters of the Law, said "You should have practiced the latter [weightier matters], without neglecting the former [tithing]" (Matthew 23:23).

It's a form of worship to honor the Lord with your money and wealth, so don't neglect Him in hard times Don't retreat in difficult times and withhold unduly. Remember the tithe, honor Him, and you will actually gain from your giving, even in a time of lack.

JULY 12

"He who works his land will have abundant food,
but he who chases fantasies lacks judgment." — 12:11.

In 1982, I was in a fantasy world, having joined some men and brothers in what we planned to be a business venture—a "Christian" venture. We started with grand plans, but ended in failure. We were going to provide jobs for believers, and instead lost our own. We were going to give to missions, and instead came into need ourselves. What went wrong?

In spite of my noble plans, the business world was and still is a fantasy for me. It isn't where the Lord has called me. He wants to give me through a ministry what I wanted to get from a business. Seeing this company as a golden goose, I lacked judgment and ended up in poverty when my goal had been prosperity!

Today's verse alludes to the fact that you've been given a plot of land from the Lord. You must work, cultivate, subdue, and harvest it. If you accept that land and are faithful, you'll prosper and have plenty of food, as today's verse tells you. If you covet another field that the Lord has not chosen for you and try to work it, you'll have a difficult time.

Consider Abraham and Lot. When it came time for them to part, for their herdsmen were not getting along with one another, Abraham let Lot choose where he wanted to go. In Genesis 13:10-11, it says, "Lot looked up and saw that the whole plain of the Jordan was well watered, like the garden of the Lord....So Lot chose for himself the whole plain of the Jordan and set out toward the east."

Lot chose according to what looked good. Perhaps he had always wanted land like that which he saw. The only problem with his choice was that it took him to the gates of Sodom and Gomorrah. His choice cost him his wife (who was turned into a pillar of salt as they fled Sodom's destruction) and later his daughters (who also chose poorly and had children by their father).

Abraham, on the other hand, worked the land that Lot didn't take and the Lord blessed him. He walked in faith and faithfulness, and had plenty of food. Knowing that the Lord would bless him no matter what the land looked like, he only had to work where the Lord wanted him, and his provision would be secure.

Are you struggling with what field to work in? Don't walk by sight or by what looks best for you. Choose according to the will of God. Your field may seem small or incapable of supporting you, but that's not the issue. The issue is your faith in God who chose the field for you. Give yourself to your plot of land and you'll succeed; choose your own plot and you'll fail. Get out your shovel and start working your field today. Your success in life depends on it.

JULY 13

"He who walks with the wise grows wise,
but a companion of fools suffers harm." — *13:20.*

Experience is the best teacher, or so the saying goes. But in reality, it isn't always the best way to learn. The best way to learn is to find someone who has gone through it and learn from them! Why make the same painful mistakes that someone else has already made?

Discipleship—or "mentoring" as it is known in the secular world—was the means to train new believers in the early church. Converts were called disciples, and walked for a season with those who were more experienced in the ways of the Lord. In some sense, a believer is always a disciple of the Lord, learning from Him. There's also a practical, "earthly" side of discipleship that is all but lost in the church today.

Saul was Gamaliel's disciple and learned Pharasaism from him. When he was duly trained, he was released to his own ministry. After Saul became a believer, he kept this concept and trained Timothy, Titus, and others. He didn't throw out this student/teacher relationship because the Holy Spirit was now involved. Paul knew the value of this relationship and continued it in the early Church.

In Paul's last epistle, he wrote Timothy to continue this discipling process. "The things you have heard me say in the presence of many witnesses entrust to reliable men who will also be qualified to teach others" (2 Timothy 2:2). Paul wanted Timothy to train men just like Paul had trained him. He knew leaders wouldn't just emerge in the Church. They would come out of a close relationship between teachers and students.

You can't be a disciple solely by reading or attending church. You will learn that way, but you won't be fully developed. In all probability, you'll avoid dealing with some issues in your life and your blind spots will keep you from yielding some things to God's scrutiny. You'll tend to keep your idiosyncrasies, and they can detract from what the Lord wants to make you.

I encourage you to walk with the wise as today's verse also urges you to do. Spend time with older, more experienced saints who can impart life's wisdom to you. Don't repeat the mistakes of the past but learn from those who have already made them. Find men or women who are willing to impart their lives to you and seek their advice and counsel. Your work, marriage, family, and walk will benefit from that relationship. It matters with whom you spend your time, so spend it where you will get the greatest return.

JULY 14

"A simple man believes anything,
but a prudent man gives thought to his steps." — 14:15.

Not long after I was saved, I read Exodus 15:26: "If you listen carefully to the voice of the Lord your God and do what is right in his eyes, if you pay attention to his commands and keep all his decrees, I will not bring on you any of the diseases I brought on the Egyptians, for I am the Lord, who heals you." I read that before my wife and I had children, and in my mind I equated measles, chicken pox, and mumps with the diseases of Egypt. I thought about this for a while, and then decided that this promise was for me and my family.

My children are now in their teens, and have never had any of those diseases. God has given us faith for this promise, and it has come to pass. I didn't have to "work up" the faith or claim it repeatedly. This promise was something I considered over time, and accepted it after meditation and thought. You might say that I saw it, chewed, swallowed, and digested it.

That's how faith is. It isn't emotional, although it involves the emotions. It isn't an exercise of the will, but it is a choice. It isn't super spiritual, for it is within reach of all mankind. Faith is a quiet confidence in God and His word.

"Now faith is being sure of what we hope for and certain of what we do not see" (Hebrews 11:1). There's a process that helps you become sure of what God promises. You've heard people claiming, in faith, all kinds of things—healing, financial blessings, salvation for loved ones, and possessions. They've seen something, or heard someone else's testimony and decided to make that promise their own. I've counseled many whose faith was "shipwrecked" after they didn't receive what they had been claiming.

I have always appreciated the father who brought his son to Jesus for healing. In Mark 9:23 Jesus tells the father, "Everything is possible for him who believes." In verse 24 "The boy's father exclaimed, 'I do believe; help me overcome my unbelief.'" He believed, but also considered his steps and knew he had some unbelief. Yet his unbelief didn't keep his son from being healed. He didn't try to be something he wasn't, and he admitted his lack of faith to Jesus. The good news is that Jesus accepted him where he was and healed his boy.

Be honest with God and don't confess something you don't believe. Don't launch out in faith, only to find you are in presumption. Give thought to the promises of God and let them become real to you. Don't try to use your faith to manipulate God, but use your faith to discover His purpose for you. When you are convinced, you won't have to give yourself a pep talk. You'll have an inner strength that comes from trusting in the Rock of your salvation.

"A man finds joy in giving an apt reply—
and how good is a timely word." — 15:23.

I had just hung up the phone with a man in the church who had lost his job and was unable to find another. His finances were tight, and his electricity was about to be shut off. I told him I would bring a check to his wife's place of employment to help them out. That was a timely word for him, and it brought him great joy.

To receive a timely word is a great thing, and can save your life. The Apostle Paul wrote, however, that it is "better to give than receive." Paul, instructing the Corinthian church concerning their public meetings, said, "When you come together, everyone has a hymn, or a word of instruction, a revelation, a tongue or an interpretation. All of these must be done for the strengthening of the church" (1 Corinthians 14:26). The writer of Hebrews wrote that believers should "encourage one another daily" (Hebrews 3:13).

Barnabas was a man who was always ready to give an apt word. In fact, his name literally meant "Son of Encouragement" (Acts 4:36). His ministry was to encourage and strengthen the saints. By being sensitive to people and their needs, he could deliver the right word into their situation.

Barnabas is first mentioned in Acts 4 for selling a piece of property and giving it to the apostles for the needs of the brethren. He was an encouragement as he gave. He is next mentioned in Acts 9 where he brought Saul before the believers and testified of Saul's conversion. This helped the Jerusalem church to accept Saul, whom they had been resisting. The Lord used him to open the doors for those called into the ministry.

In Acts 13, the Holy Spirit chose Saul and Barnabas to start Gentile churches. The Spirit used this encourager as a pioneer to people not yet touched by the Gospel. Later, Saul and Barnabas parted ways after a dispute over John Mark, who was Barnabas' cousin. Barnabas probably was willing to overlook Mark's weaknesses to keep him on the ministry team. To the end, Barnabas was an encourager, able to see the potential in everyone and working to help strengthen the people of God.

You can't give a timely word unless you are listening to the Holy Spirit. The Spirit knows where people truly are, and can tell you, if you are interested. You also can't encourage if you are looking for encouragement yourself, for your focus then is not outward but inward.

Ask the Spirit to show you who you can encourage today. Look for someone who needs a timely word, someone loaded down with life, and then lighten their load. Find your joy not in receiving a word, but giving one. Seek the ministry that Barnabas had—the ministry of encouragement—and God will use you to no end.

JULY 16

"A wise man's heart guides his mouth,
and his lips promote instruction." — 16:23.

Your heart, not your brain, is your communication center. Jesus was clear about this when He addressed the Pharisees in Mark 7:6-7: "Isaiah was right when he prophesied about you hypocrites; as it is written: 'These people honor me with their lips, but their hearts are far from me. They worship me in vain.'"

Later when His disciples questioned Him about this, He replied,

Don't you see that nothing that enters a man from the outside can make him "unclean"? For it doesn't go into his heart but into his stomach, and then out of his body....What comes out of a man is what makes him unclean. For from within, out of men's hearts, come evil thoughts, sexual immorality, theft, murder, adultery, greed, malice, deceit, lewdness, envy, slander, arrogance and folly (Mark 7:18-22).

It's your heart where sin originates—not just "big" sins like theft, adultery, or murder but also "little" sins like envy, slander, and foolishness. It's the heart that is "deceitful above all things and beyond cure" (Jeremiah 17:9). It's the heart that guides your lips, for Jesus said in Matthew 12:34, "For out of the overflow of the heart the mouth speaks."

It's critical that you fill your heart with good things if you want to be able to answer according to the need of the moment. You can memorize *what* to say, but if your heart isn't right, it won't help you know *when* to say it.

The first step toward a heart that can guide your lips is honesty with God. The temptation is to tell the Lord what you think He wants to hear instead of the truth. God "desire[s] truth in the inner parts" (Psalm 51:6). Be truthful with Him. If you're sad, tell Him. If you're jealous, angry, or bitter, confess it to Him, for He already knows what is there. If He were going to "punish" you, He would already have done so.

The truth isn't for His benefit, it's for yours. Recognizing the truth of what's in your heart is the first step to getting rid of it. Hiding it is folly, for eventually it will come out anyway as the overflow of your heart pushes it out into the open, usually through what you say.

Seek a clean heart. Weed out the bad, and replace it with the good things of the Lord. Let the overflow of your heart be love, joy, kindness, and mercy. If your mouth is guided by those things, you'll be known for gracious speech. You'll promote instruction since people will want to hear from you. Don't hide your heart from the Lord because He already knows what's there. Clean it up, and watch your ability to speak improve.

JULY 17

"The crucible for silver and the furnace for gold,
but the Lord tests the heart." — 17:3.

I became a believer in 1973. The morning after my salvation, I awakened to a startling presence in my bedroom. I knew someone was there, and I heard the Lord speak to my heart. He told me I would leave the church I was attending, go into full-time ministry, and give my life to His service. Based on what I had sensed since I was young, I knew that this service was to be a pastor.

I went into ministry in 1978 as the youngest of a 20-man church staff. For 11 years I served on almost every committee there was. I was church administrator, public relations director, and associate pastor. During those 11 years, I only preached twice. There were times I felt like I was watching the baggage as the others went off to war. I knew I was to be a pastor, but what I was doing wasn't fulfilling that call.

The Lord was testing me during those 11 years, training and delivering me from ambition and conceit. The word *test* refers to the process of "testing" precious metals. Silver and gold ore are submitted to intense heat to purify them. As they are heated and become molten, the impurities rise to the top where they can easily be skimmed off. The Lord turned the heat up on me, and certainly found plenty of impurities to remove. In 1989, 16 years after my "call," I came to Orlando to pastor a church. By then my exuberance, pride, and arrogance had been burned off, and my testing, while not finished, was far enough along that the Lord could use me.

During those 16 years of testing, I always found great comfort in the story of Joseph who had a dream from the Lord that his brothers would bow down to him. He knew he was destined for greatness. But before that happened he had to go through the testing process. He was sold into slavery by his brothers. The Lord then

> Called for a famine upon the land; He broke the whole staff of bread. He sent a man before them, Joseph, who was sold as a slave. They afflicted his feet with fetters, he himself was laid in irons, until the time that his word came to pass, the word of the Lord tested him" (Psalm 105:16-19 NAS).

Joseph received his word but instead of it coming to pass immediately, he found himself in prison and chains! Why? So that he could be tested and purified for God's use. Eventually, he became the second most powerful man in the world! His family did bow down to him, and he spent many years in fruitful service. He came to appreciate his testing, for he told his brothers when it was all over, "You intended it to harm me, but God intended it for good to accomplish what is now being done, the saving of many lives" (Genesis 50:20).

Your testing isn't designed to harm you, but to prepare you. Don't faint and don't be surprised at the fiery ordeal you are in. The greater your destiny, the greater the preparation or testing process. One day you'll be grateful for what it did.

JULY 18

*"A poor man pleads for mercy,
but a rich man answers roughly." — 18:23.*

My son had just messed up, doing something dumb and getting into trouble at school. I listened to the principal's report, barely able to contain my anger. I began to question my son and found he had no excuse for what he had done. I was about to "lower the boom" on him, but decided instead to have mercy. We talked, I disciplined him, but I didn't raise my voice (or at least I don't think I did).

The next day I messed up, responding to someone in a way that wasn't proper. They smiled at me, went on with the conversation, and overlooked my blunder. As I was praying, the Lord showed me that, had I not responded in mercy to my son, the person would not have responded graciously to me. I had reaped what I had sown!

A rough response to another person usually comes from feeling like you have it all together in that area. How could they have been so dumb? You watch the news and wonder how someone could have been so foolish to do what they did. Your memory may be too short to recall how you too have done foolish things, and how fortunate you were that the cameras or reporters weren't there when you did.

It would be good to keep in mind that you are a priest, ministering to the Lord and to others on His behalf. The writer of Hebrews wrote.

Every high priest is selected from among men and is appointed to represent them in matters related to God, to offer gifts and sacrifices for sins. He is able to deal gently with those who are ignorant and are going astray, since he himself is subject to weakness. This is why he has to offer sacrifices for his own sins, as well as for the sins of the people (Hebrews 5:1-3).

For a priest to answer roughly is for that priest to forget that he too is beset with weakness. As today's verses states, the rich—those who feel that they are above failure or sin—will give a sharp response. The poor—those who know and have experienced their own failure—will extend mercy because they know they have needed and will need mercy.

Paul instructed, "If someone is caught in a sin, you who are spiritual should restore him gently. But watch yourself, or you also may be tempted" (Galatians 6:1). Paul wants those who "restore" to do so with care, for they aren't above problems themselves.

Do you answer roughly or with mercy? Do you minister from a position of superiority or with a knowledge of your own weakness? Do you have a critical spirit? Then remember from where you have come, and be mindful of what you are still capable of doing. If you do that, you will minister gently and the words of your mouth will bring healing and not condemnation.

JULY 19

"It is not good to have zeal without knowledge,
nor to be hasty and miss the way." — 19:2.

Jesus and Peter offer two contrasts in the study of zeal. Both were passionate men who did what they had to do with all their heart. But Peter's zeal was without knowledge and often reckless, while Jesus' zeal accomplished the will of God on every occasion. Sincerity isn't enough when you're doing the will of God, for you can be sincere and still miss His will.

Consider Peter first. In Matthew 16:22, he rebuked Jesus for talking about the cross! Peter was so excited and zealous after his revelation of who Jesus was that he presumed to teach Jesus about other aspects of His ministry. Peter's zeal had gotten him into trouble, and Jesus sharply rebuked him for his presumption

Shortly after that, Jesus took Peter with Him to the mountain where Jesus' transfiguration occurred. This time Peter took it upon himself to speak when Elijah and Moses appeared. What could Peter possible add to a meeting where Jesus, Moses, and Elijah were conversing! His zeal was great, however, and he spoke sincerely but hastily. The Father's voice interrupted Peter and said, "This is my Son, whom I love; with Him I am well pleased. Listen to Him!" (Matthew 17:5).

Finally, Peter was asked by the temple collectors whether Jesus paid the temple tax. Peter zealously and confidently replied that He did. When he returned to Jesus, the Lord helped him understand that the Son does not have to pay the tax. The Lord then sent Peter to catch a fish that had the amount of the temple tax in its mouth! (see Matthew 17:24-27).

Jesus, on the other hand, combined zeal and knowledge. He was never hasty, but instead waited to know what the will of God was, and then He launched out in the power of godly zeal. For example, Jesus beheld that woeful situation at the temple for years, yet He didn't drive out the money changers until the visit before His death. A zealous show of force before that perhaps could have caused the crowds to rally to His support and make Him king. Instead He waited and in the right hour moved with zeal.

Psalm 69:9 says, "Zeal for your house consumes me." Jesus' zeal for God led Him to the cross. Jesus wasn't consumed with careless, unbridled zeal that took Him in just any direction. When it was His time to go to Jerusalem to die, "He resolutely set His face to go" (Luke 9:51 NAS). Jesus even went to His death with zeal.

The cause of Christ has been hurt by undisciplined zeal, and by those who have lost their zeal to do God's will. You need zeal, but it must be directed. You must learn to harness it so that it brings all the energy you need to do the Lord's work. If you have zeal, combine it with knowledge. If you have lost it, get it back so you can once again work with enthusiasm.

JULY 20

"A man's steps are directed by the Lord.
How then can man understand his way?" — 20:24.

When my son was in kindergarten, he had a school program at 11:00 one morning, which I promised to attend. I went to work and got busy. My boss asked me to drive across town on an errand, so I took the company truck and set out. Traffic was terrible everywhere, and I made numerous detours through back streets to get where I was going. Suddenly I found myself in front of my son's school and it was 10:58! I had totally forgotten about his program, yet traffic and all those detours had brought me to his school's doorstep.

I learned that day how the Lord can direct my steps, even when I'm unaware of His guidance. I thought I was flowing with traffic, but instead He was getting me where I needed to be, when I needed to be there. The Lord may not take the most direct route, but He always chooses the correct route for you and gets you to His appointed place at the right time.

"And we know that in all things God works for the good of those who love him, who have been called according to his purpose" (Romans 8:28). This verse tells me that God is a master baker. He takes all the ingredients of your life, mixes them together, and gets the desired results. You have to accept Romans 8:28 as a statement of faith, for there are times when your way seems so disjointed and without meaning that it seems that things are out of control. Your definition of good doesn't correspond with God's definition, and you can easily despair when you can't figure out what the Lord is doing or where He is taking you.

David wrote in Psalm 27:13-14, "I am still confident of this: I will see the goodness of the Lord in the land of the living. Wait for the Lord; be strong and take heart and wait for the Lord." He was still confident even though he had plenty of reason to lose his confidence. It didn't seem like things would work out. He couldn't always understand how he would become king, how Saul would be removed, and why things went the way they did. But he retained his confidence, and did indeed see the goodness of the Lord in the land of the living.

The writer of Hebrews wrote to "not throw away your confidence; it will be richly rewarded" (Hebrews 10:35). Let your confidence be restored today that God is in control. He is leading you, whether you feel it or not, in the way you need to go. Perhaps you know where you're going and where God has called you, but you don't understand the road on which He is taking you. Remind yourself that the Lord is directing your steps. You may not understand, but you can be confident that He hasn't abandoned you to the side roads of life. You may not like it at times, but you're on the main highway and well on your way to your appointed destination.

JULY 21

"All a man's ways seem right to him,
but the Lord weighs the heart." — 21:2.

The father before me asked me if I would meet with his son. I had performed the wedding ceremony for this son and his wife, but their marriage was now in trouble. The father told me of the problems his son was having, and the son's behavior wasn't good. My mind went back to our premarital counseling sessions. I had some reservations about the marriage, but the son insisted that he had heard from the Lord. This marriage, he had asserted, was the will of God.

Now there were health and money problems, and the son was acting irresponsibly. I went to meet with him and reminded him of his "vows." He wasn't too pleased to hear me remind him of our earlier conversations. His way had seemed right to him, but now the Lord was weighing his heart to reveal what was there. His motives and intentions were being tested, and he wasn't passing the test.

It's true that my initial reservations had been correct, but now was not the time to discuss those. He had made the commitment, and now he had a marriage to preserve. The good news is that he chose to do what was required to see it work and today they're doing much better.

Peter had also confidently boasted of his ways, which seemed so clear to him. During the Last Supper, Jesus said to him,

Simon, Simon, Satan has asked to sift you as wheat. But I have prayed for you, Simon, that your faith may not fail. And when you have turned back, strengthen your brothers (Luke 22:31-32).

The Lord was about to weigh Simon's heart and reveal what was really there. But Simon was confident that he already knew what was there. He had figured out his way and thought he would walk on no matter how bad it got.

"But he replied, 'Lord, I am ready to go with you to prison and to death.' Jesus answered, 'I tell you, Peter, before the rooster crows today, you will deny three times that you know me'" (Luke 22:33). Peter dismissed this prediction, for he was certain of his loyalty and ready to prove it. Yet the Lord was correct and a few hours later, Peter was weeping because he did exactly what the Lord had predicted.

You can be fooled easily when it comes to your own heart. Jeremiah wrote, "I the Lord search the heart and examine the mind" (Jeremiah 17:10). God reveals what is truly in your heart because you don't always know. In fact, God uses His Word to do the job, the Word which is "living and active. Sharper than any double-edged sword, it penetrates even to dividing soul and spirit, joints and marrow; it judges the thoughts and attitudes of the heart" (Hebrews 4:12).

Don't be so confident in your self-assessment, but let the Lord and His Word test you to see what's there. Give God room to weigh your motives to make sure they are righteous and holy. Let God weigh your heart, and learn to trust His perspective of what is really there.

JULY 22

"So that your trust may be in the Lord,
I teach you today, even you." — 22:19.

Today's verse says that the goal of wisdom is faith. Every teaching you hear should be judged on whether it increases your trust in the Lord. God's wisdom doesn't come only to intellectually stimulate the mind. It also comes to stir the heart to faith and action. Since "without faith it is impossible to please him" (Hebrews 11:6), wisdom must produce faith if God is to be pleased.

Abraham is "the father of all who believe" (Romans 4:11). He perhaps more than anyone in the Bible epitomizes the walk of faith. The Lord revealed Himself to Abraham and taught him about faith. You also need to be instructed so that you may trust in the Lord. To help you learn, Abraham's walk of faith is best summarized in Romans 4.

> He is our father in the sight of God, in whom he believed—the God who gives life the dead and calls things that are not as though they were. Against all hope, Abraham in hope believed and so became the father of many nations, just as it had been said to [or taught] him, "So shall your offspring be." Without weakening in his faith, he faced the fact that his body was as good as dead—since he was about a hundred years old—and that Sarah's womb was also dead. Yet he did not waver through unbelief regarding the promise of God, but was strengthened in his faith and gave glory to God, being fully persuaded that God had power to do what he had promised. That is why "it was credited to him as righteousness" (4:17-22).

The one aspect of this account that impresses me is how Abraham soberly assessed his situation. He didn't deny the deadness of his body or of Sarah's womb, nor did he turn his back on reality. He didn't try to work up a positive confession and claim that their bodies were alive. He quite frankly said, "We're dead."

Abraham said that because he knew their deadness didn't really matter. The important thing for Abraham was the promise of God that he would have children. When he considered his deadness, he also considered the power of God to make alive. When he compared his deadness to that power, he was convinced that God could overcome all obstacles to bring His promise to pass.

You may be dead in some area. Wisdom wants to teach you today to go ahead and face your deadness. You can even say, "I'm dead" and not negate the promise of God. If God has promised you prosperity and times are lean, you can say so and still be standing on the promises of God. Faith never forces you to deny reality. It calls you instead to a higher reality—the word of God. Be like your father Abraham and let wisdom teach you to trust in God, no matter how bleak it looks. Your faith will please your heavenly Father, and you will in time receive the reward for your faith.

JULY 23

"There is surely a future hope for you,
and your hope will not be cut off." — 23:18

Jeremiah was a prophet with a sobering word and people didn't particularly like to see him come near. He was chosen to tell the people of Judah that the end of their kingdom was at hand. He brought word that the Babylonians were coming to carry Judah into exile. As you would expect, he was not greeted with parades and open arms. He was imprisoned, persecuted, and scorned.

This word had its affect on Jeremiah. All he could see was death, pain, and destruction. He had brought a word of doom and it had become a part of him and his outlook. In Jeremiah 32, the prophet was put into prison by the king for prophesying. The king wanted to shut him up. Still he spoke the word of the Lord that Judah would not escape the hand of Babylon. The city was already surrounded, and the people were hoping that God would intervene. Jeremiah was telling them it was over—God would not help them.

While in prison, however, a peculiar thing happened to Jeremiah. His cousin came to visit him and asked Jeremiah to buy a field in Anathoth. Real estate did not seem like a good investment at that time since the land was about to be ravaged and plundered by foreigners. Even though things looked hopeless, the Lord told Jeremiah to buy that field and invest in the future. "For this is what the Lord Almighty, the God of Israel says: 'Houses, fields and vineyards will again be bought in this land'" (Jeremiah 32:15). In the midst of hopelessness, God offered a glimmer of hope. "As I have brought all this great calamity on this people, so I will give them all the prosperity I have promised them" (Jeremiah 32:42).

It seems that God's judgment is always tempered with mercy, seldom being as bad as it could be. His people need to maintain this perspective. It's all right to have hope for the future. No matter how bad things may become, the future is in God's hands. He can turn it from judgment to mercy. How it is today is not necessarily how it will be tomorrow.

There are modern economists, analysts, and prophets who paint a bleak picture of what is coming. Along with that, the end-time theology of some is severe and pessimistic. Yet the Lord may want you to invest in the future, that same future that looks so dark. If nothing else, you're to invest in the age to come. If all seems lost, you can still do good, knowing that you will receive your reward in the next world. If your hope is lost for this age, your hope isn't completely cut off. The resurrection will come, and you'll be rewarded for your deeds done in this age.

Even if you are carrying a gloomy outlook concerning the present or future, be hopeful. The best is yet to come, and God can bring it to pass out of the worst of situations. Look today to invest something in hope. You're not investing in the future, but in the God of your future. You'll be saying that God is in control of your destiny, and you'll not be disappointed.

JULY 24

"Finish your outdoor work and get your fields ready;
after that, build your house." — 24:27.

Today you will be faced with many things you could do. There are urgent matters and there will undoubtedly be unexpected interruptions. Then there are long-term projects that have been on your heart for some time. All these can bring the tension that comes from facing a long "to-do" list with no idea of where to start.

The verse for today speaks to that very problem of needing to set priorities. The person who can set priorities, and focus on them in the midst of life's craziness, is the person who will be productive and satisfied. The person who goes from crisis to crisis, without any thought to what is most important, is foolish and short-sighted. The fields are those things that will produce a crop for you in the future; your house is what may make you feel good today, but can be done later after your "field work" is done.

Being able to set priorities, Jesus did what the Father told Him and that became His number one priority at any time. Jesus said, "When you have lifted up the Son of Man, then you will know who I am and that I do nothing on my own but speak just what the Father has taught me. The one who sent me is with me; he has not left me alone, for I always do what pleases him" (John 8:28-29).

Jesus did what the Father told Him to do, and He gave greatest attention to what would do the most good in the long run. You could argue that had Jesus remained on earth longer, He would have been able to heal and help more people. But the cross was His highest priority. According to today's verse, He didn't "build his house first," but rather prepared His fields. He wasn't short-sighted, but focused on what He could do that would bring the greatest return.

You also have things to do to which you must learn to devote time. In other words, you're busy building your house. You've done those things that are most pressing, but are they the most productive? When harvest time comes, will you have any crops coming in? In the future, when you need that second language, you won't know it. You'll miss the money and opportunities that a new book could have produced had you taken time to write it. If you're not careful, you'll be able to invest in your grandchildren only what you could have invested in your "field"—your own children—but were too busy to do.

Ask yourself today whether you're building your house or preparing your fields. Are you working toward short-term relief of pressing problems, or long-term projects that will bring results? Ask the Spirit to help you set your priorities today, and then give yourself to something that won't produce results for months or even years. Don't be pulled into the little things of today, but give yourself to the big things of tomorrow. Once your fields are prepared, then you can go about the less critical tasks that may be nice, but yield less important results.

JULY 25

"If you argue your case with a neighbor,
do not betray another man's confidence." — 25:9.

Go into a bookstore today, and you'll be bombarded with books written by some to expose the faults and abuses of another. Children write about parents, wives about former husbands, workers about ex-supervisors, government officials about political leaders, and athletes about other athletes. The abused are encouraged to go public with their stories as part of the healing process, and the wronged are considered justified when they expose those who wronged them. It's the spirit of the age, but it isn't necessarily godly behavior.

On a smaller scale, I've counseled many people who have not attended my church. They didn't feel comfortable going to their own pastor or Christian friends, for fear of gossip and public exposure of their private wounds and faults. They had every right to be concerned. The church should be the place where people go when they make mistakes or when they are facing their dark side. Instead, the church sometimes puts an impossible standard of righteousness on its members. They consequently shy away from walking in the light for fear of the results. If this were a problem only in the world, it would be one thing. But it's a problem in the body of Christ, and must be addressed as a serious lack of integrity.

I can remember my father telling me how his uncle had confided in him, telling my father something on his deathbed that my father has never told anyone. I've even asked him to tell me what it was, but he has refused. I admired that when I was a child, and I admire it today. I have sought to be a confidant to people like my dad was to my uncle. I want people to trust me with their dark side and to have confidence that their secrets will stay just that—secret. I don't want to reveal what they said, even if it will help me or make me look smart or spiritual in some situation.

Galatians 6:2 exhorts, "Carry one another's burdens." James 5:16 instructs, "Confess your sins to each other and pray for each other so that you may be healed." 1 Peter 4:8 says, "Love each other deeply, because love covers a multitude of sins." God wants a people who know how to bear and cover, not unload and uncover. God wants to use you to help other people bear their marriage, family, financial, and personal problems. He is looking for those who won't be shocked by what they hear, but moved to love and compassion.

Don't reveal the secrets of another, whether it be in prayer or conversation. Be a person in whom others can have confidence. There are many looking for a friend with whom they can be themselves, and some hope they can find that in the church of Jesus Christ. Don't disappoint them when they come by making a commitment to be one who loves and knows how to cover.

JULY 26

"Like one who seizes a dog by the ears
is a passer-by who meddles in a quarrel not his own." — 26:17.

Yesterday you considered how to be one who can bear the secrets of others. Today you consider how not to be a busy-body. One tendency is not to get involved with people, and the other is to get so involved that you begin to meddle in areas that are none of your business. The Spirit wants to teach you the balance between those two tendencies

While recently visiting a friend who was having some problems, I observed some things that weren't quite right in his home. I returned to my home to pray, but felt no need to share it with him, for I considered that to be "strife" not belonging to me. In my younger days, I was quick to offer opinions to all who were within earshot. I would confront someone in a minute if I felt I saw something they needed. As I have grown in the Lord, I've changed that habit, now looking for "quarrels" that are mine, and avoiding those that are not.

I have used one verse to help me decide whether the quarrel is mine or not and it says, "Always be prepared to give an answer to everyone who asks you to give the reason for the hope that you have" (1 Peter 3:15). If someone asks me, that means they are probably interested, so I'm going on their turf at their invitation. If they ask me about what to do, I feel better about telling them. My wife may ask me now why I didn't say anything when we were involved in some sticky situation. My reply is often, "No one asked me."

My second guideline is whether I sense the Spirit prompting me to say anything. Jesus said what He heard the Father saying. I'm not Jesus, but I am working at responding according to the Spirit's lead. There are times when people ask me and I still don't respond. If you pick up a dog by the ears, he may bite you. Today's verse warns that some people ask for input, but will bite you when you respond. I'm not interested in getting bitten. I have enough teeth marks to last a lifetime.

I'm still looking for "quarrels," but only those that the Spirit has assigned to me. There are tough problems that I know the Lord wants me to address. There are other problems I see, but they are not part of my quota. I'm trying to learn to leave them alone.

Today's verse is an exhortation to mind your own business. Jesus taught not to "give dogs what is sacred; do not throw your pearls to pigs. If you do, they may trample them under their feet, and then turn and tear you to pieces" (Matthew 7:6). Knowing the truth doesn't give you the automatic green light to share it. Sharing truth can be bad for both the truth and you—you can both get trampled in the process. Learn to be quiet and wait for the Spirit's confirmation that this is your quarrel. You will suffer enough dog bites in life; don't go looking for any more.

JULY 27

"Do not forsake your friend
and the friend of your father." — 27:10.

Jonathan and David are perhaps the best example in the Bible of friendship and loyalty being walked out. They became close when David served Jonathan's father, King Saul, as a court musician and their friendship withstood all kinds of trials. Even though Jonathan was in line for the throne, David was anointed to be the next king. Jonathan rejoiced, however, in his friend's good fortune, and looked forward to the day when he could serve David as the second in command.

Saul tried to poison his son's mind against David, but Jonathan refused to be affected and even went off secretly to encourage David. Jonathan didn't listen to the accusations, nor did he believe that David had conspired against him to steal the throne. Jonathan died in battle alongside his reprobate father, and then it was David's turn to manifest his love and friendship toward his fallen friend.

When David ascended the throne, he inquired if there were any of Jonathan's descendants whom he could bless. He was told that there was one son, Mephibosheth, who was lame but who had survived the civil unrest after Saul's death. David brought this young man to his court, sat him at the royal table, and took care of him with a financial allowance.

Friendship and loyalty are godly traits. God Himself is faithful and loyal to His own, and carries that loyalty over generational lines. Exodus 33:11 tells how "the Lord would speak to Moses face to face, as a man speaks with his friend." James wrote that Abraham was "called the friend of God" (James 2:23). The Lord's loyalty to Solomon was in large part due to the special relationship his father David had with the Lord.

As Jesus was concluding His earthly ministry, He defined an important shift in His relationship with His disciples. "I no longer call you servants, because a servant does not know his master's business. Instead, I have called you friends, for everything that I learned from my Father I have made known to you" (John 15:15). It's interesting that Jesus would make this distinction, wanting His men to know of His love and affection for them.

Today's verse warns you not to forsake your father's friends. Your heavenly Father is a friend to many on the earth. His people are not only His servants, but His friends. You are required to be their friends as well, learning to stand with your friends. Be like Jonathan and David. It's a godly trait to stay loyal to friends in the midst of their and your human weaknesses. God is a good friend and wants you to be one, too. Determine to bless a friend of yours today.

JULY 28

"He who keeps the law is a discerning son,
but a companion of gluttons disgraces his father." — 28:7.

The purpose of the law in the life of the believer has been debated for a long time. I regularly hear people say that today we live under grace and not law. Legalism is considered a bad thing, and so many make every effort to live by the Spirit and not by the rules of the law. Today's verse praises the son, however, who keeps the law, calling him discerning. The person who ignores the law is called the friend of gluttons—those who are undisciplined and seek to feed themselves with no restrictions or thought of the consequences.

Jesus' words in Matthew 5:17-20 concerning the law are most important.

Do not think that I have come to abolish the Law of the Prophets; I have not come to abolish them but to fulfill them. I tell you the truth, until heaven and earth disappear, not the smallest letter, not the least stroke of a pen, will by any means disappear from the Law until everything is accomplished. Anyone who breaks one of the least of these commandments and teaches others to do the same will be called least in the kingdom of heaven, but whoever practices and teaches these commands will be called great in the kingdom of heaven. For I tell you that unless your righteousness surpasses that of the Pharisees and the teachers of the law, you will certainly not enter the kingdom of heaven.

Without question, some of the law is no longer in affect. For instance, you no longer have to kill a lamb at the temple. Dietary laws don't pertain to the believer, although they still make good sense from a nutritional standpoint. And special care for the Levites is no longer your concern.

The moral aspects of the law, however, are still applicable. Adultery and murder are still forbidden. In fact, Jesus went on to say that not only was the ban on adultery still applicable, but the thought of it was also considered sin. He didn't do away with the law. If anything, He made it more restrictive and demanding.

The difference today is that the law is fulfilled in the power of the Spirit, and not the power of human will. Everyone must come to see that God's law is holy, and man has no power whatsoever to keep it. A spiritual glutton is someone who eats whatever he wants whenever he wants. He is "free" to follow his spiritual instincts apart from any law. But the discerning son is hemmed in by the law. He isn't free to do what he wants, but follows God's law as the Spirit directs. There's a big difference between those two philosophies of life.

You're under the law, not to gain salvation, but to please God. You're under law to love your neighbor and to give mercy. If you're a discerning son, you'll realize that. If you're a companion of gluttons, you'll rejoice in your freedom only to find yourself following your flesh in the things of God. Ask God to help you be a discerning son or daughter, and then get on with keeping the righteous law of God.

JULY 29

"A man's pride brings him low,
but a man of lowly spirit gains honor." — *29:23.*

My wife was recently telling me of something one family member said that offended another member. It was said in pride, and it offended the pride of the other party. There was now an offense, and a wall had gone up between the two.

The book of Proverbs regularly addresses man's pride. It clings to all men, and is the root of most disputes and problems. John wrote,

If anyone loves the world, the love of the Father is not in him. For everything in the world—the cravings of sinful man, the lust of his eyes, and the boasting of what he has and does—comes not from the Father but from the world (1 John 2:15-16).

Boasting and pride are the foundation upon which man's kingdom is built. Satan in his pride fell from heaven, and his spirit has found a home in the hearts of men. Unfortunately, your pride is not dealt with when you meet the Lord. James addressed believers when he wrote,

Who is wise and understanding among you? Let him show it by his good life, by deeds done in the humility that comes from wisdom. But if you harbor bitter envy and selfish ambition in your hearts, do not boast about it or deny the truth. Such "wisdom" does not come down from heaven but is earthly, unspiritual, of the devil. For where you have envy and selfish ambition, there you find disorder and every evil practice (James 3:13-16).

I once had a wise man tell me, "If it hurts, it's not dead." When you lose the promotion and it hurts, your ambition to get ahead was not dead. Another man once said that we think that our flesh is dead only to find out later that it had only fainted. It comes back to life when you are insulted, overlooked, or frustrated. God wants to deal our pride a death blow, so that it won't hurt when we're humbled.

The way to deal with pride is found in 1 Peter 5:6: "Humble yourselves, therefore, under God's mighty hand, that he may lift you up in due time." You can humble yourself, having some say in how quickly and thoroughly your pride is dealt with. Humility is a decision. The only other option is humiliation—God will humble you if you choose not to humble yourself.

The good news from today's verse is that humility comes with a promise. If you humble yourself under God's hand, He will exalt you. God can use the humble, and He is looking to use those who aren't concerned with who gets the credit for the work done. If there is disorder in your life, is there pride and selfish ambition? If there is turmoil in your relationships, is conceit a factor? Examine your motives today, and ask the Lord to help you see the blind spots of pride. Then humble yourself and wait for God to promote you. A lowly spirit gains honor, and God wants to honor you when you meet his basic requirement—humility.

JULY 30

*"There are those who curse their fathers
and do not bless their mothers." — 30:11.*

I was sitting with a member of my church, and we were praying about some problems he was having in his walk with the Lord. I asked this young man about his family, and found out that he had not talked to his father in five years. He didn't even know where his father was. I then asked how long he was prepared to carry this grudge. He told me, "For the rest of my life." That night he began to face his hatred and walk in forgiveness. He was ready at last to face his past.

You can only live in the "today" of life. You can't bring the future or the past into "today" and be successful. Stress, anxiety, and breakdowns come in when the past or future become bigger than "today." You can't try to ignore or bury what has happened to you, but the only way to deal with the past is "head on." If you bury the past in your heart or mind, it's like the hand reaching from the grave in a horror movie. You can't bury it deep enough that it will ever go away.

To fully live in today, you must face the past, admitting that a person hurt you. You must come to grips with any anger, bitterness, resentment, or rejection you still have. Psalm 51:6 tells you that the Lord "desire[s] truth in the inward parts." This truth of what you are holding is not for the Lord's benefit—He already knows what's there. The truth is for your benefit so that you can acknowledge it, repent, let it go, and ask the Lord to heal it.

Jesus said, "You will know the truth and the truth will set you free" (John 8:32). Knowing and facing the truth of your past is not to torment you but to set you free. Until you face it, you aren't really free but bound to the past. When the past floods into your consciousness, you aren't free to respond today as the Lord would want.

Start by asking the Lord to show you your heart. Is there hurt, bitterness, or anger hidden inside? Against whom are you angry? Then tell the Lord where you are. If you're angry, tell Him. Then forgive the person or persons who wronged you. I have found that parents are very often the source of these problems. Your mind tells you that you ought to love them, but the heart very often harbors resentment for some of the things they did or didn't do. Be especially honest about them.

Finally, ask the Lord to forgive you. You must realize and acknowledge that you may have sinned in response to someone else's sin. Their wrong deed does not justify your wrong response. This is not an easy process, and you may need to enlist the help of your spiritual counselor or friends to help you. Dealing with the past will enable you to live today, the only day that you were created to live in successfully.

JULY 31

"Her husband is respected at the city gate,
where he takes his seat among the elders of the land." — 31:27.

I once heard it said that God is looking to use people who aren't concerned with who gets the credit for the work. I remember as a young pastor preparing a memo for my superior. I worked long and hard, and presented it to him—all five pages of it—on my stationary. He read it, said it was just what he wanted, and then asked if I would transfer it to his letterhead. I was crushed!

I wanted people to know that I had done the work. Wanting my name to be on that memo, I desired the recognition and praise that I knew would come from that work. I worked my way through that request, and did put the memo out in his name.

After I did that, I was reading Proverbs 31 and noticed today's verse. Here was an account of a godly woman. She was diligent and a hard worker. Yet it seemed to me as if the credit for her labor went to someone else. She is the one put forth as a model worker, and her husband got to sit at the gate. Here was someone doing the work and her husband, while undoubtedly working hard himself, got the public notoriety.

John the Baptist found himself with the same situation. He had the attention of all Israel. Large crowds came to see him, and he was the talk of the land. Then Jesus came along. Some had tried to declare that John was the Messiah. Others were jealous that Jesus was now getting all the public notice after John had ministered so effectively prior to Jesus' arrival on the scene. John put the concerns to rest about Jesus getting more credit than he. He simply told his followers, "He must become greater; I must become less" (John 3:30).

As I have matured, I have taken comfort from Paul's admonition to "give yourselves fully to the work of the Lord, because you know that your labor in the Lord is not in vain" (1 Corinthians 15:58). God is watching what I do. If man doesn't recognize it, God will. What I do in secret will be trumpeted from the housetops! I work hard, and trust my reputation and recognition to Him. My labor for man may be in vain, but if I work for Him, nothing I do will go unnoticed. I also recognize that God will exalt some over me and may use me to help get them there!

AUGUST 1

"My son, if sinners entice you, do not give in to them." —1:10.

Whenever I read this verse, I think of my children. They attend public schools now and come home with graphic stories of what's going on in classrooms and hallways. I'm amazed at the language used by their peers and the sin that entices them at such a tender age. Facing these realities, my wife and I are constantly trying to help them recognize the nature of the pressure on them to conform. I try to be watchful of whom they are "hanging around" with, for I notice a difference in them if they're around certain people.

Peer pressure is a problem not only for the young, but also for the mature. Paul wrote, "Do not be misled: 'Bad company corrupts good character'" (1 Corinthians 15:33). Earlier in that epistle he wrote these instructions:

I have written you in my letter not to associate with sexually immoral people— not at all meaning the people of this world who are immoral, or the greedy and swindlers, or idolaters. In that case you would have to leave this world. But now I am writing you that you must not associate with anyone who calls himself a brother but is sexually immoral, or greedy, an idolater or a slanderer, a drunkard or a swindler. With such a man do not even eat (1 Corinthians 5:9-11).

It's important who your friends are. Arthur Pink wrote, "A person is not only known by the company he or she keeps, but is molded thereby."* You need to build relationships with those who are strongly committed to the Lordship of Jesus Christ. I can understand why Paul urged the Corinthians not to spend time with the sexually immoral. He goes on to urge them, however, not to associate with slanderers, the greedy, or idolaters! This seems strict, but Paul knew how susceptible we are to the influences of others. Knowing this, he taught that we should build friendships only with those who are leading godly lives.

Today's verse urges you to recognize the pressure of your peers, and not to give in to it. If others are less than truthful on their tax forms, don't think it's all right to do the same. If others give in to a materialistic lifestyle, don't try to keep up with them. If everyone else complains on the job, don't join in just because it's the thing to do. Keep your focus on the Lord and His commands, and avoid those who will pull on you to join their lifestyle. "Do not conform any longer to the pattern of this world, but be transformed by the renewing of your mind" (Romans 12:2).

The Lord even wants to be Lord of your relationships. He knows who you are and what it will take to maintain your holiness. Let God help you to choose your friends and associates. Work at being transformed instead of conformed. The people you spend time with will help you one way or the other.

*Arthur W. Pink, *The Life of David*, Baker Book House, page 326.

AUGUST 2

"He holds victory in store for the upright." —2:7.

I've always been a big sports enthusiast. While never a gifted athlete, I always played hard to win, for losing was distasteful to me. If I played well, but my team lost, I would take no consolation. I could never understand those who lost and walked away happy, saying they enjoyed the competition. For me, to play was to play to win, and anything less was hard to comprehend.

When I became a believer, I was impressed with the nature of the battle between good and evil. Jesus fought the powers of darkness and emerged victorious. I see the book of Revelation as a book of victory, for the Lamb came out the winner in every confrontation with His enemies. He rules on the throne, and could not be overcome by death itself.

The Lord wants you to be a winner. You are to confront the world, the devil and your own weaknesses, and overcome them all. "In all these things we are more than conquerors through him who loved us" (Romans 8:37). You aren't called just to play the game, but to win through the blood of Jesus Christ.

The book of Revelation holds many promises for those who overcome—for those who win the battle. You will "eat from the tree of life" (Revelation 2:7), "not be hurt at all by the second death" (2:11), be given "some of the hidden manna" (2:17), be given "authority over the nations" (2:26), "be dressed in white" (3:5), become "a pillar in the temple of my God" (3:12), and be given "the right to sit with me [Jesus] on my throne, just as I overcame and sat down with my Father on his throne" (3:21).

The Lord holds victory in store for you. He doesn't want you just to enjoy the game, but He wants you to win. William Temple, Archbishop of Canterbury during World War II, wrote, "At the root of all your being, your intellectual studies, the games you play, whatever it is, the impulse to do them well is and ought to be understood as being an impulse towards God, the source of all that is excellent."*

Don't be afraid to win, and don't feel guilty as you try to be or do your best. Your desire to succeed is God-given. If you're willing to pay the price for your success—to overcome all obstacles to win—then you'll receive some magnificent promises. If you remain passive, then you'll miss out on the victory the Lord holds in store for you. Decide you'll be a winner in the things of God, and you'll enjoy the spoils that are the inheritance of the overcoming saint.

*William Temple, *Christian Faith and Life*, Macmillan Co., NY 1931, p.18

AUGUST 3

*"Have no fear of sudden disaster or of the ruin that overtakes the wicked,
for the Lord will be your confidence." — 3:25-26.*

I'm well acquainted with fear for it has ruled one side of my family for generations. There is fear of the unknown, being poor, accidents, driving in bad weather, the future, and sickness. When I was young, I almost drowned so I know the fear of water. Fear of failure has driven me at times to work too hard and with the wrong motives.

Fear can paralyze you. It can cause you to do nothing when something needs to be done. Or it can cause to do the wrong thing when several options are available. Paul wrote to his disciple Timothy, "God did not give us a spirit of timidity [fear], but a spirit of power, love and of self-discipline" (2 Timothy 1:7).

Many times in the Old Testament, the Lord commanded His people not to fear. His command did not indicate an absence of things that would cause fear. Instead, the Lord was warning that a problem was coming and that His people would have to chose between fear and trust in Him. If the Lord commands you not to fear, then you must also have the ability to control fear when it confronts you.

When I read a fearful economic report, or if I'm anxious over a meeting I have organized, I decide not to fear. I choose not to fear that sudden disaster may come. I'm learning not to put my confidence in my ability to plan, or in the government to control inflation, or in science to harness the environment. I'm learning to overcome fear by putting my confidence in Him who is all powerful. When I have a thought that some accident may befall my children, I commit them to Him who is my confidence.

You're not at the mercy of the elements or fate. "For you died, and your life is now hidden with Christ in God" (Colossians 3:3). Think of it. Your life is hidden in Christ. If something reaches you, it has to pass through Christ to get to you. You have no need to fear the unknown or the future. For a trial or bad time to reach you, it must first pass through your protector, in whom your life is hidden. Thank you, Lord!

This doesn't mean that fearful things don't confront you, or that difficult times won't come your way. It simply means that, when they do, they've passed through the outer guard of your life. They passed inspection, and Jesus gave them permission to proceed. You may be shaken, but you can be confident that God is at work and in control. He won't let anything pass to you through Him that is more than you can handle.

Deal with your fears and anxieties by facing them for what they are. Then reassure yourself that your life is hidden in Christ. For something to reach you, it must come through Him. Your confidence is in your border guard, the one who is the outer defense of your life. Put your trust in Him and put your fears to rest. He is surely in control.

AUGUST 4

"When you run, you will not stumble." — *4:12.*

Several years ago, I went to see a friend run a six-mile race. It was a hot, summer day and the runners were sweating profusely. While the runners were "amateurs," they were running their hearts out and it looked like it would be a photo finish. Just as the runners neared the finish line, one of the lead runners stumbled and fell across the line, losing the race in the process. Since the race was on asphalt, that runner received some serious scrapes and bruises as a trophy. Needless to say, she was embarrassed and made a quick exit from the race site.

There are times when the Lord will have you run. With a full schedule, you'll be under pressure, convinced that things are moving too fast. You may even think things can't get any worse—but they may! The promise for you is found earlier in today's chapter: Wisdom will guide you and keep you from stumbling while you are running. You store up wisdom in slow times, so that you'll be prepared to run and not stumble in fast times.

Jeremiah encountered this problem. He was preaching righteousness, but the wicked were prospering. As he cried to the Lord for justice, the Lord responded, "If you have raced with men on foot and they have worn you out, how can you compete with horses?" (Jeremiah 12:5). The Lord was telling Jeremiah that it was going to get worse. Jeremiah was wearied by his trials, but no relief was in sight. The Lord was teaching him to run with horses!

It's easy to underestimate how fast and long you can run in the Lord. Paul and Barnabas were "strengthening the disciples and encouraging them to remain true to the faith. 'We must go through many hardships to enter the kingdom of God,' they said" (Acts 14:22). That was strange "encouragement"! To tell someone that many hardships are ahead hardly seems like a positive word. Yet that's what the Lord told Jeremiah and that's what Paul and Barnabas told the believers.

When you run—when trials put you on a treadmill—you learn that the Lord is capable of sustaining you. You also learn to respond to His government and kingdom. Then when the trials are over, you realize that the Lord sustained you. You further realize that in your weakness, His strength was made perfect and His wisdom pulled you through. You may say like Jacob, "My years have been few and difficult" (Genesis 47:9), but you will also be like Jacob who "worshiped as he leaned on the top of his staff" (Genesis 47:31). You'll recognize that the Lord delivered you from all your troubles, and you will worship because of it.

As a believer, you will run. You will find yourself in difficult situations, but wisdom will sustain you. Teaching you how to act and what to do, wisdom will pull you through times tougher than you had ever imagined. When you run, you will not stumble. You'll rather run the race and finish the course set out for you. Don't be afraid of falling, for He will preserve and keep you in the busiest and most difficult of times.

AUGUST 5

*"Lest strangers feast on your wealth,
and your toil enrich another man's house." — 5:10.*

Divorce has reached epidemic proportions in the modern world. In my daughter's class, only one-third of her classmates live with both their natural parents. A large percentage of people today have been previously married, and invariably seek counsel concerning the complexity of their new lives. Battles over the children, alimony, child support, stepparents, visitation rights, court orders, and custody are all too frequent. These battles are very painful and often bitter, as people see their money, time, and children going to the house of a "stranger."

Enriching the "stranger," however, is a dilemma faced not only by those who are divorced. The pursuit of modern wealth and status has caused men and women to work long and hard. A pastor recently told me that the area in which he lives requires such a commitment to meet the cost of living that it was difficult to get anyone to volunteer for church activities. By the time his families traveled to and from work (and in most families, both the husband and wife worked), they had little time or energy for anything else. The best of their time and effort was going to the house of another, a "stranger," and not the house of God. Their work was enriching others and not the body of Christ. People are coming to church to rest from their labors, not to find more pressure and work.

This pressure to maintain a standard of living is real and needs to be balanced with a strong faith in the Lord's ability to provide. Solomon wrote, "Unless the Lord builds the house, its builders labor in vain. Unless the Lord watches over the city, the watchmen stand guard in vain. In vain you rise early and stay up late, toiling for food to eat—for he grants sleep to those he loves" (Psalm 127:1-2).

Jesus continued this teaching by saying, "Do not worry, saying, 'What shall we drink?' or 'What shall we wear?' For the pagans run after all these things, and your heavenly Father knows that you need them" (Matthew 6:31).

These verses can free you from the pressure to produce, for the Lord can give to you even in your sleep. When you have this settled, you can then free yourself to work less and have time to invest in God's house. Luke 21:5 says, "Some of his disciples were remarking about how the temple was adorned with beautiful stones and with gifts dedicated to God." The temple of God—the body of Christ—will be built in the same manner, as living stones freely dedicate themselves to God's use. "The whole body, joined and held together by every supporting ligament, grows and builds itself up in love, as each part does its work" (Ephesians 4:16).

You have a part to play in building the body of Christ. Don't give the best you have and are to the house of a stranger. Save something for the Lord. Dedicate yourself to contributing something to the house of your Father. If you do, your Father can provide for you in your sleep. Check out your priorities, and make any necessary adjustments to start investing in the house that will remain forever.

AUGUST 6

"There are six things the Lord hates,
seven that are detestable to him: haughty eyes." — 6:16-17.

Religious people can be haughty. They consider their doctrine, their traditions, and their services superior to those in other groups. Some use only a certain version of the Bible and look down on those who use another. Others manifest spiritual gifts and go so far as to question someone's salvation who does not manifest the same gifts.

The greatest area of pride, however, is doctrine. Some believers hold their doctrinal revelation superior to all others, and this often breeds pride and competition among groups. They believe God's special blessing is on them because they are correct. If God's blessing is not evident in another group, they reason it's probably because the other group is wrong.

Today's verse tells us that the Lord hates those who view their world through the eyes of pride. Pride is always wrong, but it's especially terrible when it accompanies spiritual things. If you take pride in what you have freely received from the Lord, you manifest an attitude that you earned what you have. You act like you deserve what in fact the Lord has given you in His grace.

John the Baptist said, "A man can receive only what is given him from heaven" (John 3:27). Jesus said, "Freely you have received, freely give" (Matthew 10:8). When the Lord blesses someone or some group of people, He does so in His grace and out of His sovereign will. It doesn't necessarily reflect the goodness of the recipient, but of the giver. After all, God spoke through a donkey in the Old Testament. That certainly wasn't an indication of the donkey's spirituality, but of the madness of the prophet whom the donkey addressed!

Paul wrote the Corinthians, who were blessed with all spiritual gifts, but also had some serious moral and spiritual problems in their midst. He told them, "We do not dare to classify or compare ourselves with some who commend themselves. When they measure themselves by themselves and compare themselves with themselves, they are not wise. We, however, will not boast beyond proper limits" (2 Corinthians 10:12-13).

You do well to heed the exhortation of the prophet Micah: "He has showed you, O man, what is good. And what does the Lord require of you? To act justly and to love mercy and to walk humbly with your God" (Micah 6:8). Don't make yourself feel worthy by comparing yourself to someone else. Be humble, and realize that the Lord has blessed you out of His goodness, not out of yours. Don't walk with haughty eyes, but be merciful and gracious. The Lord has been merciful to you and expects you to return the favor to others.

Those that see through haughty eyes are of no use to the Lord and their pride causes the Lord to actually resist them. Commit today to give thanks to the Lord for His favor, which is unmerited. That will help you to maintain a humble heart as you enjoy the blessings of God.

AUGUST 7

"I have covered my bed with colored linens from Egypt." — 7:16.

I have a good friend who operates a drug and prison ministry. He himself was involved in the drug scene many years ago, which eventually led him to prison. After his release, he began to go back into schools to tell of his experiences and warn others. His presentation is effective among young people because it is realistic.

In his presentation, he tells young people that drugs do indeed give pleasure. For a season, they make you feel good and help you escape from the unpleasant realities of life. He goes on to tell from personal experience, however, that drugs also take. And his main point is that in the long run, what they take is much more than what they give.

When young people hear this, they can relate to what he is saying, for many know by experience that drugs do give them something. To deny the pleasure they give while appealing to young people to stay off drugs because they are "bad" is not something this generation can relate to. When they hear someone testify how he ended up in prison after a life of drugs is something young people can and do identify with.

Today's verse is taken from a chapter that relates how a "wayward woman" seduces her victim. She tells her man that where she is taking him looks and feels good, and that is the truth. To deny the pleasures of sin is to deny reality, for sin does bring some measure of pleasure. But that pleasure is passing and leads to ultimate destruction. It's hard to see that when the pleasures have not passed.

The writer of Hebrews says that Moses "chose to be mistreated along with the people of God rather than to enjoy the pleasure of sin for a short time. He regarded disgrace for the sake of Christ as of greater value than the treasures of Egypt" (Hebrews 11:25-26). Egypt does hold treasures such as worldly wealth, creature comforts, prestige, power, and fame. To deny that is to deny the truth. The real truth is that they are passing pleasures that last only for a short time.

Jesus asks you to forsake these real pleasures for the eternal rewards that only He can give. It's a hard decision for some. Your efforts to evangelize should not ignore this fundamental truth, for your appeals to the cross have some stiff competition. Even believers struggle with this, for Paul wrote, "Many live as enemies of the cross of Christ. Their destiny is destruction, their god is their stomach, and their glory is in their shame. Their mind is on earthly things" (Philippians 3:18-19). He was not talking about unbelievers, but those who at some time called on the name of Christ.

Are you an enemy of the cross? Have the passing pleasures of sin—being "right" at all costs, pride, rebellion, greed, or ambition—beguiled you? Have the colored sheets of Egypt captured you with their beauty and attractiveness? It would be good today to trade the treasures of Egypt for the riches of the cross. There may not be any immediate returns, but the eternal rewards are tremendous.

AUGUST 8

"I was there when he set the heavens in place,
when he marked out the horizons on the face of the deep." — 8:27.

Chapter eight is a discourse from wisdom speaking as a man. For me, it has always seemed like the words of Jesus. Wisdom for the Greek was a system, but for the believer, wisdom is a person. Greeks sat around all day, while slaves did their work, and "spent their time doing nothing but talking about and listening to the latest idea" (Acts 17:21). Believers, on the other hand, went out armed with God's wisdom and turned the world upside down. Philosophy is still the main pursuit of some, but the believer in right relationship with the Lord is out doing new things, with fresh insight and revelation from the Master.

Jesus is "the power of God and the wisdom of God" (1 Corinthians 1:24). He "has become for us wisdom from God—that is, our righteousness, holiness, and redemption" (1 Corinthians 1:30). In Him "are hidden all the treasures of wisdom and knowledge" (Colossians 2:3). Wisdom is understanding of what to do with godly knowledge. Jesus gives you the ability to apply your knowledge about God in a practical way. Your knowledge and wisdom aren't a system for living life, but a relationship that guides life. There is a major difference.

Solomon understood this. In 1 Kings 3, the Lord appeared to Solomon in a dream and said, "Ask for whatever you want me to give you" (verse 5). Solomon asked for a "discerning heart to govern your people and to distinguish between right and wrong" (verse 9). The Lord was pleased and responded, "I will give you a wise and discerning [listening] heart" (verse 12). Solomon went on the receive this wisdom, and Proverbs was written because the Lord answered his prayer.

But notice, the Lord equated wisdom with a listening or discerning heart. The Lord wants to give you more than a system of beliefs. He wants to talk to you and teach you how to do everything you do. He wants to empower you to do new things. Anyone can do what someone else has done by copying their actions. That isn't wisdom, for wisdom is listening to the voice of the Lord, or better yet, being led by the Holy Spirit. "Those who are led by the Spirit of God are sons of God" (Romans 8:14). You notice that the book of Proverbs is time and again addressed to "my son"—a living wisdom speaking to a listening son.

Are you relying on what someone else has done and learned, or do you have a vital, listening relationship with the Lord? Are you operating in wisdom, or in the revelation of the past that belonged to another day or someone else? Pray Solomon's prayer today, confident that God's wisdom is available to you right now, right where you are. It's the same wisdom that was present when the Lord ordered creation. It's fresh and living, and will help you to accomplish the will of God and even do new things in your own world. Your heritage isn't to learn the collective wisdom of the Greeks, but to draw on the limitless wisdom of your God. Begin today to seek and apply that wisdom, and then set out to do new things for the Lord to His glory.

AUGUST 9

"Instruct a wise man and he will be wiser still;
teach a righteous man and he will add to his learning." — 9:9.

My wife jokingly informed me the other day that we were getting old. Some young people in our church were excitedly telling us of some new concept they had learned. We both nodded our heads, but felt that they were young and would learn. I didn't think they really had anything to teach me. My wife's statement surprised me, for I remembered how it was when I was on the other end. When I was young, I felt many "mature" believers could not receive what I had to say. They had "arrived," and were beyond learning from such as me.

I determined after my wife said that to open myself afresh to learn from those older and younger than me in years and in the Lord. I recalled 1 Corinthians 10:12, which states, "So, if you think you are standing firm, be careful that you don't fall!" I don't want to think I'm a pillar of truth, only to find myself standing still as others pass me in their walk. I want to grow and increase in my comprehension of the Lord and His ways until I go home to be with him.

With that in mind, I set out on a brief Bible study on the word *increase*, and I found two familiar passages. The first is in Colossians 1:10: "And we pray this in order that you may live a life worthy of the Lord and may please him in every way: bearing fruit in every good work, growing in the knowledge of God." One way to be worthy of the Lord and to please Him is to grow and increase in His knowledge.

You should constantly be learning more about the Lord and His ways. To stop learning is to stagnate and die. Your life is a walk with the Lord and not a race with an end. There is an end for you, but even in death, you will come to know then what you now "know in part" (1 Corinthians 13:12). Your existence is meant to be spent in knowing Him more fully.

The second passage I found is in 2 Peter 1:5-9:

For this very reason, make every effort to add to your faith, goodness; and to goodness, knowledge; and to knowledge, self-control; and to self-control, perseverance; and to perseverance, godliness; and to godliness, brother kindness; and to brotherly kindness, love. For if you possess these qualities in increasing measure, they will keep you from being ineffective and unproductive in your knowledge of our Lord Jesus Christ.

Not only are we to possess these qualities, but they are to be found in increasing quantities. This growth will keep us effective and productive in the knowledge of God. If you have stopped progressing and growing, begin anew to be a learner. It's part of your destiny to be a learner for life, and for the life to come.

AUGUST 10

"He who gathers crops in summer is a wise son,
but he who sleeps during harvest is a disgraceful son." — 10:5.

When I lived in Florida, I heard people say how much they missed the season changes in the North. When they said that, I used to think of just how many seasons I have seen come and go in the Lord. Solomon wrote about this in Ecclesiastes 3:1-8:

> There is a time for everything, and a season for every activity under heaven: a time to be born and a time to die, a time to plant and a time to uproot, a time to kill and a time to heal, a time to tear down and a time to build, a time to weep and a time to laugh, a time to mourn and a time to dance, a time to scatter stones and a time to gather then, a time to embrace a time to refrain, a time to search and a time to give up, a time to keep and a time to throw away, a time to tear and a time to mend, a time to be silent and a time to speak, a time to love and a time to hate, a time for war and a time for peace.

The first problem with change is that it is filled with uncertainty. A psychologist once wrote that all people see all change as loss, and it is usually accompanied by anger. When things change, you become disoriented and even upset over the shifting circumstances. You're no longer comfortable in your environment and that brings insecurity. The smallest things in a time of change can be stressful.

The other problem with change isn't so much in struggling with the change, but rather in knowing what season you are in. Is it time to laugh or cry? Build or tear down? Mourn or dance? Today's verse tells you it's a disgrace to be found doing the wrong thing in a given season. It takes spiritual discernment to understand this, and only those sensitive to the Lord and His purposes will know what season it really is.

When the kingdom was turned over to David from Saul, 1 Chronicles 12:32 says that the sons of Issachar came to him, men "who understood the times and knew what Israel should do." The sons of Issachar knew it was time to make a change from Saul's to David's leadership. They came prepared for the change, and surrendered themselves to it.

The Lord brings change so that your security won't be in your surroundings but rather in Him who does not change. Change causes you to press into the Lord, and to seek His help during times of uncertainty. It makes you confess, like the psalmist, "My times are in your hands" (Psalm 31:15).

Are you in transition? Then trust the Lord. He knows where you are, and can help you in the most difficult of times. Seek His mind to know what season you're in, and then give yourself to it with the Lord's help. Be a modern son of Issachar. Change isn't just an occasional event; it's a way of life. In light of this, learn to trust the things that change to Him who changes not.

AUGUST 11

"The integrity of the upright guides them,
but the unfaithful are destroyed for their duplicity." — 11:3.

Another business scandal has rocked the American business world. Two top executives of a large drug store chain were found to have manipulated the company value to be $350 million higher than it actually was! For good measure, they also embezzled $11 million! That's a lot of money to steal! I wonder where they hid it all. Undoubtedly these two were great businessmen who built a large empire of stores. They had already made millions of dollars in salary and stock options. Their unfaithfulness and duplicity destroyed them, however, and they will spend many years in prison.

Today's verse speaks to your need for integrity—a set of principles that will guide your life in every situation. There are times when you need a word from the Lord to provide guidance; there are other times when you need to rely on what you know to be right, and act accordingly.

Balaam is an example of an Old Testament prophet who had no integrity. He didn't have a set of principles that would guide his life and ministry. You can read in Numbers 22 how Balak, the king of Moab, summoned Balaam for the express purpose of putting a curse on the nation of Israel. Balak was willing to pay Balaam for his services. When emissaries came to seek Balaam, he told them he could not go with them, for the word of the Lord was for him to stay put.

Balak persisted and sent a second group of dignitaries, and Balaam hinted that "even if Balak gave me his palace filled with silver and gold" (Numbers 22:18), he could not go with them. The prophet, giving in to a greedy heart, inquired of the Lord a second time, to see if the Lord had changed His mind. This time the Lord told him to go. With great expectation, Balaam went to the king. On the way, Balaam's donkey actually spoke to him, trying to address the prophet's lack of integrity. The prophet engaged his donkey in conversation, seemingly unimpressed with the fact that his beast was talking to him, and continued on his way.

When Balaam arrived, he tried three times to curse Israel. Each time, however, he could only bless them as he opened his mouth. His greed wasn't rewarded, his faithlessness was exposed, and later he perished by the sword as Israel entered the land. Instead of operating from his integrity, he sought the Lord's guidance about an issue that should have been obvious to him from the beginning. Because he lacked integrity and sought a word from the Lord—a word he hoped would free him to pursue his own interests—he was destroyed.

Do you operate from a set of principles from God's Word? Or, when confronted with the chance for personal gain, do you seek the Lord for a word when your decision should come from your integrity? Let your integrity be your guide, and don't follow the path of destruction. Set some standards of behavior and follow them, regardless of how you could benefit by ignoring them.

AUGUST 12

*"The slothful does not roast his prey,
but the precious possession of a man is diligence."* — *12:27 (NAS)*

I'm not a hunter. The thought of tramping around in the woods in freezing temperatures looking for an animal whose meat I don't like to eat isn't exactly pleasant. There are many avid hunters, however, and I'll allow them their enjoyment. I remember being at the home of a man when he received the mounted animals he had killed during an African safari. He was so excited to see his animals and gladly shared the story behind each kill.

Imagine a hunter who would pack up his gear and set out on a similar expedition. He would probably leave before dawn to drive to his favorite hunting grounds. Parking his vehicle, he would walk deep into the woods to a place that had favorable conditions for finding what he was hunting. Having found a suitable hiding spot, he would then wait for his game. Imagine that the animal suddenly appeared, and the hunter "bagged" it with one shot.

Wouldn't it be ludicrous for the hunter, after all he went through, to walk back to his vehicle and go home! This would not be the sport of hunting, but a cruelty to the animal and a wasted expedition. Every hunter wants to eat his prey, or at least have a trophy to show others from the hunt itself.

You are just like that foolish hunter if you don't have diligence in your life. For instance, let's say that you get an idea, perhaps to go back to school. You send away for catalogs and go visit the campus. You fill out the applications and are accepted to attend. You do everything necessary to go, but then for whatever reason don't proceed. Your lack of diligence kept you from roasting your prey. Your idea and creative inspiration went for naught. You caught your prey, but after looking at it, left it on the ground and walked away.

Procrastination is the opposite of diligence. Putting off until tomorrow what can be done today destroys many great and noble ideas. Being unable to make your ideas top priority is, according to today's verse, sloth. A modern translation for sloth is laziness.

Have you been talking about writing a book? Then begin today to write it. Have you wanted to learn a second language? Start learning a few words now. Do you have an idea for an invention? Get with someone who can help you translate your idea into reality. Add diligence to your creativity, and be a hunter who carries through with the hunt from the kill to the meal.

AUGUST 13

"The way of transgressors is hard." — 13:15 (KJV).

Several days ago we discussed the life and ministry of Balaam the prophet. Balak, king of Moab, wanted to hire Balaam to curse Israel, the enemy of Moab. We saw how Balaam's lack of integrity caused him to give in to greed and go with Balak's delegation. Balaam wanted the "fee for divination" (Numbers 22:7) that the king had sent with his emissaries.

As Balaam was traveling to his job as a "consultant," the Bible says Balaam got up in the morning, saddled his donkey and went with the princes of Moab. But God was very angry when he went, and the angel of the Lord stood to oppose him. Balaam was riding his donkey, and his two servants were with him. When the donkey saw the angel of the Lord standing in the road with a drawn sword in his hand, she turned off the road into a field. Balaam beat her to get her back on the road (Numbers 22:21-23).

Balaam had transgressed the original word of the Lord to him not to go with these people. When Balaam asked a second time, to try to change the Lord's mind, the Lord relented and told him to go. But now the Lord was opposing him. When the Lord opposes transgressors, they are indeed opposed but that still didn't stop Balaam.

"Then the angel of the Lord stood in a narrow path between two vineyards, with walls on both sides. When the donkey saw the angel of the Lord, she pressed close to the wall, crushing Balaam's foot against it. So he beat her again" (Numbers 22:24-25). The way of this transgressor was getting more difficult, but he was determined to press on, spurred on by the financial reward that was just ahead.

"Then the angel of the Lord moved on ahead and stood in a narrow place where there was no room to turn, either to the right or to the left. When the donkey saw the angel of the Lord, she lay down under Balaam, and he was angry and beat her with his staff" (Numbers 22:26-28). Due to his transgression, Balaam was inconvenienced, delayed, and then physically hurt. He was in a fit of rage because things weren't going well. Things never go well when you oppose God's will; the way of a transgressor is indeed a hard one.

Contrast this with the life of the righteous, which is also difficult but for other reasons. The Lord helps the righteous in their troubles and does not oppose them. What is the source of your resistance? If it's a "painful trial" (1 Peter 4:12) common to all believers, then rejoice. If it's the difficulty of one who is transgressing God's will, then repent. If you aren't sure, ask the Lord for wisdom and "it [wisdom] will be given" (James 1:5). Spiritual people—even prophets like Balaam—can transgress. Thanks God that the resistance can be removed when you submit to the will of God. Submit today and let your resistance be what conforms you to the image of His Son, and not the resistance that is common to all transgressors.

AUGUST 14

"Where there are no oxen, the manger is empty,
but from the strength of the ox comes an abundant harvest." — *14:4*.

I expected George Washington or Thomas Jefferson to appear at any time. My family and I had the chance to vacation in Williamsburg, Virginia, several years ago. Williamsburg is a restored colonial community brimming with history. While there, I saw an ox for the first time as it drew a cart through the colonial streets. What an animal the ox is! It's the size of a cow, but is one, big, lean muscle. It was dragging a cart filled to capacity as if it were empty.

When I saw that ox, I thought of today's verse. I could only imagine what that ox must eat every day. And I can't begin to imagine how messy his stall must be! It must take a lot of work to clean it up and maintain that animal, but, in its day, the ox was able to work and make the farmer's life more productive. I was able to relate that to my own life.

A few years ago, my family needed a bigger home, but I was afraid to purchase one because it would be more trouble to take care of. I also needed a computer for my work, but I was afraid of the time and effort it would take to master it. I also had the tendency to avoid working with certain people who were gifted and skilled, but had certain idiosyncrasies that I did not like. In each case, I was trying to keep my manger clean. I was trying to keep my life ordered, structured, and free from problems and inconveniences. But in each case, much increase would have come from my learning to live with a "messy stall" brought by each of those situations.

Eventually we moved into a bigger home and it became a haven for guests. Once we even hosted a beautiful wedding for a couple in our church and their 60 guests! My computer, while adding a new dimension to my life that required a lot of effort, has increased my productivity to levels I never thought possible. My new flexibility has allowed me to work with all kinds of people that I would have avoided in the past. These people have created some interesting problems for me to get used to, but they've also increased my ability to oversee projects requiring teams of people with diverse gifts and personalities.

Sometimes you can keep your life, family life, and ministry nice, neat, and ordered. You can fall into a convenient schedule and not have to deal with unexpected or unpleasant interruptions. In other words, you can have an empty, clean ox stall. There are times, however, when you need an ox. You may need a new car, tool, or staff member. You've avoided getting one because it would be too much trouble, and you're comfortable at your current level of commitment and effort.

Increase is a godly principle. The parable of the talents shows that those who are faithful to increase what they have are rewarded. Those afraid of what it takes to increase are considered fearful, and lose what they have. Don't be afraid of your ox, but welcome it. The ox may mess up your life, but in the long run will bring increase that honors God.

AUGUST 15

"The Lord detests the sacrifice of the wicked,
but the prayer of the upright pleases him." — *15:8.*

I jumped out of bed and grabbed the alarm clock, wanting to blame it for my troubles. It was 6:45 and I had slept through the men's prayer meeting. Of all the disciplines in my Christian walk, prayer has been the most difficult to master. There have been times when I have gotten up early, and my prayer life has flourished; at other times I could not get out of bed to save my life. There have been times when I was sure that the Lord heard my every word; other times it seemed like my words dribbled down my chin and onto the floor.

I'm sure there were people when today's verse was first written who also struggled with their prayer life. Perhaps they went on to make lavish sacrifices at the temple. They brought the finest animal, oil, or grain to give to the Lord and His servants. Their heart, however, wasn't right. They thought the impressiveness of their sacrifice would make up for what they lacked. Today's verse says that the Lord detested such sacrifices.

There can be no substitute for the prayer life of those who love the Lord. There's no sacrifice, good deed, or devotional practice that can take the place of prayer. It's not just that prayer accomplishes much good (which it does). It's more than the fact that prayer puts you in touch with the Lord of the universe. You are told in this verse that prayer, your prayer, is pleasing to God.

It still excites me that I can do things that please God. I can actually pray and the Lord will receive pleasure from my so doing. My God, who is above all and needs nothing, is pleased when I talk and pour out my heart to Him. That someone like me can please a God like Him is awesome! When God is pleased, He is moved to action. I need God to act on my behalf, so I need to pray.

Acts 10 provides a graphic picture of your prayer life. Cornelius, a Roman centurion, was "devout and God-fearing; he gave generously to those in need and prayed to God regularly" (10:2). An angel appeared to Cornelius one day and said to him, "Your prayers and gifts to the poor have come up as a remembrance before God" (10:4). Cornelius was chosen as the first Gentile convert because he prayed regularly. He was an upright man and continually pleased the Lord with his prayers. When God looked to usher in the Gentile church era, He chose a man who gave and prayed.

I'm trying to pray less to make my needs known, and more as a habit that pleases the Lord. I'm also trying to be less wordy, and more worshipful. Furthermore, I'm trying to be less demanding and more appreciative. But most of all, I'm trying to be more regular. Who knows, maybe an angel will visit me, bringing me word that my name is constantly on God's mind because I pray. What a great testimony that would be.

AUGUST 16

"When a man's ways are pleasing to the Lord,
he makes even his enemies to be at peace with him." — 16:7.

When David finally became king of all Israel, he conducted some military campaigns and then brought the ark to Jerusalem. After that was completed, 2 Samuel 7:1 says, "The Lord had given him rest from all his enemies." The Lord let David know that this time of peace was from Him. "I have cut off all your enemies from before you" (2 Samuel 7:9) and "I will give you rest from all your enemies" (2 Samuel 7:11)." That was the word of the Lord to David. Since David's ways were pleasing to the Lord, the Lord brought him peace.

Peace doesn't just happen. It's the result of conforming your thoughts, will, and actions to whatever pleases the Lord. Yesterday you read that your prayer life brings pleasure to the Lord. Today's verse reminds you that all your ways must please Him in order for the "peace of God, which transcends all understanding" (Philippians 4:7) to be yours. In fact, for your prayers to be heard, 1 John 3:22 says, "We receive from him anything we ask, because we obey his commands and do what pleases him."

How can you be sure if your ways are pleasing to the Lord? Fortunately, the word of God tells you: "Children, obey your parents in everything, for this pleases the Lord" (Colossians 3:20); the support that the Philippians sent to Paul was "an acceptable sacrifice, pleasing to God" (Philippians 4:18); your worship can be nothing less than offering your body as a "living sacrifice, holy and pleasing to God—this is your spiritual act of worship" (Romans 12:1); and your prayers for others should have the same goal that Paul had when he wrote, "We pray this in order that you may live a life worthy of the Lord and may please him in every way" (Colossians 1:10).

Paul had a simple goal in life: "We make it our goal to please him, whether we are at home in the body or away from it" (2 Corinthians 5:9). You will please the Lord not just by what you do, however, but also by who you are. Hebrews 13:20-21 says, "May the God of peace...equip you with everything good for doing his will, and may he work in us what is pleasing to him, through Jesus Christ, to whom be glory for ever and ever. Amen."

Set it as your life's goal to please the Lord. If your enemies are overwhelming you, examine your ways. Don't necessarily attack your enemies—whether internal or external—but ask the Lord to show you if there is some action or attitude that is not pleasing to Him. Correct what He shows you, and then claim the promise of victory that is for all who please Him.

AUGUST 17

"Of what use is money in the hand of a fool,
since he has no desire to get wisdom?" — *17:16.*

Jesus encountered a young man one day who "ran up to him and fell on his knees" (Mark 10:17). He was eager to have a personal audience with Jesus and ask him a question for which he thought he had the answer already. He asked Jesus, "Good teacher, what must I do to inherit eternal life?" (verse 17).

Jesus first asked the man why he called Him "good." "No one is good— except God alone" (verse 18). Jesus was asking him whether he was trying to get on Jesus' good side, or whether he had revelation that Jesus was the Son of God. Jesus decided to further test him and continued, "You know the commandments" (verse 19). The man declared that "all these I have kept since I was a boy" (verse 20). There was some obvious self-righteousness in his response.

Then Mark says, "Jesus looked at him and loved him. 'One thing you lack. Go, sell everything you have and give to the poor, and you will have treasure in heaven. Then come, follow me.' At this the man's face fell. He went away sad, because he had great wealth" (verses 21 and 22).

This young man was a righteous man. He had obeyed the commandments all his life and was interested in the things of God. Yet he was a fool. He had money, but he wasn't willing to use it to come to a closer relationship with God. He wasn't willing to trade his money for wisdom—the wisdom that would come from making Jesus the Lord of his finances.

I baptized a man one time who left his wallet in his back pocket. I asked him if he wanted to remove it, and he said no. He symbolically wanted to take his possessions and his money into the kingdom of God. Have you done the same thing? It isn't enough to keep the commandments—do not kill, steal, or commit adultery. You must learn to use all that you have to lay up treasures in heaven.

Recently I took an offering in our church for a special speaker. One man had just $62 in his checking account but the Lord directed him to give $50. He struggled but wrote the check. He no sooner dropped it into the offering basket when my secretary brought him $100 given to her by someone specifically for him. After that happened, he was glad he had obeyed the Lord! He had used his money to store up treasure, and God released some of that treasure to him almost immediately.

Use the wealth— whether great or small—that God has given you to buy wisdom. A fool hoards his money, but the wise use it to purchase godly wisdom. Commit all you have to the Lord, and then spend, keep, or distribute it as He directs. By so doing you will store up treasures in heaven and wisdom on earth. That's a good deal.

AUGUST 18

*"A fool finds no pleasure in understanding,
but delights in airing his own opinions."* — 18:2.

I was sitting in an airport boarding area when three people—a man, woman, and their college-age daughter—made it a point to come sit by me as I was doing some computer work. They began to talk in loud tones, sharing their opinions with one another about a number of subjects. They wanted me to know, for whatever reason, what their opinions were on politics, AIDS, and life in general.

I considered moving to another area, and then I prayed whether I should say something. I didn't sense the Lord giving me any direction on how to respond, and they eventually boarded their plane. Everything in me wanted to counter them with my opinions and somehow shut them up, but I had this strong sense that I was to sit there patiently and endure their opinions.

When I'm confronted with people like that, I pray that the Lord will keep me from being that same way. I don't want to force people to listen to my views when they haven't asked me. I don't want to be so arrogant that I speak with absolute certainty. Yet I also want to be bold in my witness. I don't want to be so afraid of offending that I say nothing at all, for some people will be offended at anything.

Jesus never had this problem, for He always knew what to say. That was because He was a good listener, not only to people, but to His heavenly Father. Jesus said in John 8:26, "What I have heard from him [the Father] I tell the world." Jesus did not minister with His own agenda, but rather He was here to do and say the Father's will. He also told His disciples, "I do not speak of my own accord, but the Father who sent me commanded me what to say and how to say it" (John 12:49).

The Father not only told Jesus *what* to say, but He also gave Him directions of *how* to say it. There are times when you know you have something to say, but you stumble over how to present it. You *need* a word of wisdom to know how to *give* your word of wisdom. First of all, you must surrender your right to speak your own views. Your opinions are just that, and may or may not coincide with the Lord's views on a given subject.

After you surrender your "right" to be heard, you must then seek the Lord for what to say. When confronted with a situation, pray silently. Ask the Lord if He wants you to say something. If so, ask Him to instruct you how to say it. Work on submitting your tongue to the Master, and then seek His help in speaking His words with grace and in a tone pleasing to Him. There may be times when you have something pertinent to say, but the Lord may tell you to be quiet.

A fool enjoys sharing his own opinions; a wise man enjoys sharing the word of the Lord. A man of understanding goes one step further and shares the word as the Lord would have it shared. Be a spokesman for God, and follow Jesus' example. Your speech will never be the same.

AUGUST 19

"A man's wisdom gives him patience;
it is his glory to overlook an offense." — 19:11.

The book of Proverbs was written to give you wisdom, which is the ability to use knowledge in a supernatural manner. You don't receive wisdom just to make you smarter than other people. It comes to make you more like Jesus. Jesus had many great qualities, and the most impressive, perhaps, was His patience and self-control in the face of incredible opposition.

Peter preached, "God anointed Jesus of Nazareth with the Holy Spirit and power, and he went around doing good and healing all who were under the power of the devil, because God was with him" (Acts 10:38). All this good led Jesus to the cross. The people He had helped turned against Him and His closest followers abandoned Him to the will of the Jewish leaders.

When they crucified Jesus, He did not curse or revile, nor did He vow revenge. Instead His wisdom gave Him patience and helped Him to overlook the offense. He said, "Father, forgive them, for they do not know what they are doing" (Luke 23:34). He immediately began to talk with the two criminals with whom He had been crucified. While the people and soldiers were dividing His clothes, sneering at him, and mocking Him, Jesus was promising one criminal, "Today you will be with me in paradise" (Luke 23:43). What an example of ministry! Jesus was in agony, hanging naked before family, friends, and foes, and yet He was looking beyond His own pain and relieving the pain of another.

Jesus left you an example to follow when you are hurt or offended. It's not to the glory of God to hold onto your offense. It's to His glory that you overlook it. Paul wrote to the Colossian church to "bear with each other and forgive whatever grievances you have against one another. Forgive as the Lord forgave you" (Colossians 3:13). He wrote that because he knew close relationships would bring offense. Fellow believers will say and do things to hurt you. It's your glory to overlook those hurts.

1 Corinthians 13:5 says that love "keeps no record of wrongs." Your wisdom isn't just to increase your head knowledge or your grasp of God's Word. Your wisdom will make you more like Jesus, and part of that is learning to deal with someone who offends you. It's not to your glory to confront everyone who has hurt you; it's your glory to grow in patience. As you go today, walk in glory. Don't let your day be ruined by those who wrong you. Look past them to Jesus, who learned how to do that very thing. He looked past the offense, saw His Father, and "entrusted himself to him who judges justly" (1 Peter 2:23).

AUGUST 20

"The Lord detests differing weights,
and dishonest scales do not please him." — 20:23.

In 1974, I was a graduate student working in the admissions department at a local university. I was quite busy with school work and my job, and often did papers and worked on my thesis at my desk. One morning I was in prayer and felt the Lord tell me to write a check and send it to the supply department. The check was to pay for all the paper clips, tablets, and pens I had used to work on my school work. Those office supplies were not intended for personal use, but I had freely used them. I had also used the postage machine for a few personal letters.

Panic set in. What would the person think who received my check? I was admitting to having stolen office supplies. Would they tell my boss? Could I lose my job? I delayed for several days, hoping that the Lord would relent and change His mind. When it was clear that there was no way out, I wrote a $25 check, sent it with a note, and prayed. The next day, the supply department called and I almost fainted. The man called to verify my check and what office I worked in. He deposited the check with not another word said.

Today's verse speaks to integrity in business. It literally applied to those merchants who measured out spices or other items sold by weight. The merchandise would be put on one side of a scale, and metal weights on the other side. When the weight of the merchandise was equal to the specified weights, the scales would balance. An unscrupulous merchant could alter and lighten the weights. By doing so, the merchant would sell less than the expected weight, charge the same price, and make more money. The buyer would probably never know the difference.

When the Lord confronted me, I was using a "dishonest scale" on my job. I wasn't treating what belonged to another with integrity. I was preaching honesty, and appearing to be what I was preaching. But I was using deceptive weights when it came to my own actions. I was justifying what I did because I was busy, and it was "only" a few tablets and supplies that wouldn't be missed. I had lightened the weights on one end of the scale, and it appeared that my employer had an honest employee. He really had one who was not afraid to pilfer his supplies.

Paul wrote Titus to "teach slaves to be subject to their masters in everything, to try to please them, not to talk back to them, and not to steal from them, but to show that they can be fully trusted, so that in every way they will make the teaching about God our Savior attractive" (Titus 2:9-10). Paul was urging employees and employers to use honest scales. Do a full day's work for a day's pay by putting in your allotted hours. Don't steal. Make sure you provide what you promise, and what the customer expects. All this is to be done for one reason—so that God and His doctrine will have a good reputation.

Commit to absolute honesty in business, realizing that your behavior there is a direct reflection of your God. Show by your deeds that God is above reproach, and bring glory to Him in even the smallest of business dealings.

AUGUST 21

"There is no wisdom, no insight,
no plan that can succeed against the Lord." — 21:30.

Haman was the villain in the book of Esther. He was the king's right-hand man and that position brought him prestige, money, and power. He attempted to use that power to wipe out the people of God, however, and his efforts brought him to ruin.

Haman was consumed with anger toward Mordecai, Queen Esther's cousin. Haman had been given a place of honor above all the officials of the land, and it was customary for the other officials to kneel down and honor him. Mordecai, being a Jew who worshiped no man, refused to kneel, and Haman set out for revenge. "He scorned the idea of killing only Mordecai. Instead Haman looked for a way to destroy all Mordecai's people, the Jews throughout the whole kingdom of Xerxes" (Esther 3:6).

This man petitioned the king (and also paid a large amount of money into the king's treasury) to issue a decree to destroy the Jews. The king did so, and the edict went out that on the thirteenth day of the twelfth month, all the Jews were to be killed and their property seized.

Today's verse tells us that there is no plan or wisdom that can succeed against the Lord. God was already one step ahead of Haman. Esther, herself a Jew, was already queen. She had won the favor of her husband the king, who didn't know her nationality. Mordecai urged Esther to make herself known and, after fasting and praying, she did so. During a banquet for the king and Haman, Esther revealed Haman's treachery. The result was that Haman was hung on the very gallows he had built to hang Mordecai.

What was true for Mordecai and Esther is still true for you today. God is with you, and no plan will succeed that sets itself against you. Paul wrote,

> If God is for us, who can be against us....For I am convinced that neither death nor life, neither angels nor demons, neither the present nor the future, nor any powers, neither height nor depth, not anything else in all creation, will be able to separate us from the love of God that is in Christ Jesus our Lord (Romans 8:31, 38-39).

You can rest secure in God's power, for there is none like Him in all the heavens and earth. The enemies of God—your enemies—may seem to have the upper hand for the moment, but their victory will be short-lived. They will be undone through the very plans they designed to undo you! Walk in confidence and security knowing that your God rules over all. Don't be anxious or worry, for He holds the outcome of all things in His mighty hands.

AUGUST 22

"A good name is more desirable than great riches,
to be esteemed is better than silver or gold." — 22:1.

The story of Jesus and Zacchaeus is found in Luke 19. Zacchaeus was a tax collector short in stature. He was hated by his fellow Jews, because he collected taxes for the Roman government. Every tax collector was assessed a quota to collect, and could keep everything over and above the quota. This made tax collectors wealthy but despised men. They had silver and gold, but they also had a bad name.

As Jesus came through Jericho, Zacchaeus climbed a sycamore tree to get a better view. "When Jesus reached the spot, he looked up and said to him, 'Zacchaeus, come down immediately. I must stay at your house today.' So he came down at once and welcomed him gladly" (Luke 19:5-6). The people "began to mutter, 'He has gone to be the guest of a sinner'"(verse 7).

The Lord was reaching out in love to this man who had his priorities all wrong. Zacchaeus had hoped to get a good name by accumulating wealth. He also hoped to be a successful business man, but instead found the scorn of his neighbors. He was stuck in this life he had created. Jesus came to save him and help him to set his priorities straight. "Zacchaeus stood up and said to the Lord, 'Look, Lord! Here and now I give half of my possessions to the poor, and if I have cheated anybody out of anything, I will pay back four times the amount.' Jesus said to him, 'Today salvation has come to this house, because this man, too, is a son of Abraham'" (verses 8-9).

Zacchaeus put his faith in Jesus that day, and he received the good name of Abraham. He gave away his riches and in return got a name that was esteemed; he was considered by God a son of Abraham.

The third commandment says, "You shall not misuse the name of the Lord your God" (Exodus 20:7). This doesn't pertain to cursing as most people think. It rather cautions people not to take the name of the Lord and do nothing with it. It warns not to become familiar with this good name, and then go about with a life that is unchanged and shows no godly fruit. Zacchaeus didn't misuse the name of the Lord. He didn't go out and try to get more money, using God's name as his justification. He didn't become a "born-again" tax collector. He was not guilty of misusing the name of his God but chose a good name over riches. (He took definite steps to make his behavior consistent with one who bore the name of Abraham.)

It's never too late for you to set your priorities right with the Lord. Perhaps you have pursued success, fame, or money at the expense of your reputation. Maybe your ministry has grown, but your children have suffered. It's not too late to get it right. The Lord sought Zacchaeus, and He is seeking you. He wants to give you His good name, and it's worth infinitely more than what you've been pursuing. Today you can become a child of Abraham if you put your trust completely in the good name of Jesus Christ.

AUGUST 23

"Listen, my son, and be wise, and keep your heart on the right path." — 23:19.

As I looked out the plane, I saw a smog cloud hovering over Los Angeles, but nothing could dampen our enthusiasm. The Lord had miraculously provided a family vacation, and we rejoiced as we landed. We arrived with a lot of excitement, but not much cash, a condition that had plagued us for more than a few days. The next morning I prayed about our financial situation, asking the Lord whether this was a result of some mistake on our part, or was this something God was using to develop and train us?

That day we went to an amusement park with barely enough money for that one day. While standing in line, a woman turned around and gave us four free tickets! Once in the park, we purchased a meager lunch. When we went to our table, another woman came and insisted we had left a large order of food at the counter. We did not, but she forced us to take it and then disappeared into the crowd!

I heard the Lord "speaking" through these events. He was answering my prayer by showing that He was in control. He had our situation well in hand, and would provide for all our needs. To be honest, I would have rather had $10,000 in cash, but tickets and hot dogs would do for now.

Today's verse commands you, as a child of God, to listen and keep your heart on the right path. God can (and will) speak to His children through circumstances and with His voice. You must be ready to listen, and then direct your heart in the way the Lord commands. Jesus called Himself the shepherd of the sheep in John 10. He said that the sheep follow a shepherd because "they know his voice. But they will never follow a stranger; in fact they will run away from him because they do not recognize a stranger's voice" (John 10:4-5). Your shepherd wants to talk with you. Isaiah wrote a passage that was a prophetic description of Jesus:

> The Sovereign Lord has given me an instructed tongue, to know the word that sustains the weary. He wakens me morning by morning, wakens my ear to listen like one being taught. The Sovereign Lord has opened my ears, and I have not been rebellious; I have not drawn back (Isaiah 50:4-5).

Jesus prayed that the Father would open His ears and give Him the ability to hear His voice. Jesus acknowledged that what He did hear was due to the Father opening his ears. What Jesus heard, He did, not drawing back even from the cross. In fact the next verse says, "I offered my back to those who beat me, my cheeks to those who pulled out my beard"(verse 6).

Listen for the voice of God, for He is answering the cries of your heart. Pray that He will open your ear every morning to teach you. When you hear—and you will hear—don't shrink back from what He says. Set your heart on the right path no matter how difficult or painful. You are His sheep and your Shepherd is talking. Don't follow the voice of a stranger, but rather respond to the voice of love, the voice of Him who laid down His life for the sheep.

AUGUST 24

"For waging war you need guidance, and for victory many advisers." — 24:6.

King David was a man after God's own heart, having waited since his anointing as a youth to become the King of Israel. "When all the elders of Israel had come to King David at Hebron, the king made a compact with them at Hebron before the Lord, and they anointed David king over Israel" (2 Samuel 5:3). The Lord was finally bringing to pass what He had promised!

Trouble, however, was just over the horizon as the Philistines, the enemies of Israel, were marching against David to ruin his coronation. David barely had time to enjoy his new office before he had to go to war. David could have marched right out in the excitement of his new position. Or he could have been on a spiritual "high" and rushed out, confident of the Lord's blessing. That, however, was not the case. Instead, "He inquired of the Lord. The Lord answered him, 'Go, for I will surely hand the Philistines over to you'" (2 Samuel 5:19).

David was victorious because he sought guidance before he waged war. He didn't presume to know God's will, but sought it carefully and deliberately. The story, however, doesn't end there, for those stubborn Philistines came back for another battle! David could have gone out in the power of the previous word he had received from the Lord. But instead he again "inquired of the Lord, and he answered, 'Do not go straight up, but circle around behind them and attack them in front of the balsam trees'" (2 Samuel 5:23). This time the Lord gave him a new strategy, and once again he was victorious.

You too are involved in a spiritual war and can't presume to know who your enemies are, or how they can be defeated. When you are fresh from a spiritual success, you're often most vulnerable to presumption. At that point, you can easily assume that the Lord is with you and that anything you do will succeed. That, however, is not the case.

Yesterday you read of your need to listen to the voice of the Lord. The same lesson applies today for the Lord wants to speak and guide your steps. Don't enter a business deal with confidence just because you have some experience. Don't minister to someone the way that has always "worked" for you just because you've always done it that way. Don't put your confidence in past victories, but rather seek the Lord's guidance even for things that have become second nature to you.

David was on top of his world when God's enemies marched against him. It would seem to have been clear what he was to do. Yet he sought the Lord, and you must do the same thing. Don't assume to know God's mind. Ask Him and then have the faith that He will respond. Do what He says and you'll say what David said: "The Lord has broken out against my enemies before me" (2 Samuel 5:20).

AUGUST 25

"Like an earring of gold or an ornament of fine gold
is a wise man's rebuke to a listening ear." — 25:13.

I was a new Christian on fire for the Lord. I was working my first job as part of a college admissions staff, none of whom were believers. I witnessed to them in the strongest terms, and wasn't tolerant of their actions or attitudes. My boss would often ask me the question, "Did God make man or man make God?" and I would launch into a vehement defense of my God.

One day this same boss came into my office and closed the door, asking to have a word with me. He sat down across from my desk and began to rebuke me, telling me that my work wasn't what it could be. He said the staff felt I was very critical of them, not exhibiting "Christian love" as he put it. He was firm, yet kind and fatherly. This was the same man who mocked God—or so I thought—and everything in me wanted to tell him where to go (at least out of my office).

I knew, however, that he was speaking the truth and that the Lord had sent him to me. I was out of control, trying hard to convince people I was a believer rather than trying to show them. It was true that my work had not been the best, because I resented being paid so little. I felt superior to those I worked with, so I was critical and intolerant. I couldn't respond to him that day, and after he left my office I wept bitter tears. Through him, the Lord had rebuked me and I was hurting.

I knelt down next to my desk and asked God to forgive me, asking him to help me be a better worker. When I composed myself, I went to my boss and thanked him for his courage and grace. I apologized for my shortcomings and vowed to do better. I went on, with his help, to improve my performance greatly. When the opportunity came, that man recommended me for a job that tripled my salary!

This man wasn't a righteous man, but God used him. By the grace of God, I had a listening ear at that point so that I didn't miss what the Lord was trying to say. The Lord often will use people to rebuke you and set you on a course that is pleasing to him. King David knew this, and wrote in Psalm 141:5, "Let a righteous man strike me—it is a kindness; let him rebuke me—it is oil on my head. My head will not refuse it." What a bold statement! David was asking the Lord to send people who would correct him, and he was promising that he wouldn't find excuses to dismiss what they were saying.

Can you pray what David prayed? Will you commit to receive any that come to you today and listen to what they have to say? That requires humility, grace, and faith. Pray that God will give you a listening ear that can hear the rebuke of the wise. Then accept the fact that the Lord may use other people to speak His corrective word to you.

AUGUST 26

"The words of a gossip are like choice morsels;
they go down to a man's inmost parts." — 26:22.

Churches can be nesting grounds for gossip and rumors. Because churches attract people who see one another regularly, there's a tendency for the people to talk about other people in the church. When you get close to people, you see them as they are in their weaknesses. It's easy to "compare notes" with someone else about the problems or faults of another. Even if it's all true, it constitutes gossip.

Jesus was familiar with this problem, because He lived in a community where people grew up together. Everyone knew everyone, and then Jesus became famous and was the talk of Israel. This made him the target for gossip. In John 8, Jesus was in a heavy discussion with the Pharisees. They said to Jesus in verse 41, "We are not illegitimate children." I have always interpreted this to mean that the Pharisees were saying, "We are not illegitimate like you." Perhaps they knew the circumstances around Jesus' birth and were drawing the wrong conclusion. That was some of the gossip going around about Jesus.

Then in verse 48 they said, "Aren't we right in saying that you are a Samaritan and demon-possessed?" In their private discussions, they had concluded that Jesus was a halfbreed Samaritan with demonic problems. Again they were talking about Jesus when He wasn't there and coming to some awful conclusions that were spread in casual conversation.

Today's verse states that gossip is like a smorgasbord full of great food—both are hard to pass up. To hear the latest tidbit about someone is almost impossible to resist. Today you should make up your mind not to talk about anyone not present unless it is positive. Praise them or pray for them, but don't be the source or recipient of information about them, even if it's true. Paul wrote to Corinth, "I fear that there may be quarreling, jealousy, outbursts of anger, factions, slander, gossip, arrogance, and disorder" (2 Corinthians 12:20). Gossip has no place in the body of Christ.

Maybe you are in a place where you are the subject of the gossip. Your weakness has been blown out of proportion and it's the talk of the town. What should you do? Do what Jesus did. He did not address the gossip. He knew that truth always triumphs and He went about His business. They said Jesus was in league with the devil, yet He didn't stop to defend Himself or try to set the record straight. He Himself said, "Blessed are you when people insult you, persecute you and falsely say all kinds of evil against you because of me" (Matthew 5:11). Jesus was blessed when people did that, and so are you. Let it go and let God even the score. People may eat the gossip, but in the end, it will turn sour in their hearts.

AUGUST 27

"He who tends the fig tree will eat its fruit,
and he who looks after his master will be honored." — 27:18.

"God, there has to be more than this!" I remember crying that one night as I knelt by my bed in prayer. I had been serving as an assistant to my pastor for four years. He was and is a great man of God, and has fathered me in the Lord. I moved to be with him and served him as he traveled in ministry. I cared for his house, watched his children, paid his bills, and kept watch over the flock when he was gone.

But I wanted my own ministry. I had received promises from God to that end, and all I was doing (or so it seemed) were meaningless, trivial tasks that anyone could do. I wanted to preach, teach, and maybe even travel. I wasn't even studying theology. I was just working to assist this one man and it seemed totally unfair.

When I cried to the Lord, I soon saw today's verse. I was tending the fig tree that God had chosen for me. It was only one tree, but God had hand-picked it for me. If I would tend that fig tree, I would eat its fruit. If I would look after my "master," one day I would be honored. I jumped up with excitement. If I would continue to sow into his life, I would reap it back again. I used that verse whenever I got restless, and God has been faithful to bring it about.

Today I'm doing everything I ever wanted to do in the ministry and more. I'm preaching, teaching, pastoring, traveling, writing, studying, and counseling. I've been given my own "trees" and God has given me men and women who are learning to tend my trees so they can receive their own. Don't be afraid to serve someone else's vision, fearing being "used." Honor your master, whoever he or she may be. Tend their fig tree and one day you will get your own.

Galatians 5:13 says, "You, my brothers, were called to be free. But do not use your freedom to indulge the sinful nature; rather, serve one another in love." 1 Peter 5:6 instructs you to "humble yourselves, therefore, under God's mighty hand, that he may lift you up in due time." Determine to serve the Body and especially those over you. Service requires humility, for it's often done behind the scenes and may directly benefit someone else. You have God's promise, however, that, if you humble yourself under His hand, He will personally exalt you in due time.

My road to the ministry led through serving another man's vision for several years. My personal testimony includes the truth of today's verse. Honor your master, and you will be honored. Serve with grace and receive that same grace back at a later date. You may not like figs, but the honor is tremendous.

AUGUST 28

"He whose walk is blameless is kept safe,
but he whose ways are perverse will suddenly fall." — 28:18.

Have you ever gone to a church meeting and witnessed someone drop dead as they presented their offering? That would be a meeting you would not soon forget! The Bible records such a meeting in Acts 5:

> Now a man names Ananias, together with his wife Sapphira, also sold a piece of property. With his wife's full knowledge he kept back part of the money for himself, but brought the rest and put it at the apostle's feet. Then Peter said, "Ananias, how is it that Satan has filled your heart that you have lied to the Holy Spirit and have kept for yourself some of the money you received for the land? Didn't it belong to you before it was sold? And after it was sold, wasn't the money at your disposal? What made you think of doing such a thing? You have not lied to men but to God." When Ananias heard this, he fell down and died. And great fear seized all who heard what had happened (Acts 5:1-5).

Ananias came to the meeting and pretended to give all the proceeds from the sale of his property to the church. If he would have said, "We sold a piece of property for this much, and we are giving eighty percent," he would have been truthful. Instead he wanted the glory and notoriety as if he were giving all. He wanted to appear more generous than he truly was.

Later his wife came in and she was questioned as to the price of the land, and whether they were giving it all to the church. When she verified her husband's lie, she died, too. That meeting had not one death, but two! Verse 11 says, "Great fear seized the whole church and all who heard about these events." You can understand why!

Today's verse says that those who go off in strange ways will fall. Their fall will not be gradual, but sudden. You must be diligent to keep your ways blameless. Don't let some "little" fault grow to such a habit that it causes you shame and embarrassment. Don't let the leaven of sin come in and puff you up to look like you're something when you're not. Ananias and Sapphira wanted to impress people with their giving, but they were not as generous as they seemed. God, who is never mocked, exposed their perversity and sudden was their fall.

Examine your ways today. Are they blameless or is there some besetting sin— lies, lust, or greed—that has gone unchecked? If there is something, and the Holy Spirit will show you (if you are serious), then repent. Ask God to remove that perverse way. Don't wait until the crash, but take steps to avoid the fall today, before it's too late. There is safety in integrity—take refuge there now before it's too late.

AUGUST 29

"Where there is no vision, the people perish." — 29:18 (KJV).

Another person called to tell me they were leaving the church, and I was depressed and discouraged. I had heard it said that if you give someone a job to do in the church, they will stay put. Everyone that had left my church, however, had a job to do but still they were leaving. It was frustrating and disturbing.

As I analyzed the situation, I found that each person was indeed busy. They were not, however, committed to the overall purpose of the church. They didn't share my vision for what we were doing and why the church existed. They were fine people, and we parted on good terms. But they could not stay because they didn't share the same vision.

Where does vision come from? If I understand it correctly, it comes from faith. Faith gives you the ability to see the invisible. It takes you from the realm of the seen to that of the unseen. I'm not saying that the people who left had no faith. They needed to seek the Lord in faith to get a vision that would excite them. When they found it, they would give their lives to it. Vision has that much power.

The king of Aram wanted to find Elisha, the Old Testament prophet so "he sent horses and chariots and a strong force there. They went by night and surrounded the city" (2 Kings 6:14). Elisha's servant panicked, asking, "Oh, my lord, what shall we do?" (verse 15). The servant lacked vision and was perishing for lack of it. Elisha comforted him and said, "Don't be afraid. Those who are with us are more than those who are with them. And Elisha prayed, 'O Lord, open his eyes so he may see'" (verses 16-17).

Elisha knew that unless the servant's eyes were opened, he would not be able to function. So Elisha prayed and the Lord answered his prayer. "Then the Lord opened the servant's eyes, and he looked and saw the hills full of horses and chariots of fire all around Elisha" (verse 17). What a vision! That servant would never be the same because his eyes were taken off what he could see and instead focused on the unseen. He had vision, and he faced the Arameans with confidence in the unseen Lord of all.

You may not have much vision. Perhaps you're so bound to the visible that you're slipping spiritually. If that's true, do like Elisha and ask God to open your eyes. You might also pray what Paul prayed: "I pray also that the eyes of your heart may be enlightened in order that you may know the hope to which he has called you, the riches of the glorious inheritance in the saints, and his incomparably great power for us who believe." (Ephesians 1:18-19). Don't pray it for other people; pray it for yourself! In faith, ask God to show you and He will. If you're perishing because you don't have vision, you don't have to stay in that predicament. Ask God to open your eyes, and you will see what He sees. It will turn your life around!

AUGUST 30

"Do not slander a servant to his master,
or he will curse you, and you will pay for it." — 30:10.

I was watching sports highlights late one evening, and saw a fight break out between two baseball teams. The star player on one team was hit by a pitch purposely thrown by the opposing pitcher. Immediately the players from both sides were on the field punching, grabbing, holding, and kicking. The announcer said it went on for thirty minutes!

As I watched in amusement, I felt the Holy Spirit speak to me, "I wish my people were more like that." I dismissed it as a thought coming from the lateness of the hour. But the Lord persisted, and I had to ask Him to explain. As I meditated, I realized that the players were protecting their own. They weren't going to stand for the "enemy" doing anything to hurt their star. If that pitcher did it to one, it was as if he did it to all.

I understood that the body of Christ needs to protect its own just like that team tried to do. When the enemy knocks down a brother, we need to storm the field. We need to pick up a fallen comrade and be quick to his or her defense. All too often, however, we distance ourselves from those under attack, and are ready to switch teams if they make a mistake or fail.

When I first believed, I was convinced that the gift of suspicion, which I had in abundance, was a gift of the Holy Spirit. I was wary of everyone who was doing anything for the Lord. I was jealous of anyone who had more than I had in the Lord. One day I was asked my opinion about a certain minister. Without hesitation, I began to freely share my thoughts, emphasizing all the areas where I disagreed with him. I was not a team player.

Shortly thereafter I was reading the book of Romans, and the Lord hit me right between the eyes with Romans 14:4: "Who are you to judge another man's servant? To his own master he stands or falls. And he will stand, for the Lord is able to make him stand." Later in the same chapter, Paul wrote, "You, then, why do you judge your brother? Or why do you look down on your brother? For we will all stand before God's judgment seat....Therefore let us stop passing judgment on one another" (verses 10, 13).

Then I saw today's verse, and my conviction was complete. I saw that I was slandering a servant of God, not just to others, but to God! From that time on, the Lord has tried to work in me graciousness and kindness toward my fellow servants, for they are all His servants. We are on the same team and have the same manager. I determined to stand with my teammates and not slander them. I may not agree with them, but I decided to attack the devil and not my fellow believers.

You should determine to do the same. When the enemy throws a high, hard fast ball at your brother, don't applaud, but be ready to storm the field in your brother's defense. Remember who your real enemy is today, and then stand with your teammates in the Lord.

AUGUST 31

"Speak up and judge fairly; defend the rights of the poor and needy." — 31:9.

Senator Stanko had a nice sound to it, or so I dreamed. My goal early in life was a political career. I came to know the Lord through contacts I had made as I was preparing my campaign to become a Model Cities Commissioner, a position created by President Lyndon Johnson's war on poverty in the 60s. My plan was to use that election victory to launch my career. I won that election, but the residents protested my student status. The results were actually thrown out and I lost the new election by just nine votes! My political dreams were shattered!

I tried to stay politically active from that point, but the Lord had different plans. I had always identified closely with the perceived agenda of one political party, and tend to vote for their candidates. The Lord, however, was not interested in whether I was a Republican or a Democrat. I soon learned that the Lord had His own agenda, and I was now dead to the things of the world. I've never missed voting in an election, but I now do so as a voter registered in the Lamb's book of life.

The church and you as part of it are to be a prophetic voice to this generation, actually being God's spokesperson. You must maintain your allegiance to God's Word, and speak it to members of all political parties. Both conservatives and liberals put man at the center of things—the former tend to say that man can handle his own problems without government, while the latter generally feel that more government involvement is required to heal the hurts of man. Both sides are wrong! There is only one answer to man's woes—the gospel of Jesus Christ—and anything else is just a band-aid put on a major wound.

Politicians will attempt to court believers as another minority group among their followers, but you are not to go along. Your trust is to be in the Lord and not in any form of government. Psalm 146:3-4 states, "Do not put your trust in princes, in mortal men, who cannot save. When their spirit departs, they return to the ground; on that very day their plans come to nothing."

Don't rely on the government what the church is to do. You are to speak for the oppressed, defending the lowly and poor. A secular institution cannot understand or provide justice. Only those who understand God and His law can do so. Speak up, and when you do, speak to all political parties. You owe allegiance to one, and He is the Lord. No political party can carry out the Lord's agenda. Only the church can do that.

Take courage to speak out wherever you see injustice.

SEPTEMBER 1

*"Listen, my son, to your father's instruction
and do not forsake your mother's teaching." —1:8.*

There I was, a guest in someone's home, sick and wanting to be someplace, anyplace else. My wife and I had traveled with our pastor to another city where he was ministering. We were sitting in the living room of the host pastor, and he had assembled a group of people together to sing and worship. For two hours, I sat there while they sang songs (mostly hymns) that I had never heard. Not only was I ill, but I was a bit perturbed that they weren't singing some of the newer music written for my generation.

I've come a long way since that night when I pouted in that pastor's home. I've come to realize that my journey with the Lord isn't complete without an appreciation and understanding of those brothers and sisters who have gone before me. I need them, their insight, and their testimony if I'm to carry on in their footsteps.

Jesus said, "My mothers and brothers are those who hear God's word and put it into practice" (Luke 8:21). You have many mothers and fathers in the faith who went before you. They gave their lives so that today you can enjoy freedom to proclaim the Gospel, own a Bible, and be free from a state-run church. In your family tree are those who gave their lives to break with the norm to establish godly traditions in their churches, homes, and governments.

You don't stand alone as you walk with the Lord. You are "surrounded by such a great cloud of witnesses" (Hebrews 12:1) that you can't ignore the historic church. Don't look down on the past from the superior position of the present. What God is doing in you, He has done in countless millions before you. You don't exist apart from them. They have passed the baton on to you, and you must run the way they ran—with faith, courage, and zeal. They often overcame greater obstacles than you ever will, and their stories will serve to challenge your faith.

Today's verse encourages you not to ignore the instruction of your spiritual parents. Many have gone before you, and they left a legacy for you. Don't ignore them and feel like they have nothing to say to you. Commit yourself to learn from them. Sing their songs and read their devotional books. Appreciate them for the pioneers that they were. Then determine to leave your own legacy to the next generation.

You're not part of something that began with you, but of something that began long ago. You're to preserve it, add to it, and pass it on. So this Sunday, sing some verses of a hymn you don't know, and learn to tolerate it, or maybe even like it. Don't judge the past, but embrace it and you will enhance the value of what the Lord has done for you today.

"For the upright will live in the land,
and the blameless will remain in it." —2:21.

I was in jail again, doing a "life" sentence one visit at a time to minister to the inmates. As I fielded questions, the inevitable issue of the end times came up. The men had heard all the theories concerning the beast, the number "666," the tribulation, and the rapture. I answered and responded as best I could, but was overwhelmed with the pessimism and fatalism that prevailed in the men. The book of Revelation and biblical prophecy had the men's attention, and it had won their imaginations and intellectual efforts.

The disciples were preoccupied with the end as well. After Jesus' resurrection, they asked Him, "Lord, are you at this time going to restore the kingdom to Israel?" (Acts 1:6). Jesus' reply was enlightening:

It is not for you to know the times or dates the Father has set by his own authority. But you will receive power when the Holy Spirit comes on you; and you will be my witnesses in Jerusalem, and in all Judea and Samaria, and to the ends of the earth (Acts 1:7-8).

Jesus told them to stay focused on their mission and not to get sidetracked by speculation over things that have no specific answer. He warned them not to let anything keep them from their appointed task of presenting the Gospel to the world. They took heed, and proceeded to turn the world upside down with their preaching and witnessing. Their outlook was optimistic, even though they faced huge obstacles from idolatrous Romans and hard-hearted Jews.

You have a choice of whether you will be an intellectual Christian or an active Christian. Now, intellectual and theological studies are wonderful, if they lead to Christian character and action. If they simply lead to more studies and doctrinal speculation, then they are a waste of time. The apostle Paul was a learned man, but his learning did not lead him to a pessimistic world view. He understood that "the earth is the Lord's and everything in it" (Psalm 24:1). Paul knew what Nebuchadnezzar learned the hard way, that "the Most High is sovereign over the kingdoms of men and gives them to anyone he wishes and sets over them the lowliest of men" (Daniel 4:17).

Whatever your stand on the return of the Lord—and the good news is that He will return—you should be optimistic about the future. The blameless and upright will be rewarded. In fact, Jesus said the meek "will inherit the earth" (Matthew 5:5). The meek will not be run over by some world government, but instead will usher in the government of God. I don't understand how or when that will take place, but I know it will.

Armed with that knowledge, I refuse to live in fear and pessimism over the devil or his antichrist. Instead I walk and preach a victorious Gospel that says, "Repent, for the kingdom of heaven is near" (Matthew 4:17).

SEPTEMBER 3

"Trust in the Lord with all your heart
and lean not on your own understanding." — 3:5.

It was a dream come true. There we were sitting in the grandstands on Colorado Boulevard in Pasadena, California as the Rose Bowl parade passed in front of us. Since I was a child, I had vowed that "one day" I would see it in person. And there I was! It was spectacular. The bands, the flowers, and floats with the Southern California mountains as a backdrop were everything and more I had thought they would be.

King David sponsored a lavish parade that would have rivaled any ever held. After he became king of all Israel, David decided to bring the ark of the covenant back to Israel. The ark had been in the land of the Philistines, and David, rightly so, wanted to return it to the people of God.

David again brought together out of Israel chosen men, thirty thousand in all. They set the ark of God on a new cart and brought it from the house of Abinadab. David and the whole house of Israel were celebrating with all their might before the Lord, with songs and with harps, lyres, tambourines, sistrums and cymbals (2 Samuel 6:2-3).

What a procession! Thirty thousand chosen men, led by King David, with the ark on a new cart, were returning the ark to its rightful place. But then tragedy struck the parade.

When they came to the threshing floor of Nacon, Uzzah reached out and took hold of the ark of God, because the oxen stumbled. The Lord's anger burned against Uzzah because of his irreverent act; therefore God struck him down and he died there beside the ark of God (2 Samuel 6:6-7).

What happened here? Why would God have struck down a man who was trying to serve his king and God? The answers are found in today's verse. David and his men had leaned on their own understanding. They brought the ark up on an ox cart, which is just how the Philistines had done it. As Paul wrote, "They are zealous for God, but their zeal is not based on knowledge" (Romans 10:2).

The will of God was plainly revealed: the ark was to be covered, staves were to be inserted in the rings in its ends, and it was to be carried on the shoulders of the Kohathites. Nothing had been said about placing it on a "new cart": that was a human invention, and contrary to the instructions of the Lord. David's desire was holy, his motive was pure, but he went about things in a wrong way.*

You are not free to serve God as you chose to serve Him. To please Him you must do it *His way* and according to His word. See where you are leaning on your own understanding, and repent today of any "good ideas" that have crept into your walk. Then determine, with God's help, to trust in His ways in all that you do.

*The Life of David by Arthur W. Pink, page 291.

247

SEPTEMBER 4

"Wisdom is supreme; therefore get wisdom.
Though it cost you all you have, get understanding." — 4:7.

Yesterday you saw David's triumphal parade turn into a funeral march. Uzzah, one of his choice men, had been struck down after touching the ark. When the oxen stumbled, Uzzah reached out to steady their cargo. When he did, he died. David, who had the best of intentions, was confused. The Bible says,

> Then David was angry because the Lord's wrath had broken out against Uzzah, and to this day that place is called Perez Uzzah. David was afraid...and said, "How can the ark of the Lord ever come to me?" (2 Samuel 6:8-9).

David parked the ark in someone else's home until he could figure out what went wrong. He continued to seek the Lord for wisdom in the midst of his confusion.

Today's verse encourages you to do the same. Have you ever had a time when you were serving the Lord, doing what you thought He wanted, yet things were not going well? Perhaps you had been generous, but your financial picture was as bad as ever. Maybe you were serving the church, and people and leaders seemed to ignore you, or take you for granted. Or have you loved and served your spouse, only to have that spouse harden his or her heart against you?

When that happens, you can get angry and fearful. It's easy to say, "I tried that and it didn't work!" Cynicism can creep in and tell you that serving the Lord is too hard, or God is impossible to figure out. When this happens, you might be tempted to pull back from the Lord, not wanting to invest any more of your best efforts.

David was at that place, but he didn't stay there long. Instead he sought the Lord and found wisdom and understanding. His zeal without knowledge had cost him one of his best men, so he turned to the Lord for insight. In 1 Chronicles 15:2, David said, "No one but the Levites may carry the ark of God, because the Lord chose them to carry the ark of the Lord and to minister before him forever." Later in verses 12-13 he said,

> You are the heads of the Levitical families; you and your fellow Levites are to consecrate yourselves and bring up the ark of the Lord, the God of Israel, to the place I have prepared for it. It was because you, the Levites, did not bring it up the first time that the Lord our God broke out in anger against us. We did not inquire of him about how to do it in the prescribed way.

If it seems like God is resisting you, it's time to humble yourself. Declare a fast and pray. Study the word of God. Ask the Lord to show you where you are. Are you serving Him the way He wants to be served? Are you raising your children according to His word. Are your marriage and business life in line with His commands? David was angry and afraid, but when he took time to get wisdom and understanding, he saw the error of his ways. God is a good God. Seek Him and His wisdom, and change your ways to please Him. It's worth whatever effort you make.

"I would not obey my teachers, or listen to my instructors.
I have come to the brink of utter ruin." — 5:13-14.

These last several days we have studied David's struggle to bring the ark back to Israel. After the tragic death of one of his men, David sought the Lord concerning the proper way to bring up the ark. Undoubtedly he sought the insight of the Levites who had been given custody of the ark. When he did bring up the ark according to their advice and the word of God, his mission was successful.

David's grandson wasn't as wise. Rehoboam inherited the kingdom after Solomon's death. The people came to him and asked for relief from the heavy burden that Solomon had put on them due to his massive building projects. Rehoboam sought counsel from his teachers and instructors.

King Rehoboam consulted the elders who had served his father Solomon during his lifetime. "How would you advise me to answer these people?" he asked. They replied, "If today you will be a servant to these people and serve them and give them a favorable answer, they will always be your servants." But Rehoboam rejected the advice the elders gave him and consulted the young men who had grown up with him and were serving him (1 Kings 12:6-8).

The young men advised that he assert his authority even more, and increase the burden on the people. That's what Rehoboam did, and the people rebelled. Ten tribes defected to Jeroboam, and the kingdom of Israel was never the same. The glory days of David were over because this young man refused to listen to his instructors.

As you build in life, you must learn to seek out instructors and listen to them. My marriage, children, finances, ministry, and walk with the Lord are what they are in large part because of the input I've received. I've carefully chosen teachers whose lives I wanted to imitate. I've sought their input and have benefited greatly. I can think of times when I wanted to carry out my own plan, only to receive godly counsel that changed my mind. In the end, I was glad it did.

The choice is yours. Be like David and seek the counsel of the godly, or be like Rehoboam and pursue your own agenda. Is your marriage going through a difficult time? Seek counsel. Are your finances stretched thin? Seek counsel. Having family problems? Seek counsel. Struggling in ministry? Seek counsel. Planning a ministry or business expansion? Seek counsel.

To ignore or avoid your instructors is foolishness. Hear their instruction and then act on it. Utter ruin is the inheritance of those who reject the Lord. God wants you to prosper and succeed in every area of life. He will send you people who can help you do just that.

SEPTEMBER 6

"When you sleep, they will watch over you." — 6:22.

It was a business meeting that will live in my mind for the rest of my days. I was in a meeting of elders and church leaders. I urgently voiced my opinion, but the moderator tried to move on to the next item. I objected and then tried to block the meeting's progress. I was so disrespectful and rude that the leader had no option but to adjourn the meeting, and we were only on the second item of business. He was mad, and I had, quite frankly, acted like a donkey—stubborn and obstinate.

Later, I was mortified at my behavior. How could I have been so arrogant? I carried that guilt all day, and could not face my friends. That night, however, I had a dream. A former pastor appeared in my dream and told me everything was all right. He instructed me to ask forgiveness of those involved and not to let this condemnation overwhelm me. I awakened, and I felt wonderful. As quickly as I could, I sought forgiveness from my brothers, and we got on with the business at hand.

Today's verse tells you that the Lord can minister to you even in your sleep. Your body may rest, but your spirit never does because while you rest, the Lord can speak to your spirit. He can counsel, comfort, direct, and rebuke. In fact, when your flesh is at rest and unable to interfere, the Lord can actually speak to you more clearly.

Think of how many times dreams were given to guide people in the Bible. Jacob had a dream and saw the angels of God ascending and descending a heavenly ladder. Joseph had a dream that he would rule his brothers. Pharaoh dreamed about a pending famine. Joseph, Mary's husband, was continually directed by dreams concerning Jesus' birth and early life. The Magi were warned in a dream not to return to Herod. Paul was instructed to go to Macedonia in a dream.

Sometimes the best thing you can do is go to sleep. Don't stay up fretting over what direction you should take. Don't lose sleep over some dilemma you are in. Psalm 127:2 says, "He gives [blessings] to His beloved in sleep" (AMP). You might be tempted to rely on your five senses as the only way to get revelation and guidance. The Lord, however, never slumbers nor sleeps and can speak to you even when your senses are at rest.

Pay attention to your dreams. Pay special attention to what is on your mind when you first awaken in the morning. Take seriously that verse of Scripture, person's name, or word of direction that you're thinking about when you open your eyes. Remember, the Lord has been ministering to you in your sleep. He can provide for you 24 hours a day—even as you slumber. Before you fall asleep tonight, ask the Lord to speak to you and then commit it to Him. Enjoy your rest and in faith expect the Lord to work on your behalf while you get your body rested to carry out His will.

SEPTEMBER 7

"He was going down the street near her corner,
walking along in the direction of her house." — 7:8.

Hunger had become a way of life. I had lost so much weight my shoes were slipping off my feet. No, I wasn't ill, but rather I was involved in a 40-day fast. In addition to food, I fasted from television for that period. The fast was in January, so I missed the Super Bowl broadcast. What spirituality!

After the fast was over, I began watching television again and was amazed at what I saw. I felt assaulted. The ads, sensuous pictures, and show content attacked my spirit. I hadn't felt that before since I was accustomed to seeing that day after day before my fast. I became more aware after the fast of how I needed to avoid certain shows and images if I was to walk in holiness.

Today's verse isn't against television, nor am I making an appeal for you to get rid of your set. Today's verse does, however, paint a picture of someone falling into sin. It shows a young man knowingly walking in the direction of an immoral woman, a prostitute. The man didn't sin when he encountered the woman. Rather he fell when he walked in her direction. He should have avoided that area, knowing a problem lurked there for him. Instead he proceeded and paid the penalty.

You, too, have limitations. There are areas that the enemy tries to use against you. If money is a temptation for you, you don't need to be counting the church cash offering by yourself. If pornography is a weakness, you need to avoid certain places—airport newsstands, streets in your town, and cable television—that you know contain what draws you. If alcohol is a weakness, avoid going alone to restaurants that also have lounge areas.

Jesus taught that you must do all you can to avoid sin.

If your right eye causes you to sin, gouge it out and throw it away. It is better for you to lose one part of our body than for your whole body to be thrown into hell. And if your right hand causes you to sin, cut it off and throw it away. It is better for you to lose one part of your body than for your whole body to go into hell (Matthew 5:29-30).

Jesus is telling you to be ruthless when it comes to sin. Change your habits, and go out of your way to avoid temptation. Deal with whatever causes you a problem. Don't flirt or make peace with it. Any precaution you must take—as difficult as it may be—is better than the wages of sin because "the wages of sin is death" (Romans 6:23).

While going out of your way to avoid sin may be inconvenient, it isn't nearly as bad as experiencing death! The end of sin is death, and you have been called to enjoy abundant life. Determine therefore to avoid whatever causes you to sin. Be ruthless and uncompromising. Don't be tricked into a false security in your ability to avoid sin. Stay away from temptation, and sin will stay far away from you!

SEPTEMBER 8

"By me kings reign and rulers make laws that are just." — 8:15.

"Here we go again," or so I thought. I was conducting a question-and-answer session in prison and questions about Jesus' Second Coming were raised. There were questions of the millennium and who the antichrist was. I patiently responded that I didn't know about either, but I did share the one thing I was certain of. In the next life, I told them, you will rule with Christ.

It may be hard for you to think of yourself as royalty. It's a whole lot easier to speculate concerning the end times. The truth is, however, that you are a son or daughter of the King. That makes you a prince or princess. You're an heir to the throne and the inheritance that is stored up for the royal family. You're being trained and prepared for royal duties. I don't quite understand what those duties will be, but the Bible is clear that you will have them.

Now your duties today may seem to be totally unrelated to any royal destiny you have. You need to remember, however, how the Lord prepared his royal servants in the Scriptures. Joseph was trained to rule by running a jail. Moses was trained by serving as a shepherd. David was also trained as a keeper of sheep. Even Jesus' ministry was built on the foundation of His work as a carpenter, and He worked as a carpenter longer than He ministered.

Jesus said, "I tell you the truth, at the renewal of all things, when the Son of Man sits on his glorious throne, you who have followed me will also sit on twelve thrones judging the twelve tribes of Israel" (Matthew 19:28). There will be purpose and work in the next age. You are learning and being conformed to the image of Christ now to get you ready for what is ahead. You will rule.

Consider the following quote:

It is work [in the next life] as free from care and toil and fatigue as is the wing-stroke of the jubilant lark when it soars into the sunlight of a fresh, clear day and, spontaneously and for self-relief, as well as a matter of obedience to the ruling will of God. It is work according to one's tastes and delight and ability. If tastes vary there, if abilities vary there, then occupations will vary there.*

Today's verse tells you that kings and princes rule through the use of wisdom. You need wisdom not just for what is before you today, but for what is to come. You're being prepared right where you are and by what you are doing to rule with Christ. Act like a person of destiny. You're part of the royal family and you're being trained. There is work ahead in the next age. Isn't the pursuit of wisdom a worthy pursuit for nobility? Then get on with the learning process and get ready to sit on the throne.

*The Biblical Doctrine of Heaven, p. 192

SEPTEMBER 9

"Stolen water is sweet; food eaten in secret is delicious!" — 9:17.

It was a sad story I have heard again and again. I was on the phone consoling a young woman whose husband had been imprisoned. He was facing a long sentence, and she was facing the reality of raising her young family without the companionship of her loved one. He was accused of some illegal business dealings and was in serious hot water. The man was a believer and not malicious. He just thought that the Lord would protect him. He had a secret sin and for a while, it seemed like there would be no repercussions. Suddenly the boom was lowered, and his world collapsed.

Today's verse contains words from a woman named "Folly." She stands against wisdom. She, like wisdom, cries out to men and urges them to act. She, however, appeals to deceit and darkness, whereas wisdom appeals to truth and light. Adam and Eve faced this temptation. They sinned and then tried to hide from God. They ate food in secret. It was pleasant food, but it brought them death.

The first thing Adam and Eve did was to sew fig leaves together to hide their nakedness. They attempted the first known "cover-up." Then they hid from God. Imagine the foolishness of the creature trying to hide from the Creator behind some bush or tree! That's what they tried to do, and that's what folly does to you— it destroys your judgment so that you do one foolish thing after another.

The temptation to sin in secret can be very strong. You can be so easily tricked into thinking that no one is watching. Being aware that the Lord is mindful of what you do, you know that He will forgive you. Nothing bad will come of it. Someone once said, "It's easier to get forgiveness than permission." With that in mind, you proceed and pay the penalty.

There are always consequences. The Lord warned Israel of this when He said, "But if you fail to do this, you will be sinning against the Lord; and you may be sure that your sin will find you out" (Numbers 32:23). He warned,

> Because you have rejected this message, relied on oppression and depended on deceit, this sin will become for you like a high wall, cracked and bulging, that collapses suddenly, in an instant. It will break in pieces like pottery, shattered so mercilessly that among its pieces not a fragment will be found for taking coals from a hearth or scooping water out of a cistern (Isaiah 30:12-14).

The answer to this problem is found later in Isaiah. "In repentance and rest is your salvation, in quietness and trust is your strength" (30:15). Repent and turn away from any secret sin. Deal with what is in you before what is in you deals with you. Don't wait until the wall collapses to pieces. Get it straight before the crash. Bread eaten in secret may taste good, but it will turn to rottenness in your stomach. Listen to wisdom, reject folly, and your wall will stand secure and strong, safe from the crash that comes as a consequence of sin.

"The memory of the righteous will be a blessing." — 10:7.

I will never forget Hilma Hightower. She was a wonderful woman in her mid-fifties. As a member of my congregation, she was always an encouragement to my family and me. She was kind, soft spoken, and gracious, yet strong and spiritual. We counted her and her family among our closest friends and associates. Naturally we were devastated when she was diagnosed with the cancer that took her life so prematurely.

I will also never forget her funeral. It was a joyous yet somber time as we gathered to mourn and rejoice at the promotion of our sister and friend to her eternal reward. After the funeral I returned to my office, closed the door, and reflected on what had just taken place. I cried tears of sorrow at her passing, and realized how futile my plans and "busy-ness" were. Her death had put it all into perspective for me.

Mrs. Hightower was a righteous woman. Her grace in the midst of trial, her sensitivity to others, and her words of encouragement left good memories. No one remembered so much what she accomplished. They remembered who she was and that left pleasant memories.

I still have an armchair in our bedroom that Mrs. Hightower gave my family. I have told my wife that we will never get rid of that chair. When I sit in it, I think of her. It symbolizes the ability a believer has to bless people even after death.

I vowed that day in my office over ten years ago to try to leave behind pleasant memories as well. I determined to be a blessing to people in more ways than I had been in the past. I decided never to close my door or my time to those who needed me. I set a goal to put the needs of people first and trust the Lord for my projects and plans. I've not always succeeded, but I'm trying to leave a godly legacy of memories that others can discuss and remember long after I'm gone.

Later I was reading Hebrews 11 and found the real key to leaving godly memories. "By faith Abel offered God a better sacrifice than Cain did. By faith he was commended as a righteous man, when God spoke well of his offerings. And by faith he still speaks, even though he is dead" (Hebrews 11:4). I realized it was Mrs. Hightower's faith that had so impacted my life. It was her quiet trust in the Lord that had blessed me and was still blessing me today.

Your testimony is what people will remember. Your faith exploits will be what they talk about. It won't be your doctrine, building projects, money, or business deals. People will remember your faith. Do you want to be remembered after you are gone? Then be like Abel and offer to God sacrifices of faith. Trust in Him and others will imitate your faith, and tell good stories of you long after you are gone.

SEPTEMBER 11

"The righteous man is rescued from trouble,
and it comes on the wicked instead." — 11:8.

We sat up into the wee hours of the morning intently listening to every story as a minister friend told us of his trip to Africa. Stories of Africa would not be complete without a lion story, and he told us of his visit to a game reserve where he learned that a lion can scale a six-foot fence carrying a full grown ox in his mouth!

Daniel in the Old Testament had his own lion story as well. It seems that Daniel carried out his duties in such a way as to stir up the jealousy of his peers.

Now Daniel so distinguished himself among the administrators and the satraps by his exceptional qualities that the king planned to set him over the whole kingdom. At this, the administrators and the satraps tried to find grounds for charges against Daniel in his conduct of government affairs, but they were unable to do so. They could find no corruption in him, because he was trustworthy and neither corrupt nor negligent (Daniel 6:3-4).

Daniel's enemies contrived a scheme that they thought would bring about his demise. They urged the king to ban any prayer in his kingdom for 30 days. These men spied on Daniel and turned him in when he began to pray. The king had no choice but to punish Daniel for his disobedience to the decree. "So the king gave the order, and they brought Daniel and threw him into the lions' den" (verse 16).

The word that disturbs me in today's verse is "rescued." That word means that trouble will come my way. I'm not exempt from it. The promise is that I will be delivered or rescued from it. Daniel experienced the reality of this verse. He found himself in trouble, and needed the Lord to save and rescue him. The king who put Daniel into the den acknowledged this when he said, "May your God, whom you serve continually, rescue you!" (verse 16).

God's promise proved true. When the king rushed to the den the next morning, he called out, "Daniel, servant of the living God, has your God, whom you serve continually, been able to rescue you from the lions?" (verse 20). Daniel told the king that he was all right. In fact, the lions never opened their mouths. God truly rescued Daniel. Then the other half of today's promise came true.

At the king's command, the men who had falsely accused Daniel were brought in and thrown into the lions' den, along with their wives and children. And before they reached the floor of the den, the lions overpowered them and crushed all their bones (verse 23).

Don't fret when evil men plot against you, but just concentrate on staying righteous. Don't let bitterness or anger creep in. Serve the Lord no matter what men do to you. If you do, whatever they plan for you will come upon them. Remember Daniel and follow in his footsteps. You may have to face the lions, but you will be rescued from their might. What a mighty God you serve!

SEPTEMBER 12

"The words of the wicked lie in wait for blood." — 12:6.

Yesterday you read about Daniel and the lions' den. Daniel's enemies were out to get him. They just didn't want to hurt him, they wanted to kill him. They talked the king into passing a law prohibiting prayer to anyone but the king for 30 days under penalty of death. Once they had that law backing them up, they spied on Daniel and then reported him to the king when he prayed. The king had no choice but to commit Daniel to the lions' den.

You also have an enemy. He is Satan, and he has many demonic sidekicks. They aren't out just to hurt you or ruin your prayer life. The forces of evil aren't set on disrupting your spirituality. They are out to destroy you. Jesus told you that the devil's desire is to "kill, steal and destroy." Peter told you, "Your enemy the devil prowls around like a roaring lion looking for someone to devour" (1 Peter 5:8). When you put your faith in Christ, you got an enemy for life.

To ignore this truth can be fatal. To turn your back on an enemy that is armed and dangerous is foolish. Paul warned the Ephesian church concerning the reality of the war that goes on:

> Finally, be strong in the Lord and in his mighty power. Put on the full armor of God so that you can take your stand against the devil's schemes. For our strug-gle is not against flesh and blood, but against the rulers, against the authori-ties, against the powers of this dark world and against the spiritual forces of evil in the heavenly realms. Therefore put on the full armor of God, so that when the day of evil comes, you may be able to stand your ground, and after you have done everything, to stand (Ephesians 6:10-13).

Paul warned that the day of evil will come. He urged the church to be armed and ready, for the battle will not be trivial but serious. He concluded that passage with a call to prayer: "And pray in the Spirit on all occasions with all kinds of prayers and requests. With this in mind, be alert and always keep on praying for all the saints" (Ephesians 6:18).

Jesus knew about prayer and spiritual war. You are told in Hebrews, "During the days of Jesus' life on earth, he offered up prayers and petitions with loud cries and tears to the one who could save him from death, and he was heard because of his reverent submission" (Hebrews 5:7). Jesus faced a real death threat from His enemies, and He prayed fervently to counter that threat. If Jesus did that, can you do any less?

Your enemy lies in wait for your life. There can be no peaceful coexistence. Understand his intention, and then fight him with all the weapons you have. Your life depends on it.

"Righteousness guards the man of integrity." — 13:6.

I could hear them as I sat on our front porch. The lions roaring in the distance sounded like something out of a Tarzan movie. We were not on safari nor at some game reserve. My wife and I lived about three miles from the city zoo when we were first married. From that distance I could still hear the lions in that zoo roaring at night. I was glad those lions weren't roaming my neighborhood, but instead were safely contained in a cage.

As we read a few days ago, Daniel didn't have that advantage. He wasn't sitting on his front porch while the lions were locked away. Daniel found himself in the cage with them. He didn't experience their fierceness from a distance, but rather saw it "up close and personal." Daniel didn't have a whip and a chair either. He went into the lions' den equipped with one thing—his integrity. And his integrity was enough to keep him from harm.

When Daniel's enemies conspired against him, "They could find no corruption in him, because he was trustworthy and neither corrupt nor negligent" (Daniel 6:4). Daniel walked in righteousness, carrying out his duties in holiness and efficiency. When the wicked rose against him, he could rely on his past record as a means of escape. The Lord looked on his flawless performance, and Daniel could tell the king, "My God sent his angel, and he shut the mouths of the lions. They have not hurt me, because I was found innocent in his sight. Nor have I ever done any wrong before you, O king" (Daniel 6:22).

Integrity and righteousness are powerful shields. They will protect you from harm, keep you from accusation, and defend you should accusations come. Righteousness is the best defense the accused can have, for it's in righteousness that the Lord assumes the role of your protector. He is the best public defender in the universe.

Daniel was neither "corrupt nor negligent." If you want God to help you, first of all maintain correct behavior in the affairs of life. Pay your taxes. If you sell something, make sure it's in good working order. Give a good days work for your wages. Be faithful to account for any cash you may handle for the church or on the job.

But good behavior isn't enough to protect you from the lions. You must also not be negligent. Keep your promises, letting your word be your bond. Keep your appointments, and pay your bills on time. Keep your home, car, and other possessions in good working order and appearance. Don't neglect your responsibilities.

I hope the lions don't get any closer to you than they got to us when we lived in our first home. But if they do, then I hope you will have a shield of righteousness and integrity that can shut their mouths. Let people say of you that you are neither corrupt nor negligent—it's the best defense known to man.

"When calamity comes, the wicked are brought down,
but even in death the righteous have a refuge." — 14:32.

Earlier in his life, Daniel had some friends who were faced with a calamity. The king had erected a statue of gold and ordered everyone to worship it when the orchestra began playing. The king had a reputation for taking action against anyone who disobeyed him, so the people had a strong incentive to do just as he said.

Daniel's friends, however, refused to bow down. They were good Jews, and they had been taught to worship no one but God. When the band started playing, they remained standing. As usual, there were some nearby who, having seen their refusal to bow down, immediately told the king.

"Furious with rage, Nebuchadnezzar summoned Shadrach, Meshach and Abednego" (Daniel 3:13). The king was incensed and asked if it was true that they did not worship. "But if you do not worship it, you will be thrown immediately into a blazing furnace. Then what god will be able to rescue you from my hand?" (verse 15). When faced with impending doom, the three men were resolute. They responded,

> We do not need to defend ourselves before you in this matter. If we are thrown into the blazing furnace, the God we serve is able to save us from it, and he will rescue us from your hand, O king. But even if he does not, we want you to know, O king, that we will not serve your gods or worship the image of gold you have set up (verses 16-18).

These three men knew the truth of today's verse. They knew that, even in death, they had a refuge. They were facing a terrible dilemma and their young lives were hanging in the balance. They were convinced of God's ability to deliver them, but they did not know whether He would choose to do so. They faced death rather than compromise their service to God—and God honored their faith.

It's interesting that those who threw them into the furnace perished. The furnace was so hot that the men who carried them to their supposed doom were burned to a crisp. The three men, however, had a refuge in the fire. They were not delivered *from* the fire but *in* it. There's a big difference.

You may not receive full recompense for the wrongs you have received in this life. You may face some struggles that are unfair. You need the same resolve these three men had. They had faith, but they were determined to serve God if it killed them. They knew what was right, and they risked their lives. Remember, we have another life to live. If the score isn't settled here, it will be settled there. Give yourself, therefore, to the service of God and know that He is a refuge even in death. You will be saved, but it may take longer than you expected. Take refuge in the Lord, and trust Him for the results.

SEPTEMBER 15

"The cheerful heart has a continual feast." — 15:15.

I had done it again. We were at a party and I had teased and joked around with people beyond what was appropriate, saying some things that I now regretted saying. In my attempt to be funny, I had gone too far. I was feeling low, so I sank down to my knees beside my bed. I prayed for the Lord to forgive me, asking him to help me discipline my tongue and to take away this desire I had to be funny.

I felt the Lord tell me that He would not take away my humor, for that was His gift to me. He would, however, teach me how to use it, for it was a great tool to strengthen me and others. I then turned to Nehemiah 8:10: "The joy of the Lord is your strength." From then on, I determined to study humor, get to know my "gift," and use it for the glory of God.

Today's verse tells you that joy provides its own food. There's something about laughter and cheer that sustains you. I saw a study once that said a child smiles hundreds of times per day, but the average adult smiles less than ten! No wonder that disease and mental disorders are the adult norm. Life for the grown-up has become too serious.

This can even be true for spiritual people. You're dealing with eternal truths, and a person's eternal destiny is the most serious of topics and concerns. But there is joy in serving the Lord. He knows you by name, forgives your sins, helps and provides for you, and guides your steps. Hallelujah! He's a strong fortress in time of trouble. He's on your side. If that doesn't make you happy, I don't know what will.

Paul knew the importance of joy so he commanded the Philippians to rejoice. That's right. He ordered them to have joy. "Rejoice in the Lord always. I will say it again: rejoice!" (Philippians 4:4). If Paul ordered you to rejoice, it must be within your power to have joy. Otherwise he could be asking you to do something that was inappropriate or impossible. Joy isn't a feeling; it's a decision. To decide not to have joy is to decide to lose some of your strength, for your joy is your strength according to Nehemiah.

As I have studied humor, I've learned one important thing: to laugh at myself. Everyday, I make some dumb mistakes. I've said some bloopers in the pulpit that would make you laugh. Humorous things that have happened to me as I travel have kept people in stitches. If I can laugh at myself and my world, I know I will have all the strength I need to carry out whatever God wants me to do. Smile and laugh more today. Let your heart be cheerful. In that cheer is a continual feast for you and those around you. Don't miss out on this banquet. Dig in and enjoy it.

SEPTEMBER 16

"The Lord works out everything for his own ends —
even the wicked for a day of disaster." — 16:4.

This couldn't be happening. The business some men and I had started—the one that we had dedicated to the Lord—was going under. We had spent our capital and now were facing the inevitable: We were going out of business, and I was left to pay for the office and phone leases since my signature was on the contracts. It was in the midst of that dilemma that I asked the Lord what my purpose in life was. "If it wasn't politics or business, what was it?" I asked. I felt the Spirit respond that it was to "bring administrative order out of chaos"—the chaos similar to that found in Genesis 1:2 where "the earth was formless and empty." That phrase has stuck with me ever since, serving as a guide to my life and ministry.

Everyone is born for a reason because God is a God of purpose. He doesn't reveal Himself to us just for the sake of fellowship. He reveals Himself with purpose. Paul described his conversion experience to King Agrippa with these words: "The Lord replied, 'Now get up and stand on your feet. I have appeared to you to appoint you as a servant and as a witness of what you have seen of me and what I will show you'" (Acts 26:16). Paul knew from that time what the Lord wanted of him. He knew his purpose.

Paul wrote to the Galatians, "They saw that I had been given the task of preaching the gospel to the Gentiles, just as Peter had been given the task of preaching the gospel to the Jews" (Galatians 2:7). Paul's purpose was clear to him, and Peter's purpose was also clear to Paul. Both had a God-given purpose, and they functioned in it effectively. Paul's purpose was so clear to him that he refused to baptize people. "For Christ did not send me to baptize, but to preach the gospel" (1 Corinthians 1:17). Paul's focus allowed him to say "no" to things not related to his mission in life.

You have a purpose in life, a mission that only you can accomplish. It can be summarized in one phrase or verse of Scripture, and it contains the reason why you exist. When I see chaos or something that needs order, I know I'm on holy ground. I know my purpose and am free to flow in it with all the creativity and gifts God has given me.

This may be a new concept for you. There's a specific task you can do that no one else can. Even Pharaoh had a purpose, for it says in Exodus 9:14, "I have raised you up for this very purpose, that I might show you my power and that my name might be proclaimed in all the earth." If God had a purpose for Pharaoh, how much more for you, His beloved child. It can be a major step for you to realize that you have a purpose. Meditate on the fact that God has a job for you to do. If you can't summarize it, then ask the Lord to make it clear to you starting today. Over time, you will be able to state it clearly and simply. Define it and you are well on your way to doing it.

*"A rebuke impresses a man of discernment
more than a hundred lashes a fool." — 17:10.*

Yesterday you saw that you have a purpose to fulfill that no one else can accomplish. The more I study the Bible, the more I see that God is a God of purpose. He doesn't reveal Himself to you to make you feel good, or just to save you from your sins. He has a plan, and that plan includes you. If you stray from your purpose, He will rebuke or chastise you. If you're a discerning person, you will understand what He is saying and get back on track.

The apostle Paul tried to avoid his God-given purpose. The Lord had appeared to Saul on the Damascus road—not just to convert him, but to reveal His purpose for Saul's life. On that day, Saul saw his purpose—to preach the Gospel to the Gentiles. At first, however, Saul hesitated and the Lord had to rebuke him.

In Acts 22, Saul returned to Jerusalem after his Damascus-road experience. While praying in the temple, he fell into a trance and heard the Lord say: "Quick! Leave Jerusalem immediately, because they will not accept your testimony about me" (22:18). The Lord wanted Saul to leave the comfortable environs of the temple for the uncertainty of the Gentile world.

Saul didn't want to go and dragged his feet. He responded by politely arguing with the Lord, implying that he knew better:

Lord, these men know that I went from one synagogue to another to imprison and beat those who believe in you. And when the blood of your martyr Stephen was shed, I stood there giving my approval and guarding the clothes of those who were killing him (22:19-20).

Saul was in essence saying, "Let me stay here. I will be effective. You don't understand. These people know me. They will surely recognize what You have done in my life."

The Lord was not impressed. He rebuked Saul and rejected his reasoning in verse 21: "Go, I will send you far away to the Gentiles." This rebuke was all Saul needed. He fled for his life, and embarked on one of the most successful ministries the world has ever seen. He gave up his dreams and goals, discerned God's purpose, and gave himself to it with all that he had.

Today's verse says that a gentle rebuke does more for the wise man than a severe beating does for a fool. Yesterday you read that everyone has a purpose. The Lord wants to guide you into that purpose, and He can do it by gentle or extraordinary means. Be sensitive to the Lord's voice and rebuke. Has a recent failure been the Lord's direction out of a particular activity in which you have been involved? Has God used a lack of finances to point you in a certain direction better suited to your God-given purpose? Is the Lord speaking to you about some course adjustment, and are you obeying that voice? Don't wait for your world to fall apart before you hear the Lord. Discern His purpose now and follow it with all your heart.

SEPTEMBER 18

"The name of the Lord is a strong tower;
the righteous run to it and are safe." — 18:10.

There I was weeping in our backyard. The pressure was too great, or so I thought. I was under tremendous pressure from family and friends due to my decision to follow what I believed was the will of God. Kathy and I—recent newly-weds—had changed churches and that had caused quite a stir. I retreated to our small, cramped backyard to get my bearings. Was I acting in arrogance? Had I really heard from the Lord? Was it right to cause so much pain? These and other questions pressed hard on my mind. I cried out to the Lord for help. As I did, I opened my Bible to Mark 3. The verses consoled and strengthened me:

Then Jesus entered a house, and again a crowd gathered, so that he and his disciples were not even able to eat. When his family heard about this, they went to take charge of him, for they said, "He is out of his mind" (Mark 3:20-21).

Jesus' family thought He was crazy! They wanted to step in and care for Him because they thought Him incapable of caring for Himself. What an encouragement to my young and fragile faith. If they thought Jesus was out of His mind, could I expect different treatment?

Today's verse tells you where your safety and refuge are. When I was down and out, the Lord became my strength. He led me to His Word and strengthened my hand and way. He was more than able to protect and defend me.

King David learned this valuable lesson in his life long before I did. There was a time when he and his men were in the land of the Philistines before he had become king. When they returned home from the Philistines, they found their city "Destroyed by fire and their wives and sons and daughters taken captive. So David and his men wept aloud until they had no strength left to weep....David was greatly distressed because the men were talking of stoning him; each one was bitter in spirit because of his sons and daughters" (1 Samuel 30:3-6).

What did David do? What would you do in a similar situation? Would you try to talk your way out of this dilemma? Would you launch a counterattack? Defend yourself that it wasn't your fault? Become depressed? David ran into the name of the Lord and took refuge in God. He got alone somewhere, poured out his heart, and allowed the Lord to comfort and direct him. It says, "David found strength in the Lord his God" (1 Samuel 30:6). The Lord gave him specific instructions of what to do. On the way to recover their families, David "happened" to find a dying slave from the party that had raided his home. That slave led him to the place where David was able to recapture all that was his.

The name of the Lord is a strong tower, so learn to run into it. Talk to Him and then listen for His voice. Allow Him to encourage and strengthen you. Learn to hide in His name for no one can touch you there.

"He who is kind to the poor lends to the Lord,
and he will reward him for what he has done." — 19:17.

I was in dangerous territory. I was reading the Bible, asking the Lord to quicken something to me. I felt impressed to go to the epistle of James, which is seldom a pleasant experience for me. James wrote about pride and ambition, and the Lord always seemed to direct me to that epistle when He was dealing with those shortcomings in my life. This time, however, I went there for a different reason.

I directed my attention to James 1:27: "Religion that God our Father accepts as pure and faultless is this: to look after orphans and widows in their distress and to keep oneself from being polluted by the world." After some study, I saw that this was the only reference to "religion" in the New Testament. The definition had nothing to do with church activities, doctrine, a denomination, or the sacraments. James said that religion was connected to action, and the specific action referred to was the care of orphans and widows.

James' world differed from modern society. There was no social security or welfare. Older women were not employable, and a retirement pension was unheard of. So a woman without a husband and children without parents were destitute unless some family member could help out. James was clearly stating that religious service reached its fulfillment when it helped those who were without any other means of help.

After reading this, Kathy and I discussed whether we knew any true widows. One woman came to mind who had been widowed early in life. She had raised her children, and they were all in the ministry. She had lived a simple and holy life, and was living on a fixed income. We knew her birthday was coming up, so we sent her a card with a check for as much as we could afford. We wanted to be "religious."

The response was overwhelming. We got a beautiful thank you from the widow, but we got a greater response from the Lord. We received several significant financial blessings in the weeks that followed, and we knew that it was attributable to that act of kindness to a widow.

Today's verse encourages you to be kind to the poor. The media can dull your senses to the fact that there are poor people in your neighborhood or church who are in desperate need. When you help them, you're lending money to the Lord! The Lord always pays His debts, and the interest rate is astounding. Don't let your religion be limited to what church you attend or doctrine you believe. Let your religion be what you do with what you believe.

Pray today that the Lord will show you someone in need. Then minister to them as unto the Lord. The Lord who is watching will bless you, and the people to whom you give will be blessed as well. Become a religious person in the best sense of the word. Become one who meets the needs of the needy.

SEPTEMBER 20

"A sluggard does not plow in season;
so at harvest time he looks but finds nothing." — 20:4.

I'm no farmer. The closest I got to a farm was the my first-grade field trip. Just the thought of getting up before dawn to work was unpleasant to me even as a young child. I had no desire to see the sun come up. I figured that a sunset looked the same as a sunrise, so I would study the sunset and sleep in.

I do understand enough to know that a farmer will harvest what he plants. If he plants wheat and conditions are right, he will harvest wheat. If he plants corn, he will harvest corn. If the farmer decides to farm "in faith" and trust the Lord for what comes up, he will harvest nothing. He may look for a harvest, but he will find weed-filled fields.

That principle applies to all of life. You must plant if you're going to harvest. I was reminded of this as I was praying about the church I pastored. I was bemoaning the apparent lack of growth and progress we were experiencing and wondering when things would begin to "bust loose" as the church growth experts had promised. The Lord directed me to today's verse, and encouraged me to continue to plow and sow. I wanted to see the harvest. The harvest, however, can't be rushed. It must follow a definite course.

Jesus taught,

This is what the kingdom of God is like. A man scatters seed on the ground. Night and day, whether he sleeps or gets up, the seed sprouts and grows, though he does not know how. All by itself the soil produces grain—first the stalk, then the head, then the full kernel in the head. As soon as the grain is ripe, he puts the sickle to it, because the harvest has come (Mark 4:26-29).

We were building the church according to Kingdom principles, and this principle would hold true. First we plant the seed, then the stalk, head, and full kernel come forth. I had to follow and be patient with that process.

So we launched out on a new plowing and seed-sowing season. We started a daily radio program. We ordained a man called to the ministry, even though we didn't see where the money would come from (we haven't missed a paycheck to him, yet). We decided to continue our prison and jail ministry, although it had brought little fruit. We began to fast every Monday as a congregation.

You too must learn to plow. Are you looking to the harvest, but seeing nothing? Then ask whether you have plowed and sown enough seed. If you have not, then look to begin anew. Have you sown enough Word in your children? Maybe a daily Bible study is in order. Have you given enough seed above your tithe? Consider giving to people or causes that you have been wanting to help. Is your ministry stale and flat? Consider a fast, with prolonged periods of prayer and Bible study. Today is the season to plow, so that when you look for the harvest down the road, it will be there in abundance.

SEPTEMBER 21

*"A wise man attacks the city of the mighty and
pulls down the stronghold in which they trust." — 21:22.*

I was one of the few white faces walking the streets of a black neighborhood early one morning. It was Saturday, and some of the men from my church had assembled to pray in the community where we were holding our Sunday services. We decided to walk the streets and pray for the town's problems, which included a serious drug problem. We felt that the best thing we could do.

We came to a small restaurant that was known for its drug traffic. Ironically, it was across the street from the town hall! About 15 of us assembled in the empty lot next to the restaurant. We prayed against the spirit of drugs and bound the activity of the enemy, praying strong and aggressive prayers.

Imagine our joy when six weeks later that restaurant closed down. The bulldozers came in and leveled it. When we inquired why, no one had a good reason. The owner had decided to shut down. Today there's a shopping center on that site and what once was a destructive center of illegal activity has become a productive center of community development. We know that we had a role in that transformation.

We have gone back to the streets since then. We actually laid hands on the town hall the day the city held its mayoral election. At 6:30 a.m., we looked like we were holding up the side of the building! We prayed for a specific, godly candidate and he won.

There are times when you must go on the offensive. It's all too easy to become passive concerning the status quo, and even assume that it's the will of God for that bad situation to persist. Aggressive, active prayer is the only thing that can pull down the stronghold of the enemy. Someone once said that prayer is like an intercontinental ballistic missile—it can be launched from any position (kneeling, sitting, standing), travel long distances, and not be stopped by any known defense. We launched missiles at the fort of the enemy in that town and pulled down his stronghold.

Jesus said, "The kingdom of heaven has been forcefully advancing, and forceful men lay hold of it" (Matthew 11:12). While men argue over the exact meaning of that verse, people who understand how to violently attack evil advance the kingdom of God. You don't have to be mean, arrogant, or belligerent to be forceful. You can be mild mannered and loving, yet be tenacious in your pursuit of the Kingdom.

What area can you attack today? Toward what can you launch some prayer missiles? What have you become accustomed to that needs to be attacked and torn down spiritually? Don't be afraid to go on the offensive. Go after the enemy where he lives, and see his world come tumbling down in Jesus' name.

SEPTEMBER 22

"The sluggard says, 'There is a lion outside!'
or 'I will be murdered in the streets.'" — *22:13.*

It looked so innocent and harmless. My wife kept pointing out a piece of our house siding that was discolored. It was close to the ground and looked to me like it had been splashed by dirt from the rain. I put off looking into it, coming up with all kinds of excuses. "I don't know how to fix it," "I don't know where to get another piece of siding," and "It's only a small piece" were my favorite excuses that kept me from doing anything about it.

Then one day I went over and pulled on that piece of siding. To my shock, that piece represented the doorway to termites that had infested my entire garage. The only thing holding up that side of the house was the garage-door frame. I went on to find that my termite policy did not cover replacement costs, and I was faced with a $2,000 repair bill. Procrastination had almost cost me my house.

Today's verse speaks about procrastination. But instead of calling it procrastination, it refers to the procrastinator as a sluggard. I like procrastination better because it sounds more dignified. The sluggard comes up with all kinds of outlandish excuses for not doing what is required. But the excuses are a smoke screen for the real reason why something isn't being done, and that is laziness.

Sit down now with a pencil and paper. List all the projects and ideas that you've been putting off. I mean everything. Include the book that you have talked about writing; the addition to the house; the room that needs to be painted; the garden you've talked about planting; the class courses you need to take; the computer you want to learn to use. You know what those projects are.

Next to each item write the reason or reasons why you haven't done them. Is it time? Money? Education? Family? Fear? Then study that list. What can you eliminate from your schedule to make room to do that project. How much television can you give up? Can you go to bed later or get up earlier? How do you use your Saturdays? Lunch hours? Commute time to work?

The goal here is to eliminate the excuses that bind you. You must get over the laziness that presses you and keeps you from producing. When you write down your excuses, study how you can overcome them. The apostle Paul learned how to "press on toward the goal to win the prize for which God has call me heavenward in Christ Jesus" (Philippians 3:14). You must press on through those excuses that cause you to procrastinate. When you do, you'll reach new levels of accomplishment that will be gratifying and rewarding. If you don't, you'll sound much like the sluggard quoted in today's verse.

The choice is yours. Don't let your fictitious lion in the street stop you from doing the will of God, but face him and move on to do great things for God.

SEPTEMBER 23

"Do not move an ancient boundary stone
or encroach on the fields of the fatherless." —23:10.

It was dark and foggy on the interstate as we made our way north. When our children were young, we would often start out in the small hours of the morning if we were making a long trip. On this particular trip, we had been driving for hours and stopped at a fast food restaurant for breakfast. We went to the drive-in window, and encountered one hassle after another.

After waiting an inordinate amount of time and seeing our order get confused several times, the woman (who obviously needed some help) gave me back too much change. I was so aggravated that I pulled out, not bothering to return the money she had mistakenly given me. I told my kids what had happened and they expressed their disapproval. It was only a dollar or two, I responded, and there had been so many hassles that I just wanted to get back on the road. They were not impressed, and at their young age knew the proper action I should have taken. Since we were not returning in that direction, I made sure I gave back the money by placing it in the church offering (with a little extra added to it).

Today's verse cautions you to maintain integrity in the affairs of life. It speaks to those who would take advantage of the weak for their own personal gain. I had taken advantage of that ill-equipped waitress and had kept money that wasn't mine. The verse goes on to say that God will defend those who are taken advantage of. Life presents many opportunities that test your integrity. You can't afford to take shortcuts in the name of business or behind the guise of tough negotiations. The Lord is watching and will reward you according to your motives.

I recently had to return a suit I bought nearly one year ago because it had a flaw in a pant leg that finally tore. The manager told me I could return the whole suit for another one by bringing in the receipt. I went home and, to my surprise, found the receipt. My first thought, however, was not to show the receipt in hope of getting a more expensive suit in exchange. I was planning to encroach on their field and take a piece of their land for my own advantage. I'm glad to say that reason prevailed. I brought the receipt in and got a brand new suit.

How about you? Are you encroaching on the field of another? Are you receiving cable television service for which you aren't paying? Do you "borrow" someone else's computer software to copy on your own computer? Does your library contain volumes borrowed from another person? Does your workshop have tools loaned to you in good faith? Have you cut a business deal deliberately withholding information that, if shared, would help the other party and hurt you? Ask the Lord to show you where you've encroached on someone else's field and then seek to make it right.

SEPTEMBER 24

"By wisdom a house is built,
and through understanding it is established." — *24:3.*

I hung up with the realtor and shook my head in disbelief. I had just told her that we would close on our house in six days and that the money to close would be here by then. That "money" amounted to $10,000, and I had no idea where it would come from! I only knew the Lord had led us that far, and I believed He would not disappoint us.

The whole process of purchasing that home had been a wonderful adventure in faith. We had put our other house up for sale but nothing was happening. I am convinced that faith requires action, so I decided to look for and find our new house whether the old house had a buyer or not. My family went looking and, to our surprise, fell in love with the first house we saw. It was everything we wanted and more.

We went home and waited for someone to buy our old house. Still no one came. So again, I decided to act in faith. We submitted a bid (on the house we loved) contingent on the sale of our old home. We put a deadline on the deal, and stood to lose our earnest money if the old house didn't sell. After some exciting and tense days, we got an offer on our old house 36 hours before the deadline! Kathy and I signed the agreement at 9:30 p.m. in the parking lot of a movie theater where our realtor had tracked us down.

The sale of our old house left us $10,000 short of what we needed to close on the new home. With six days before the purchase was to be final, we needed a miracle. I remember praying, "Lord, we've done all we can do. The rest is up to You." The Bible says, "Everyone who trusts in him will never be put to shame" (Romans 10:11), and we were not. Someone came forward, loaned us the money for the purchase, and we moved into our dream home that truly was a gift from the Lord.

Not long after we moved in, a friend gave us a house-warming gift: A painting of our new home with today's verse written in next to the house. We hung that painting in our hallway, and I will always think of that house when I see today's verse. We got that house because the Lord gave us wisdom and understanding of what to do. That house was so special not only because of its beauty, but also because of what the Lord taught us as we bought it.

Years later the Lord required that house from us. When we moved to pastor in Orlando, we lost that house. We were unable to sell it for 18 months, and then sold it for less than the purchase price. But there are still only pleasant memories surrounding that home. After all, "The Lord gave and the Lord has taken away; may the name of the Lord be blessed" (Job 1:21).

I pray that the Lord will give you wisdom and understanding today that will enable you to step out in faith and see Him move on your behalf. Whatever your "house" is, may it be filled with the knowledge that God helped you get it.

SEPTEMBER 25

"A word aptly spoken is like apples of gold in settings of silver." — 25:11.

"We're on the air," and so began my television debut. I had been asked to serve on a panel for a local cable television station to discuss the role of women in the church. I had prepared my material, and thought I was in for a nice, pleasant time. Instead, the program turned into a spiritual wrestling match.

I shared the set with quite a panel. First, there was a woman leader from a non-Christian sect who called the apostle Paul a male chauvinist. Then there was a fighting fundamentalist with a large-print Bible, who quoted Scripture and attacked the woman. Finally, there was also a Catholic theologian. The show took phone calls and people were calling in attacking both the woman and my fundamentalist brother. For 20 minutes I said nothing. At the break, the fundamentalist rebuked me for not jumping into the battle.

I was sitting there praying. I didn't want to participate in this media circus and was asking the Lord for an apt word. Finally, the host asked me for some input. I responded that I was uncomfortable with the tone of the debate. I said that, while my church did not ordain women, we certainly valued their role in the church. I gave some examples of women in the Bible who had been in ministry, and tried to raise the level of the discussion.

At first there was silence, but then the peace of God settled in. The attitude of the woman and my brother changed. The incoming calls became constructive and kind. The remainder of the show was given over to constructive discussions. As we were signing off, the woman leader publicly thanked me and said, "This man was the only one who acted in a Christian manner tonight." With that over with, I got in my car and went home, vowing not to return any time soon.

Today's verse paints a vivid word picture of gracious speech. Picture an apple made of gold placed on a silver tray. That's what an apt word looks like. It's attractive, valuable, and something that people admire. It's given a place of honor and stands out against more common conversation. An apt word injects something precious into ordinary talk.

Paul encouraged the Ephesians to "not let any unwholesome talk come out of your mouths, but only what is helpful for building others up according to their needs, that it may benefit those who listen" (Ephesians 4:29). Make that your goal today. Let your words benefit your spouse, children, neighbors, brethren, and co-workers. Ask God to help you give an apt answer in a difficult situation. Picture that apple of gold in a setting of silver, and see if you can match your words to that image. Seek to offer words that will beautify any conversation, and take your discussions to a new level of grace.

SEPTEMBER 26

"Like a lame man's legs that hang limp
is a proverb in the mouth of a fool." — 26:7.

It was a beautiful day, perfect for watching baseball. I had my father's hand as we walked to old Forbes Field in Pittsburgh. We were going to a game, always an exciting time for me. The road to the stadium was usually lined with beggars, who offered pencils in return for a contribution.

On this particular Sunday, a boy younger than I was so in awe of the surroundings that he tripped over a man without legs who was sitting and begging on the sidewalk. The man's money and pencils went flying, and everyone was embarrassed as they scurried to retrieve the man's belongings. I had never noticed that legless man before, but I will never forget the image of seeing that boy tumble over his body.

Today's verse tells you that a proverb in the mouth of a fool is useless. It is unable to get to where it is going just like a person without legs. You can say the right words, even quote the Bible, but if you don't have the character to go along with the words, the proverb does no good. In Jesus' day, the religious leaders taught from the sacred writings. Yet when Jesus came along, "the crowds were amazed at his teaching, because he taught as one who had authority, and not as their teachers of the law" (Matthew 7:28-29). Jesus had power behind His proverbs and the people recognized the difference immediately.

How can you get this authority? Paul wrote to the Colossians to inform them of the source of this power: "Let the word of Christ dwell in you richly as you teach and admonish one another with all wisdom" (Colossians 3:16). The word of Christ must work in you if it's to be effective when it comes out from you. Memorizing verses isn't enough. Those words must work in you and must become flesh before they'll be effective. Someone once said that you'll impart who you are and not what you say. You can preach on peace and be nervous. The people to whom you preach will receive your nervousness—you'll impart who you are.

Paul went on to write, "Let your conversation be always full of grace, seasoned with salt, so that you may know how to answer everyone" (Colossians 4:6). Do you want your proverbs to have power? Then let the Lord work grace into you. Learn to be gracious, making your words be compassionate. Don't be a know-it-all believer. Learn how to listen with empathy. Then learn how to season your speech with salt.

Don't dump all you know on someone. Rather make them thirsty for more. Give them an opportunity to ask based on what they hear from and see in your life. Don't tell them their kids are misbehaving; let them ask why your children behave so well. In other words, use wisdom with your proverbs. If you do, people will marvel at you, like they did at Jesus, because you'll have power—the power of the word made flesh—behind what you say.

"Better is open rebuke than hidden love." — 27:5.

It was a scene I will never get used to. A prison for men is one thing. The environment is rough, but the men seem able to handle it and adapt. A jail for women, on the other hand, is a different story. Some of the women to whom I minister look like my sister or mother! While some are pretty hard, most of them seem so frail and for the most part they seem out of place.

During one weekly Monday Bible study in a local jail, a shy, petite woman was sitting on the front row. She had a puzzled look on her face, and I thought some typical, basic question was forthcoming. Instead this woman directed my attention to Deuteronomy 28, and asked how a loving God could release curses on His people as that chapter describes. I stumbled a bit as I answered, and went home to do some homework.

Deuteronomy 28 is a tough chapter. It first outlines the blessings that come from obeying the commands of the covenant. Those first 14 verses contain some wonderful blessings—healthy children, successful businesses, leadership positions, and general prosperity. The next 54 verses, however, contain some frightening curses, the consequences for not obeying the commands of the Lord.

Those curses include confusion, diseases, drought, defeat at the hand of enemies, lack of success, seizure of property, foreign oppression, crop failure, plagues, and exile to a foreign land. Every calamity known to man is promised to those who choose to ignore the commands of the Lord. I could see why that woman was struggling with this chapter. I was beginning to struggle myself!

Then I came across today's verse. It tells you that open rebuke—some visible sign of concern, even if it's a stern one—is better than passive love that remains hidden. As I studied Deuteronomy 28, I began to see the love of God for His people, even in His curses! While there was an aspect of punishment in His open rebuke, He also showed His great love for His people. History shows that the Lord did rebuke His people. But it also shows that when His people realized the foolishness of their ways and turned back to Him, He was gracious and glad to receive them. The goal of God's rebuke was not to harm, but to bring His people to their senses. His open rebuke, if it works to bring His people back, really is better than the Lord loving His people yet remaining silent as they stray into error.

You may be experiencing the Lord's rebuke. Don't see it only as the Lord's harshness. In His sternness, He is trying to turn your heart toward Him. Have you transgressed His commands? Have you done all that you can do to obey Him? If not, then humbly call out to Him for His forgiveness and help. His open rebuke is far better than His ignoring you and allowing you to go your own way. Humble yourself and you will return to the blessings found in Deuteronomy 28:1-14.

SEPTEMBER 28

*"He who rebukes a man will in the end gain more favor
than he who has a flattering tongue." — 28:23.*

It was another 10:30 bombshell. The home meeting I was leading was known for its late-night sessions. It seemed that people waited as long as possible before they shared problems or prayer needs. When the bombshell hit, we would spend as long as needed to pray, counsel, encourage, and even rebuke. We were young and idealistic, and the rebukes were often hard-hitting and direct. People often went home mad and upset, but those meetings were never dull!

The Lord used those meetings to train us all, and today—almost 20 years later—many of those people are among my closest friends. While those meetings made us mad, afterward they yielded fruit in our lives. It was common for us to bring good testimonies to the meeting that followed those with 10:30 explosions.

My home meetings have mellowed since then, and today they don't resemble those early "free-for-alls." But I still value the necessity of rebuke in building the church and people. Rebuke is never easy to give or receive. Correction is a sensitive subject and often unpleasant business. If done correctly, however, it will bring you favor after the message has had time to sink in.

I rebuke my children because I love them and want what is best for them. We have a close relationship and I always marvel at how much stronger our relationship is after I have rebuked them. Then there have been times when I have had to sit down with a church member or friend, and correct them as their pastor. That hasn't been easy, but it's challenged them and me to walk in love and to be sensitive to others and their feelings. Failing to rebuke or confront someone—especially a friend—is not done out of love for the other person, but rather self-love. You're protecting yourself, not wanting to be unpopular or "the heavy."

Paul wrote to the Ephesians to be "speaking the truth in love [so that] we will in all things grow up into him who is the head. Each of you must put off falsehood and speak truthfully to his neighbor, for we are all members of one body" (Ephesians 4:15, 25). The foundation for rebuke is love. If I love someone, I'll proceed to correct them and trust the Lord for the results. If I'm not sure of my love, then I'll hold back until my motives are clear. I'm not a rebuking machine, but it's part of my job as a believer and leader. It's part of your job, too.

There may be a person or situation that is eating you up. You spend a lot of time worrying or thinking about it. Wouldn't it be easier to sit down and talk with the person, telling them how you feel? Don't expect them to throw their arms around you and thank you, but give the Lord some room to work, and afterward you'll win their favor.

"A man who remains stiff-necked after many rebukes
will suddenly be destroyed—without remedy." — 29:1.

It couldn't be true. We were watching a national news broadcast, and there was a well-known evangelist being exposed for serious misconduct. It was a sad day for the body of Christ. Later reports revealed that this problem had existed in his life for many years. I have to believe that the Lord had spoken and even rebuked him for his sin, yet he, for whatever reason, didn't deal with it. The result was sudden destruction. There has been no remedy for his fall, for today he is virtually unheard of in Christian circles.

These past few days we have studied the concept of the rebuke. If you refuse to listen to rebuke, today's verse pictures you as stiff-necked. You're rigid, not having the ability to look around. You're not flexible, and in need of a good spiritual chiropractic adjustment. The rebuke is designed to do just that—loosen you up so that you can continue to grow and be conformed to the image of Christ.

You need the same attitude that was in David. He wrote in Psalm 141:5, "Let a righteous man strike me—it is a kindness; let him rebuke me—it is oil on my head. My head will not refuse it." You've seen this verse before in this book, and will probably see it again. It represents a radical attitude that opens yourself to criticism. It says, "I want all that you have, Lord. Send it by whomever you wish. I'll not refuse it." That's not the attitude in the church today. It's rather, "If you correct me, I will go someplace else."

Peter and Paul had a serious confrontation. Paul wrote in Galatians 2:11, "When Peter came to Antioch, I opposed him to his face, because he was in the wrong." Peter was a famous apostle and leader, as was Paul. Yet Peter had fallen into hypocrisy, refusing to eat with Gentile believers. Paul rebuked him and Peter received it. I know he received it because he wrote about Paul in 2 Peter 3:15: "Just as our dear brother Paul also wrote you with the wisdom that God gave him." Peter didn't get mad at Paul or hold a grudge. His "head" received the rebuke, and he called Paul "dear."

Who will you be like? Will you be like King David and Peter, who knew how to receive and were therefore qualified to give a rebuke? Or will you be like the person in today's verse? Will you humbly take a rebuke, or become like a person in a neck cast? If you're serious about your walk, then rebuke is part of the package. If you consistently ignore rebuke, your world is in jeopardy of coming down and there will be no re-building. You're not above rebuke. Accept it as a way of life, and let it do its work. Ignore it and you risk a serious fall. The choice is obvious but not easy.

SEPTEMBER 30

"I am the most ignorant of men;
I do not have a man's understanding."
— 30:2.

This is what the Lord says: "Let not the wise man boast of his wisdom or the strong man boast of his strength or the rich man boast of his riches, but let him who boasts boast about this: that he understands and knows me, that I am the Lord, who exercises kindness, justice and righteousness on earth, for in these I delight," declares the Lord (Jeremiah 9:23-24).

My pastor once told me, "It's hard to be humble when you're good." We just visited a church that was growing and prospering, and we noticed an arrogant edge in the leadership and people. Their attitude seemed to be that they deserved the blessing of the Lord because they had the correct doctrine and were doing the right things. They were wonderful people, who were in fact doing many good things. They were guilty, however, of boasting in their wisdom and insight.

Today that church exists no more. One day God breathed on it and it faded away. All their wisdom and good ideas, projects and programs, dreams and goals melted. What happened to this fellowship? The answer lies in today's verse.

Paul warned the Galatians, "If anyone thinks he is something when he is nothing, he deceives himself. Each one should test his own actions. Then he can take pride in himself, without comparing himself to somebody else" (Galatians 6:3-4). When you compare yourself to another church, ministry, or person, you're on dangerous ground. When you think that you've figured out the Lord, you make yourself the equal of God. When you reduce God to a formula—"I did this; therefore God must do this"—you make God someone whom you can manipulate with His own principles.

The Lord poses the same question to us that Paul posed to the Corinthians: "For who makes you different from anyone else? What do you have that you did not receive? And if you did receive it, why do you boast as though you did not?" (1 Corinthians 4:7). Whatever you have or have become, God did it. You didn't earn it; it was the result of His grace. You need to stay humble and say like the writer of today's verse, "I am ignorant." Compared to God, you are.

Don't take yourself or your success too seriously. Keep in mind this simple formula found in the words of Micah the prophet: "He has showed you, O man, what is good. And what does the Lord require of you? To act justly and to love mercy and to walk humbly with your God" (Micah 6:8). Walk humbly with God and rejoice that you know Him and His ways. Keep your perspective and appreciate the grace of God. It has brought you this far and, if you rest in it, will bring you into all that He has for you.

OCTOBER 1

"Then they will call to me but I will not answer;
they will look for me but will not find me." —1:28.

Today is the beginning of a new month. On the first of the month, I try to determine an area I can study during the coming month. What spiritual discipline can I work on? I look at my prayer life one month at a time. How was my prayer life last month? What steps can I take to improve it? With that in mind, why don't you and I embark on a 31-day study of prayer, starting today?

What if you began praying, however, and the Lord didn't answer? To think that you could call on the Lord and He would not respond is a sobering thought. We're a people who expect the Lord to hear and answer. Moses asked the people, "What other nation is so great as to have their gods near them *the way the Lord our God is near us whenever we pray to Him?"* (Deuteronomy 4:7 emphasis added). That's our experience and it's a wonderful heritage.

Today's verse does warn, however, that conditions may be right for the Lord not to respond. Isaiah wrote, "Seek the Lord while he may be found; call on him while he is near. Let the wicked forsake his way and the evil man his thoughts" (Isaiah 55:6-7). There is a time when the Lord "may be found." He makes Himself available to you by His grace. If you choose not to respond to Him, over time He may make Himself less accessible.

Isaiah urged the people to seek and forsake—seek the Lord and forsake evil. Your prayer life must be one of seeking Him and His face only. Jeremiah wrote to the exiles, "You will seek me and find me when you seek me with all your heart" (Jeremiah 29:13). David instructed his son Solomon,

Acknowledge the God of your father, and serve him with wholehearted devotion and with a willing mind, for the Lord searches every heart and understands every motive behind the thoughts. If you seek him, he will be found by you; but if you forsake him, he will reject you forever (1 Chronicles 28:9).

Your seeking must be wholehearted for the Lord to take notice. The good news is that "the Lord is near to all who call on him, to all who call on him in truth" (Psalm 145:18). Let this month be a month when you seek the Lord with all your heart. Put aside any hindrance to your seeking, and do nothing that would risk the Lord turning a deaf ear to you. Be like King David when he said, "Your face, Lord, I will seek. Do not hide your face from me, do not turn your servant away in anger" (Psalm 27:8-9).

Set this month aside as "seek the Lord" month. Don't take for granted that the Lord hears and answers. Renew your efforts to seek His face, and keep a record of what you pray, hear, and see. Set aside some days for prayer and fasting. Get off by yourself for an entire day this month to do nothing but pray. This is a day of new beginnings. Let it begin with a renewed commitment to prayer.

OCTOBER 2

"And if you call out for insight and cry aloud for understanding...." —2:3.

My grandmother had a picture of Jesus hanging in her hall. It was a portrait of an angelic-looking man with brown, flowing locks and an illuminated look. When I was young, I thought it was an actual picture of what Jesus looked like. That image of Jesus has been duplicated in Hollywood movies many times over as Jesus is constantly portrayed as a meek, gentle-looking man with long hair and a holy countenance. I wonder if that picture of Jesus hasn't done more harm than good.

Jesus was God, but He was also a man, who probably worked as a carpenter. He was human in every way except sin. The movies that show Jesus floating over the ground, barely touching it with his feet, are not accurate. This image has caused people to emulate that style, mistakenly thinking it to be holy and correct.

You can read in the Gospels that Jesus was a man of prayer, staying up all night to pray on several occasions. If Jesus fulfilled His earthly mission by relying on His being God, then why the need to stay up all night? Was He just enjoying the Father's fellowship? Perhaps, but I doubt if that alone would cause Him to miss a night's sleep. I believe that Jesus stayed up all night doing what today's verse encourages you to do—call out and cry aloud to the Father.

"One of those days Jesus went out to a mountainside to pray, and spent the night praying to God. When morning came, he called his disciples to him and chose twelve of them, whom he also designated apostles" (Luke 6:12-13). It seems that Jesus stayed up all night calling out for wisdom to know whom He was to choose. If Jesus did that, do you suppose that you will need to do it also? When faced with a difficult decision, will you get by with any less than Jesus?

The writer of Hebrews paints a more accurate picture of Jesus than my grandma's old portrait ever could:

During the days of Jesus' life on earth, he offered up prayers and petitions with loud cries and tears to the one who could save him from death, and he was heard because of his reverent submission. Although he was a son, he learned obedience from what he suffered and, once made perfect, he became the source of eternal salvation for all who obey him (Hebrews 5:7-9).

Learn to pray like Jesus prayed. Shout out and cry, seeking the Lord with all the energy you can muster. Don't be religious—and don't try to copy that picture. Be yourself and call out to God. You will be heard when you call out and cry aloud to the God who hears and can save.

"In all your ways acknowledge him, and he will make your paths straight."
— *3:6.*

I frantically felt through my pockets, only to realize that it wasn't there. Then I looked through everything I had worn recently to no avail. I'd lost my favorite pen. It was a gift and had sentimental value. Finally and as a last resort, I prayed and asked the Lord to help me find it. Several days later it turned up in some out-of-the-way place. I had acknowledged my dependence on the Lord, and He had heard my request and helped me.

You may feel that a pen isn't worth praying for and that God has more important things on His mind than my possessions. I see it another way. I'm dependent on God for everything. He's my provider, protector, and helper. I realize my need for Him more than ever. I've prayed for godly spouses for my children since they were babies. I've prayed for His help as I study. I've sought Him for wisdom to know where to get my car repaired. Today's verse says to acknowledge Him in all your ways, and I've consistently, although often imperfectly, tried to do that.

Paul wrote to the Philippian church,

Do not be anxious about anything, but in everything, by prayer and petition, with thanksgiving, present your requests to God. And the peace of God, which transcends all understanding, will guard your hearts and your minds in Christ Jesus (Philippians 4:6-7).

I studied this passage in the Greek and the word "anything" literally means "anything." "In everything" means "in everything!" There's no hidden meaning there. Paul told them (and you) to pray in every situation. By doing so, you acknowledge your dependence on God, and He works to straighten out the paths before you that may seem crooked.

One of the beautiful by-products of a fruitful and comprehensive prayer life is peace—not just any peace, but the peace that passes all understanding. This peace makes you think, "Why am I so peaceful now? Things are pressing in, yet I have confidence and rest." That's the kind of peace that comes from presenting your requests to God. If you lack peace and are anxious, have you really dispatched that burden to the Lord in prayer?

If your paths are crooked before you and you can't see where you're going, this is no time to pray what I call "now-I-lay-me-down-to-sleep" prayers. This is no time to be timid or immature in prayer. You must acknowledge your need for Him in the strongest terms. That will take time and energy. If you'll make your needs known, He will straighten your paths and you'll have peace. This is a great deal— you trade anxiety and crooked paths and He gives peace and grace. Make the trade today.

OCTOBER 4

"Listen, my sons, to a father's instruction;
pay attention and gain understanding."— 4:1.

Whilst it be true that none but the One who inspired the Holy Scriptures can open to any of us their hidden depths and rich treasures, yet it is also true that He places no premium upon sloth. It is the prayerful and meditative reader who is rewarded by the Holy Spirit's illumination of the mind, giving him to behold wondrous things out of God's Law. "The soul of the sluggard desireth, and hath nothing; but the soul of the diligent shall be made fat" (Proverbs 13:4). If, then any verse of Scripture is really to speak to our hearts, there has to be not only a crying unto God for the hearing ear, but there must be a girding up the loins of our minds and a careful pondering of each word in the verse.*

It's not enough to cry out to God for wisdom. You must learn to listen for the answer. It may come through circumstances, another person, a book, or through the written word of God. Today's verse commands you to listen and pay attention. That requires a quieting of the spirit that blocks out all distractions. It also requires a diligence in seeking that focuses your energies toward God and His voice.

Perhaps your Bible reading isn't as fruitful as you would like. Maybe you read a passage dutifully, only to reach the end and realize that you didn't understand or remember what you read. Do you go back and re-read it? Or do you press on due to time restraints, only to skim over the next verses as well? Part of your prayer life is to pray over the word of God. You must learn to listen to what the Lord is saying to you from the Word of life.

David wrote,

My heart is not proud, O Lord, my eyes are not haughty; I do not concern myself with great matters or things too wonderful for me. But I have stilled and quieted my soul; like a weaned child with its mother, like a weaned child is my soul within me (Psalm 131:1-2).

David said his soul was composed like a weaned child. That has meaning if you consider what an unweaned child is like. Have you ever seen a two- or three-year old that is still on its mother's milk? When that child wants to be fed, it reaches and grabs for its mother in a way so demanding that's embarrassing to watch.

When you want something from the Lord, you can act the same way. You can grab and claw at God talking so much that you fail to listen. You can be so preoccupied with your needs that you find yourself unable to concentrate on hearing God's voice. You're so anxious about your problem that you read through the Word but it doesn't penetrate. Determine today to compose your soul and don't act like a unweaned child. Take your time as you pray and read, listening for the voice of the Lord. Pay attention, for your answer may be before your very eyes.

*Arthur L. Pink, *The Life of David*, 1981, page 345.

278

"My son, pay attention to my wisdom, listen well to my words of insight."—5:1.

"Your yard looks wonderful," my neighbor said. "It's so much better than when you moved in." When we moved in, our yard was a sea of weeds and dead grass. Due mostly to my wife's efforts, it's now green with pretty flower beds and a lot less weeds. My wife likes flowers and a well-landscaped yard. When I hear the word "landscaping," I hear work and I try to distance myself from them both. I was unable to escape all of the work, however, and had to give myself to some weeding and fertilizing.

Jesus talked about giving yourself to the same—weeding and fertilizing—if you're to listen and hold onto God's word. In Matthew 13, Jesus taught the parable of the sower, which would perhaps better be called the parable of the four soils.

A farmer went out to sow his seed. As he was scattering the seed, some fell along the path, and the birds came and ate it up....When anyone hears the message about the kingdom and does not understand it, the evil one comes and snatches away what was sown in his heart. This is the seed sown along the path Matthew 13:3-4,19).

The first problem with listening or receiving the seed of the Kingdom is busyness. The seed falls on the path, and that path tends to get worn down through activity. It's unfit to grow anything because there's so much foot traffic there. Since the seed is constantly jostled and kicked around, it can never take root. When this happens, the evil one is able to come and steal away the seed. The problem is with you, because you allowed conditions to be favorable for him to come and steal. You were too busy to hold onto what the Lord was trying to show you.

Jesus goes on to describe the second soil condition.

Some [seed] fell on rocky places, where it did not have much soil. It sprang up quickly, because the soil was shallow. But when the sun came up, the plants were scorched, and they withered because they had not root....What was sown on rocky places is the man who hears the word and at once receives it with joy. But since he has no root, he lasts only a short time. When trouble or persecution comes because of the word, he quickly falls away (13:5-6, 20-21).

The second problem with listening is the trouble that can come with it. The Lord can show you some pretty scary things—give away what you have; do something you know will offend family, friends, or business associates; or publicly admit some wrongdoing. When you pray for wisdom and get it, it can scare you to death. What you at first received with joy, can be given away to the scorching sun of trouble and you find yourself in a worse predicament—rejecting God's solution.

Determine to deal with your soil so that you can get and hold on to God's word. As you pray this month, also work on your ability to retain your answers. Let your busy paths see new growth and let your shallow soil have depth so that God's word won't be stolen or scorched.

OCTOBER 6

"How long will you lie there, you sluggard?
When will you get up from your sleep?"— 6:9.

Every day "it" is on my to-do list, assigned the primary place above all else. I write down prayer on my list, yet it stays on my list undone more times than I care to admit. Since I'm not a morning person, I enjoy lying in bed after I awake, especially when it's cold out. I'm more of a night person, and often I "put off" prayer until later. The only problem is that often "later" never comes.

The biblical evidence for praying early in the morning is overwhelming, yet simple. The pressures of the day haven't begun and it's time that is freer from distractions. Consider these verses:

• "Morning by morning, O Lord, you hear my voice; morning by morning I lay my requests before you and wait in expectation" (Psalm 5:3).

• "Evening and morning and noon, I cry out in distress" (Psalm 55:17).

• "Awake, my soul! Awake, harp and lyre. I will awaken the dawn" (Psalm 57:8).

• "In the morning I will sing of your love" (Psalm 59:16).

• "In the morning my prayer comes before you" (Psalm 88:13).

• "Awake, harp and lyre! I will awaken the dawn" (Psalm 108:2).

• "I rise before dawn and cry for help" (Psalm 119:147).

• "Let the morning bring me word of your unfailing love" (Psalm 143:8).

David wrote all but two of those verses. It's obvious that he was in the habit of getting up early, before sunrise.

Ernest B. Gentile, in his book *Awaken the Dawn!*, outlines the reasons for praying early: "For me a consistent early morning prayer schedule provides the answer to all four of these hindrances [to prayer]: time pressure, administrative jumble, weakness of the flesh, and lack of fresh content [in prayer]."* Andrew Murray wrote, "If I commit myself for the day to the Lord Jesus, then I may rest assured that it is His eternal almighty power which has taken me under its protection and which will accomplish everything for me."**

As you commit to prayer this month, get out of bed earlier. Don't be a sluggard in God's eyes. Set two alarm clocks. or have someone call you to help get you up. Maybe you need to go to bed earlier. Another suggestion would be to read either of the two books quoted above. Do what you must to establish an early-morning prayer time. Don't let your bed rob you of prayer, but let your prayer life rob you of sleep. Sleep may rest the body, but prayer rests the soul. You need your spiritual rest, so get up and pray!

*Ernest B. Gentile, *Awaken the Dawn!* (Portland, OR: Bible Temple Publishing, 1990), pages 16-20.
**Andrew Murray, *The Prayer Life* (Grand Rapids: Zondervan, new edition 1988), page 15.

OCTOBER 7

"Keep my commands and you will live;
guard my teachings as the apple of your eye."— 7:2.

The day before yesterday we began to discuss the parable of the sower as it related to prayer. We saw that it could also be referred to as the parable of the four soils. We read about the first two types of soil. Let's now consider the other two.

Other seed fell among thorns, which grew up and choked the plants....What was sown among the thorns is the man who hears the word, but the worries of this life and the deceitfulness of wealth choke it, making it unfruitful (Matthew 13:8, 22).

The word of God has a lot of competition in our heart. It's often one voice among many. There's a duty voice, a family voice, a guilt voice, a business voice, and a self voice. All these put pressure on you to do certain things.

The parable pays special attention to the deceitfulness of riches as it chokes out God's word. You may not have much money and feel that this doesn't pertain to you. But the verse isn't talking about a lot of money. You can be so anxious over money, retirement, rent and car payments, debt and the like that you can't hear the voice of God! It doesn't refer to large amounts of money—it refers to the cares of life that issue from any amount of money.

Then the parable finishes with the final soil type: "Still other seed fell on good soil, where it produced a crop—a hundred, sixty or thirty times what was sown....But what was sown on good soil is the man who hears the word and understands it. He produces a crop, yielding a hundred, sixty or thirty times what was sown"(13:8; 23).

The Lord wants you, according to today's verse, to keep His teaching as the apple of your eye. He expects you to prepare your soil to receive His commands, understand them, and allow them to bear fruit. That's one goal of your prayer life.

Deal with your soil. How much do money matters cause you anxiety? Are you uptight with your business, rising early to get the jump on your competitors? Have the cares of this life—car, children, spouse, house, and even church problems—choked out God's voice? Have you allowed good things to consume you and keep you from your Lord? Then start today to weed and fertilize. Whatever soil type you have, deal with it accordingly; let your busy paths replenish themselves; let your shallow soil grow deeper; and pull out your weeds and thorns.

Let your focus this month be on seeking God's face, and don't let anything interfere with that. You can be sure that things will try. Treat them like weeds and cut them off at the root. Allow nothing to hinder your ability to receive God's seed. Guard yourself and your relationship with the Lord. Keep Him as the apple of your eye, and you will yield a crop, 30, 60, or even 100 times what was sown. Your prayer life can bring that kind of return, if you take the time to cultivate it faithfully.

OCTOBER 8

"Listen, for I have worthy things to say;
open my lips to speak what is right."— 8:6.

The restaurant was filled as usual with lunch traffic. I had arrived early to get a seat, and saw the church member I was to meet coming through the front door. He sat down at our booth, and immediately said, "I almost canceled because I knew you were going to ask me, 'What is the Lord saying to you?' I haven't heard anything, but we still need to talk." This man knew me well, for I usually begin each pastoral session with the same question, "What's the Lord saying to you?"

The Lord is always "broadcasting." Is your antenna up and radio on? He wants to speak to His people as a group and individually. I always try to summarize in my own mind what the Lord is saying to me, and I can usually find a key phrase, ministry gift, habit, verse, or flaw about which the Lord is speaking.

Many verses in the book of Proverbs tell you to "listen." Why would you be told to listen unless you could actually hear? Isaiah wrote about listening:

How gracious he will be when you cry for help! As soon as he hears, he will answer you. Although the Lord gives you the bread of adversity and the water of affliction, your teachers will be hidden no more; with your own eyes you will see them. Whether you turn to the right or to the left, your ears will hear a voice behind you, saying, "This is the way; walk in it" (Isaiah 32:19-21).

You should spend as much or more time listening in prayer as you do speaking. After all, prayer is communication, and effective communication is never one-sided. Zechariah and Elizabeth, parents of John the Baptist, found this out. They were praying for a child even though they were old. They persevered and one day Zechariah went into the temple to offer incense. As he did,

An angel of the Lord appeared to him, standing at the right side of the altar of incense. When Zechariah saw him, he was startled and was gripped with fear. But the angel said to him: "Do not be afraid, Zechariah. Your prayer has been heard" (Luke 1:11-13).

His prayer had been heard and God was responding. It was time for Zechariah to listen.

The angel told Zechariah that they would have a child, but this great man of God didn't believe the angel's report! He was comfortable with speaking to God, but didn't know how to listen and receive. His discipline was, "Now you will be silent and not able to speak until the day this [John's birth] happens" (Luke 1:20). Zechariah would lose his ability to speak to God until he learned how important it was to listen to God. You must learn the same lesson.

Are your prayers stagnant? Maybe you have lost your ability to talk so you'll learn how important it is to listen. And if you're praying for answers, don't fall into unbelief when they come. Expect a response, for the Lord has many wonderful things to say to you.

"Come, eat my food and drink the wine I have mixed."— 9:5.

Above the clatter of dishes and noise of conversation, I've done some of my finest pastoring. It's common for me to meet those I pastor for breakfast or lunch in some local restaurant. That gives us a chance to eat, enjoy some fellowship, and dialogue over some problem or opportunity. Today's verse invites you to a restaurant for some food prepared by someone else. No, it's not actual food for the stomach, but it can be food for the soul.

Jesus' disciples came to Him one day and asked, "Lord, teach us to pray, just as John taught his disciples"(Luke 11:1). Both John and Jesus taught their disciples to pray. You may also need to learn how to pray. The good news is that there's an abundance of "food and mixed wine" for you to feast on. The feast consists of the prayers contained in the Bible.

One of my favorite prayers is found in Ephesians 1:17-19:

> I keep asking that the God of our Lord Jesus Christ, the glorious Father, may give you the Spirit of wisdom and revelation, so that you may know him better. I pray also that the eyes of your heart may be enlightened in order that you may know the hope to which he has called you, the riches of his glorious inheritance in the saints, and his incomparably great power for us who believe.

That's a great prayer that you can pray for yourself, family, or friends at any time. Another great prayer is found in Colossians 1:9-10:

> Since the day we heard about you, we have not stopped praying for you and asking God to fill you with the knowledge of his will through all spiritual wisdom and understanding. And we pray this in order that you may live a life worthy of the Lord and may please him in every way.

That passage is "wine and food," for it represents an inspired prayer that is still effective. I regularly pray that prayer for the people I pastor.

Another favorite is in Hebrews 13:20:

> May the God of peace, who through the blood of the eternal covenant brought back from the dead our Lord Jesus, that great Shepherd of the sheep, equip you with everything good for doing his will, and may he work in us what is pleasing to him, through Jesus Christ.

I have an assignment for you. Begin to collect prayers found in the Bible and begin to use them in your prayer life. Substitute specific names where a "you" is used and pray them for yourself or others. Add these prayers to your prayer list. These prayers are indeed the "food and mixed wine" of wisdom. If they were good enough for Paul and the early Church, they should be good enough for you. Dig in and enjoy the rich feast that has been prepared just for you.

OCTOBER 10

"The lips of the righteous nourish many."— 10:21.

I wasn't at all encouraged. The church I pastored was struggling, finances were tight, and the pressure of ministry was overwhelming. At my lowest point, however, the Lord sent me a phone call that encouraged me. During this call my friend simply informed me that he had been praying for me all that week. What a blessing to know that the Lord had put me on his heart. I can only imagine how much worse that week would have been without those prayers.

Your lips have the ability to nourish and sustain many people. First, you can encourage them, telling them how much you appreciate them and their work. You can find something positive that will strengthen them. The writer of Hebrews wrote to "encourage one another daily" (Hebrews 3:13). That's one way that your lips can nourish many.

The second way, however, is through your prayer life. The apostle Paul knew the value of this nourishment, and he was constantly asking for it. He told the Colossians, whom he had never met, to "devote yourselves to prayer, being watchful and thankful. And pray for us, too, so that we may proclaim the mystery of Christ" (Colossians 4:2-3). He asked the Thessalonians to "pray for us" (1 Thessalonians 5:25). He asked them also to "pray for us that the message of the Lord may spread rapidly and be honored, just as it was with you. And pray that we may be delivered from wicked and evil men, for not everyone has faith" (2 Thessalonians 3:1-2).

Paul asked the Ephesians to

> Pray also for me, that whenever I open my mouth, words may be given me so that I will fearlessly make known the mystery of the gospel, for which I am an ambassador in chains. Pray that I may declare it fearlessly, as I should (Ephesians 6:19-20).

Finally, the writer of Hebrews (who I believe was Paul) also asked the brethren to "pray for us" (Hebrews 13:18).

You have the ability to nourish many, even if you don't say a word to them. You can pray and they will be sustained. If you don't have a list, put one together of all the people you need to pray for on a regular basis. Don't rely on your memory. And remember what you learned yesterday. Use the prayers found in the Bible—even the ones discussed today—as you pray for those on your list.

You can make the difference in someone's life, and prayer can make that difference. Paul also wrote to "pray in the Spirit on all occasions with all kinds of prayers and requests. With this in mind, be alert and always keep on praying for all the saints" (Ephesians 6:18). Take Paul's command seriously and start nourishing people from the bread line of your own prayer life.

OCTOBER 11

"Through the blessing of the upright a city is exalted,
but by the mouth of the wicked it is destroyed."— 11:11.

Television cameras and reporters were everywhere and excitement crackled in the air. I was famous, and my political career was on the rise. Having just been elected a Model Cities Commissioner, I was a hot item. I had an interest in urban affairs, and this was to be my spring board to bigger and better things. To my dismay, however, the election results were thrown out over a technicality, and I lost the next election by nine votes! What a short-lived career!

Shortly after that I met the Lord, and my entire life changed. From that time, politics has been a closed door for me, but my burden for cities is still there. I now understand how I can better be a blessing to the area in which I live. That blessing is released through prayer.

Paul wrote Timothy about this very topic:

I urge, then, first of all, that requests, prayers, intercession and thanksgiving be made for everyone—for kings and all those in authority, that we may live peaceful and quiet lives in all godliness and holiness (1 Timothy 2:1-2).

Paul told Timothy to pray for the political leaders. I doubt if leaders then were any more righteous than today, but that wasn't the point. Paul wanted people to pray for the leaders, because he knew the truth of today's verse: Only righteous people who pray can exalt and bless the area in which they live.

There's a feeling among many that politics is a dirty business. Corruption and inefficiency have led many to abandon any hope for the political arena. But regardless of the spiritual condition of leaders, you are to pray for them. You are to bless them and the city in which you live and worship.

Jeremiah had to deal with this same issue. He wrote to the Jewish exiles who were living in the land of Babylon to pray for that city: "Seek the peace and prosperity of the city to which I have carried you into exile. Pray to the Lord for it, because if it prospers, you prosper" (Jeremiah 29:7).

Those to whom Jeremiah wrote had been forcibly removed from their homes and relocated to Babylon. They had no love for this pagan, idolatrous city in which they now lived. But Jeremiah instructed them to pray. If he told them to do that, can you do any less?

Your prayer list should include a list of the local officials in your city or town. You should be praying for the mayor, council, police chief, school board, and other local officials. Expand that list to include state and national politicians. Both Paul and Jeremiah knew that by praying for them to prosper, the church and its members would prosper as well. Don't take an apathetic or adversarial posture toward your political leaders. Pray for them, and you'll be doing the will of God.

OCTOBER 12

"Diligent hands will rule, but laziness ends in slave labor."— 12:24.

I was lying on my face before the Lord, crying out over my lack of spiritual fruit. I wasn't leading many people to the Lord and the church wasn't growing. With some self-pity and a whole lot of self-righteousness, I was reminding the Lord how hard I had worked and how diligent I was. Answers to problems are seldom complex, and the Lord spoke into my heart a simple statement that morning: "You don't have more fruit because you don't pray."

That was it. I was not praying. I didn't heed what Samuel had said to Israel, "Far be it from me that I should sin against the Lord by failing to pray for you" (1 Samuel 12:23). James wrote, "Anyone, then, who knows the good he ought to do and doesn't do it, sins" (James 4:17). I knew to pray; I wanted to pray and had seen prayer answered, but I wasn't praying. Because I wasn't diligent to pray, I was in "slave labor." I was in bondage to my calendar and duties. Today's verse says I was lazy.

Wesley Duewel wrote:

> There is probably no single sin that you and I ought to acknowledge with deeper shame than the sin of prayerlessness. Perhaps never in the history of the church have we church leaders and our congregations been busier and more organized in church activity. But where is the power that attracts the unsaved, that causes them to tremble in the presence of God, that brings them to real repentance and transformed lives, and that then makes them a part of an actively witnessing community? Being busy is not enough.

> Never has the cause of God needed more visible illustration of the possibilities and power of prayer than does the church in our age. It is prayer power that makes saints and that produces holy character, ethical living, and fruitful witnessing. God forgive our prayerlessness and call us again to a life of prevailing prayer.

> Jesus longs to save you from a defective spiritual life and a defective prayer life. He must become more personally real to you. You must value His infinite love more than ever before. You must reciprocate His longing for communion with you. Be willing to take time to share His prayer burden with Him as He intercedes at the right hand of the Father. The resurrected, enthroned Lord Jesus, your great Intercessor, through His Holy Spirit, will teach you the life and power of prayer. May the Spirit fill you with the spirit of intercession.*

What an awesome privilege and responsibility to "share His prayer burden." Join forces with the great Prayer Warrior today and be diligent to rule on your knees in prayer.

*Wesley L. Duewel, *Mighty Prevailing Prayer* (Francis Asbury Press: Grand Rapids, Michigan, 1990), pages 34-35.

OCTOBER 13

"The sluggard craves and gets nothing,
but the desires of the diligent are fully satisfied."— 13:4.

Yesterday we talked about being lazy and prayerless. I want to see many things happen in the Lord, but my tendency is not to take the time to pray. If I do, I want to pray just a few times and see results. I'm not always interested in prevailing prayer over a long period of time. Today's verse speaks to that tendency in me. I'm lazy, but I want to see and have a lot of things. But my desires will never be fully satisfied if I don't pray.

Jesus encouraged His followers to pray.

Keep on asking and it will be given to you; keep on seeking and you will find; keep on knocking (reverently) and the door will be opened to you. For everyone who keeps on asking receive, and he who keeps on seeking finds, and to him who keeps on knocking it will be opened. Or what man is there of you, if his son asks him for a loaf of bread, will hand him a stone? Or if he asks for a fish, will hand him a serpent? If you then, evil as you are, know how to give good and advantageous things to your children, how much more will your Father Who is in heaven (perfect as He is) give good and advantageous things to those who keep on asking Him! (Matthew 7:7-11, Amplified).

The Amplified Version captures the true meaning of Jesus' words. Those who keep on asking will receive what they ask. This speaks of a diligent and persistent prayer life that focuses on the object and prays until an answer is received. God likes this kind of persistence. He is not offended. In fact, He hides Himself at times to draw you into a life of persistent prayer. Jesus encouraged such prayer:

Then Jesus told his disciples a parable to show them that they should always pray and not give up. He said: "In a certain town there was a judge who neither feared God nor cared about men. And there was a widow in that town who kept coming to him with the plea, 'Grant me justice against my adversary.' For some time he refused. But finally he said to himself, 'Even though I don't fear God or care about men, yet because this widow keeps bothering me, I will see that she gets justice, so that she won't eventually wear me out with her coming.' And the Lord said, 'Listen to what the unjust judge says. And will not God bring about justice for his chosen ones, who cry out to him day and night? Will he keep putting them off? I tell you, he will see that they get justice, and quickly. However, when the Son of Man comes, will he find faith on the earth?'" (Luke 18:1-8).

Will the Son of Man find faith in you when He returns? Will He find you crying out to Him diligently? Will you be found asking, seeking, and knocking? The desires of the diligent prayer warrior will be fulfilled. Press into God today, and determine to seek Him as long as it takes to get "justice." Don't give up, but be diligent and see the salvation of God.

OCTOBER 14

"Knowledge comes easily to the discerning."— 14:6.

In high school, I enjoyed biology class. My favorite part was dissecting the various creatures. I still remember taking apart a worm, starfish, and, of course, a frog. One or two students would get sick, others would dread the experience, but I loved the whole process. There was no doubt that when we were done, we no longer had a frog or worm, just the parts thereof.

Some believers treat prayer like I treated that frog I dissected. They analyze its parts and "take prayer apart" in such a way that they have nothing left when then are through. They have the components of prayer, but they don't have prayer. If a teaching on prayer doesn't lead you to pray more effectively, then you don't have much of a teaching. You can so analyze prayer and the correct way to pray that you are uptight about the how's and why's of prayer.

Prayer isn't complex. It's talking with the Father and listening for His direction and response. There's no "wrong" way to pray. As you mature in the Lord, your prayer life will mature as well. But along the way, don't be uptight over the "how to's." Jesus taught His disciples how to pray. He taught them to pray out of their relationship with their Father, but He didn't give them a formula. Too many have taken the Lord's prayer and been content to pray it word for word. That isn't prayer, but rather the pattern for prayer.

Paul wrote to the Roman church, "In the same way, the Spirit helps us in our weakness. We do not know what we ought to pray, but the Spirit himself intercedes for us with groans that words cannot express" (Romans 8:26). Your prayer life is to be Spirit-led. You often don't know how or what to pray in a given situation, but the Spirit is ready and willing to lead you if you allow Him the freedom to direct your prayer life.

When I pray, I try to listen for the Spirit's leading. One day I'll focus a great deal of time on one subject; on other days, I feel impressed to pray for the people I pastor by name. When someone's name or face comes to mind during the day, I assume that the Spirit wants me to pray for them, trying to hear what He wants me to pray for. Today's verse tells you that knowledge—even about what to pray—is easy to the discerning. If you learn to discern the Spirit, your prayer life will dramatically improve.

Start out by confessing that you don't know how to pray. Acknowledge your weakness and ask the Spirit to direct you as you pray. From that point, what comes into your mind and heart in most cases will be from the Spirit of God. Learn to be less rigid and more flexible as the Spirit directs your prayer, and your prayer life will take on new vigor and strength.

OCTOBER 15

"The Lord is far from the wicked,
but he hears the prayer of the righteous."— 15:29.

When I first moved to Florida, the state experienced a terrible drought. There was very little rain for almost an entire year. Water levels were so low that car washing was banned and a rationing system was enforced to control lawn irrigation. Stricter restrictions were about to be implemented when the rains finally came. That drought taught me how I took rain for granted. Now when it rains, I try to thank God for His provision.

That year in Florida with little rain was a minor inconvenience, however, when compared to the drought during Elijah's ministry. James tells us,

> The prayer of a righteous man is powerful and effective. Elijah was a man just like us. He prayed earnestly that it would not rain, and it did not rain on the land for three and a half years. Again he prayed, and the heavens gave rain, and the earth produced its crops (James 4:16-18).

What a dramatic intervention in the affairs of men! One man prayed, and it didn't rain for a long time. Today's verse tells you that God hears the prayer of the righteous. God certainly heard Elijah's prayer. You may think, however, that Elijah was a prophet and that he had a special prayer connection, but that is not the case. James wanted you to know that Elijah was just like you. His prayers had power and were effective because he was a righteous man.

This should give you tremendous confidence when you pray. God hears you! Your words have power, so try not to pray for trivial things. Stop praying only for things that affect you and yours and start praying big prayers. For instance, choose one nation of the world and pray for that nation. Lay your hands on the globe where that nation is. Pray for the Gospel to be released on all flesh there.

Or get the names of all the elected and appointed officials in your area. Pray for them by name and intercede on their behalf. You can also get your church directory and pray for those listed. Pray for their prosperity and welfare. The God of the universe is listening, so don't pray silly or small prayers. You have the same power in you that Elijah had when he changed the course of history through prayer. Your prayer power is like having a nuclear weapon. Don't use it to hunt rabbits; use it to change the world and destroy the works of the enemy.

Jesus told His followers, "If you believe, you will receive whatever you ask for in prayer" (Matthew 21:22). What a promise! Don't waste that promise on selfish or shortsighted things. Join with Elijah and pray powerful and effective prayers.

OCTOBER 16

"In his heart a man plans his course, but the Lord determines His steps."
— 16:9.

As I walked out the door, I promised my four-year-old son that I'd see him at his school program later that morning. He had talked about that program for days, and was really looking forward to my being there. As soon as I got to work, however, I got involved in my day and forgot all about the program. Later in the morning, my boss came in and asked me to take the van and run an errand, which I set out to do.

I encountered terrible traffic and used all the back roads and short-cuts I knew. I was a little upset over how hard it was to get where I was going. I made one final turn and suddenly there I was, in front of my son's school! I looked at my watch, and it was two minutes before his program was to start. I parked the van and ran into his classroom only to have the teacher tell me how much my son had been talking about my being there. I kept thanking God for His mercy in getting me there in spite of myself.

That day taught me just how God can determine my steps. Without ever interfering with my free will, and in His power, He got me where I needed to go. I planned my course, but He directed my steps. That truth gives me great confidence when I pray. Everything is not up to me. God's working with me. He knows my frailty and is ready and willing to set the course of my steps. Someone once told me to pray as if everything depends on God, and then work as if everything depends on me. I can do that because I know God will direct me as I "move out" to do His will. He's for me and not against me.

The apostle Paul knew this truth is his life and ministry. He was constantly asking for prayer that doors of ministry would open. At one point, "Paul and his companions traveled throughout the region of Phrygia and Galatia, having been kept by the Holy Spirit from preaching the word in the province of Asia" (Acts 16:6). I don't know how the Spirit prevented Paul from going to Asia, but He did.

"When they came to the border of Mysia, they tried to enter Bithynia, but the Spirit of Jesus would not allow them to do so" (Acts 16:7). Again Paul was planning his course, but the Lord continued to direct his steps. Finally,

> During the night Paul had a vision of a man of Macedonia standing and begging him, "Come over to Macedonia and help us."After Paul had seen the vision, we got ready at once to leave for Macedonia, concluding that God had called us to preach the gospel to them (Acts 16:9-10).

Don't be uptight if God seems to be resisting you. Keep on praying, and then keep on moving. A moving car is easier to steer than a parked one. God has promised to direct your steps, but He never promised to direct your inactivity. Pray and work, and the Lord will surely bless your efforts.

OCTOBER 17

"A bribe is a charm to the one who gives it;
wherever he turns, he succeeds."— 17:8.

The line was long, the lights were out, and the language was strange. In the midst of a power outage, I was working my way through the customs line in a South American airport. I had brought quite a few boxes full of donations for the mission work there. As I came before the inspection official, he asked me to open every box!

The friend whom I was visiting later told me that the official had taken so long in hopes of receiving a bribe from me. A bribe is a shortcut and is given to bring about a desired end. The inspection official was willing to forego the time and trouble of looking through everything (a shortcut) to let me go through (the desired result). When I didn't offer anything, he proceeded to take his time.

Today's verse tells you that a bribe brings favor, at least in the short run. In the context of every day life, I've also tried to use a bribe. Instead of travailing in prayer, I've tried everything else to make something respond. I've tried to use my intelligence. At other times, I've redoubled my efforts to work harder. I've preached harder, studied longer, and tried new techniques. I've thrown a "bribe"—money, expertise, people—at a difficult situation and temporarily it may have improved. But the effects of a bribe are short-lived, and I often find myself back in the same predicament.

Prevailing in prayer until God's answer is given involves the investment of time. Any prayer answer worthy of prevailing prayer is worth all the time that you can invest in it. It may involve time spent in prayer on repeated occasions as well as a priority on your heart, so that you return to his special petition whenever you have free time. Persevering prayer takes time.*

There are no short cuts in the spiritual life. Prayer is the key, but often I want to try anything else that can open the door.

Jesus did not "bribe" His way through life; He prayed His way through. He didn't rely on His divinity; He prayed. "One of those days Jesus went out to a mountainside to pray, and spent the night praying to God. When morning came, he called his disciples to him and chose twelve of them" (Luke 6:12-13). Jesus prayed all night before He chose the twelve. Jesus lost sleep over prayer. He didn't do personality evaluations or interviews to choose the Twelve; He prayed.

Oh Lord, forgive me for my prayerlessness. Forgive me for trying everything else except prevailing, time-consuming prayer. I have been confident in my own abilities, and have tried to use them to bring me success. But true success comes only from You. I ask that You fill my heart with the desire to pray. Empower me to persevere. I want Your success and not my own. Teach me to pray. Amen.

*Wesley L. Duewel, *Mighty Prevailing Prayer* (Francis Asbury Press: Grand Rapids, MI), page 158.

OCTOBER 18

"From the fruit of his mouth a man's stomach is filled;
with the harvest from his lips he is satisfied."— 18:20.

It was cold and the snow from the night before was beautiful—the perfect day for skiing. My wife and I were chaperoning a church youth group in Colorado, and the morning activities were about to begin. As I was boarding our bus, I was asked to go pray for a young lady who had been injured the day before.

I went to see her and sensed she was hurting in more ways than her injured back. She had been recently widowed and was on the trip at the recommendation of her pastor. She didn't want to be there, and told me she had decided to come, but vowed not to meet or mingle with anyone new. There she was, bed-ridden since she had arrived, and her vow had come true—she had not met anyone!

That incident confirmed to me once again that words have power in them. This young woman had uttered something in a moment of anguish. She didn't set out to fall and hurt herself, but something was released when she spoke that commitment not to socialize. Today's verse tells you that you will eat what you say, so it's wise to bring forth a good crop of words.

Jesus spoke of this truth in Matthew 21:

Early in the morning, as he was on his way back to the city, he was hungry. Seeing a fig tree by the road, he went up to it but found nothing on it except leaves. Then he said to it, "May it never bear fruit again!" Immediately the tree withered. When the disciples saw this, they were amazed. "How did the fig tree wither so quickly?" they asked. Jesus replied, "I tell you the truth, if you have faith an do not doubt, not only can you do what was done to the fig tree, but also you can say to this mountain, 'Go, throw yourself into the sea,' and it will be done" (21:18-21).

It's noteworthy that Jesus' teaching on faith is set in the context of His looking for fruit on the tree. Jesus is always looking for fruit, even in your prayer life. He wants you to use the awesome power of your tongue to unleash a host of blessings. He wants you to be aggressive in prayer and call things that are not as though they are.

"You will pray to him and he will hear you, and you will fulfill your vows. What you decide on will be done, and light will shine on your ways" (Job 22:28). You have a role in fulfilling your destiny. You have the power to declare a thing in prayer and see it through to its end. That's both exciting and sobering, for it makes prayer a serious matter, one worthy of your time and concern. Get busy using your tongue for good, and eat an abundant harvest of answers to your prayers.

OCTOBER 19

"He who gets wisdom loves his own soul;
he who cherishes understanding prospers."— 19:8.

"One day Jesus was praying in a certain place. When he finished, one of his disciples said to him, 'Lord, teach us to pray, just as John taught his disciples'" (Luke 11:1).

Jesus' disciples saw Him praying and they wanted to pray like He did. There's something contagious about prayer. If you're like me, your desire to pray increases when you're around others who pray. When you hear their testimonies of answered prayer, you want to go home and pray. The desire to pray, however, doesn't automatically produce a rich prayer life. The disciples were challenged by Jesus' prayer life, but that challenge confronted their ignorance. They asked Jesus to help them know how to pray.

Today's verse tells you that if you get wisdom and understanding, you will prosper. If you apply this to prayer, your understanding of how to pray will bring you success. So let's examine what Jesus told His followers.

But when you pray, do not be like the hypocrites, for they love to pray standing in the synagogues and on the street corners to be seen by men....When you pray, go into your room, close the door and pray to your Father, who is unseen. Then your Father, who sees in secret, will reward you (Matthew 6:5-7).

Find a place you can use regularly for prayer and set it aside as a "holy" place. Then see prayer as something borne out of your relationship to your heavenly Father. Don't make it stiff and religious, using King James' English. Talk to your "dad" about what's on your heart. Don't use your chances to pray in public as a time to show off your spirituality—just use them as a time to address your Father in front of His other children.

"And when you pray, do not keep on babbling like pagans, for they think they will be heard because of their many words. Do not be like them, for your Father knows what you need before you ask him" (Matthew 6:7-8). Be confident when you pray. You're not trying to convince God to give you what you need. You're talking to Him who knows the secrets of your heart! There's no right formula to get God to do what you want. You're expressing your dependence on Him for all things, and you have His promise that He's committed to your provision.

If your children need milk, they ask you for milk. They don't ask and ask and beg and plead. They know you love them and will provide. God is the same. As you mature in the Lord, let your prayer life mature with you. Continue to learn how to effectively talk with God, and you'll prosper and succeed through prayer.

"Who can say, 'I have kept my heart pure; I am clean and without sin?'"— 20:9.

I was starving and we were only half way through a 40-day fast. I was eating one meal a day, and I was dropping weight quickly. My clothes were hanging on me, and my shoes were slipping off my feet. Those were the least of my problems, however. I was going through an intense time with the Lord and He was using that time to confront the true condition of my own heart. I could not get out of Psalm 50 during that fast.

What right have you to recite my laws or take my covenant on your lips? You hate instruction and cast my words behind you. When you see a thief, you join with him; you throw in your lot with adulterers. You use your mouth for evil and harness your tongue to deceit. You speak continually against your brother and slander your own mother's son. These things you have done and I kept silent; you thought I was altogether like you. But I will rebuke you and accuse you to your face (Psalm 50:16-21).

These were strong words, but I needed them. At that time, I had begun to trust my own righteousness. I was confident in what I had learned about God. My doctrine was correct, and the blessing on my life was because I had made the right decisions. I was confident and a bit arrogant. As I entered the fast, however, God began to show me my wretchedness. I was reminded that my righteousness was as filthy rags, and God was not impressed. During that time, I also studied Luke 18.

To some who were confident of their own righteousness and looked down on everybody else, Jesus told this parable: "Two men went up to the temple to pray, one a Pharisee and the other a tax collector. The Pharisee stood up and prayed about himself: 'God, I thank you that I am not like all other men— robbers, evildoers, adulterers—or even like this tax collector. I fast twice a week and give a tenth of all I get.' But the tax collector stood at a distance. He would not even look up to heaven, but beat his breast and said, 'God, have mercy on me, a sinner.' I tell you that this man, rather than the other, went home justified before God. For everyone who exalts himself will be humbled, and he who humbles himself will be exalted" (verses 9-14).

Humility is the foundation on which you can approach the Lord in prayer. The blood of Jesus—not your own righteousness or spirituality—has paved the way into the presence of God. Today's verse asks who can claim that they are holy and right. The answer, of course, is no one. You have bold access to the throne of grace, but the access word to that throne is the name of Jesus. Don't be proud, and don't be so humble that you never deliver your petitions to God. Approach Him in an attitude of meekness and humility and God will hear you every time. Approach like the Pharisee and God will turn a deaf ear to remind you of your true spiritual condition.

OCTOBER 21

"Better to live in a desert
than with a quarrelsome and ill-tempered wife."— 21:19.

As America went to war with Iraq, I marveled at the terrain as I watched the newscasts. There was endless desert with no vegetation or life. The war had to be conducted in winter, for the heat of summer would have been oppressive. As it was, the soldiers had to consume large quantities of water to be able to handle the conditions.

As I watched, I kept thinking of today's verse. The Spirit was saying that it would be better for a man to live under those conditions than to live with a nasty wife. That's hard to imagine! Enduring heat and all that goes with it are preferable to nagging and contention in the home. Don't get mad at me—I didn't write that verse. I've done enough family counseling, however, to know that it's true. I also believe that the verse has a special meaning in the context of prayer.

The church is the bride of Christ. It's to be presented to Him without spot or wrinkle. Too often, however, the church has been a belligerent and argumentative wife. She's gone about her business and has produced endless splits and doctrinal differences. The church has marketed and profited from the business of religion, but hasn't given the world access to the Spirit of God. Rather than "live" with this quarrelsome spouse, the Lord has abandoned her to spiritual dryness and lack of fruit. God has lived up to the reality of today's verse.

Jesus confronted this reality and acted out today's verse.

Jesus entered the temple area and drove out all who were buying and selling there. He overturned the tables of the money changers and the benches of those selling doves. "It is written," he said to them, 'My house will be called a house of prayer, but you are making it a den of robbers.'" The blind and the lame came to him at the temple, and he healed them. But when the chief priest and the teachers of the law saw the wonderful things he did and the children shouting in the temple area, "Hosanna to the Son of David," they were indignant (Matthew 21:12-15).

Jesus said that God's house is to be a house of prayer, not commerce. He drove out the businessmen and in essence said that it would be better for no one to be here (a desert) than for the status quo to continue. He then showed by example what the house of God should be—a house of healing—and the leaders became indignant.

The church, God's modern temple, should also be a house of prayer. You and I should be producing the fruit of prayer, and healing a hurting world. Anything else we do should be secondary. Let's abandon our quarreling and business so we can pray in unity. If we don't, God would rather live in a desert than tolerate His contentious bride.

OCTOBER 22

"A prudent man sees danger and takes refuge,
but the simple keep going and suffer for it."— 22:3.

When I came home, I knew something was up. There were no lights on outside my house, and no one came to open the garage door to let me in. I stumbled in the darkness and walked around to the front door, trying to find my keys. My wife finally came to the door, and told me that she had had quite a night. Our son had gotten into some trouble, and she had to spend the evening sorting out the problem.

As we talked, she told me that the Lord had spoken to her three weeks earlier, warning her. She prayed and dismissed it, thinking that she was just being negative and overly concerned. She now knew that what she heard had been the Lord, and regretted not having taken more definite steps to head off this trouble.

I am convinced that the Lord tries to warn when trouble looms. My problem is that much of my prayer life is taken up with my requests, and too little is given over to listening and seeing "in the Spirit." Today's verse tells me that a prudent man will see danger. I don't know how that will happen apart from a prayer life that moves from the seen to the unseen. "So we fix our eyes not on what is seen, but on what is unseen. For what is seen is temporary, but what is unseen is eternal" (2 Corinthians 4:18).

Elisha had a servant who was fretting over what was seen. His prayer life was probably occupied with what was before him. The king of Aram had surrounded the city where Elisha lived, trying to capture the prophet.

When the servant of the man of God got up and went out early the next morning, an army with horses and chariots had surrounded the city. "Oh, my lord, what shall we do?" the servant asked. "Don't be afraid," the prophet answered. "Those who are with us are more than those who are with them." Elisha prayed, "O Lord, open his eyes so he may see." Then the Lord opened the servant's eyes, and he looked and saw the hills full of horses and chariots of fire all around Elisha (2 Kings 6:15-17).

Elisha had learned to see and operate according to the unseen. According to today's verse, he was a prudent man. He had learned, probably through prayer, to see the unseen. He took refuge in the Lord when the danger came, and was unmoved. That's how I want to be.

Learn to use your prayer life to get God's perspective. My wife and I are praying to get God's perspective on our son's problem. There is plenty that we "see" that concerns us, but we want to walk in the unseen. That has brought us to our knees and God is helping us. He will help you, too, but you must cooperate and accept His perspective no matter how hard the seen presses in on you. Ask God to open your eyes, and you will see the help that surrounds you everywhere you go.

OCTOBER 23

*"Do not join with those who drink too much wine
or gorge themselves on meat."*— 23:20.

I've often wondered if there is such a thing as spiritual gluttony. I've seen and counseled so many who are consumed with self. Everything they do and say has them at the center. They've gotten a lot of spiritual attention and food, and the more they get, the more they want.

Paul encountered believers just like that. He wrote to the church at Philippi,

> Join with others in following my example, brothers, and take note of those who live according to the pattern we gave you. For, as I have often told you before and now say again even with tears, many live as enemies of the cross of Christ. Their destiny is destruction, their god is their stomach, and their glory is in their shame. Their mind is on earthly things (Philippians 3:17-19).

The cross of Christ dealt with the problem of self. Jesus said, "If anyone would come after me, he must deny himself and take up his cross daily and follow me" (Luke 9:23). The cross must also be applied in your prayer life; otherwise you can pray selfish and carnal prayers.

I've worked over the years to reduce the number of "my's" and "I's" in my prayer time. I still make my needs known to God. But I've incorporated many other prayer requests that don't benefit me in the slightest. I've tried to sense what's important to the Lord, and pray those things as well.

The church is not to be a "bless me" club, made up of those who are trying to grab all the spiritual goodies possible. In the history of the church, those who have given themselves to the deepest prayer life have also been the most active in ministry to the poor and downtrodden. They've come out of the presence of God ready to minister and give away what they have received. They have seen the burden of God as they prayed, and the burden was that "it is more blessed to give than receive" (Acts 20:35).

James, the brother of our Lord, had a tremendous burden for social justice. He wrote,

> What good is it, my brothers, if a man claim to have faith but has no deeds? Can such faith save him? Suppose a brother or sister is without clothes and daily food. If one of you says to him, "Go, I wish you well; keep warm and well fed," but does nothing about his physical needs, what good is it? In the same way, faith by itself, if it is not accompanied by action, is dead (James 2:14-17).

Prayer isn't just for your needs, but also to sensitize you to the needs—and your role in meeting those needs—of your brothers. Pray with an eye toward action, or you risk the danger of becoming a spiritual glutton. Give away some of your "food," and your prayer life will take on new life and meaning.

OCTOBER 24

"Rescue those being led away to death;
hold back those staggering toward slaughter."— 24:11.

Over the years, I've watched the "gloom and doom" prophets condemn the wicked. The world is going to hell (which it is) and all must "turn or burn." While I agree with the message, I have seen little weeping over the condition of the lost. It almost seems as if the Church has enjoyed its superior position. My own problem in regard to the lost has been apathy—I'm busy, and their problem is their problem.

The Lord told Ezekiel, "I looked for a man among them who would build up the wall and stand before me in the gap on behalf of the land so I would not have to destroy it, but I found none. So I will pour out my wrath" (Ezekiel 22:30-31). It is written in Isaiah, "The Lord looked and was displeased that there was no justice. He saw that there was no one, he was appalled that there was no one to intercede; so his own arm worked salvation for him" (Isaiah 59:15-16).

The judgment of God is real, but He doesn't rejoice that any will be lost. Moses was confronted with this dilemma. "'I have seen this people,' the Lord said to Moses, 'and they are a stiff-necked people. Now leave me alone so that my anger may burn against them and that I may destroy them. Then I will make you a great nation'" (Exodus 32:9-10). Moses didn't rejoice in that message, even though the people had been a burden to him.

Moses asked the Lord to relent. He stood in the gap for the people and begged God for mercy: "Then the Lord relented and did not bring on his people the disaster he had threatened" (Exodus 32:14). The Psalmist tells us, "He said he would destroy them—had not Moses, his chosen one, stood in the breach before him to keep his wrath from destroying them" (Psalm 106:23).

Part of the prayer ministry of the church is to stand in the gap. You're to be like Moses and ask God for mercy, not judgment. God loves the world, but He will judge it in time. But He longs to have mercy, and marvels that you, who have received His mercy, are not quick to share it—and pray for it—with others. God is not mad at the world. He loves it so much that He gave His Son so that no one would perish.

Today's verse urges you to stand in the gap. Ask the Lord for a new burden for the lost. Repent if you've been like Jonah, wanting to see the world perish. God had mercy on you; now ask Him to have mercy on others. Help save those who are staggering off to death. Pray for them today and stand in the gap. God will be pleased as you do what Moses and Jesus did in their roles as priests.

"Like the coolness of snow at harvest time is a trustworthy messenger to those who send him; he refreshes the spirit of his masters."— 25:13.

I was exhausted, and the mile markers seemed to pass by slowly as I drove the truck northbound. But I was praising God, for He had just used me literally to save a family member from a desperate situation. I felt like that entire weekend had been a mission for God. I still rejoice that I was available then for Him to use, and I don't know any finer feeling than being used by God in a tough situation.

Today's verse tells you that a trustworthy messenger refreshes the one who sends him. I'd like to think I "refreshed" God when He used me then. I was an available messenger, went in His name and power, and accomplished the mission. I felt His pleasure when it was all over.

Prayer is making yourself available to God. It's surrendering to Him, so that He can reveal His will. He may direct you to call, write, visit, intercede, or encourage. You come into His presence to hear His will and find out how to carry it out. As you do, you'll please Him by your obedience. What a wonderful opportunity to bless the God who has blessed you.

Ananias was a man we know little about. He appeared as part of Saul's salvation experience.

In Damascus there was a disciple named Ananias. The Lord called to him in a vision, "Ananias!" "Yes, Lord," he answered. The Lord told him, "Go to the house of Judas on Straight Street and ask for a man from Tarsus named Saul, for he is praying. In a vision he has seen a man named Ananias come and place his hands on him to restore his sight" (Acts 9:10-12).

Ananias was concerned for he knew Saul was a persecutor of the church. But the Lord reassured him, and he went as a faithful messenger to restore Saul's sight.

That is the essence of availability in prayer. Little did Ananias know what he was doing, or how Saul would be used of God. Ananias was just a faithful messenger, doing what God revealed for him to do. He refreshed the heart of God that day and changed the course of history—all because he was committed to be a faithful messenger.

You can do the same thing. Make yourself available to God, asking Him to use you. Tell Him you will go wherever He wants you to, and believe that He will show you. The job you do may change the course of history! Determine to be a faithful messenger, knowing that as you are, you're blessing God through your obedience.

OCTOBER 26

"The sluggard buries his hand in the dish;
he is too lazy to bring it back to his mouth."— 26:15.

The Bible is direct and to the point. If you're lazy, you're called a sluggard. You're not called unmotivated, unfocused, or a procrastinator. God's answers are not complex, even if the problem is. Laziness is an enemy of your prayer life. "Many prayers are granted by God but given up by the ones praying because they stopped praying before the answer arrived. Undelivered prayers help no one. Without the dynamic of persistence much prayer remains unanswered."*

Consider Daniel, who fasted and prayed for three weeks. Daniel wasn't a sluggard when it came to prayer but was motivated and diligent. The angel Gabriel appeared to him and said,

> Do not be afraid, Daniel. Since the first day that you set your mind to gain understanding and to humble yourself before your God, your words were heard, and I have come in response to them. But the prince of the Persian kingdom resisted me twenty-one days. Then Michael, one of the chief princes, came to help me, because I was detained there with the king of Persia. Now I have come (Daniel 10:12-14).

God heard Daniel on the first day. It took three weeks, however, for Gabriel to overcome the spiritual opposition that came against him. If Daniel had been a sluggard—if he would have put his hand into the dish but not completed the process of eating—the answer might never have come. Today's verse encourages you to follow through with what you have begun. In the context of prayer, that is critical.

Wesley Duewel lists several reasons why you need to give God time to answer your prayer:

1. Sometimes demonic resistance delays God's answer until you and heaven prevail.

2. Sometimes it takes time for separate parts of complex situations to fit together.

3. Sometimes it takes time for God to coordinate circumstances to bring pressure on a person until that one becomes willing to do what God wants him or her to do.*

With this in mind, have you abandoned some prayer project? Is there a person you were praying for whom you gave up on? Is there some situation—family, business, or church—that didn't seem to yield to your prayers and you consequently abandoned the fight? Today's verse encourages you to complete what you started. Don't grow sluggish, but be fervent in your prayers. Be like Daniel and persevere until the breakthrough comes. It will come, if you don't surrender to discouragement or laziness.

*Wesley Duewel, *Mighty Prevailing Prayer* (Grand Rapids: Francis Asbury Press), page 150.

OCTOBER 27

"Be sure you know the condition of your flocks,
give careful attention to your herds."— 27:23.

I've seen it in the counseling room again and again. Someone is experiencing lack and it has created pressure on them and their family. When I inquire about their prayer life and how they are praying about this problem, they are usually meek and passive. They believe that to ask for provision aggressively—money, cars, homes, equipment—is somehow selfish and unspiritual. Granted it can be abused, but the Lord wants you to ask without shame or condemnation for the things you need. That isn't selfishness; it's just common sense.

Today's verse encourages you to pay attention to your "flocks and herds." Those herds represented the shepherd's livelihood. They were his source for food and clothing. The income from their sale gave him the other necessities of life. He wasn't told to ignore them; he was told to watch them carefully. Even Jesus taught His disciples to pray, "Give us this day our daily bread" (Matthew 6:11).

Jack Hayford wrote:

God is concerned for daily detail, and we should ask about it. The most important thing about this is not the discovery that we can ask for God's help in the mundane matters of our personal lives. The most important thing is that we are told to. The message is plain. We must ask about day-to-day matters as well as large essential matters. Back-to-back with prayer that the Almighty's will be worked on earth, we should not overlook the simplest matters of life.

By God's grace we come to realize that the work of our own hands provides nothing. Not that God has appointed us to laziness, but "God helps those who help themselves" isn't in the Bible. "Ask for your day to day need" is. And full understanding in prayer leads us to consult the Father about the smallest matters in life...which become the largest if neglected in prayer.*

Someone once said, "The smallest matters often become the largest if neglected in prayer." How true that is. Don't neglect the practical needs you have. Having bold access to the throne of grace, come before your God boldly and ask for your needs. He is not too busy, nor is He bored with your requests. You are His joy, not His burden, so don't feel guilty that you have needs. God created you with those needs, and He fully expects to meet them for you. Jesus reminded His followers:

Look at the birds of the air; they do not sow or reap or store away in barns, and yet your heavenly Father feeds them. Are you not much more valuable than they? Who of you by worrying can add a single hour to his life? (Matthew 6:27).

You are more valuable to God than all of creation. Ask Him for your needs and allow Him the joy of a Father in providing for His beloved child.

*Jack Hayford, *Prayer Is Invading the Impossible* (Plainfield, NJ: Logos International), p.101-2.

OCTOBER 28

"The wicked flees when no one pursues,
but the righteous are as bold as a lion."— 28:1.

I had been traveling and had not seen my children much in days. I went into my five-year old daughter's bedroom to kiss her and pray for her. As I entered, I detected the smell of peppermint in the air. My first thought was that her toothpaste must be pretty strong. As I approached her bed, she had that guilty look on her face that told me, "I've done something wrong."

Upon closer examination, I found a candy cane under her pillow. I had not come in with the purpose of catching her in the wrong, but the guilty flee when no one pursues. She was guilty and could not receive my loving visit. There was a barrier between her and me, and it was caused by her guilt and disobedience.

The same can happen in prayer. You can have such a sense of guilt and unworthiness that it affects your prayer life. I've heard people tell the Lord over and over again how sinful they are, and unworthy of His blessings. It has become a ritual, a sort of spiritual superstition for them to start out their prayer time in this manner. Or they apologize for asking God for anything, bringing a sense of guilt and condemnation into the presence of God.

You must shake any of off these tendencies! You have no reason to be guilty in the sight of God. Paul wrote,

> Therefore, if anyone is in Christ, he is a new creation; the old has gone, the new has come! All this is from God, who reconciled us to himself through Christ, and gave us the ministry of reconciliation, that God was reconciling the world to himself in Christ, not counting men's sins against them (2 Corinthians 5:17-19).

God doesn't hold your sins against you, so you can face God without guilt!

"In Whom, because of our faith in Him, we dare to have the boldness (courage and confidence) of free access—an unreserved approach to God with freedom and without fear" (Ephesians 3:12 AMP). You have bold access to God. Because you do, "Let us then approach the throne of grace with confidence, so that we may receive mercy and find grace to help us in our time of need" (Hebrews 4:16).

You are "the righteousness of God" (2 Corinthians 5:21). Act like it when you pray by being bold and adventurous. Don't use your time to recite your weaknesses and failures. God is aware of them all, and some that you don't even know about. That's not the basis upon which He accepts you. You're accepted before Him in Christ, who is your righteousness. Christ was perfect, and based on His perfection, you can pray boldly to God.

Don't be timid in prayer. Find the help you need by crying out to God. He longs to hear from you and help you because He cares for you.

"When the wicked thrive, so does sin,
but the righteous will see their downfall."— 29:16.

There's an attitude that I notice in believers regularly. The attitude is that a person can't pray when they are in trouble because they didn't pray before the trouble came. It's like a drowning man who rejects a life jacket because he wasn't wearing one before he fell into the water. It makes no difference what happened before the disaster came or who was to blame. There's always time to pray, and God hears the cry of the distressed.

James instructed, "Is any one of you in trouble? He should pray" (James 5:13). Peter was in trouble in Acts 12. King Herod had James, the brother of John, killed. He saw that James' death pleased the Jews, so he seized Peter also, and put him in jail. "Herod intended to bring him out for public trial" (Acts 12:4).

In this passage, we see part of what today's verse describes. The wicked were thriving and had the upper hand, and it looked bleak for the church. "So Peter was kept in prison, but the church was earnestly praying to God for him" (12:5). The church began to pray, and I think Peter prayed as well. If the man who arrested you had just killed your ministry associate, you would probably pray, too.

The good news is that the latter part of today's verse also came to pass.

The night before Herod was to bring him to trial, Peter was sleeping between two soldiers, bound with two chains, and sentries stood guard at the entrance. Suddenly an angel of the Lord appeared and a light shone in the cell. He struck Peter on the side and woke him up. "Quick, get up!" he said, and the chains fell off Peter's wrist (Acts 12:7).

Peter walked out of jail and went to the place where the church was praying. When he arrived, they didn't believe it was him! The servant girl announced that Peter was at the door, and they responded, "You are out of your mind!" (12:15).

Prayer works! And prayer when you are in trouble, regardless of what got you in trouble, also works. Psalm 18:6 says, "In my distress I called to the Lord; I cried to my God for help, from his temple he heard voice." Psalm 50:15 states, "Call upon me in the day of trouble; I will deliver you, and you will honor me." And Psalm 118:5 reports, "In my anguish I cried to the Lord, and he answered by setting me free."

If you're in distress, call out to God. If the wicked have increased around you and have you trapped, call on Him. If you've been lax in prayer, don't let that keep you from praying now. It's never too late. What's more, He promises that though the wicked increase and prosper, you'll see them come down. After Peter was released, Herod was struck down. Not only was Peter delivered, but an enemy of the church was sent to his eternal sentence. Prayer works. It's powerful. Avail yourself of it today, and stand and see God work on your behalf. And don't let your past prayer failure stand in the way of coming before God today.

OCTOBER 30

"I have not learned wisdom, nor have I knowledge of the holy one."— 30:3.

Another excuse that you may offer for an inadequate prayer life is your lack of spirituality or knowledge. Today's verse quotes from the sayings of Agur son of Jakeh. I don't know who this man was or what he did for a living. He started out with a rather negative perspective on his own spirituality stating that he didn't have wisdom or knowledge.

I've had people tell me that their prayer life is insignificant. The real prayer power, they say, rests with those who are more spiritual—their pastor or some other believer. Like Agur, they say that they don't feel very spiritual or that God is not that interested in what they have to say.

There's a fascinating story in 2 Chronicles 33 about a king of Judah named Manasseh.

> Manasseh was twelve years old when he became king, and he reigned in Jerusalem fifty-five years. He did evil in the eyes of the Lord, following the detestable practices of the nations the Lord had driven out before the Israelites. He rebuilt the high places...he also erected altars to the Baals and made Asheroth poles. He bowed down to all the starry hosts and worshipped them. He built altars in the temple of the Lord....He did much evil in the eyes of the Lord, provoking him to anger (2 Chronicles 33:1-6).

In summary, Manasseh was an evil man. Like Agur in today's verse, he didn't have wisdom or knowledge. So the Lord dealt with Manasseh.

> The Lord spoke to Manasseh and his people, but they paid no attention. So the Lord brought against them the army commanders of the king of Assyria, who took Manasseh prisoner, put a hook in his nose, bound him with bronze shackles and took him to Babylon (33:10-11).

Manasseh was in trouble and deserved all that he got and more. He had rejected God, and the Lord had rejected him. But an interesting thing took place after that.

> In his distress he [Manasseh] sought the favor of the Lord his God and humbled himself greatly before the God of his fathers. And when he prayed to him, the Lord was moved by his entreaty and listened to his plea; so he brought him back to Jerusalem and to his kingdom. Then Manasseh knew that the Lord is God (33:12-13).

God heard this evil, wicked king when he prayed. This man had made a shambles of his life, yet the Lord heard and restored him. What a testimony to God's mercy and grace. You can pray no matter how "ignorant" you are of God and His ways. Just begin to pray in your own words and from right where you are. Your God, who is compassionate and merciful, will hear and answer. Remember Manasseh and then humble yourself and pray. God will not turn a deaf ear.

OCTOBER 31

"Speak up for those who cannot speak for themselves,
for the rights of all who are destitute."— 31:8.

What does Jesus do at the right hand of the Father? Has that question ever crossed your mind? I wonder if He just sits there and watches the affairs of the world, kind of like watching a baseball game. Or does He talk with the Father? Or is "at his right hand" just a figure of speech?

I do know one thing that Jesus does, and that is pray. Hebrews 7:25 says, "He is able to save completely those who come to God through him, because he always lives to intercede for them." No matter what else Jesus does, He prays. More specifically, He prays for His own. Today's verse is a command to the king to speak up for those who cannot. Jesus fulfills this kingly role, for He prays and intercedes.

I have already admitted that prayer has sometimes been a low priority for me. When faced with so many things that I can do, I have often chosen to do everything but pray. When I have two hours and five things to do, I will all too often neglect prayer because I can do other things that seem to bring immediate result. I can mark two phone calls and one report off my to-do list and that makes me feel like I've accomplished something. Prayer gets things done in the invisible realm, and that's why I put it off.

I don't know all that Jesus does now, but I know He prays. He went through all that He did here to ascend to the Father so he can pray. If it's important enough for Jesus to give Himself to prayer, should you and I not do the same? Should I not be "speaking up" for those who can't? Is not my time well spent when I spend it crying out to God on behalf of others?

Paul wrote to "pray continually" (1 Thessalonians 5:17). I can't pray 24 hours a day, but I can be ready to pray at all times. I can pray instead of watching television, writing a letter, or going to a sporting event. I can be ready to pray when someone's name comes to my mind. I can see that prayer needs to be done not when everything else is finished, but is a high priority in the heart of God as evidenced by Jesus' active prayer life today.

Dear Lord, thank You that You allow me to share in the precious activity of prayer. Forgive me for my lack of diligence. I have missed many opportunities as I have been wrapped up in my own busy-ness and activity. Teach me to pray. Give me the desire to pray. Guide me when I pray. Open my eyes to see all that can be done through prayer. Help me to speak up in prayer for those who cannot speak for themselves, that they too may come to know You and the joys of communicating with a loving Lord and Father. Amen and amen.

NOVEMBER 1

*"We will get all sorts of valuable things
and fill our houses with plunder"* — *1:13.*

Last month we studied prayer. This month, as we prepare for December and the season for giving, perhaps it would be appropriate to study finances and giving. The book of Proverbs has a great deal to say about money, and you and I will do well to heed its wisdom. After all, money is a part of everyone's life, and a proper understanding of it is essential for spiritual success.

When I minister in prisons, I meet many men and women who were caught stealing. They didn't steal just to have a lot of "stuff" around. In most instances, they needed what they stole to support their drug habit. They weren't thieves as such; rather they had an addiction that they somehow needed to support.

The prophet Malachi warned Israel not about physical but spiritual theft. There were many in Israel during his day who were in "spiritual" prison because they had robbed God. They had plundered what was God's, and had used it for some other reason. They would not have considered themselves thieves, and certainly would not think of stealing something directly from God. Yet Malachi identified their problem as theft, and confronted their need to repent.

Malachi wrote, "Will a man rob God? Yet you rob me. But you ask, 'How do we rob you?' In tithes and offerings. You are under a curse—the whole nation of you—because you are robbing me" (Malachi 3:8-9). Don't dismiss this as merely the Old Testament. This is the word of God, and it still applies today.

When Jesus addressed the Pharisees, He said,

Woe to you, teachers of the law and Pharisees, you hypocrites! You give a tenth of all your spices—mint, dill and cummin. But you have neglected the more important matters of the law—justice, mercy and faithfulness. You should have practiced the latter, without neglecting the former" (Matthew 23:23).

Jesus didn't tell the Pharisees not to tithe, but to keep the practice of tithing in proper perspective. Tithing was the proper financial response to God's increase, and was to be done along with the "weightier" matters of the Law.

Is your house filled with plunder? Have you taken from God (and notice Malachi said in tithes and offerings) and used it for personal things? Have you been irregular in the giving of tithes and offerings? If you answer "yes," then determine this month to change by giving to God what is His. You may have to sell something you have in order to get it right with the Lord. Do whatever it requires to not be found with plunder taken from God.

On this first day of the month, set your course to do the will of God. If you do, God will fill your house with His blessings, and you won't be found with spiritual plunder that belongs to Him.

NOVEMBER 2

"Then you will understand what is right and just and fair —
every good path." — 2:9.

Picture this with me. A service is going on and the preacher has finished his message. As he ends, a prosperous young man comes forward to the altar to ask the preacher a question. The man is well dressed and the preacher imagines that he's a lawyer or some other successful professional. The man is sincere and polite, and obviously has some church background.

"Preacher," he asks, "how can I be sure that I have eternal life?" The minister is taken back, for this is a serious question. In response, the minister asks, "Have you kept the commandments?" The young man replies that he has since he was a boy. The preacher looks at him and tells him, "I see that you have a lot of things. Sell what you have and give it to the church's ministry for the poor." The young man is offended and begins attending another church where the pastor is not so judgmental and money-hungry.

Of course, this is actually the story of the rich young man found in Mark 10. That young man found out that God wants to get involved with every area of life—even finances. The young man was hoping that keeping the Law would be enough. He had been doing that since youth. But

> Jesus looked at him and loved him. "One thing you lack," he said. "Go sell everything you have and give to the poor, and you will have treasure in heaven. Then come, follow me." At this the man's face fell. He went away sad, because he had great wealth (Mark 10:21-22).

This man's love for and attachment to his money brought something between him and his God. In fact, his possessions had become his god, and now he was faced with the command to abandon that god and follow the true and living God. It was a sad day for him. I'd like to think that later he returned to follow the Lord, but there's no record that he did.

Materialism is the order of the day in modern society. Bigger homes, better cars, new gadgets, the latest technology, exotic vacations, and fashion updates are the goal of individuals and families alike. The economy is the number one concern for a majority of people. In the midst of this, Jesus' command is still the same: make Him Lord of your finances as you follow Him.

Today's verse says that the Lord will show you what to do with your life and money. If you commit them to Him, He will direct your paths. Pray over your finances and ask the Lord to guide your spending, saving, and giving. Constantly work at keeping your finances in His hands. He's the only financial advisor who knows the future, and He can direct your investments to a place where heavenly rewards will be the dividends. Submit to His direction, and you'll do what the rich young ruler could not—put the Lord before money.

NOVEMBER 3

"For she [wisdom] is more profitable than silver
and yields better returns than gold." — 3:14.

I was huffing and puffing on the court, enjoying our church's new multi-purpose gym. It was the first evening I had been able to attend men's basketball, and I was having a good time. Suddenly one of the men I pastored came running in and told me to go right home. The house next to ours was on fire.

When I got home, it was worse than I imagined. Flames were shooting out of my neighbor's house, scorching a pine tree 30 feet up its trunk. One of their vehicles was still in the garage, engulfed in flames. My family was on our front lawn, my children in their pajamas, watching as firemen desperately tried to control the fire. When it was all over, the house and its contents were a loss. It had happened so close to our home, and we were all pretty shaken by it.

That night, safely tucked in our own home, we thanked the Lord for His protection. We once again committed all that we had to Him for His care and protection. After we put the children back to bed, Kathy and I talked about what we would do in the event of a fire in our home. When we tried to think of what we would "grab," we came to one conclusion—we couldn't think of one thing that was so dear to us that we couldn't lose it. There were pictures and things of sentimental value, but we didn't have anything that was worth running after to save.

When we came to that conclusion, we realized that what we had was more precious than possessions, for the Lord has been good to us. He's given us righteousness, peace, and joy in the Holy Spirit. He has revealed Himself to us, and has made His magnificent promises available to us. While He has given us some material things (for which we are grateful), they don't have a hold on us. If we were able to save our children from a similar fire, we would carry with us all that we held dear and worth saving.

It's a good exercise to commit your possessions to the Lord on a regular basis. Remind yourself that it's His car, home, furniture, and television set that you are using. If something happens to one of these, do you treat it as His, or get upset as if it were your own? The unseen things that the Lord gives you—peace, love, patience, and the other fruit of the Spirit—yield greater returns than any material possession you may have.

Today's verse reminds us of this truth. If you find wisdom and are rightly related to the Lord, you have the most valuable thing there is. Don't fret over possessions and don't put your trust in how much silver and gold you have. Sit down (as a family if you're married) and commit your "stuff" to God. Give Him the computers, Nintendo games, cars, and VCRs. Then determine to "seek first his kingdom and his righteousness" (Matthew 6:33). Your house may burn and your car may fall apart, so why look for satisfaction there? Your investment in the Lord will yield greater returns. Get your priorities straight—see the Lord as your greatest possession.

NOVEMBER 4

"My son, pay attention to what I say; listen closely to my words." — 4:20.

In the past, my wife would stay away from me when I paid the bills. I would sit down thinking that everything was all right. As I began to write checks, I would soon see that there wasn't as much money as I had thought (or at least it wasn't going as far as I hoped). By the time I was done, I'd be mumbling and talking to the checkbook, ready to bite anyone who came within striking distance. It wasn't a pretty sight.

I don't know when I changed, but I did. I'm not as uptight about finances as I once was, although it's still sometimes a struggle to make ends meet. I remember one time around Christmas when I sat at my desk working on the finances. I was praying over my bills and felt impressed to write a $100 check to a widow. I didn't have $100 to spare, but obeyed the Lord. It was such a blessing to that widow that I got blessed, too. I was glad I had listened to what the Lord prompted me to do, and I've sent her money every holiday season since then.

I've already told you about the time I discovered termites in my home. The only thing holding up the end of the home that contained the garage was the framework around the garage door! To top it all off, I found out that the termite policy I had wouldn't cover the repairs. I was stuck with a $2,000 bill, and had no money.

That set me into a tizzy! I prayed and cried out to God. I was trying to get out of debt, and it didn't seem like He was helping me. At that time I was also preparing to minister at another church, but I couldn't concentrate. Those termites were driving me crazy. Having prayed for hours, I was still upset and angry.

Then the Lord spoke: "You have made those termites bigger than I am." It was such an unusual thought that I knew it had to be from the Lord. I repented, for that's exactly what I had done. I'd made one of God's smallest creatures bigger than its Creator. Having allowed those bugs to overwhelm my faith, I asked God to forgive me. He went on to miraculously provide for the house repairs.

Let the Lord speak to you about your finances. Do you think you are generous, or does God think you are generous? Are you anxious over your money? And if you are, is God anxious also? Are you giving Him the chance to guide your decisions, or do you only include Him on certain ones? Are you making your situation bigger than the Lord? Today's verse encourages you to pay close attention to what He says, for God will almost always share His perspective with you. Are you willing to listen?

Don't walk in the wisdom or counsel of the ungodly when it comes to your finances. Listen to God, and you'll always have the wisdom you need where finances are concerned.

NOVEMBER 5

"Lest you give your best strength to others,
and your years to one who is cruel." — 5:9.

It was October 19, 1987, otherwise known as "Black Monday." The stock market plummeted and so did the net worth of many people. One prominent business leader lost $1 billion as his company's stock dropped in value. I can remember the nervousness that followed as many speculated whether a crash similar to the one that led to the Great Depression was to follow.

I slept very well the night of October 19 because my value didn't change one iota. Having lost no money that day, I went to work the next day and continued on with my life as if nothing had happened. Now if the national economy would have collapsed, I'd have certainly been affected. But I serve a different economy—a transcendent economy—and it operates on a totally different set of rules.

Many give their strength to others and their years to one who is cruel. They give it all to business, the stock market, or some cause. A sudden downturn causes their stock or savings to fall, their job to be eliminated, or their pension to disappear. They find themselves bitter over the way events unfolded. The world and its system can be cruel, and compassion isn't consistent with its way of doing business.

Jesus warned us to invest our strength, time, and money wisely.

Do not store up for yourselves treasures on earth, where moth and rust destroy, and where thieves break in and steal. But store up for yourselves treasures in heaven, where moth and rust do not destroy, and where thieves do not break in and steal. For where your treasure is, there your heart will be also (Matthew 6:19-21).

We can't ignore this principle. I'm amazed how many people opt for investments that bring ten-percent interest when investing in the kingdom of God can bring a 300-percent return! When Black Monday came, my money was tied up in another Kingdom. My return doesn't depend on the Dow Jones average, inflation, or the price of gold, but on the faithfulness of my God. It was a good feeling to know that I had invested in the right place.

David wrote, "I was young and now I am old, yet I have never seen the righteous forsaken or their children begging bread. They are always generous and lend freely; their children will be blessed" (Psalm 37:25-26). I've tried to base all of my financial decisions around that truth, deciding to lay up treasures in heaven. Don't fall for the latest investment trap or trend, but stay with the one that's time-tested. The Lord promises to be generous to those who show themselves the same—what better guarantee do you need?

NOVEMBER 6

"Yet it stores its provisions in summer and gathers its food at harvest." — 6:8.

I'm not against savings, pensions, retirement plans, or investments. I believe it's important to gather what we can when we can. There are many wonderful investment counselors who are also believers, and their programs and recommendations are sound. We're wise to follow their proposals. Today's verse encourages us to store provisions when we can, and use them when we must.

While it's wise to store up, it's not wise to trust in what we store. Our trust must always be in the Lord. If by chance our storehouse is ruined, our security need not be. If the Lord blesses us with abundance, we're blessed. If He doesn't, we're still blessed, for He has promised to provide for us no matter what.

Take Elijah as an example. Here's a man who declared a famine. Elijah may have been impressed for a while at what he was able to do. But one day he realized he had to survive in a land that he had just declared to be under a drought! The Lord had already provided for his needs, however. "You will drink from the brook, and I have ordered the ravens to feed you there" (1 Kings 17:4).

But eventually the brook dried up. "Then the word of the Lord came to him. 'Go at once to Zarephath of Sidon and stay there. I have commanded a widow in that place to supply you with food'" (1 Kings 17:9). Elijah had no savings or investments. Yet the Lord provided for him. In fact, Elijah went to see this widow and asked her to use her last "savings" to feed him. When she did, her "jar of flour was not used up and the jug of oil did not run dry" (1 Kings 17:16). God miraculously provided for them all.

Can you imagine today's headlines: "Fundamentalist prophet commands widow to use up savings. He took her last dime. Hear the shocking truth at eleven." But God wasn't concerned with her savings. He's able to provide however He chooses. He's not limited to provide where there's no food stored up.

If you have something set aside, realize that it's the Lord's; He gave it to you in the first place. He was your source for that abundance, and is still your source, whether you continue to save it or have to spend it. Don't take your eyes off Him. Commit what you have to His care. If He directs you to use it, then do so. After all, it's His, and He can do with it what He wants. When you think of it, can $30,000, $100,000, or more really provide security for you? Put your trust not in the provision, but in the God of the provision. Your trust will be in the right place, and you'll be able to face the future with confidence.

"My husband is not at home; he has gone on a long journey." — 7:19.

I never wanted much from life—just to go to Harvard Business School and make $250,000 a year! I also dreamt of being a famous trial lawyer, working late at the office to prepare for the big case. That case would require all my time and energy and then bring me fame and fortune. There's only one problem with that dream: Fame and fortune are often obtained at the expense of other things, such as family, friends, and a meaningful spiritual life.

Those in the ministry have been just as guilty as those building a successful business empire. I've counseled with many preacher's kids (p.k.'s) who are wounded today because the church and the needs of the people always came first. The father was distant, having given his best to the people, only to have nothing left for his family. While I've not always been successful, I've tried to give my family my time. I've traveled, but I've planned so that family time was also included. There are times when my wife has been a ministry "widow," but I've made up for it at other times.

What price are you paying for success? Is it worth it? Your children will never be this age again. The little league and soccer games, the school plays, the PTA meetings, the school open houses will all be gone before you know it. The summer vacations will soon be impossible to plan, for everyone will be going their own way. Will you then give to your grandchildren what you should have given to your own children? That will be fulfilling, but never an adequate substitute.

Does your job or ministry come before your spouse? Your spiritual life? Your other relationships? Do you draw your identity from what you do, or from who you are? Are you working as if it all depends on you? If so, remember what the psalmist wrote:

I lift up my eyes to the hills—where does my help come from? My help comes from the Lord, the Maker of heaven and earth. He will not let your foot slip—he who watches over you will not slumber; indeed, he who watches over Israel will neither slumber nor sleep. The Lord watches over you—the Lord is your shade at your right hand; the sun will not harm you by day, nor the moon by night. The Lord will keep you from all harm—he will watch over your life; the Lord will watch over your coming and going both now and forevermore (Psalm 121:1-8).

Does your spouse say what the spouse said in today's verse? Are you away from home too much? Has your pursuit of success (and money) taken over? If so, read Psalm 121 again. The Lord will watch over you, so stop working so hard and smell the roses along the way. Keep your home life in order, and trust God for the results you're so diligently pursuing. In the end, you'll be glad you did.

NOVEMBER 8

"With me are riches and honor,
enduring wealth and prosperity." — *8:18.*

I grew up in a church where poverty was a blessing for some. Men and women took vows of poverty, and were considered spiritual for doing so. It was thought that money and wealth were a great temptation, and to be avoided. This created a lot of confusion over money; everyone knew it was important and those who took the vows of poverty asked for it regularly. Yet the desire (or need) for money was often accompanied by great guilt.

Today's verse should help clear up how the Lord feels about wealth. We're told that if we find wisdom, she brings riches, prosperity, and "enduring wealth." Those words are a promise from the Lord. There aren't only spiritual riches, but also natural riches. God isn't afraid of money, or of giving it to you and me. Paul didn't caution us against money itself; rather he wrote, "The love of money is a root of all kinds of evil" (1 Timothy 6:10).

Those who believe that money and wealth are evil must then explain Deuteronomy 8. Moses was preparing the people for the promised land, and he gave them these instructions:

> For the Lord your God is bringing you into a good land—a land with streams and pools of water, with springs flowing in the valleys and hills; a land with wheat and barley, vines and fig trees, pomegranates, olive oil and honey; a land where bread will not be scarce and you will lack nothing; a land where the rocks are iron and you can dig copper out of the hills. When you have eaten and are satisfied, praise the Lord your God for the good land he has given you. Be careful that you do not forget the Lord your God, failing to observe his commands, his laws and his decrees that I am giving you this day. Otherwise, when you eat and are satisfied, when you build fine houses and settle down, and when your herds and flocks grow large and your silver and gold increase and all you have is multiplied, then your heart will become proud and you will forget the Lord your God....You may say to yourself, 'My power and the strength of my hands have produced this wealth for me.' But remember the Lord your God, for it is he who gives you the ability to produce wealth, and so confirms his covenant, which he swore to your forefathers, as it is today (Deuteronomy 8:7-14, 17-18).

Why would this be God's will in the Old Testament and not in the New? Paul explained that the desire to get rich is the trap. The riches that God gives are to confirm His covenant with His people. They're not to be sought after; they're to be received. Since the Lord wants to prosper you, don't feel guilty, and don't reject it when it comes. Receive it from your Father's hand, and use it for His glory.

NOVEMBER 9

"She has prepared her meat and mixed her wine;
she has also set her table." — 9:2.

There I was on my first ministry trip for the Lord. I was a new believer, only several months old in the Lord. I went with my pastor to visit someone out of state to encourage them in their walk. We stayed several days, and at the end of our stay, the host came to me and tried to give me some money. That had never happened before, and I didn't know what to do. I politely refused it, thinking it was the spiritual thing to do.

My host then turned to my pastor who gladly received the offering. When we got on the plane to go home, my pastor asked me why I didn't take the money. I stumbled around for words, and then he gave his perspective. "It was pride," he said. "You didn't feel right taking something from someone else out of pride." He was right.

It's surprising that pride will stand in the way of what the Lord wants to give us. Today's verse says that wisdom has set her table to feed those who will come. That's how the Lord works. He sets a table before us. We didn't earn that table and we're not asked to pay for the spread we're given. It's a gift of God, and we're told just to give thanks. Why do some work and receive $200, and others work the same amount of time and get $2,000? It's the gift and grace of God. It has nothing to do with the amount of work, but it has everything to do with God's grace.

Did you realize that you don't work to eat? Yes, I know what Paul wrote about almsgiving: "If a man will not work, he shall not eat" (2 Thessalonians 3:10). But that represents instruction for a certain situation. We work to extend the kingdom of God wherever God chooses to place us. God as our Father is committed to provide for our needs.

Now you can have a "works" mentality. You can believe that everything you have depends on our ability to work. If you work longer or harder, God will give you more. That's the wrong mentality. God longs to spread a table before you. What parent requires their children to pay for what's before them? It's their right as children and the joy of the parents to give it. The same is true of your heavenly Father.

The reason we don't see this provision, this table set before us, could be due to pride. James wrote, "You do not have because you do not ask God" (James 4:2). You may want to earn what you have, and see your job, pension, or other means as your source. But God is your source. He has fixed a lavish banquet for you. See beyond your job to your Father who desires to provide for you. Once that principle is deep in you, ask for what you need. Not to do so is pride, and God always resists the proud, but gives grace to the humble.

NOVEMBER 10

"The blessing of the Lord brings wealth,
and he adds no trouble to it." — 10:22.

If wealth is evil, the writer of Proverbs was a deceived man because he thought wealth was a blessing. Time and time again he affirms God's desire to give wealth to His people. The enemy has confused the people of God and put them on the defensive when it comes to money. Money isn't evil. Men who use the money are often evil, but the money itself is clean. Money can't sin; men with money sin. Are you justified in rejecting God's financial blessing for you because it may be abused or wasted?

People sometimes avoid money because of the trouble it can bring. I say, "Lord, send me some of that potential trouble!" Yes, there can be trouble, but there can also be tremendous blessing as well. Today's verse promises that the wealth God gives will be without trouble. That's what I want.

I long to see the church, missions, and outreaches adequately funded. I long to see the servants of God rewarded financially for their labors. I have often planned what I would do with a large amount of money. I have told the Lord what I would give and to whom. The wealth that God gives brings no trouble; it brings provision and gratefulness to God.

Again, let yourself be convinced of this principle. Read what Moses said in Deuteronomy 28:

If you fully obey the Lord your God and carefully follow all his commands I give you today, the Lord your God will set you high above all the nations on earth. All these blessings will come upon you and accompany you if you obey the Lord your God. You will be blessed in the city and blessed in the country. The fruit of your womb will be blessed, and the crops of your land and the young of your livestock—the calves of your herds and the lambs of your flocks. Your basket and your kneading trough will be blessed. You will be blessed when you come in and blessed when you go out....The Lord will send a blessing on your barns and on everything you put your hand to. The Lord your God will bless you in the land he is giving you....The Lord will grant you abundant prosperity—in the fruit of your womb, the young of your livestock and the crops of your ground—in the land he swore to your forefathers to give you (Deuteronomy 28:1-6,8-11).

If God doesn't want to prosper His people, then Moses was confused along with the writer of Proverbs. Get it straight in your heart today that God wants to bless and prosper you. Don't be double-minded concerning that issue. Tell the Lord today that you'll receive all He has for you. Then receive and use it under His direction and guidance. Oh, what joy will be released when you become a channel of God's wealth to those around you!

315

NOVEMBER 11

"A generous man will prosper;
he who refreshes others will himself be refreshed." — 11:25.

My father in the Lord is a generous man. I assisted him for years, and had oversight for his finances. I would see what he gave, and be overwhelmed and challenged. I would try to give like he did for, after all, the Bible says to "remember your leaders...consider the outcome of their way of life and imitate their faith" (Hebrews 13:7). I tried to give like he gave and it got me in some financial trouble.

I realized that the problem was my definition of "generous." I saw the amount that he gave and considered that to be the standard of generosity. When I couldn't give like he gave, I wouldn't give. Other times I gave beyond my means. That wasn't generosity—it was stupidity!

Paul instructed the Corinthian church about giving:

> And here is my advice about what is best for you in this matter....now finish the work, so that your eager willingness to do it may be matched by your completion of it, according to your means. For if the willingness is there, the gift is acceptable according to what one has, not according to what he does not have (2 Corinthians 8:10-12).

I've learned to see that a $2 offering from one person can be generous. If a man only has $5 to his name, $2 represents 40% of what he has. Another person may give $25 because that's what he or she always gives as an offering. If that person has $1,000 in the bank that's available to be given, then $25 isn't a generous offering. That insight has set me free. God doesn't want me to go into debt to try to match someone else's generosity.

Jesus taught this principle:

> As he looked up, Jesus saw the rich putting their gifts into the temple treasury. He also saw a poor widow put in two very small copper coins. "I tell you the truth," he said, "this poor widow has put in more than all the others. All these people gave their gifts out of their wealth; but she out of her poverty put in all she had to live on" (Luke 21:1-4).

Jesus was watching the people as they gave, just as He watches today. He saw some large gifts going into the treasury, but they didn't impress Him. It was the "small" offering that caught His attention, because that offering was generous. The other offerings were "duty" offerings, representing a fraction of what the givers had. The widow gave 100% and the Lord singled her out for special attention.

Today's verse urges you to be generous. When you are, you'll be refreshed. Don't ever hold back a "small" offering just because it's insignificant. Take every opportunity to be generous, no matter what the amount. Your Lord, who is watching, will reward you according to what you've given, not according to what you didn't have to give. Be generous, and receive refreshment from the Lord.

NOVEMBER 12

*"From the fruit of his lips a man is filled with good things
as surely as the work of his hands rewards him." — 12:14.*

"I'll never be able to afford that." That's what I said when I was handed the
$2,000 estimate to repair the termite damage to my house. I was depressed and
discouraged, and my mind was filled with thoughts of doom and gloom. And I
couldn't figure out how those little critters had caused so much damage. I had no
savings, no room in my budget, and no one from whom I could borrow the money.
It seemed hopeless.

Maybe you've been there, too. It's so easy to be negative when it comes to
finances. You can get locked into a mentality that says your income is your limit.
You can wish for a new car, computer, new clothes, or a college education, but you
don't have the money. Since you don't have it, it seems impossible. But it's not
impossible for the Lord.

When you're faced with an impossible situation, you must watch what you say.
Don't be so ready to come out with a negative confession. Yes, it looks bleak and
no, you don't have the money yet. God, however, can provide in miraculous ways,
and you must watch how you speak. What you say may come true!

God had promised Abraham and Sarah a child. They were getting old and it
seemed like the child was an impossibility. Paul wrote,

Against all hope, Abraham in hope believed and so became the father of many
nations, just as it had been said to him, "So shall your offspring be." Without
weakening in his faith, he faced the fact that his body was as good as dead—
since he was about a hundred years old—and that Sarah's womb was also
dead. Yet he did not waver through unbelief regarding the promise of God, but
was strengthened in his faith and gave glory to God, being fully persuaded that
God had power to do what he had promised (Romans 4:18-21).

It's all right to acknowledge the reality of your situation. Abraham faced the
"fact" that he and Sarah were beyond child-bearing age. But he didn't let that fact
affect his faith. The promise of God was more certain than the fact he considered!
You may be broke, but the truth is, "And my God will meet all your needs according to his glorious riches in Christ Jesus" (Philippians 4:19). The truth is that "the
Lord will accomplish what concerns me [and you]" (Psalm 138:8 NAS).

Be careful what you say and don't let unbelief rule your tongue. Today's verse
tells you that your tongue can work for you just like your job. Don't release your
mouth to speak the negative. Rather speak out the promise of God, and see His
provision. Abraham did that, and you're a child of Abraham. Speak faith no matter
how bad it looks, and be watching for the promise of God to come true.

NOVEMBER 13

"From the fruit of his lips a man enjoys good things." — 13:2.

What you say is like a tree: It brings forth fruit. Good words spoken bring good fruit; negative words produce bad fruit. That's a reality of life. When you speak cutting words to someone, the fruit is tension, pain, and sorrow; encouraging words bring righteousness, peace, and joy. You must learn to apply that same principle to your finances. If you say God can't do it, He probably won't. If you speak faith—"And without faith it is impossible to please God" (Hebrews 11:6)—then it releases the Lord to act on your behalf.

In the time of Elisha the prophet, Israel was under siege. The city was surrounded by the Aramaeans, and the people were starving to death. Women had actually resorted to eating their offspring! You might say that their financial situation was a bit bleak. Death was the next step from where they were.

Then Elisha the prophet spoke: "Hear the word of the Lord. This is what the Lord says: 'about this time tomorrow, a seah of flour will sell for a shekel and two seahs of barley for a shekel at the gate of Samaria'" (2 Kings 7:1). In other words, the prophet was announcing that tomorrow food would be available at low prices. He was saying that the Lord was going to miraculously provide for His people!

But the people were in a "siege" mentality. Things had been bad for so long that they didn't see any way out. "The officer on whose arm the king was leaning said to the man of God, 'Look, even if the Lord should open the floodgates of the heavens, could this happen?'" (2 Kings 7:2). With his mouth he uttered a negative statement full of unbelief. The prophet responded to his words by saying, "You will see it with your own eyes," answered Elisha, "but you will not eat any of it!" (2 Kings 7:2).

The next day, when the word of the Lord came to pass, the people rushed out of the city to get the food the Arameans had left as they fled. This officer saw the provision, but the people trampled him to death as they ran to get their groceries. That officer harvested the bad fruit of his words, and it cost him his life.

You may also find yourself in a siege mentality. Things have been tight for so long that you may assume they will always be like they are today. Don't give in to that perspective. God can change and prosper your world in no time at all. Don't say, "I can't afford that." Rather say, "I can't afford that, but the Lord can." Ask the Lord to provide it for you. Keep on asking in faith, and believe God for the impossible. Your words have a role to play in how God moves in your life. Choose your words carefully, and make sure that the fruit of your mouth works for you, not against you.

NOVEMBER 14

"Fools mock at making amends for sin,
but goodwill is found among the upright." — 14:9.

The water was icy cold that January in Pennsylvania. The church I was attending had a large trough in the basement for baptisms. We would use a hose to fill that trough on Sunday mornings and then baptize new believers. On this particular morning, one man approached that cold trough, introduced himself, and gave a brief testimony. As I prepared to baptize him, he announced that he had his wallet in his back pocket. I told him we would hold it for him, but he declined. He said he wanted to take it into the waters of baptism as a symbol of his money coming under the Lordship of Jesus.

I've never forgotten that man. He saw a connection between his salvation and his money. He knew that the Lord wanted to rule all his life, even his finances. Zacchaeus also understood this connection. His story is found in Luke 19.

Jesus was in Jericho where Zacchaeus was the chief tax collector. Zacchaeus got rich collecting taxes from his people, the Jews, to give to the Romans. This earned him the hatred of his peers. Jesus called to Zacchaeus while he was in a sycamore tree trying to get a good view; Jesus then went to Zacchaeus' house to enjoy a meal with him and probably his friends and associates.

People scoffed at Jesus because he met with such a "sinner." Zacchaeus rejoiced, however, and made a fascinating statement: "Look, Lord! Here and now I give half of my possessions to the poor, and if I have cheated anybody out of anything, I will pay back four times the amount" (verse 8). Jesus didn't rebuke him for fanaticism but instead said, "Today salvation has come to this house, because this man, too, is a son of Abraham. For the Son of Man came to seek and to save what was lost" (verses 9-10).

Today's verse states that the wicked laugh at the need to make restitution for sin. Zacchaeus understood immediately that his new-found relationship with the Lord necessitated that he make up for his financial sins. He gave away half of what he had, and went back to set the record straight with those whom he had taken advantage of. Jesus praised him for his actions, and identified his motive for doing so as faith—thus He called him a son of Abraham.

The Lord requires strict financial dealings in all that you do. Don't take the extra can of cola that comes from the machine by accident. If you paid for one, take only one. Don't use cable television if you're not paying for it, even if the signal continues to come through. If you know you have financial matters in your past that need attention, take care of them. Give a special offering to your church for the amount of your past wrongdoing, and add twenty percent to it (the Old Testament amount for restitution). Don't bring tainted money into the kingdom of God. Make amends for your financial sins, and do it gladly just like Zacchaeus did.

NOVEMBER 15

"Better a little with the fear of the Lord
than great wealth with turmoil." — 15:16.

"Someone in the crowd said to him, 'Teacher, tell my brother to divide the inheritance with me'" (Luke 12:13). That was the request made of Jesus then, and inheritance is still an issue that divides many families. How often I've heard and read of brothers and sisters fussing over a will and the money that was left by mom or dad. I've already vowed and told my sister that I won't, under any circumstances, get into a dispute over our parents' estate when they pass on. My sister has lived in the same city as my parents and has cared for them. Whatever she deems correct in light of my parents' wishes will be fine with me.

Jesus responded to the person who asked Him to settle their family squabble, "Man, who appointed me a judge or an arbiter between you?" (Luke 12:14). Jesus was saying just what today's verse tells you: Better to be right with God and have a little, than have great wealth with tension and pressure surrounding that wealth. The person who wanted to get Jesus to side with him was mocking God. He was trying to use the Lord to pressure his brother into giving him what he wanted from the family estate. That person wanted to use God as an attorney, and Jesus refused to get involved. In fact, He clearly identified the real problem present in that person's life.

"Then he said to them, 'Watch out! Be on your guard against all kinds of greed; a man's life does not consist in the abundance of his possessions'" (Luke 12:15). Jesus inferred that the one requesting help with the family will was greedy. Note that Jesus said there were all kinds of greed and covetousness. This was one kind, and Jesus came down hard on it.

Today's verse is not saying there's anything wrong with wealth. The verse is drawing an analogy between two options. If you have the option of having a little and being right with God, or having a lot with turmoil, it's better to choose the little. Better to be right with God than to suffer from greed. Better to be wronged and have God on your side than to be "right" and have God against you.

Paul wrote, "Put to death, therefore, whatever belongs to your earthly nature: sexual immorality, impurity, lust, evil desires and greed, which is idolatry. Because of these the wrath of God is coming" (Colossians 3:5-6). God condemns greed and calls it idolatry. Jesus warned the person who sought legal advice, and He warns you, to keep watch and guard against it.

Do you covet something more than the Lord? Are you willing to forfeit money or even what's "rightfully" yours to stay in right relationship with God? Ask God to reveal any greed or covetousness that may be in your heart. Repent and be willing to settle for the little with fear of God. In the end, you'll have more than money or wealth could ever buy.

NOVEMBER 16

"Better a little with righteousness than much gain with injustice." — 16:8.

The book of Proverbs contains so many verses that speak to greed and wealth. Yesterday we saw how much better it is to have a little with the fear of God. Today we see the same thing: Better to have a little with righteousness than to gain great wealth through injustice and unrighteousness.

It's important to note that this verse doesn't exalt poverty or condemn wealth; the verse compares two possible options. It says if these are the only two options available to you, it's best to choose the first one without any sense of loss.

After Jesus addressed the greed of the person who asked Him to get involved in the dispute over the family will, Jesus told the crowd a parable.

The ground of a certain rich man produced a good crop. He thought to himself, "What shall I do? I have no place to store my crops." Then he said, "This is what I'll do. I will tear down my barns and build bigger ones, and there I will store all my grain and my goods. And I'll say to myself, 'You have plenty of good things laid up for many years. Take life easy; eat, drink and be merry.'" But God said to Him, "You fool! This very night your life will be demanded from you. Then who will get what you have prepared for yourself?" This is how it will be with anyone who stores up things for himself but is not rich toward God (Luke 12:16-21).

The person in this parable was satisfied with what he had. Seeing his possessions as something to be kept and used at his disposal, his life had meaning only in the abundance of what he owned. His whole world was consumed with getting and then keeping what he had accumulated. While he was rich, he had one major problem; he was poor toward God. He kept what God gave him through a kind of injustice. Since there was no thought of sharing or storing up riches in heaven by investing his goods here on earth, the parable (and God) calls this man a fool. You too are a fool if you are doing the same thing.

Paul instructed Timothy to instruct those with wealth:

Command those who are rich in this present world not to be arrogant nor to put their hope in wealth, which is so uncertain, but to put their hope in God, who richly provides us with everything for our enjoyment. Command them to do good, to be rich in good deeds, and to be generous and willing to share. In this way they will lay up treasure for themselves as a firm foundation for the coming age, so that they may take hold of the life that is truly life (1 Timothy 6:17-19).

Wealth has no life, but obedience to God has life abundantly. See your wealth not as life, but as a means to life—the life that flows from the Spirit of God to those who see Him, and not wealth, as their source.

NOVEMBER 17

"Better a dry crust with peace and quiet
than a house full of feasting, with strife." — 17:1.

Again today's verse is making a comparison, not an endorsement. It's not advising that you eat three-day old bread! Nor is it saying that you're holy if you eat beans out of a can. If those were the only two options available to you at any given time, then choose peace over strife. If the choice is between a little and a lot, and the "lot" has a price tag of tension and turmoil, today's verse urges you to choose the little.

Proverbs weaves this theme into its many verses. It tells us again and again to keep our priorities straight. Jesus preached the same theme, and He returned to it again and again. Continuing on with the story of the man who sought Jesus' "legal" help, Jesus instructed His disciples:

> Therefore I tell you, do not worry about your life, what you will eat; or about your body, what you will wear. Life is more than food, and the body more than clothes. Consider the ravens; They do not sow or reap, they have no storeroom or barn; yet God feeds them. And how much more valuable you are than birds! Who of you by worrying can add a single hour to his life? Since you cannot do this very little thing, why do you worry about the rest? Consider how the lilies grow. They do not labor or spin. Yet I tell you, not even Solomon in all his splendor was dressed like one of these. If that is how God clothes the grass of the field, which is here today, and tomorrow is thrown into the fire, how much more will he clothe you, O you of little faith! And do not set your heart on what you will eat or drink; do not worry about it. For the pagan world runs after all such things, and your Father knows that you need them. But seek his kingdom, and these things will be given to you as well (Luke 12:22-31).

Matthew wrote in his gospel to "seek first his kingdom and his righteousness" (Matthew 6:33). You must seek to know and do God's will and the rest of life will take care of itself. If you seek abundance for its own sake, you'll be putting something before God. If you seek His kingdom first, God promises to provide for all your needs.

Are you worried about life and your provision? Commit yourself to do God's will and get your eyes off what you need or don't have. Instead focus on righteousness, peace, and joy, even it if means giving away some things or doing without for a season. Better a little where God is than much where He isn't. Get your priorities straight today. You're not here for the money; you're here to do God's will.

NOVEMBER 18

"The wealth of the rich is their fortified city;
they imagine it an unscalable wall." — 18:11.

I put my hand into my pocket; it was empty and that was a strange feeling. No matter how tight things had been, I always had at least a few dollars in my wallet. But now I was flat broke with not a penny to my name. Later that day someone handed me a couple of dollars and I noticed how much more secure I felt with just that little bit of money in my pocket.

That's how wealth can be. You can have money in your checking account and feel pretty safe and secure. If you have six months income stored up, your sense of security can skyrocket. Today's verse speaks to this phenomenon: Financial security can make calamity seem far off and increase your sense of peace and security.

Jesus urged (and urges) His followers to put their trust in God and not in the uncertainty of money. He finished His discourse in Luke 12 with these words:

Do not be afraid, little flock, for your Father has been pleased to give you the kingdom. Sell your possessions and give to the poor. Provide purses for yourselves that will not wear out, a treasure in heaven that will not be exhausted, where no thief comes near and no moth destroys. For where your treasure is, there your heart will be also (Luke 12:32-34).

Jesus knew that money and wealth were subject to change. The "moth"—inflation, sudden economic changes, bad decisions—can eat it up. The "thief"—the unexpected, unscrupulous people, bad business deals—can steal it in a short time. Rather than seeing money as an end, Jesus saw it as a means to an end. He taught that wealth could be used to "buy" real treasure that couldn't be destroyed or eroded.

You have to admit that money is a source of great blessing or tension. If you use it to bless people, it's a blessing. If you use it to get more money, and that plan fails, you're filled with anxiety and the pressure can be overwhelming. Determine today to use your money for the right thing. Use it to meet your needs and then use the rest to build up a "nest egg" in heaven. Invest in the kingdom of God where the return is 30, 60, or 100 fold. Don't be afraid, but sell some of your unneeded possessions and give the proceeds to those in need.

When you do this, your heavenly Father is watching. He's keeping account and will reward you with heavenly treasures. Have you put your trust in those few dollars sitting in your pocket? Take your trust and put it in God, and then let your money decisions reflect where you've put your trust. Put your treasures in the right place, and then let your heart follow along.

NOVEMBER 19

"He who obeys instructions guards his life,
but he who is contemptuous of his ways will die." — 19:16.

It was a can't-miss opportunity, a sure investment. A brother in the Lord told me about a business venture that he was investing in, and he wanted me to go in with him. I didn't have much money, but I felt a sense of loyalty to him and saw that the business had potential. I sought advice, prayed about it, but felt a definite "no" from my counselors and my spirit.

Several years later, that "sure" business went belly-up. It folded and many who invested had to pay a high price for their gamble. Then I was glad I had obeyed my instructors, for I was watching those who had invested go through the agony of losing money in a bad deal.

The word of God has much to say about money, as we've seen from this month's theme. Money can be a source of peace or death, according to how and where we use it. We need to be instructed from the Word concerning God's will for our money if we're to enjoy the peace money can bring.

Why don't you embark today on an in depth study of the Bible and all that it says about money? Get a notebook and set aside a section for your notes and insights about money, including Old and New Testament verses. Also begin to read more books on the topic. By so doing you'll be guarding your soul from the distress that comes from misusing your money.

For instance, begin with Paul's instructions to the Corinthian church:

And now, brothers, we want you to know about the grace that God has given the Macedonian churches. Out of the most severe trial, their overflowing joy and their extreme poverty welled up in rich generosity. For I testify that they gave as much as they were able, and even beyond their ability. Entirely on their own, they urgently pleaded with us for the privilege of sharing in this service to the saints. And they did not do as we expected, but they gave themselves first to the Lord and then to us in keeping with God's will (2 Corinthians 8:1-5).

Paul saw the Macedonian opportunity to give as "the grace God has given." Out of their poverty, they had "overflowing joy" as they gave. They gave "beyond their ability." Without any pressure, they "pleaded" with Paul for the chance to give. And they didn't just give money to soothe a guilty conscience; they first gave themselves and then their money as proof of their surrender to the will of God. Those verses contain instruction about giving and the attitude that goes with it. Study them and the others you find, and let the Word judge and change your heart as you give.

NOVEMBER 20

"Make plans by seeking advice; if you wage war, obtain guidance." — 20:18.

Imagine for a moment that you've been away on a ministry or business trip. You've been gone for quite a while and have finally returned to your family and home. You drive into the garage, open the door expecting a warm welcome, only to find the house ransacked and your family gone! You discover that a thief has come and taken all you held dear in life. What a shock that would be!

That's exactly what happened to King David and his men when they returned to their home base of Ziklag in 1 Samuel 30:

Now the Amalekites had raided the Negev and Ziklag. They had attacked Ziklag and burned it, and had taken captive the women and all who were in it, both young and old. They killed none of them, but carried them off as they went on their way. When David and his men came to Ziklag, they found it destroyed by fire and their wives and sons and daughters taken captive (1 Samuel 30:1-3).

Not only were their loved ones taken, but all their possessions were gone as well. The same thing has happened to believers, and it may have happened to you. Your enemies (Satan and his hosts) are busy doing what they do best. Jesus said, "The thief comes only to steal and kill and destroy" (John 10:10). They've stolen what belongs to the people of God and they must be forced to give it back. You have a major role to play in the return of what the enemy has taken from you.

Today's verse urges you to get advice when you war so that you can be successful just as King David was in his campaigns.

David said to Abiathar the priest, the son of Ahimelech, "Bring me the ephod." Abiathar brought it to him, and David inquired of the Lord, "Shall I pursue this raiding party? Will I overtake them?" "Pursue them," he answered. "You will certainly overtake them and succeed in the rescue" (1 Samuel 30:7-8).

If you think the enemy has stolen what is yours, then seek out those wise in spiritual war and get advice. Don't walk in your own understanding alone, but enlist the help of those who know how to fight the enemy.

The good news is that David was successful. "David recovered everything the Amalekites had taken, including his two wives. Nothing was missing: young or old, boy or girl, plunder or anything else they had taken. David brought everything back" (1 Samuel 30:18-19). And David brought back extra: "He took all the flocks and herds, and his men drove them ahead of the other livestock, saying, 'This is David's plunder'" (1 Samuel 30:20).

If you attack him to get it back, the devil must restore what's yours and add some to it. Proverbs 6:31 says, "Yet if he [a thief] is caught, he must pay sevenfold." Command the enemy to give you back what is yours with a seven-fold increase. Pray fervently and diligently. Get those who know how to fight to pray with you. Don't leave what is yours in the camp of the enemy, but fight to get it back.

NOVEMBER 21

"If a man shuts his ears to the cry of the poor,
he too will cry out and not be answered." — 21:13.

You've seen it time and again. An emaciated, pathetic-looking child in some far-off land is shown on the news or in a commercial. These are victims of some famine, war, or other natural disaster, and your heart breaks—at first. After seeing that scene regularly, however, you can develop a callous around your heart. It's not that you don't care; it's that you can't carry that burden for very long. The needs are too great, and the need and your seeming inability to do very much can cause you to retreat into a world where those images can't penetrate.

Today's verse urges us, however, to maintain a sensitivity to the poor. There are many needs and we can't begin to meet them all. The Lord can help us discern the cries that are for our ears, and then reward us in our own day of need. I've tried to remember Galatians 6:9-10 when it comes to the poor: "Let us not become weary in doing good, for at the proper time we will reap a harvest if we do not give up. Therefore, as we have opportunity, let us do good to all people, especially to those who belong to the family of believers."

These two verses encourage us to keep on doing good while keeping our priorities in order. We are to do good to all, but first and foremost to those in the household of faith. When my church or church organization identifies a ministry to the poor that's geared to fellow believers, I feel on solid ground when I give to it. I can't meet all the world's needs, but I can help a poor brother or sister. That's a high priority in my life.

Paul instructed the Corinthians about giving as they prepared to send an offering to Judea to relieve the needs of a famine there. Their priority was to do good to the household of faith. Paul wrote:

Our desire is not that others might be relieved while you are hard pressed, but that there might be equality. At the present time your plenty will supply what they need, so that in turn their plenty will supply what you need. Then there will be equality, as it is written, "He who gathered much did not have too much, and he that gathered little did not have too little" (2 Corinthians 8:13-15).

Paul wasn't asking them to give beyond their means; rather, he made an appeal that they would hear the cry of the poor, and answer it as they could. Notice that they would do this "so that in turn their plenty will supply your need." That's the principle today's verse speaks to. Give when someone is in need, and when you're in need, it will come back to you. Ask the Lord today to help you hear the cry of your poor brother, and then help meet his need. One day, he may be able to do the same for you.

NOVEMBER 22

"A generous man will himself be blessed,
for he shares his food with the poor." — 22:9.

The Thanksgiving holiday is a time for food. Whether people give thanks or not, they usually sit down with family and friends to a feast. Thanksgiving is also a time for sharing. Few families eat alone, and many special programs exist that feed the poor and homeless. One aspect of giving thanks is sharing, and this holiday gives the perfect opportunity to do so.

You and I shouldn't wait for this one day to give thanks and share. In fact, Thanksgiving has diminished in importance for me since I met the Lord. I find myself offering thanks to God regularly, and I look for opportunities to share my food with the poor all during the year. I find that I'm not motivated by guilt during the holidays to give to the poor because that's something I try to do regularly.

The Corinthian church didn't celebrate Thanksgiving Day as we know it, but they did share their food with the poor. They prepared a special offering for their suffering brethren in Judea, and took up this offering over a long period of time. Paul wrote them to encourage their faithfulness in completing what they had started:

Remember this: Whoever sows sparingly will also reap sparingly, and whoever sows generously will also reap generously. Each man should give what he has decided in his heart to give, not reluctantly or under compulsion, for God loves a cheerful giver. And God is able to make all grace abound to you, so that in all things at all times, having all that you need, you will abound in every good work. As it is written: "He has scattered abroad his gifts to the poor; his righteousness endures forever" (2 Corinthians 9:6-9).

One part of giving is the blessing that comes to the giver. If you give sparingly, Paul said, you'll be blessed sparingly in return. You may wonder why you don't see more spiritual and physical blessings in your life. Could the reason be that you have sowed too little? If you plant three flower seeds in your bed, you'll get three plants at the most. If you throw out handfuls of seed, you'll get a lot more flowers. It's the same with giving. Are you planting one seed at a time, or are you putting seed out by the bushel?

Jesus taught this same principle when He said, "Give and it will be given to you. A good measure, pressed down, shaken together and running over, will be poured into your lap. For with the measure you use, it will be measured to you" (Luke 6:38).

Don't wait for it to be given to you, but rather give out of what you have. Determine to share your food with the poor. Increase your sensitivity to the needs of others. See their need as your opportunity to sow and then sow generously. It will indeed come back to you in many ways!

NOVEMBER 23

"Cast but a glance at riches, and they are gone,
for they will surely sprout wings and fly off to the sky like an eagle." — 23:5.

Soon IRS tax time will be upon all Americans. If you're like me, you'll sit down, look at your income statement, and wonder where it all went. I go one step further and actually try to come up with my annual expenses for food, car, housing, and the like. It seems that what comes in goes right out again. Like today's verse says, it's as if your money gets wings and flies away.

Money and wealth (and the increase of both) aren't meant to be permanent fixtures in your life. Money, as we have discussed in previous days, is a means to an end. It can be used to store up treasures in heaven, but money itself can't be taken there. Jesus told the parable of the unjust steward and then said, "I tell you, use worldly wealth to gain friends for yourselves, so that when it is gone, you will be welcomed into eternal dwellings" (Luke 16:9). Jesus urged His followers to use money for what it was intended—meeting daily needs and sharing with others. By so doing, His followers would be welcomed into a place of eternal residence.

Paul also addressed this issue of financial increase. He continued his instruction to the Corinthians by writing:

Now he who supplies seed to the sower and bread for food will also supply and increase your store of seed and will enlarge the harvest of your righteousness. You will be made rich in every way so that you can be generous on every occasion, and through us your generosity will result in thanksgiving to God. This service that you perform is not only supplying the needs of God's people but is also overflowing in many expressions of thanks to God. Because of the service by which you have proved yourselves, men will praise God for the obedience that accompanies your confession of the gospel of Christ, and for your generosity in sharing with them and with everyone else. And in their prayers for you their hearts will go out to you...(2 Corinthians 9:10-14).

Paul saw the increase of wealth as a means for generosity. God will increase your seed so that on every occasion you can be generous. Part of your God-given increase is to be put aside for others. It's not coming just to fatten your savings account.

Notice too what will happen when you're generous. Paul said that it will result in "thanksgiving to God." Your faithfulness and generosity will cause people to say, "Thank you, Jesus" and worship His holy name. They'll praise His name for your obedience and they'll pray for you. What a beautiful flow of thanksgiving, praise, and prayer is released when you use your money for the right thing. Commit your money to this process and see an increase of the Spirit in your life and in the lives of those you bless.

NOVEMBER 24

"Thorns had come up everywhere,
the ground was covered with weeds..." — 24:31.

We were deep in the woods as the signs took us through a guided tour of trees and plants. My family and I were outside Williamsburg, and this was an optional tour that allowed us to stay in the car and rest while we toured. The trees were tall and everything was so grown in, but I was surprised to read a sign that said this wooded area was only 20 years old and previously had been farmland! I would have thought it to be hundreds of years old by how dense it was. I saw then that it doesn't take long for a productive area to become overrun with weeds and other plant life.

The same is true for our financial life. It requires constant care and sowing to keep our fields clean, growing and productive. And when we sow, we never know when the next crop will be the best we've ever had. Every farmer plants in hope, and we give as the farmer plants—not knowing what kind of harvest will come.

The writer of Ecclesiastes spoke to that issue. He wrote:

Cast your bread upon the waters, for after many days you will find it again. Give portions to seven, yes to eight, for you do not know what disaster may come upon the land. If clouds are full of water, they pour rain upon the earth. Whether a tree falls to the south or to the north, in the place where it falls, there will it lie. Whoever watches the wind will not plant; whoever looks at the clouds will not reap. As you do not know the path of the wind, or how the body is formed in a mother's womb, so you cannot understand the work of God, the Maker of all things. Sow your seed in the morning, and at evening let not your hands be idle, for you do not know which will succeed, whether this or that, or whether both will do equally well (Ecclesiastes 11:1-6).

The writer tells you to cast your "bread" in a way that you can't control when and how it comes back to you. And he tells you to keep on sowing. You can't figure out how God works, and this next crop may be your best yet. Don't look at the wind and clouds in your life, waiting for all the conditions to be "right" before you sow. Keep sowing and don't let the weeds take over.

Lord, I recognize that I don't have because I have not sown adequately. I've wanted to have a harvest, but I've not done all I could to make the harvest come. I ask you to forgive me. I've watched the clouds and tried to figure out the wind, and I have not sown. I've eaten my seed, and now my fields are overgrown. I commit to sow again, and this time to sow abundantly. I will sow in faith, not knowing whether this or that will produce a record crop of righteousness. Help me to have the faith and commitment to do Your will. Amen.

NOVEMBER 25

"If your enemy is hungry, give him food to eat;
if he is thirsty, give him water to drink." — 25:21.

It's usually easy to give to someone who is your friend. It's special to bless someone who appreciates it, says thank you, and maybe even gives a testimony to others, mentioning your name in the process. It's a sign of maturity, however, to give to those who are less than friendly or appreciative.

You shouldn't be surprised that Jesus spoke about this kind of giving:

> Give to everyone who asks you, and if anyone takes what belongs to you, do not demand it back. Do to others as you would have them do to you. If you love those who love you, what credit is that to you? Even "sinners" love those who love them. And if you do good to those who are good to you, what credit is that to you? Even "sinners" do that. And if you lend to those from whom you expect repayment, what credit is that to you? Even "sinners" lend to "sinners," expecting to be repaid in full. But love your enemies, do good to them, and lend to them without expecting to get anything back. Then your reward will be great, and you will be sons of the Most High, because he is kind to the ungrateful and wicked. Be merciful, just as your Father is merciful (Luke 6:30-36).

While your priority is to take care of those in the household of faith, you can't neglect the needs in the world. Jesus said that even sinners take care of their own. That doesn't represent any special grace. What does represent the heart of God is to give freely to all, regardless of the recipients' worth or response. God does that regularly, for Paul told the people in Lystra, "He has shown kindness by giving you rain from heaven and crops in their seasons; he provides you with plenty of food and fills your hearts with joy" (Acts 14:17). God gives freely to all, and asks you to do the same. If you have it, you shouldn't hold it back.

On one occasion I personally invested a lot of money in a man who attended our church. This man had been in and out of jail many times. He could reach people for the Lord, but at the same time had a lot of personal problems. I helped to get his car fixed, paid his rent, bought him clothes, and did other things. After several years he left the church and treated me badly in the process. I had given to him, not to get anything back but because the Lord had led me to give. I didn't see that money as wasted; I had sown it into the Lord. I suspected as I was giving that it one day might come to that end, and I gave anyway! I don't regret one penny I gave.

Maybe God wants you to give to someone just as unworthy. Perhaps you'll know what He feels like when men whom He provides for turn their backs on Him. Don't let the people to whom you give be your focus, but let God be your focus as you give. Do it in obedience to Him, and you'll never be taken advantage of as you sow your seed.

NOVEMBER 26

"If a man digs a pit, he will fall into it;
if a man rolls a stone, it will roll back on him." — 26:27.

There's an old saying, "Be careful where you're going; you may get there." You're going somewhere in life. You're either getting closer to God and godliness, or you're not. You're either laying up treasures for yourself in heaven, or you're laying up treasures here. Furthermore, what you do has serious implications for the age to come. Today's verse urges you to be careful where you dig—you may have to live in what you dig.

Jesus told a story with the same message as is found in today's verse. It's the story of Lazarus and the rich man and it's a sobering tale:

> There was a rich man who was dressed in purple and fine linen and lived in luxury every day. At his gate was laid a beggar named Lazarus, covered with sores and longing to eat what fell from the rich man's table. Even the dogs came and licked his sores. The time came when the beggar died and the angels carried him to Abraham's side. The rich man also died and was buried. In hell, where he was in torment, he looked up and saw Abraham far away, with Lazarus by his side. So he called to him, "Father Abraham, have pity on me and send Lazarus to dip the tip of his finger in water and cool my tongue, because I am in agony in this fire." But Abraham replied, "Son, remember that in your lifetime you received your good things, while Lazarus received bad things, but now he is comforted here and you are in agony" (Luke 16:19-25).

The reality of eternal reward should be present in your thinking as you carry out your giving program. The rich man dug a pit—a pit of luxury, self-care, and indulgence. Eventually he fell into it and couldn't get out. You shouldn't dig yourself a hole, but build an eternal monument with the resources God has given to you.

There was a rich man who died and one man asked at his funeral, "How much did he leave?" Another man responded, "All of it." Paul wrote Timothy to instruct the rich "to do good, to be rich in good deeds, and to be generous and willing to share. In this way they will lay up treasure for themselves as a firm foundation for the coming age, so that they may take hold of the life that is truly life" (1 Timothy 6:18-19).

Begin to see your money as transitory at best. It's not an end in itself, but a means to an end. Don't spend your life rolling a stone, only to have it roll back on you. Use your resources to build something for the age to come. If you use your money for this age only, you may have to live in a pit for a long time to come.

"The lambs will provide you with clothing....You will have plenty of goats' milk to feed you and your family. . . . " — 27:26-27.

My daughter excitedly interrupted a meeting to inform me that one of the families in the church stopped by our home. It was Thanksgiving season, and they took that opportunity to bring us enough food to fill our refrigerator and cabinets. That's how God's provision is—unexpected and from sources we sometimes least expect. God is faithful and can provide for His people no matter what the season or situation.

A distraught woman came to the prophet Elisha one day:

"Your servant my husband is dead, and you know that he revered the Lord. But now his creditor is coming to take my two boys as his slaves." Elisha replied to her, "How can I help you? Tell me, what do you have in your house?" "Your servant has nothing there at all," she said, "except a little oil." Elisha said, "Go around and ask all your neighbors for empty jars. Don't ask for just a few. Then go inside and shut the door behind you and your sons. Pour oil into all the jars, and as each is filled, put it to one side." She left him and afterward shut the door behind her and her sons. They brought the jars to her and she kept pouring. When all the jars were full, she said to her son, "Bring me another one." But he replied, "There is not a jar left." Then the oil stopped flowing. She went and told the man of God, and he said, "Go, sell the oil and pay your debts. You and your sons can live on what is left" (2 Kings 4:1-7).

This woman was in a difficult situation. Her husband's death left her in debt, and she was broke. Her husband had served the Lord and Elisha, but hadn't planned well. He left her with no income and a lot of bills. God is faithful, however, and He heard her cry. Her help involved her faith and she was told to get as many containers as she could. She did and the oil flowed, providing for her needs.

What a great testimony she had from that day. She had seen God be true to His word, and her fame speaks to us even to this day. Can your situation be any worse than hers? Notice that Elisha did not rebuke her for being in debt. Nor did he try to meet her need from the limited resources he had. Instead he pointed her in the direction of her God who was more than adequate to meet her needs.

Today's verse and story promise you God's practical care. You can count on it. If it's not there, then seek Him until you see it. God is true to His word and will provide in miraculous ways. Get your own testimony that will tell all who hear of the goodness and faithfulness of God to provide for His people.

NOVEMBER 28

"He who gives to the poor will lack nothing,
but he who closes his eyes to them receives many curses." — 28:27.

There I was, the only white face in a sea of brown and black. I was in South America on a ministry trip and I saw poverty that shocked me. People were actually living in cardboard boxes. Children, many of them orphans, roamed the streets hungry and in search of shelter and food. They sought me out, considering me a wealthy foreigner who might give them something. The needs were so overwhelming that I left not making much difference in the great needs that existed.

My church and family now make a monthly contribution to the church there. We've gathered shipments of clothes and medical supplies to send to the people. Today's verse tells you not to close your eyes to the needs of the poor. You have so much that you take for granted that you must work at realizing there are many with much less. You're commanded to share some of yours with them.

Moses instructed the people in Deuteronomy to be sensitive to the poor among them:

> If there is a poor man among your brothers in any of the towns of the land that the Lord your God is giving you, do not be hardhearted or tightfisted toward your poor brother. Rather be openhanded and freely lend him whatever he needs. Be careful, not to harbor this wicked thought: "The seventh year, the year for canceling debts, is near," so that you do not show ill will toward your needy brother and give him nothing. He may then appeal to the Lord against you, and you will be found guilty of sin. Give generously to him and do so without a grudging heart; then because of this the Lord your God will bless you in all your work and in everything you put your hand to. There will always be poor people in the land. Therefore I command you to be openhanded toward your brothers and toward the poor and needy in your land (Deuteronomy 15:7-11).

Moses taught, "There will always be poor people in the land." Sometimes that can cause you to become hardened to their plight. Knowing that, you must work at being "openhanded" toward the poor. This requires more than guilt offerings at Thanksgiving and Christmas. The poor have needs all year round, and you should have some means to minister to them on a regular basis.

Is there a "curse" on your finances? Is the Lord trying to get your attention concerning your ministry to the poor? You can't meet all the needs out there, but that doesn't excuse you or me from trying to meet some of them. Open your eyes to the poor and hear their cry. Then give as the Lord has given to you.

NOVEMBER 29

"The righteous care about justice for the poor,
but the wicked have no such concern." —29:7.

I'm afraid that this verse doesn't generally hold true today. It seems that sometimes the wicked have more concern for the poor than the church does. Government programs for the poor abound, but too often the church's money is tied up in schools, buildings, and other programs. Those things are necessary, but are often built and carried out at the expense of ministry to the needy.

I don't know what the "justice" is in today's verse. That debate is for the sociologists. I do know that the poor are taken advantage of regularly. They live in substandard housing, have little access to education or resources necessary to escape poverty, have been the victims of discrimination, and have more than their share of crime and violence.

I'm not advocating a social gospel, but I've become more and more impressed with the effective work of the Salvation Army. William Booth, the Army's founder, preached, "soup, soap, and salvation," and in that order. He said it was hard to preach to someone with an empty stomach. Jesus responded to John the Baptist's messengers, "The good news is preached to the poor" (Matthew 11:5). Can the Gospel be preached to the poor without tending to some of the social issues that also affect them?

When Jesus sent Judas away from the Last Supper, John's Gospel says, "No one at the meal understood why Jesus said this to him. Since Judas had charge of the money, some thought Jesus was telling him to buy what was needed for the Feast, or to give something to the poor" (John 13:28-29).

Obviously Jesus was in the habit of giving money to the poor. But it can hardly be said that He gave only money. He ministered to all the needs of the poor, and the poor received Him gladly.

As you give to the poor, be aware of their plight. Money isn't the only thing they need. They need your prayers and support. Volunteer to work in a food bank. Distribute food baskets at Christmas and Thanksgiving. Maybe you can minister to the children of inmates. Perhaps you can consider being a foster parent to children whose parents can't support them or tutor underprivileged school children. You could also visit homes for the elderly who have no money to pay for their care. Take a short-term missions trip to minister to the needs of the poor. Support the ministry to the poor in some overseas congregation.

The poor very often receive the worst from this sin-plagued world of ours. Let their justice be your concern. Give generously and get involved. If you're among the righteous, then the poor are a missions field you can't ignore.

NOVEMBER 30

"Two things I ask of you, O Lord; do not refuse me before I die: Keep falsehood and lies far from me; give me neither poverty nor riches, but give me only my daily bread. Otherwise, I may have too much and disown you and say, 'Who is the Lord?' Or I may become poor and steal, and so dishonor the name of my God." — 30:7-9.

Whatever your feelings about today's verses, you must admit that the writer had a financial philosophy. He had studied the issue, and had made up his mind how he was going to pray. I don't understand his conclusions, but I respect them.

The apostle Paul also had a financial philosophy. As an apostle, Paul was entitled to live from the offerings of the people to whom he ministered. He chose not to do so. He supported his ministry by his occupation, and only occasionally received ministry offerings. Note what he wrote to the Corinthians:

> Don't we have the right to food and drink?...Or is it only I and Barnabas who must work for a living? Who serves as a soldier at his own expense? Who plants a vineyard and does not eat of its grapes? Who tends a flock and does not drink of the milk?...If we have sown spiritual seed among you, is it too much if we reap a material harvest from you? If others have this right of support from you, shouldn't we have it all the more? But we did not use this right. On the contrary, we put up with anything rather than hinder the gospel of Christ...I have not used any of these rights....If I preach voluntarily, I have a reward; if not voluntarily, I am simply discharging the trust committed to me. What then is my reward? Just this: that in preaching the gospel I may offer it free of charge, and so not make use of my rights in preaching it (1 Corinthians 9:4-7, 11-12,15, 17-18).

You would have to say that Paul had a well-thought-out financial philosophy. If the writer of today's verses and Paul had such a philosophy, shouldn't you and I?

My own philosophy is this: I recognize that the Lord has promised to meet my needs. I'll therefore minister freely, trusting God's provision. I'll tithe on all my income, seeing the tithe as the minimum standard of giving for all believers. From there I'll generously give to as many causes and ministries as possible, faithfully fulfilling all commitments and pledges. I'll not forget my family, but will be generous with them as well. I'll be an example of faith, making decisions not only according to what is seen. I'll also work to instruct others concerning the obligation and joys of giving.

As we end this month, I urge you to write out your own financial philosophy. What verses about giving are the most meaningful for you? What have you tried to accomplish with your money? Put together a paragraph that summarizes your financial outlook. As you write it, ask yourself whether or not you're living it out. Make adjustments where necessary and honor the Lord with a consistent, faithful handling of the resources He has given you.

DECEMBER 1

"But whoever listens to me will live in safety and be at ease, without fear of harm." —*1:33.*

The soldier approached me with his machine gun resting on his shoulder. He ordered my friend and me out of the car and began to search our belongings and interrogate us. He wore U.S. Army equipment, but he was part of the Colombian army assigned to fight Marxist guerrillas and drug cartels.

That was just one more tense experience during a ministry trip to Colombia a few years ago. While I was there, a presidential candidate was assassinated. Americans were regularly kidnapped for ransom money. If that wasn't enough, a commercial airline had been bombed and blown out of the sky. Many friends and family back home expressed concern that I was going to one of the most violent countries on earth. Yet even while this soldier searched me and my belongings, I can honestly say I had perfect peace.

I gave me life to the Lord on May 18, 1973, and my life was no longer mine but His. If He chooses to claim it on a mountain road in Colombia, that is His concern. I was there because He had sent me, and I wasn't going to worry about something over which I had no control. The soldier eventually released us to go, and I went on to complete a significant ministry time there.

Today's verse promises that no harm will befall you if you listen to His voice. There are many other verses, especially among the Psalms, that seek to bring comfort and keep us from fear. "The Lord is with me; I will not be afraid. What can man do to me?" (Psalm 118:6) and "The Lord is my light and my salvation, whom shall I fear? The Lord is the stronghold of my life; of whom shall I be afraid?" (Psalm 27:1) are just a few. Perhaps the most powerful "fear not" verse is found in Psalm 91:

> I will say of the Lord, "He is my refuge and my fortress, my God, in whom I trust." Surely he will save you from the fowler's snare and from the deadly pestilence. He will cover you with his feathers, and under his wings you will find refuge; his faithfulness will be your shield and rampart. You will not fear the terror of night nor the arrow that flies by day, nor the pestilence that stalks in the darkness, nor the plague that destroys at midday. A thousand may fall at your side, ten thousand at your right hand, but it will not come near you....Then no harm will befall you, no disaster will come near your tent. For he will command his angels concerning you to guard you in all your ways (Psalm 91:2-7, 10-11).

Are you afraid? Do you have a fear of some calamity with your children? Your finances? Your relationship with the Lord? Whatever it is, face your fear today. Use today's or other verses to address your fear. God's promise to you is protection, so learn to rest in His promise today.

DECEMBER 2

*"For he guards the course of the just
and protects the way of his faithful ones."* —2:8.

Today's verse is meant to be a comforting verse. It says that the Lord is mindful of our ways and is ever watching over us. The problem comes when we take a closer look at that verse. If the Lord is watching and guarding, does that mean our path has danger on it and the Lord must protect us from that danger?

This is what the Lord said through Isaiah:

> Fear not, for I have redeemed you; I have summoned you by name; you are mine. When you pass through the waters, I will be with you; and when you pass through the rivers, they will not sweep over you. When you walk through the fire, you will not be burned; the flames will not set you ablaze....Do not be afraid, for I am with you (Isaiah 43:1-2, 5).

It's nice to think that the Lord is protecting us, until we realize that our path may lead us through the waters, the rivers, and the flames. Daniel's friends found out that God doesn't always keep you from the flames, but will walk with you through them. When they angered King Nebuchadnezzar,

> He ordered the furnace heated seven times hotter than usual and commanded some of the strongest soldiers in his army to tie up Shadrach, Meshach and Abednego and throw them into the blazing furnace. So these men, wearing their robes, trousers, turbans and other clothes, were bound and thrown into the blazing furnace. The king's command was so urgent and the furnace so hot that the flames of the fire killed the soldiers who took up Shadrach, Meshach and Abednego, and these three men, firmly tied, fell into the blazing furnace (Daniel 3:19-23).

To the king's amazement, however, he noticed an extra visitor in the furnace. "Look, I see four men walking around in the fire, unbound and unharmed, and the fourth looks like a son of the gods" (Daniel 3:25). The Lord went into the fire with the three men. He didn't save them from the fire, but rather got in there with them. And notice that they were in no hurry to get out! They met the Lord in such a special way that they had to be called out. They found themselves in a good place and didn't try to escape.

Is your way a little hot right now? God didn't promise to protect you *from* the flames but *in* the flames. You may not enjoy the heat, but you will enjoy the close fellowship with the One who is in there with you. You'll never appreciate God's ability to protect you until the flames surround and threaten to overwhelm you. Then you'll quote today's verse and cry out to Him who wants to prove Himself faithful on your behalf.

DECEMBER 3

"Then you will go on your way in safety,
and your foot will not stumble." — 3:23.

My heart was pounding as I stood before the television. My favorite football team was trying to hold onto a lead that they had enjoyed the entire game. They had gotten overly cautious and conservative, however, and had seen their lead dwindle. Instead of trying to win, now they were trying not to lose, and they were on the defensive. The inevitable happened, for the opposing team, which had the momentum, won the game.

Like sports and all of life, risk is a big factor in all spiritual progress. Abraham had to risk everything when he left his home in obedience to God's word. Joseph risked all he had when he revealed himself and his family to the Egyptians. Moses had to risk taking the people through the desert and the Red Sea on their way to the Promised Land. All risk means venturing into the unknown, and facing the unknown can bring fear with it.

Moses told the people to deal with their fears: "See, the Lord your God has given you the land. Go up and take possession of it as the Lord, the God of your fathers, has told you. Do not be afraid; do not be discouraged" (Deuteronomy 1:21). Moses gave instructions for any future battles when he said,

> When you are about to go into battle, the priest shall come forward and address the army. He shall say: "Hear, O Israel, today you are going into battle against your enemies. Do not be faint-hearted or afraid; do not be terrified or give way to panic before them. For the Lord your God is the one who goes with you to fight for you against your enemies to give you victory" (Deuteronomy 20:2-4).

Finally, Moses gave them one last exhortation: "Be strong and courageous. Do not be afraid or terrified because of them, for the Lord your God goes with you; he will never leave you nor forsake you" (Deuteronomy 31:6). Moses gave them this encouragement because they needed it. What they were facing had the potential to terrify them, so the Lord urged them not to "give way to panic" as they went on their way. They were to trust in the Lord.

Bravery is not the absence of fear. It's rather the ability to overcome fear to do what needs to be done. Today's verse says that you will "walk" in safety. You can't play it safe like a team with a big lead. You must keep on walking and your steps will not be hindered. You'll not find safety on the sidelines, but in the game itself.

Hebrews 11:34 tells you that some heroes of the faith "became powerful in battle and routed foreign armies." Notice that they didn't become powerful and then go into battle. They got their might in the battle. You can't wait until fear subsides before you do God's will. You must do it and then the fear will be taken care of. Stop playing it safe for fear of losing. Overcome your fear, step out today, and see the salvation of God on your behalf.

DECEMBER 4

"Do not forsake wisdom, and she will protect you;
love her, and she will watch over you." — 4:6.

Every now and then I enjoy watching a show about animals in the wild. I most enjoy watching the African herds and their interaction with their enemies. Watching a lion, cheetah, or tiger stalk and capture its prey is a fascinating study of how the animal kingdom functions. I suppose it's not so exciting for the animal that gets caught, but it sure makes for good television.

The believer is in a similar struggle. Peter wrote,

> Your enemy the devil prowls around like a roaring lion looking for someone to devour. Resist him, standing firm in the faith, because you know that your brothers throughout the world are undergoing the same kind of sufferings (1 Peter 5:8-9).

The devil is looking for the stray, the distracted, or the lame—anyone who gets separated from the herd. When he finds them, he's like a lion—quick to pounce and devour his prey.

Today's verse tells you that wisdom will protect you. God will always give you the supernatural insight you need to deal with your situation. Notice that wisdom will "protect" and "watch over" you. That tells you that you need constant protection. You are being "stalked' by your great enemy, and you can defeat him only with supernatural power.

Paul wrote to his beloved Corinthians about spiritual war:

> For though we live in the world, we do not wage war as the world does. The weapons we fight with are not the weapons of the world. On the contrary, they have divine power to demolish strongholds. We demolish arguments and every pretension that sets itself up against the knowledge of God, and we take captive every thought to make it obedient to Christ (2 Corinthians 10:3-5).

Be mindful of the war you are in and your need to be on watch constantly. You need spiritual weapons to fight spiritual battles and enemies. Your enemy does not fight fair, but takes advantage of the weak and helpless. He ensnares all he can by any means he can. According to Paul, the main battle is for the minds of men. We must use the word of God, prayer in the Spirit, times of fasting, and a strong prayer life to defeat the devil at his mind games.

No one likes to fight. We all would rather run and rest. But war is a fact of life, the way things are. You can't stick your head into the sand but must face the reality of the fight. Some of your problems won't change until you fight them head on. God has promised to protect you, so you can fight with courage and boldness. Determine to fight the good fight and for the next few days let's study how we can wage a good war.

DECEMBER 5

"She gives no thought to the way of life." — 5:6.

I would scratch and scratch and scratch and still found no relief. I was getting ready to move to Orlando and somehow had developed a rash on the left side of my chest and under my arm. There were no bumps or redness, but the itch was unbearable! It went on for several days and while I drove from Mobile to Orlando, I just scratched and scratched.

When I got to Orlando, I went to the pharmacy to look for anything that would bring relief. While I was walking down a supermarket aisle, the Lord spoke to me: "You have forgotten how much warfare there is in transition." I almost laughed out loud in the store. That was it. I hadn't been paying attention to what was going on. Here I was in the midst of a major change in my life, and I had been unaware of the spiritual warfare that was surrounding me. Based on past experience, I should have realized what was going on. I went home and prayed and fought that itch, and it went away in two days.

Paul wrote to the Corinthians to forgive "in order that Satan might not outwit us. For we are not unaware of his schemes" (2 Corinthians 2:11). Later he wrote that "Satan masquerades as an angel of light" (2 Corinthians 11:14). He instructed the Ephesians to

> Put on the full armor of God so that you can take your stand against the devil's schemes. For our struggle is not against flesh and blood, but against the rulers, against the authorities, against the powers of this dark world and against the spiritual forces of evil in the heavenly realms (Ephesians 6:11-12).

Your great enemy, Satan, and his cohorts are schemers. They are often behind the difficulty you encounter. Yet if you are like me, too often you don't pay attention to your way of life like today's verse says. Finances get tight and you work harder, blaming it on a poor economy. The children get sick and you buy medicine. You get depressed and stay in bed or get away for the weekend. There's nothing wrong with any of those responses, but the real source of your trouble may be powers of wickedness that attack you and yours.

Don't be an ignorant believer. Your relationship with Jesus doesn't save you from the enemy's schemes; it only makes you eligible for new ones. God will allow them to come to increase your dependence on Him and His Spirit. So don't be naive, but don't despair either. Paul told Timothy, "I give you this instruction in keeping with the prophecies once made about you, so that by following them you may fight the good fight" (1 Timothy 1:18). You must learn to "fight the good fight," and make spiritual warfare a way of life and not just a last resort.

DECEMBER 6

"Allow no sleep to your eyes, no slumber to your eyelids." — 6:4.

There's a story in Joshua 10 that challenges your faith. In that story, five kings of the Amorites joined forces to attack the city of Gibeon. The Gibeonites cried for help to Joshua and he marched up from Gilgal to fight. The rest of the account goes like this:

The Lord said to Joshua, "Do not be afraid of them; I have given them into your hand. Not one of them will be able to withstand you." After an all-night march from Gilgal, Joshua took them by surprise. The Lord threw them into confusion before Israel, who defeated them with a great victory at Gibeon (Joshua 10:9-10).

The Lord hurled large hailstones down on the Amorites and many were killed. But the battle wasn't over yet. Joshua needed more time and prayed that the sun would stand still.

The sun stopped in the middle of the sky and delayed going down about a full day. There has never been a day like it before or since, a day when the Lord listened to a man. Surely the Lord was fighting for Israel! (Joshua 10:13).

After an all-night march to the battle site, the battle continued a second night. Joshua and his troops went two nights without sleep while they engaged in spiritual war. Today's verse speaks to the urgency of that war in which all believers are involved. You must learn to fight with the same zeal that Joshua had, asking the Lord to fight with you and give you the time and energy to war, even if it means an all-night prayer time.

Spiritual warfare is a fact of life for the believer. There's no way around it. If you try to ignore that fact, the intensity of the war will eventually drag you in. Jesus was hungry in the desert, having fasted for 40 days, and came under attack from the devil. In fact, "Jesus was led by the Spirit into the desert to be tempted by the devil" (Matthew 4:1). One of the reasons Jesus went into the desert was for spiritual war.

Have you ever wondered why Jesus prayed all night as often as He did? If He was God, why the need for all-night prayer? One of the reasons was the nature of the warfare He encountered. He needed to pray all night to "pray through" the problems He was facing. Those problems included war with demonic powers, and He faced them head-on and came out the victor.

I have stayed up all night for television, fellowship, parties, driving, and sickness. Seldom have I stayed up to engage the enemy in spiritual warfare. Yet my church, family, and personal walk need that urgency now more than ever. Let's follow the example of Joshua and fight our spiritual enemies all night if necessary to see the battle won.

341

DECEMBER 7

*"Many are the victims she has brought down;
her slain are a mighty throng." — 7:26.*

The devil isn't out to *hurt* you; he's out to *kill* you. His purpose is to separate you from the love of God and cause God's creation to turn against Him. He doesn't fight fair, and he will not stop fighting just because you don't fight him. The picture of this is clear in the book of Revelation.

The devil, represented by the dragon, "stood in front of the woman who was about to give birth, so that he might devour her child the moment it was born" (Revelation 12:5). We know that the devil did indeed try to destroy Jesus through Herod. The writer of Revelation then tells that this dragon fought the angels:

> But he [the dragon] was not strong enough, and they [the evil angels] lost their place in heaven. The great dragon was hurled down—that ancient serpent called the devil or Satan, who leads the whole world astray. He was hurled to the earth (Revelation 12:8-9).

Now the devil has been cast down to the earth. The writer continues,

> But woe to the earth and the sea, because the devil has gone down to you! He is filled with fury, because he knows that his time is short. When the dragon saw that he had been hurled to the earth, he pursued the woman who had given birth to the male child....Then the dragon was enraged at the woman and went off to make war against the rest of her offspring—those who obey God's commandments and hold to the testimony of Jesus (Revelation 12:12-13, 17).

If you obey God's commands and hold to Jesus' testimony, you're the target for the devil's rage. He despises you and you must learn to fight back. The good news of how to fight is also found in this chapter of Revelation. John wrote:

> Now have come the salvation and the power and the kingdom of our God, and the authority of his Christ. For the accuser of our brothers has been hurled down. They overcame him by the blood of the Lamb and by the word of their testimony; they did not love their lives so much as to shrink from death (Revelation 12:10-11).

First of all, you'll beat back the devil through the blood of Jesus. I heard a man say once that there's more power in one drop of Jesus' blood than in all the kingdom of darkness. Thank you, Lord. Stand in what Jesus did through His death. Remind the forces of darkness that they were defeated by the cross. Then you have your testimony. Remind yourself and the forces attacking you of what Jesus has done for you. Review your testimony and take encouragement from it.

Finally, you have the assurance of eternal life. What can the devil do to you? Can he kill you? If he does succeed at that, you'll be with Jesus in the presence of God. Your final weapon in defeating him is to resist him unto death if necessary and you *will* overcome because you have no fear of death.

DECEMBER 8

"I was filled with delight day after day, rejoicing always in his presence."
— 8:30.

Imagine that you're watching an old John Wayne war movie. Picture John Wayne in a foxhole, he and his men pinned down by enemy fire. Shells are exploding everywhere, and the situation looks bleak. Suddenly John Wayne calls his men together, and tells them that they are going to attack the very hill before them where the enemy gun fire is coming from. He instructs them to follow his lead and, in the midst of heavy bombing, jumps out of his foxhole and runs straight at the enemy.

Now imagine if John Wayne and his men had decided to leave their guns in the foxhole, and went at the enemy singing and dancing! That would make a terrible John Wayne movie, but it's just how a battle took place in the Bible.

King Jehoshaphat and Judah were under attack from the Moabites and Ammonites. They were outnumbered and things looked desperate. "The people of Judah came together to seek help from the Lord; indeed, they came from every town in Judah to seek him (2 Chronicles 20:4). The king and his people prayed, and the Lord responded through a man named Jahaziel. He told the people:

This is what the Lord says to you: "Do not be afraid or discouraged because of this vast army. For the battle is not yours, but God's. Tomorrow march down against them....You will not have to fight this battle. Take up your positions; stand firm and see the deliverance the Lord will give you, O Judah and Jerusalem. Do not be afraid; do not be discouraged. Go out and face them tomorrow, and the Lord will be with you" (2 Chronicles 15-17).

The people of Judah did just that, but they went in curious battle formation. "Jehoshaphat appointed men to sing to the Lord and to praise him for the splendor of his holiness as they went out at the head of the army, saying: 'Give thanks to the Lord, for his love endures forever'" (2 Chronicles 20:21). The result was astounding: "As they began to sing and praise, the Lord set ambushes against the men of Ammon and Moab and Mount Seir who were invading Judah, and they were defeated" (2 Chronicles 20:22).

This battle was won because the people rejoiced and sang in the presence of God as today's verse describes. Paul told the Corinthians, "The weapons we fight with are not the weapons of the world" (2 Corinthians 10:4). You don't fight with machine guns and grenades. You fight with the weapons of God, and praise and worship is a powerful tool with which to fight the enemy.

Today's verse reminds you to delight in the Lord. Sing His praises, and rejoice in His presence and goodness. As you do, the spirits of darkness will flee and you'll enjoy one victory after another. Let the phrase, "Give thanks to the Lord, for his love endures forever," be on your lips today, and watch for God to fight your battles.

DECEMBER 9

"She calls from the highest point of the city." — 9:3.

When a battle is fought, everyone wants to get the high ground because it offers a view of the whole battle. Those who have this vantage point can plan and fight from a better perspective. Today's verse talks of wisdom and folly both calling out from the highest point in the city. Both are trying to get the high ground in your life. If wisdom has the high point, you'll live from God's perspective. If folly gets the high ground, you're in trouble.

This discussion of "high ground" calls to mind another story in Exodus. It seems that as soon as Israel was delivered from Egypt, they were under attack again. This is certainly symbolic of the life of the believer. If you've been saved from your sins and baptized, then you've been delivered from Egypt. But the warfare has only just begun in your life. It was that way for Israel. They learned early that they would have to fight for every inch of ground that the Lord promised them. The account goes:

> The Amalekites came and attacked the Israelites at Rephidim. Moses said to Joshua, "Choose some of our men and go out to fight the Amalekites. Tomorrow I will stand on top of the hill with the staff of God in my hands." So Joshua fought the Amalekites as Moses had ordered, and Moses, Aaron and Hur went to the top of the hill. As long as Moses held up his hands, the Israelites were winning, but whenever he lowered his hands, the Amalekites were winning. When Moses' hands grew tired, they took a stone and put it under him and he sat on it. Aaron and Hur held his hands up—one on one side, one on the other—so that his hands remained steady till sunset. So Joshua overcame the Amalekite army with the sword. (Exodus 17:8-13).

Moses went for the high ground. He wanted to get "over" the battle and see it as the Lord did. I would have thought that Joshua and the troops would have been the most important factor in that battle, but they were not. Moses on the high ground made all the difference.

In spiritual battles, you need to get the high ground. You need to fight from the superior position you have in Christ. Paul wrote that "God raised us up with Christ and seated us with him in the heavenly realms in Christ Jesus" (Ephesians 2:6). You have access to the highest place there is. If you can get there, you'll see the entire battle before you. You'll know what you're fighting and what to do.

Moses raised his hands with his staff in them. You also need to raise your hands and use the authority that God has given you in Christ. You have been given authority to tread on serpents and scorpions, but you can do that only if you're above them on the high ground. Rise above your circumstances today, and fight the good fight from your superior position. Worship the Lord, pray, and persevere on the top of the hill, where the real victories are won.

DECEMBER 10

"The righteous will never be uprooted,
but the wicked will not remain in the land." — 10:30.

This verse disturbs me. It disturbs me not for what it says, but for what it implies. It says that the righteous will never be uprooted. That tells me that after the righteous take root, someone will try to uproot them. They will then cling to this promise and survive the attack. Next this verse says that the wicked will not remain in the land. That tells me that the wicked may inhabit the land for a season, but will eventually be run off. Someone will have to run them off and that again speaks of the need for war.

If you and I are to maintain what the Lord has given us—ministries, family, jobs, finances—we're going to have to either defend it all or we may have to fight off who has it now. Israel had to displace those who were in the land that the Lord promised them. They then had to defend it many times from their enemies who wanted it back.

2 Samuel 23 gives us a record of David's mighty men. They weren't mighty because they went to a military academy. They weren't mighty just because their father or grandfather were mighty. They were considered mighty because they did mighty things. Consider these accounts:

> Next to him was Eleazar son of Dodai the Alohite. As one of the three mighty men, he was with David when they taunted the Philistines gathered at Pas Dammim for battle. Then the men of Israel retreated but he stood his ground and struck down the Philistines till his hand grew tired and froze to the sword. The Lord brought about a great victory that day. The troops returned to Eleazar, but only to strip the dead (2 Samuel 23:9-10).

Eleazar fought so long and hard that his hand muscles would not let go of his weapon. Since this was written for our instruction, is it possible that you will have to do the same?

There's something in us that doesn't want to fight. We would rather run than fight. But our cities, neighborhoods, and children won't be won to the Lord without a spiritual battle. If we want to see abortion, pornography, and drugs defeated, we will have to fight, perhaps until our hands are frozen around our sword—the Word of God.

Do you want to be known as a mighty man or woman of God? You won't get that title by memorizing the Bible. You'll be mighty by showing forth great might in battle. Don't let the enemy uproot you from your place in Christ. And don't settle for the wicked inhabiting the land. Keep fighting using all the weapons at your disposal, and let it be said of you that you are among God's mighty ones.

DECEMBER 11

"For lack of guidance a nation falls,
but many advisers make victory sure." — 11:14.

King David was successful at war because he had many advisers helping him. He knew how to seek the Lord and obey His voice, and he surrounded himself with many strong and mighty men who knew how to fight. I'm not sure whether his mighty men were the most talented, but they were the most committed. They were not perfect or from the best families. They knew how to stand and fight, however, and that made David's kingdom stand. 2 Samuel 23 tells about one of David's advisers:

> Next to him was Shammah son of Agee the Hararite. When the Philistines banded together at a place where there was a field full of lentils, Israel's troops fled from them. But Shammah took his stand in the middle of the field. He defended it and struck the Philistines down, and the Lord brought about a great victory (2 Samuel 23:11-12).

The Lord brought about a great victory through Shammah because he knew how to take a stand. He didn't retreat, but found the ground that he would fight and die for. He took his stand there and his enemies suffered for it.

I recently spoke with a dear friend who told me of a battle he fought. He was fighting a lingering sickness that awakened him in the middle of the night. One particular night his mind was attacked with negative thoughts. He was thinking what a failure he was, how insignificant his ministry had become, and a host of similar thoughts. He fought and fought but still the onslaught came. At 3:30 a.m., he got up, went to the front door, opened it, and commanded the devil, in Jesus' name, to get out of his house. He took a stand in his lentil field, and the devil had to flee. The thoughts stopped.

It's one thing to read about taking a stand, but it's another to actually take one. Paul encouraged the Ephesians:

> Therefore put on the full armor of God, so that when the day of evil comes, you may be able to stand your ground, and after you have done everything, to stand. Stand firm then, with the belt of truth buckled around your waist, with the breastplate of righteousness in place, and with your feet fitted with the readiness that comes from the gospel of peace. In addition to all this, take up the shield of faith, with which you can extinguish all the flaming arrows of the evil one. Take the helmet of salvation and the sword of the Spirit, which is the word of God (Ephesians 6:13-17).

Surround yourself with people who know when and how to fight. Find a lentil field that is yours and stop retreating before the attack of the enemy. Take your stand alone or with others and see if God doesn't bring a great victory for you.

346

DECEMBER 12

"A good man obtains favor from the Lord,
but the Lord condemns a crafty man." — 12:2.

Christmas is just two weeks away. What a wonderful yet hectic time of the year. Shopping, entertaining, family visits, decorations, Christmas cookies, special church pageants, and school programs all make this a time for memories and busy schedules. In some denominations, the days immediately preceding Christmas are called Advent. It's a time when the believers prepare their hearts and minds for the "advent"—the coming of Christ. Let us now begin to do the same.

I like the shepherds in the Christmas story. There they were, living in a field and going about their business, tending their flocks as their fathers and grandfathers had. It was business as usual for them day in and day out. But one night, their business was interrupted. "An angel of the Lord appeared to them, and the glory of the Lord shone around them, and they were terrified" (Luke 2:9). It's not known whether these shepherds were seeking the Lord. It's not certain that they were more qualified than others. The Lord simply chose to reveal His purpose to them.

After the angel had spoken to them, "suddenly a great company of the heavenly host appeared with the angel, praising God and saying, 'Glory to God in the highest, and on earth peace to men on whom his favor rests'" (Luke 2:13-14). After one angel "broke the ice," a whole host of angels came on the scene. What a night at work they were having! Now usually a "host" of angels fought God's battles. They were a band of warriors. But this host was singing. What a choir they must have made.

First they worshiped God, giving Him glory. That is to be your first response this season. Fill your house and life with festive songs that give God glory. Don't let Nat King Cole be your only musical expression this year. Surround yourself with majestic music that worships the Lord for how He intervened, not only in the shepherds' lives, but in your own. Where would you be today if God had not interrupted your business?

Then the angels brought the message you also find in today's verse. God's favor is with good men who turn their hearts toward Him. The shepherds didn't run from the presence of the angels. They didn't ignore the message. They went from there to see this child. They "returned, glorifying and praising God for all the things they had heard and seen, which were just as they had been told" (Luke 2:20).

You also need to realize that God's favor rests on you. He considers you a good man or woman because you have turned your attention to Him. Praise God this season, and don't get lost in a sea of activity. You've heard and seen many good things, just like the shepherds. Everything God told you has come true. Join with the shepherds this season and magnify the one who is just and true. The host hasn't come to fight, but to bestow God's favor on men, including you. Praise God!

DECEMBER 13

"The light of the righteous shines brightly,
but the lamp of the wicked is snuffed out." — 13:9.

The latter part of yesterday's verse states that "the Lord condemns a crafty man." Today's verse tells you that "the lamp of the wicked is snuffed out." When you read the Christmas story in light of those two verses, you have to think of King Herod. Here was a man who had his life and future planned out. He had worked hard to secure his throne, having gone so far as to have some of his family members killed to preserve his reign. He had also re-built the temple in Jerusalem and participated in the religious services of his day trying to secure the support of the Jewish people.

Yet one day, in spite of all his plans and plots, some men showed up from the east and asked, "Where is the one who has been born king of the Jews? We saw his star in the east and have come to worship him" (Matthew 2:2). Herod had been appointed king by Rome. Now he was hearing that one who has a right to the throne by birth had come. "When King Herod heard this he was disturbed, and all Jerusalem with him" (Matthew 2:3).

The Lord has a habit of disturbing the plans of men, especially those that don't include Him and His will. Herod had carefully planned his every political step, but now through a sovereign act of God's will, a new king had been born. Perhaps you've planned your future and are on a path to fulfill those plans. If they have not included the Lord, however, they're destined to fail, or at least to be a source of pain for you.

Herod tried to handle this new-born king like he did everything else. He pretended to be interested so that he could worship, but instead plotted the child's assassination. He went so far as to kill all the male children in Bethlehem, but to no avail because Joseph and Mary had been warned in a dream to flee. Jesus was safe in Egypt. Herod, however, went the way of all flesh. In spite of all his plans to reign forever, he died several years later. His lamp was indeed snuffed out and the Lord condemned him as He does all "crafty" men.

Jesus' lamp continues to shine brightly to this day. Herod tried to make a name for himself and was snuffed out. Jesus came to do the will of God and His name is exalted the world over. There's a lesson there for you. The message of this season is to submit to God and His will. Have you submitted your future to Him? Have you given to him your career, family plans, where you will live, and your dreams for your ministry? If so, then your light will shine brightly. If not, then you must submit to Him or risk resisting Him in order to see your own plans established. Surrender your life once again to Him who plans all things after the counsel of His will, and be established on a foundation of eternal righteousness.

DECEMBER 14

*"Wisdom reposes in the heart of the discerning
and even among fools she lets herself be known." — 14:33.*

Herod the Great was a fool. He was a good politician, but a fool nonetheless. In spite of his ruthless reign and cold-hearted decisions, the Lord tried to reach him. The Magi (or Wise Men as they are traditionally known) came to him first. They announced the birth of the King of the Jews saying, "We saw his star in the east and have come to worship him" (Matthew 2:2).

There were people from hundreds of miles away who knew more of what was going on in Herod's kingdom than he did. He lived right there and had access to all the tradition of Judaism, but had no idea what was going on. Today's verse points out that wisdom will make herself known even among fools. The Lord gave Herod one more chance, perhaps one last chance, to repent but he did not.

"When he [Herod] had called together all the people's chief priests and teachers of the law, he asked them where the Christ was to be born. 'In Bethlehem in Judea,' they replied" (Matthew 2:4). Herod heard the report of the Magi and the prophets and tried to use this information to further his own agenda. Instead of recognizing (and worshiping) the One who was King by birth, he tried to maintain his own throne that was his through the appointment of Rome.

Herod searched the Scriptures, but it was a selfish search. He tried to take what God was doing and turn it to personal gain.

Then Herod called the Magi secretly and found out from them the exact time the star appeared. He sent them to Bethlehem and said, "Go and make a careful search for the child. As soon as you find him, report to me, so that I too may go and worship him" (Matthew 2:7-8).

He had no intention of worshiping but of killing this rival to his throne.

This Christmas season is still full of those who try to use it for selfish gain. Stores hope to make more money than last season. The media produce godless movies and shows to lure people to watch in theaters and on television. During this one short season, people hope to find the peace and joy missing from their lives during the rest of the year. Yet the Lord continues to make His wisdom known even to fools. The story of Jesus is still proclaimed even though fools use it for their own ends.

As you approach the story of Jesus' birth, do you approach with wisdom or with selfish ends? Do you come to worship, or to find peace, gifts, and family reunions? The wisdom behind Jesus' birth is that wise men and women still worship him and give Him gifts. Don't let this holiday be self-indulgent and hectic, but rather a time for calm and peaceful meditation on the love of God and His wisdom made known in Jesus Christ.

DECEMBER 15

*"The path of life leads upward for the wise
to keep him from going down to the grave." — 15:24.*

What did the Magi see in the sky? Why did this star suddenly appear to herald the birth of the "King of the Jews?" What motivated them to travel a great distance to worship Him? Speculation abounds concerning the Magi, but today's verse certainly pertained to them. The Lord showed them the path of life, and they followed it in faith.

These men saw evidence of something that was happening hundreds of miles from their homeland. They set out, not knowing where they were going. They didn't know for sure whether the star would continue to guide them. It's doubtful whether they had ever been to Palestine before. They packed gifts in faith that they would find the King. They traveled major trade routes and were in some danger from thieves as they carried valuable gifts. These were no ordinary men. They were like Abraham who "when called to go to a place he would later receive as his inheritance, obeyed and went, even though he did not know where he was going" (Hebrews 11:8).

When they arrived in Judea, they had to inquire further as to the King's whereabouts. They persisted in their search, which took them to Herod's palace. When he told them to go to Bethlehem, they again went in faith. "After they had heard the king, they went on their way, and the star they had seen in the east went ahead of them until it stopped over the place where the child was" (Matthew 2:9). Their path was indeed "upward," for it was an uphill struggle for them to arrive at the child's house. Yet their path was also "upward" since each step took them closer to the Lord and His anointed one.

"When they saw the star, they were overjoyed. On coming to the house, they saw the child with his mother Mary, and they bowed down and worshiped him" (Matthew 2:10-11). They were overjoyed because they had reached the end of a long, hard faith journey. The Lord had been faithful every step of the way, and they worshiped. Is that not your testimony this season as well? Hasn't the Lord helped you on your journey this year? Haven't "stars"—unexpected signs—appeared for you to direct you to the child of Bethlehem?

The story didn't end there. "And having been warned in a dream not to go back to Herod, they returned to their country by another route" (Matthew 2:12). Today's verse says that the path of life keeps the wise from going down to the grave. The Magi were warned about Herod and went home safely.

Hasn't the Lord kept you from harm? He has protected you even from yourself and you read this today because of His watchful care. Rejoice this holiday season for God's mercy. He has led and protected you just like He did the Magi. You, like the Magi, have come a long way under God's watchful eye. Take this opportunity to worship Him and give Him gifts.

DECEMBER 16

*"Whoever gives heed to instruction prospers,
and blessed is he who trusts in the Lord." — 16:20.*

Have you ever noticed how prominent dreams are in the Christmas story? Joseph was told in a dream to take Mary as his wife and to name the baby Jesus. The Magi were warned in a dream not to go back to Herod. And then Joseph was given three dreams concerning the flight to Egypt and return to Nazareth. The latter three are reported as follows:

> When they [the Magi] had gone, an angel of the Lord appeared to Joseph in a dream. "Get up," he said, "take the child and his mother and escape to Egypt. Stay there until I tell you, for Herod is going to search for the child to kill him."...After Herod died, an angel of the Lord appeared in a dream to Joseph in Egypt and said, "Get up, take the child and his mother and go to the land of Israel, for those who were trying to take the child's life are dead."...But when he heard that Archelaus was reigning in Judea in place of his father Herod, he was afraid to go there. Having been warned in a dream, he withdrew to the district of Galilee (Matthew 2:13, 19-20, 22).

Joseph was able to raise his son and protect his family because he gave heed to instruction. His heart was obviously set toward hearing the Lord, and God did not disappoint him. He knew at every critical point what he was to do. When he heard from the Lord, he immediately took action for it is written: "So he got up, took the child and his mother, during the night and left for Egypt....So he got up, took the child and his mother and went to the land of Israel" (Matthew 2:14, 21). Not only did he heed instruction, but he also trusted in the Lord. Joseph perfectly fulfilled the message of today's verse, and serves as a wonderful example of a man who was obedient to the revealed will of God.

Joseph was a man of faith. He fulfilled the verse found in Hebrews 11:6, which states, "And without faith it is impossible to please God, because anyone who comes to him must believe that he is and that he rewards those who earnestly seek him." Joseph was obviously seeking the Lord in faith, and God revealed Himself to Joseph. God will reveal Himself to you this season if you seek Him in faith, believing that He will reward you with an answer.

James wrote, "If any of you lacks wisdom, he should ask God, who gives generously to all without finding fault, and it will be given to him. But when he asks, he must believe and not doubt, because he who doubts is like a wave of the sea, blown and tossed by the wind" (James 1:5-6). Joseph asked and then acted. He trusted that God was faithful to reveal His will. Don't be double-minded. If you've asked God, then trust that He is showing you. It may not be the answer you want, but if you heed His instruction, you will indeed prosper.

DECEMBER 17

"A cheerful heart is good medicine,
but a crushed spirit dries up the bones." — 17:22.

I remember going to bed in a strange house after an exhausting day. As I mentioned last month, the Lord had used me to rescue a family member from a desperate situation. It had been one miracle after another, and I was lying in bed acknowledging in my heart what the Lord had done. It's a feeling I have experienced several times—a feeling that the Lord had used me for a special project. There's no feeling like it in the world.

I'm sure I felt, to a lesser degree, what Mary felt when the angel announced that she was pregnant. After asking some basic biological questions, she declared, "I am the Lord's servant. May it be to me as you have said" (Luke 1:38). Once she said that and went to visit Elizabeth, the magnitude of what she was involved in began to dawn on her. The Lord had singled her out to be used for a very special project, and while visiting Elizabeth, she composed this song:

My soul praises the Lord and my spirit rejoices in God my Savior, for he has been mindful of the humble state of his servant. From now on all generations will call me blessed, for the Mighty One has done great things for me — holy is his name (Luke 1:46-49).

I wonder how Luke was able to record this song so accurately? He could not have met Mary until decades later. Could Mary have written this down and kept it with her all those years? Was it something she composed and then sang from that day forward? Mary sang out of her excitement and joy over God using her. She was yet to face her fiance, who would want an explanation of what happened. She was facing a hostile society that would not understand her pregnancy. But she rejoiced in the Lord, and her joy is recorded for us today.

Today's verse says that joy is good medicine. An absence of joy can actually cause physical ailments. If you lack joy, it's because you haven't sensed the exhilaration of God using you to do some special deed. You haven't found yourself on a plane praying for the person next to you, knowing that God set that appointment up. You've not given your car, computer, or other item to someone and have them weep and tell you that they were just praying for that item.

There's a joy in doing God's will that's like nothing else. It's good medicine. This holiday season, don't look for joy in traditions, Christmas cookies, snow, or a gift exchange, although there's nothing wrong with any of those. Ask the Lord to use you in a special way. Do something that, when it's done, will cause you to write your own praise chorus from the joy in your heart.

DECEMBER 18

*"The heart of the discerning acquires knowledge;
the ears of the wise seek it out."* — 18:15.

The Magi weren't the wisest men of the Christmas story. That distinction belongs to Joseph. Here was a man who found out that the girl to whom he was engaged was pregnant. The angel didn't appear to him at first as he did to Mary, so he was left for a time to figure out his response. Not much is known about Joseph, except that he was a "righteous man" and wanted to do what was required by God's law. He eventually decided to divorce Mary, but to do it quietly.

But after he had considered this, an angel of the Lord appeared to him in a ream and said, "Joseph son of David, do not be afraid to take Mary home as your wife, because what is conceived in her is from the Holy Spirit. She will give birth to a son, and you are to give him the name Jesus, because he will save his people from their sins"....When Joseph woke up, he did what the angel of the Lord had commanded him and took Mary home as his wife (Matthew 1:20-21, 24-25).

Joseph's heart was searching for what to do. He was grappling with a difficult decision, and only had his heart and the law to guide him (or so he thought). Yet when his mental and physical resources were at rest, his heart was still seeking. He was crying out to God and the angel of the Lord was sent to answer his cry. Joseph showed his wisdom by obeying what God said and not relying on what seemed to be best.

In this respect, he was like his "son" about to be born. It was written of Jesus, The Spirit of the Lord will rest on him—the Spirit of wisdom and understanding, the Spirit of counsel and of power, the Spirit of knowledge and of the fear of the Lord—and he will delight in the fear of the Lord. He will not judge by what he sees with his eyes, or decide by what he hears with his ears; but with righteousness he will judge the needy, with justice he will give decisions for the poor of the earth (Isaiah 11:2-4).

Jesus didn't trust in His own perspective, but in the one that the Spirit gave Him. He didn't judge by what He saw or heard. He judged with righteous judgment and Joseph did that as well. If Joseph had judged with his eyes, he would have divorced Mary. Instead he judged with righteousness and took Mary as his wife.

You need to be like Joseph and Jesus. You need to stop judging solely by what you see and hear. Has someone offended you? Find out in the Spirit what's really going on in their heart before you judge them. Has a situation not worked out as you had hoped? Before you blame someone or something, determine whether God is the one who has ordered your state of affairs. Let your ears seek spiritual knowledge, and don't rely solely on what you see or hear. Be like Joseph—a wise man who saw what to do in the Spirit.

DECEMBER 19

"Houses and wealth are inherited from parents,
but a prudent wife is from the Lord." — 19:14.

It's frightening to think how ignorant I was when I got married. I was 24 years old, barely out of college. I was making $600 per month and we lived in an apartment that was so small, you could stand in one place, turn around, and see it all. I had no idea what was ahead in ministry, where we would end up living, or what pressures and problems would come our way.

The Lord knew all that, however, and gave me a wonderful wife. She was the perfect fit for me. She has stood with me through it all, and was just as ignorant as I was when we married! I shudder to think of how unaware I was of her ongoing importance in my life. I thank God that He helped me make this critical decision when I could have so easily messed it up.

Joseph came to realize that the Lord had given him a prudent wife. Mary was highly favored of the Lord and a spiritual woman. Joseph and Mary were in love, but little did they know what was ahead. They would carry the stigma of Mary's pregnancy. They would have to travel to Bethlehem near the end of her pregnancy. People would invade the privacy of their home to worship the child and lay gifts at his feet.

In the middle of the night, they would have to flee to Egypt. Then they would return, only to have to settle in Nazareth, an area with a low reputation in Israel. They would lose Jesus for five days on one trip to Jerusalem. I doubt if Joseph and Mary ever thought of all that they would go through when they got married. The Lord was faithful to them, however, and they stand as examples of how God can work in and protect a marriage in the midst of extreme spiritual pressure.

This holiday season is a time for family and friends. It's a time for remembering and celebrating the past and all that the Lord has done for you. It's a season to acknowledge that the people in your life are there because God put them there. For that, you should give thanks. My family and I generally sit down and review the year and all that has happened. But above it all, we give thanks for one another and the relationships God has given us.

When you buy and give gifts this year, give them out of thanksgiving for that person. Let your gift represent how grateful you are that the Lord has brought that person into your life. Whether children, spouse, pastor, friend, employer, or employee, see them as a gift of God. And then respond to your gift with a gift. Don't just give either, but tell them what a gift from God they are to you.

DECEMBER 20

"Even a child is known by his actions,
by whether his conduct is pure and right." — 20:11.

As I write, my daughter is approaching her thirteenth birthday. When I look at her now, I think of Mary, the mother of Jesus. She was probably a teenager when the angel of the Lord appeared to her. I marvel at how nobly she responded to the startling news of her pregnancy.

Mary wasn't a theologian. She didn't wrestle with and understand the mysteries of the Jewish faith. She was a simple girl who responded to the will of God with enthusiasm and faith. Today's verse says that even a young person is known not by knowledge but by action. Mary will be forever known for what she did because her conduct was pure and right. She made a "name" for herself through her obedience.

Mary didn't develop a seminar on how to win God's favor or see angels. She didn't write a book. After the angel left, she went to visit her cousin, Elizabeth.

At that time Mary got ready and hurried to a town in the hill country of Judah, where she entered Zechariah's home and greeted Elizabeth. When Elizabeth heard Mary's greeting, the baby leaped in her womb, and Elizabeth was filled with the Holy Spirit. In a loud voice she exclaimed: "Blessed are you among women and blessed is the child you will bear! But why am I so favored, that the mother of my Lord should come to me? As soon as the sound of your greeting reached my ears, the baby in my womb leaped for joy. Blessed is she who has believed that what the Lord has said to her will be accomplished!" (Luke 1:39-45).

What a blessing Mary's visit must have been for Elizabeth. In fact, Elizabeth was filled with the Holy Spirit and saw things in the Spirit that Mary had not had a chance to tell her. Then Elizabeth's baby leapt for joy. The whole house was impacted by the visit of this simple girl. Elizabeth herself was impacted by Mary's faith. She said, "Blessed is she who has believed that what the Lord has said to her will be accomplished!" Mary's faith was a blessing to herself and others, and she spread that blessing wherever she went.

Take the opportunity this holiday season to share the good news with someone else. Go visit them and bring a blessing to their house. Maybe you can visit a hospital, homeless shelter, jail, or halfway house. Don't share with them the great doctrines of the Christian faith. Rather share with them what your faith in Christ means to you. Give a testimony of what you're trusting the Lord to do for you. Be known for your actions this Christmas season, and let your faith encourage others, as Mary's did.

DECEMBER 21

"He who guards his mouth and his tongue keeps himself from calamity."
— 21:23.

In contrast to Mary's faith is the lack of faith on the part of Zechariah, her cousin's husband. He also had an angel appear to him, but he responded to his visit with unbelief from a hard heart. Mary asked the angel a question that was biological in nature: "How will this be since I am a virgin?" (Luke 1:34). Zechariah asked the angel to prove the truth of what he said: "How can I be sure of this? I am an old man and my wife is well along in years" (Luke 1:18).

The angel responded gently to Mary and answered her question. The angel was indignant to Zechariah:

I am Gabriel. I stand in the presence of God, and I have been sent to speak to you and to tell you this good news. And now you will be silent and not able to speak until the day this happens, because you did not believe my words, which will come true at their proper time (Luke 1:19-20).

Mary went on to visit Elizabeth and sang God's praises. Zechariah was placed under "gag rule," and could not share with anyone the good news he had heard.

Today's verse tells you to put a guard on your mouth. The best way to do that is to occupy your mouth in something positive. It's striking how many people involved in the story of Jesus' birth praised God and worshiped. The one who didn't— Zechariah—brought misfortune on himself by not guarding his tongue.

Mary said, "My soul praises the Lord and my spirit rejoices in God my savior" (Luke 1:46-67). The angels sang to the shepherds, "Glory to God in the highest, and on earth peace to men on whom his favor rests" (Luke 2:14). The shepherds left after seeing Jesus, "glorifying and praising God for all the things they had heard and seen" (Luke 2:20). Simeon saw Jesus in the temple, "took him in his arms and praised God" (Luke 2:28). Anna the prophetess saw Jesus and "gave thanks to God and spoke about the child to all who were looking forward to the redemption of Israel" (Luke 2:38). And even Zechariah, after the birth of his son had his tongue loosed and said, "Praise be to the Lord, the God of Israel, because he has come and has redeemed his people" (Luke 1:68).

Use your mouth for the right thing over these next few days. Listen to and sing along with Handel's "Messiah" and other great seasonal music. Spend time in your Sunday school, church, and family speaking of the great things God has done over the past year. Put a guard over your mouth so that you won't speak negative or discouraging things. Don't focus on what you don't have, but focus on the goodness of God, singing His praises. Join your voice with all those who have seen the child and praised God through the ages. Don't bring hardship on yourself like Zechariah did, but fill your mouth with the high praises of God, from whom all blessings flow.

DECEMBER 22

"Rich and poor have this in common:
the Lord is the Maker of them all." — 22:2.

The Christmas story brought people together from all walks of life. Priests, peasants, kings from the East, Roman rulers, shepherds, prophets, and angels all played a part in the birth of Jesus. Some participated knowingly and others were unaware of their role, but the Lord used them all to make this an amazing story with many interesting characters.

The highest-ranking character who was unaware of his role was Caesar himself. The political leader of the world was sitting in Rome, far away from the action in Palestine. He was conducting his business as usual, or so he thought. "In those days Caesar Augustus issued a decree that a census should be taken of the entire Roman world. (This was the first census that took place while Quirinius was governor of Syria). And everyone went to his own town to register" (Luke 2:1-2).

This census made sense from a political point of view, but little did Caesar know that God was using that to fulfill biblical prophecy. The Messiah was to be born in Bethlehem, and Joseph and Mary had to get there in time for Jesus' birth. The Lord ordered the normal affairs of the Roman world to fulfill His will. Today's verse was certainly true at Jesus' birth. The Lord made the richest, most powerful king in Rome and the poorest shepherd in the field. They are both His by creation and He rules over them both.

What an encouragement to know that the Lord reigns! Caesar Augustus was there because God put him there. "No one from the east or the west or from the desert can exalt a man. But it is God who judges: He brings one down, he exalts another" (Psalm 75:6-7). Not only was Caesar there at God's appointment, but he was there to do God's will. Caesar had no idea where the concept came from for the census, but the Lord ordained it to do His will!

When God is ready to do something, He can move heaven and earth to do it. He can call on angels or on the kings of the world to get it done. Mary sang about it when she said,

> He has performed mighty deeds with his arm, he has scattered those who are proud in their inmost thoughts. He has brought down rulers from their thrones but has lifted up the humble. He has filled the hungry with good things but has sent the rich away empty. He has helped his servant Israel, remembering to be merciful (Luke 1:51-54).

You may be disturbed by what you see in the world. Political upheaval, wars, terrorism, and civil unrest occupy the headlines. Those in power may seem to be actively working to produce evil and death. But the message of the season is that our God reigns! He's high above it all, and is neither nervous or at a loss for what to do. There's no need for pessimism. Sing for joy as Mary did, for the rich and powerful are not beyond God's watchful eye.

DECEMBER 23

"Listen to your father, who gave you life." — 23:22.

I can still remember most of my Christmas celebrations as a child. My parents were experts at finding out what I wanted and convincing me there was no way they could get it. Invariably I would be surprised to find what I wanted under the tree. My sister would take me to downtown Pittsburgh to roam through the toy stores and view the department store decorations. Family and friends would come over unannounced for cookies and we would show them everything we got. It was and still is the best time of the year, and family made it that way.

Family figured prominently in the first Christmas as well. Mary and Joseph made perhaps their first trip together at that time. They became parents in Bethlehem and welcomed their first-born son into the world there. But why were they in Bethlehem? They were there because of their spiritual heritage.

> So Joseph also went up from the town of Nazareth in Galilee to Judea, to Bethlehem the town of David, because he belonged to the house and line of David. He went there to register with Mary, who was pledged to be married to him and was expecting a child (Luke 2:4-5).

Joseph didn't just exist in spiritual isolation. He was one of a long line of family who had served the Lord before him. The Lord used his spiritual heritage to fulfill the birth of Jesus as Joseph traveled to the city of his fathers. Today's verse encourages you to listen to your father. Joseph was following his "father" David when he went to Bethlehem. By so doing, he fulfilled prophecy: "But you, Bethlehem Ephrathah, though you are small among the clans of Judah, out of you will come for me one who will be ruler over Israel, whose origins are from of old, from ancient times" (Micah 5:2).

Have you ever skipped over the genealogies at the beginning of Matthew or especially at the start of 1 Chronicles? Why are they there? They're there because spiritual heritage is important in the Lord's eyes. You don't serve in spiritual isolation, but are continuing traditions begun by those who have gone before you, some of them giving their lives for the sake of Christ. "We are surrounded by such a great cloud of witnesses" (Hebrews 12:1). Let's be faithful to that "cloud."

During this season, it's good to celebrate your spiritual heritage and to add to it with your own traditions. Our family opens an Advent calendar almost every year. We review our past Christmas celebrations and keep the memories warm and fresh. We acknowledge those who are over us in the Lord with gifts and phone calls, and travel to visit family and friends. Trying to remember the downtrodden, we buy gifts for inmates or their children. We listen to Handel's "Messiah" and work at keeping Christ in our Christmas celebrations.

Like Joseph we try to let our spiritual heritage lead us to the birth of Jesus in our lives and hearts. During these days, see yourself as part of a large spiritual pilgrimage to Bethlehem and celebrate your heritage as a follower of the Son of God.

"And the lamp of the wicked will be snuffed out." — 24:20.

This was the life. My wife and I were enjoying a night in a Florida seacoast hotel, compliments of our congregation. It was 11:00 p.m. and we were staying just 15 miles from Cape Canaveral. Suddenly the night sky was as bright as day. A satellite was being launched and we had a perfect, unobstructed view from our hotel window. What before had been dark and ordinary was suddenly lit up by the rocket engines. It was a magnificent sight.

The shepherds had a similar experience the night Jesus was born. They were on night shift in the fields when suddenly "an angel of the Lord appeared to them, and the glory of the Lord shone around them" (Luke 2:9). The angel, like that rocket being launched, turned an ordinary dark, or perhaps moonlit night, into a spectacle. Their eyes, accustomed to the darkness, were confronted with sudden light and it took them a while, I'm sure, to actually see what was going on.

The angel appeared in the natural darkness just as Jesus came to confront the spiritual darkness of the earth. It had been 400 years since the book of Malachi had been written. The word of the Lord was a long time in coming. Israel and all the nations were languishing in spiritual darkness and gloom. They had grown accustomed to the darkness, however, and their eyes had adjusted to the dark. Now suddenly the King of glory appeared and they all had to re-adjust to this new light.

Isaiah had written 700 years earlier:

> The people walking in darkness have seen a great light; on those living in the land of the shadow of death a light has dawned. You have enlarged the nation and increased their joy; they rejoice before you as people rejoice at the harvest, as men rejoice when dividing the plunder. For as in the day of Midian's defeat, you have shattered the yoke that burdens them, the bar across their shoulders, the rod of their oppressor (Isaiah 9:2-4).

I hope that you rejoice for the light that you've received. Once you also walked in darkness, but the glory of the Lord has shone around you. The babe has come to you and yours. While you once walked in darkness, you have seen a great light, and your spiritual darkness has been turned to brightness. This is a day to rejoice as people rejoice who take in the harvest or divide the plunder. There's no reason for gloom.

Your light hasn't lasted for a few seconds or for one night. It's still with you today, showing you the way to go. The lamp of the wicked has been snuffed out and they stumble badly. The bar of your oppressor has been broken and you are freed by this marvelous light. Rejoice this day and let your joy be made full!

DECEMBER 25

"As the heavens are high and the earth is deep,
so the hearts of kings are unsearchable." — 25:3.

I have completed my Christmas ritual. I try every year to listen to Handel's "Messiah" as often as possible. At least once, I lie on my couch with only the lights from the Christmas tree and listen to the entire thing. Invariably I'll weep as I enjoy the majesty and depth of Brother Handel's composition.

The story has it that Handel was destitute when he was commissioned to write a musical history of our Lord's life. He would go out only at night so that he wouldn't meet any of his creditors. When a committee from a local church visited him with the idea for the "Messiah," he locked himself away and reportedly completed the work in 17 days. His food trays sat untouched outside his door. Today his musical score can barely be copied in 17 days. His masterpiece epitomizes what man's creative ability can accomplish when coupled with God's inspiration.

Today's verse says that the heart of a king is unsearchable. The heart of our Lord and King's would have been unsearchable had He not sent Jesus. But the birth of Jesus shows forth His loving heart for all the world to see. "For God so loved the world that he gave his one and only Son, that whoever believes in him shall not perish but have eternal life. For God did not send his Son into the world to condemn the world, but to save the world through him" (John 3:16-17).

In listening to the "Messiah," I especially enjoy the musical rendition of Isaiah 9:6-7:

> For to us a child is born, to us a son is given, and the government will be on his shoulders. And he will be called Wonderful Counselor, Mighty God, Everlasting Father, Prince of Peace. Of the increase of his government and peace there will be no end. He will reign on David's throne and over his kingdom, establishing and upholding it with justice and righteousness from that time on and forever. The zeal of the Lord Almighty will accomplish this.

Today marks the fact that a child was born. He was born to and for us. He was given to us, a gift from God, to represent God's mercy and grace. The heart of an earthly king may be unsearchable, but the heart of our King is plain for all to see. It's a heart after peace, justice, and righteousness. It's a zealous heart that accomplishes for His people what they can't accomplish for themselves.

Oh Lord, I thank you for your heart of love. I thank you for Jesus, who was sent into the world not to judge it, but to bless it. I welcome Your government in my life. I welcome the increase of peace that comes with it. You are a mighty King, and Your love is most meaningful today as I think of the gift of Your Son to the world. May I today and every day represent Your great love for the world as evidenced by the birth of Jesus. Amen.

DECEMBER 26

"Like cutting off one's feet or drinking violence
is the sending of a message by the hand of a fool." — 26:6.

The Lord used many faithful messengers during the days surrounding Jesus' birth. He sent angels to Zechariah, Mary, and Joseph. He dispatched a host of angels to the shepherds. The Magi were messengers to Herod and the Jewish leaders to announce the birth of the King. Simeon and the prophetess Anna were in the temple and they both gave messages to Joseph and Mary concerning their son and His eventual impact on them and Israel. Let us today consider Simeon:

It had been revealed to him by the Holy Spirit that he would not die before he had seen the Lord's Christ. Moved by the Spirit, he went into the temple courts. When the parents brought in the child Jesus to do for him what the custom of the Law required, Simeon took him in his arms and praised God, saying: "Sovereign Lord, as you have promised, you now dismiss your servant in peace. For my eyes have seen your salvation, which you have prepared in the sight of all people, a light for revelation to the Gentiles and for glory to your people Israel." The child's father and mother marveled at what was said about him. Then Simeon blessed them and said to Mary, his mother: "This child is destined to cause the falling and rising of many in Israel, and to be a sign that will be spoken against, so the thoughts of many hearts will be revealed. And a sword will pierce your own soul too" (Luke 2:26-35).

Simeon was a faithful messenger. He put his trust in the Lord that what God had revealed to him, he would eventually see. He spoke to Joseph and Mary in such a way that they both knew he had to be sent by God. He correctly identified Jesus as a blessing both to Jew and Gentile, and spoke of their personal pain as He fulfilled His ministry.

The world still needs to hear from faithful messengers. You need to speak to people and reveal God's knowledge of and will for them. Paul urged the Corinthians to "be eager to prophesy" (1 Corinthians 14:39). He explained that "everyone who prophesies speaks to men for their strengthening, encouragement, and comfort" (1 Corinthians 14:3). Prophecy isn't just seeing into the future, but rather speaking to people so that they know what you say is from the Lord.

Today's verse draws some analogies to a fool who delivers a message. The message of the Gospel has been entrusted to you and me. Let's be faithful with it. Let's tell the good news of Jesus' birth to the world. Even during these days after Christmas, continue to find those with whom you can share it. Pray and ask God to give you a Scripture verse or word of encouragement for individuals. When you receive something, then make sure you're faithful to give it. Don't let the Lord regret He sent the word to a fool, but rather be faithful, as Simeon was, to deliver the insight God has given you.

"Do not boast about tomorrow,
or you do not know what a day may bring forth." — 27:1.

"How could they have known?" or so I thought. Several men were praying over me, and they were delivering a prophecy. It wasn't spooky or weird. They were speaking about my life and ministry and, even though I had never met them, they were telling me things even my wife didn't know. They were telling me about my struggles and questions, and were encouraging me in the process. That has happened to me several times, and it has always served to strengthen me.

You can do the same thing. All it takes is a commitment to pray and ask the Lord to give you words of encouragement for someone else. Then it takes a commitment in faith to share what you hear. When you do, you must be open to others adjusting or correcting what you've said to make sure it's accurate. That's only part of the price you must pay to be a faithful messenger, however. The full price for speaking the word to others can be steep, as we learn from the life of Anna the prophetess.

There was also a prophetess, Anna, the daughter of Phanuel, of the tribe of Asher. She was very old; she had lived with her husband seven years after her marriage, and then was a widow until she was eighty-four. She never left the temple but worshiped night and day, fasting and praying. Coming up to them [Joseph and Mary] at that very moment, she gave thanks to God and spoke about the child to all who were looking forward to the redemption of Israel (Luke 2:36-38).

What a price Anna paid to be God's faithful messenger! She had lived a life of prayer and fasting for more than 60 years! She spent her time in the temple and constantly sought the Lord. One day, when Joseph and Mary came to have Jesus circumcised, she began speaking to them and others about Jesus accurately and in faith.

Today's verse cautions you not to boast about tomorrow, for you don't know what a day may bring forth. Anna probably never dreamed that her life would turn out as it did. Perhaps she thought she would live with her husband, grow old with him, have children and grandchildren, and then die. Instead she gave her life to being a faithful messenger. Little did she think that she would prophesy over the Christ, the anointed of God.

When you commit to be a faithful messenger, you're not guaranteed an easy ride. You may have to agonize long hours in prayer. People may not receive what you have to say. It may require periods of fasting. The goal you set for tomorrow may require a heavy price today. Are you willing to pay that price? The world needs many more Anna's who can speak the words of God. The price may be high, but the results are tremendous.

DECEMBER 28

"He who keeps the law is a discerning son." — 28:7.

I'll never forget the birth of our first-born. My feet didn't touch the ground for weeks. When he was born, his hair stood straight up in the air, looking like he had stuck his finger in an electric outlet. But I thought he was beautiful, and everyone within shouting distance had to listen to my boasting. I would just go into his room and watch him sleep. That was my boy!

For Joseph and Mary, I'm sure the birth of their first-born was a special and exciting time as well. First of all, Jesus was circumcised. "On the eighth day, when it was time to circumcise him, he was named Jesus, the name the angel had given him before he had been conceived" (Luke 2:21).

Then came the trip to Jerusalem and the temple to fulfill the Law:

When the time of their purification according to the Law of Moses had been completed, Joseph and Mary took him to Jerusalem to present him to the Lord (as it is written in the Law of the Lord, "Every firstborn male is to be consecrated to the Lord"), and to offer a sacrifice in keeping with what is said in the Law of the Lord: "a pair of doves or two young pigeons" (Luke 2:22-24).

William Hendriksen wrote:

The underlying idea of the redemption ritual was this: in the night of Israel's deliverance from the "house of bondage" all firstborn Egyptians were slain (Exodus 12:29). However, in God's holy sight not only the Egyptians but also the Israelites had forfeited their lives. Jesus too was under the sentence of death. He was born "under the Law" (Galatians 4:4) and this in the sense not only of being under personal obligation to keep the law but also of being duty-bound vicariously to bear the law's penalty and to satisfy its demand. He had no personal guilt but had of his own free will taken upon himself the sin of the world. Was the redemption fee paid at this time a symbol of the infinitely greater ransom to which the Savior was going to refer in saying, "The Son of Man did not come to be served but to serve and to give his life a ransom for many"? (Matthew 20:28)"*

Joseph and Mary were discerning children, and Jesus was a discerning Son. They all kept the law of God. Yet they weren't legalistic, but used the law to build a strong relationship with the Lord. The law doesn't bring you salvation, but once saved you're to do all the will of God and keep His commands. You do this not only from duty, but from the love of God, who gave Himself a ransom for your sins.

The story of Christmas isn't just about a Baby and gift-bearing Magi. It's about the Savior of the world who came to keep God's commands even unto death. That's the legacy He left you, and now you must do the same. Obligate yourself to do God's will and you'll perfectly fulfill the Law and the spirit of this Christmas season.

* William Hendriksen, *The Gospel of Luke* (Grand Rapids: Baker Book House, page 164.)

DECEMBER 29

"A man who loves wisdom brings joy to his father." — 29:3.

I held my hand over my heart, pretending to be under physical stress. I had walked in the den to find my two children had taken it upon themselves to do their chores! There had been no reminders and they didn't want anything special from me. They brought joy to their father.

Joseph, Mary, and Jesus brought joy to their heavenly Father. Luke writes:

When Joseph and Mary had done everything required by the Law of the Lord, they returned to Galilee to their own town of Nazareth. And the child grew and became strong; he was filled with wisdom, and the grace of God was upon him (Luke 2:39-40).

Jesus' parents were wise in keeping the Law. As Jesus grew and kept it, He was filled with wisdom and brought joy to His father, as today's verse describes.

Jesus' wisdom was made known as He began His ministry as well. "When all the people were being baptized, Jesus was baptized too" (Luke 3:21). The sinless One came with sinful people to submit to the ministry of John the Baptist. He wasn't above the people to whom He had been sent, but identified with them in every way. His wisdom and grace were so overwhelming that the Father could not contain Himself: "And as he [Jesus] was praying, heaven was opened and the Holy Spirit descended on him in bodily form like a dove. And a voice came from heaven: 'You are my Son whom I love; with you I am well pleased'" (Luke 3:21-22).

The Father burst out to express His joy and love for His Son. As Jesus had given Himself to His earthly parents, He had also been about His Father's business. He had done it with such excellence that the voice of God was heard on earth. No angel was sent this time to express the Father's will. He spoke Himself, moved by the sight of a wise Son doing His will.

Isn't that a noble goal for your own life? In the coming year, would you like to grow and become strong? To be filled with wisdom and have the grace of God on you? To pray and hear God's voice affirm you in what you are doing? Jesus didn't receive all this because He was God. There were no shortcuts. He pleased the Father through obedience. Begin now to set your heart toward the Lord in the coming year. Make this a year of growth in the Lord.

Oh Lord, as I put the holidays behind me, I set my face toward You. Speak to me in these days concerning the days to come. Help me to focus on Your will for the coming year. Fill me with a desire to pray and seek Your face. Fill me with wisdom and grace. Help me to please You in all that I do. Speak to me clearly concerning Your will for my life. I submit to Your will before I know what it is, trusting You completely and without fear. Amen.

DECEMBER 30

"Who has established all the ends of the earth?
What is his name, and the name of his son? Tell me if you know?" — 30:4.

Our friends saw my five-year-old son running down the street toward his god-parents' house. When they stopped and asked him what he was doing, he yelled, "Deborah's gone and we can't find her!" My two-year-old daughter had decided to walk to her godparents but had gotten lost. Before very long, she turned up at a friend's house one mile in the opposite direction. We, of course, rejoiced to find her safe, hugged and kissed her—and then applied the proper discipline to make that trip a costly one for her.

Jesus also got lost as a child. Joseph and Mary went up to Jerusalem every year for the feast of the Passover. When Jesus was 12, He stayed behind in Jerusalem after His family had left. They traveled one day before they realized that He wasn't with them. So they traveled one day back, and spent three days looking for Him. That means that they had no idea where He was for five days! Luke reports:

> It came to pass, that after three days they found him in the temple, sitting in the midst of the doctors, both hearing them, and asking them questions. And all that heard him were astonished at his understanding and answers. And when they saw him, they were amazed: and his mother said unto him, "Son, why hast thou thus dealt with us? behold, thy father and I have sought thee sorrowing." And he said unto them, "How is it that ye sought me? wist ye not that I must be about my Father's business?" And they understood not the saying which he spake unto them (Luke 2:46-50, KJV).

Joseph and Mary had lived with Jesus for 12 years, yet they were just now coming to an understanding of who He was. They didn't fully understand what was going on, even after all the marvelous prophecies and interventions they had beheld surrounding His birth. They were confronted with the question in today's verse: Who is the Lord and what is He doing through His Son?

You must answer that same question. It's not enough to know Jesus. He's about His Father's business, and expects you to be about it, too. You may have known Him for a number of years, but now find Him doing something in your life that you don't understand.

As a new year approaches, commit yourself to be about your Father's busi-ness. Eliminate distractions—hobbies, sports, television, memberships, and the like—that keep you from seeking the Lord. Make an effort to read one book per month that will help you in your walk with the Lord. Read through the entire Bible next year. Go to the prayer meetings sponsored at your church. In other words, go where Jesus is and stop trying to get Him to go where you want Him to be He may go with you for a while, but eventually He'll require that you go where He is—doing His Father's business in His Father's house.

DECEMBER 31

"Do not spend your strength on women,
your vigor on those who ruin kings." —31:3

When Jesus finished His stay in Jerusalem, He didn't launch out into a world-wide ministry. Luke reported, "Then he went down to Nazareth with them and was obedient to them. But his mother treasured all these things in her heart. And Jesus grew in wisdom and stature, and in favor with God and man" (Luke 2:51-52).

Proverbs 31 begins with a mother addressing her son, who is a king. She warned him in today's verse not to give himself to things that are inconsistent with being a king and leader. She urged this king not to give himself to women in a wrong manner. She knew that to be a good king, he would need to focus on the job he had and not use his position for pleasure.

Jesus understood this and gave Himself to those things that helped Him grow in wisdom and favor. I think that perhaps Mary talked with Jesus and reminded Him of those things that had been spoken over His life. She, like the mother in Proverbs 31, helped keep her son on track, so to speak, as He fulfilled the will of God.

As you approach a new year, review all the things that, like Mary, you have treasured in your heart. What has the Lord said to you in the past? Have you been faithful to them? Do you need to review them and dedicate yourself once again to seeing them fulfilled?

Then, grow in wisdom and stature in the coming year. I would strongly encourage you to start the new year with a time of fasting. Clean out the old and make way for the new. Set your entire being toward seeking the Lord. This is what Isaiah had to say about fasting:

Is not this the kind of fasting I have chosen: to loose the chains of injustice and untie the cords of the yoke, to set the oppressed free and break every yoke? Is it not to share your food with the hungry and to provide the poor wanderer with shelter—when you see the naked, to clothe him, and not to turn away from your own flesh and blood? Then your light will break forth like the dawn, and your healing will quickly appear; then your righteousness will go before you, and the glory of the Lord will be your rear guard (Isaiah 58:6-8).

Isaiah lists some great promises for those who fast with proper motives and attitude. Let your light break forth, your healing quickly appear, and let the glory of the Lord be your rear guard in the coming year. Don't waste your efforts on things that will bring trivial results. Rather invest yourself in those things that will make a difference both now and in eternity. Amen.

INDEX OF SCRIPTURES USED

367

369

371

373

374

BOOK OF PROVERBS

Chap. & Day	January	February	March	April	May	June
1	1:3	1:11	1:19	1:30	1:5	1:32
2	2:6	2:1	2:12-13	2:11	2:5	2:4
3	3:19	3:34	3:24	3:3	3:1	3:9-10
4	4:3-4	4:14	4:9	4:16	4:23	4:18
5	5:23	5:2	5:7	5:2	5:11	5:3
6	6:20	6:2	6:23	6:15	6:5	6:6
7	7:1	7:21	7:24	7:7	7:15	7:3
8	8:34	8:5	8:33	8:9	8:31	8:1
9	9:10	9:6	9:11	9:4	9:18	9:12
10	10:6	10:12	10:27	10:13	10:4	10:19
11	11:2	11:20	11:22	11:12	11:5	11:31
12	12:8	12:4	12:5	12:23	12:21	12:3
13	13:1	13:14	13:18	13:16	13:17	13:1
14	14:11	14:26	14:12	14:29	14:14	14:23
15	15:1	15:9	15:21	15:14	15:6	15:3
16	16:19	16:25	16:26	16:21	16:32	16:3
17	17:20	17:4	17:24	17:18	17:27	17:9
18	18:13	18:5	18:9	18:12	18:1	18:19
19	19:1	19:9	19:15	19:25	19:3	19:21
20	20:25	20:28	20:5	20:12	20:21	20:6
21	21:31	21:4	21:16	21:20	21:1	21:5
22	22:21	22:4	22:6	22:12	22:29	22:26-27
23	23:11	23:12	23:21	23:1	23:23	23:4
24	24:14	24:9	24:12	24:17	24:2	24:4
25	25:1	25:5	25:27	25:8	25:2	25:6-7
26	26:24	26:25	26:14	26:16	26:4-5	26:12
27	27:7	27:8	27:12	27:17	27:2	27:4
28	28:9	28:13	28:12	28:20	28:26	28:14
29	29:13	29:4	29:2	29:11	29:20	29:25
30	30:20	—	30:32	30:15	30:5	30:6
31	31:5	—	31:13-18 &25-27	—	31:1	—

377

BOOK OF PROVERBS

Chap. & Day	July	August	September	October	November	December
1	1:1-2	1:10	1:8	1:28	1:13	1:33
2	2:10	2:7	2:21	2:3	2:9	2:8
3	3:17	3:25-26	3:5	3:6	3:14	3:23
4	4:22	4:12	4:7	4:1	4:20	4:6
5	5:21	5:10	5:13-14	5:1	5:9	5:6
6	6:16	6:17	6:22	6:9	6:8	6:4
7	7:4	7:16	7:8	7:2	7:19	7:6
8	8:13	8:27	8:15	8:6	8:18	8:30
9	9:1	9:9	9:17	9:5	9:2	9:3
10	10:25	10:5	10:7	10:21	10:22	10:30
11	11:24	11:3	11:8	11:11	11:25	11:14
12	12:11	12:27	12:6	12:24	12:14	12:2
13	13:20	13:15	13:6	13:4	13:2	13:9
14	14:15	14:4	14:32	14:6	14:9	14:33
15	15:23	15:8	15:15	15:29	15:16	15:24
16	16:23	16:7	16:4	16:9	16:8	16:20
17	17:3	17:16	17:10	17:8	17:1	17:22
18	18:23	18:2	18:10	18:20	18:14	18:15
19	19:2	19:11	19:17	19:8	19:16	19:14
20	20:24	20:23	20:4	20:9	20:18	20:11
21	21:2	21:30	21:22	21:19	21:13	21:23
22	22:19	22:1	22:13	22:3	22:9	22:2
23	23:18	23:19	23:10	23:20	23:5	23:22
24	24:27	24:6	24:3	24:11	24:31	24:20
25	25:9	25:12	25:11	25:13	25:21	25:3
26	26:17	26:22	26:7	26:15	26:27	26:6
27	27:10	27:18	27:5	27:23	27:26-27	27:1
28	28:4	28:19	28:18	28:23	28:27	28:7
29	29:23	29:18	29:1	29:16	29:7	29:3
30	30:11	30:10	30:2	30:3	30:7-9	30:4
31	31:1	31:23	—	31:9	—	31:8